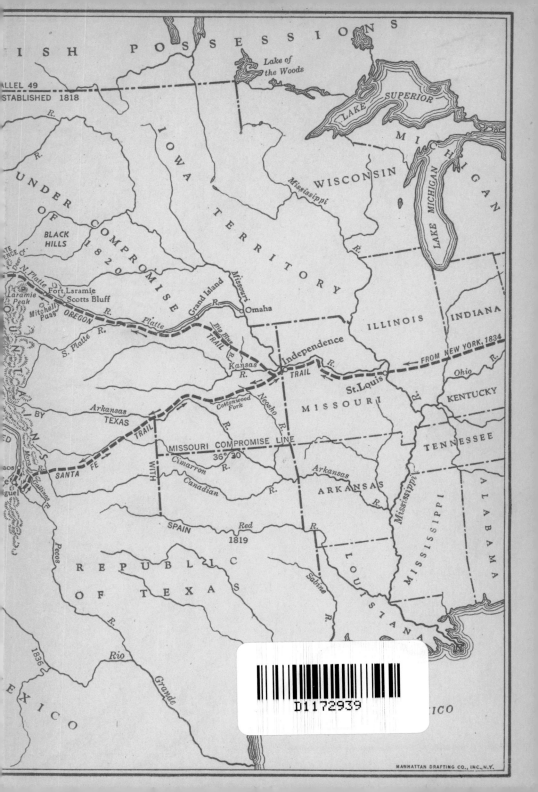

SUTTER *of* California

JOHN A. SUTTER
From the mezzotint by J. Sartain after Osgood

SUTTER
OF CALIFORNIA

A BIOGRAPHY BY JULIAN DANA

HALCYON HOUSE
NEW YORK

HALCYON HOUSE *editions are published and
distributed by Blue Ribbon Books, Inc.,
386 Fourth Avenue, New York City*

I DEDICATE THIS BOOK TO
EVERYONE WHO
LOVES
CALIFORNIA
HER PAST,
HER PRESENT
AND
HER FUTURE

PREFACE

All of us seek adventure. But few of us can afford to be heedless horizon-hasteners. Chains bind us. We may own the desire but not the daring; the disapproval of our associates hinders and deters. We may ignore John Doe as a man, but the hot voices of a multitude of John Does appal us.

This is the story of General John A. Sutter, quester after empire, one of the wandering lords of jeopardy. Adventure such as he sought is for the valiant—courageous not only against peril of body but the venom-tipped lances of criticism.

I like my heroes human. I like the authenticity which etches—even with acid on the needle-point—the indelible pictures of a man as he walks and talks and laughs and plays and plans. And, of all the important adventurers, John Sutter was one of the most human fellows who ever dared to do the things you and I dream of doing.

A biographically stuffed specimen may be fictionally pleasing; but a lack of accuracy implies a lack of artistry and knowledge. Of necessity, I have selected and arranged. I have striven to choose the facts which most clearly transmit the man's personality. To preserve the integrity of his story has been my major fervency.

I have tried to place my feet in the trail-marks of Sutter's restless roving; assimilate the mental and physical fare which his then-world accorded him; interpret him through the pages of more than twelve thousand manuscripts and a hundred books; detect the littleness and greatness of the man from written records. From Kandern to Independence I have followed him; from torrid old Taos to Wind River Rendezvous; from Fort

Vancouver to Honolulu; from Sitka to Sacramento; from Hock to Lititz, journey's present ending.

There is a hope in my heart that the real John Sutter lives again in these pages. The truthful narrative shames the printed distortions beyond the covers of this book.

In the presentation of this volume there is one certainty: it will contain errors. Assured of that certainty, I am somewhat dismayed; for the errors, whatever they may be, have persisted over two years of research, selection and rejection. For those who care to verify their mental menus I have appended a list of the more important MSS. and books which have served me in its creation. Many of the family records, temporarily in my possession, are not thus catalogued.

The Father of the Fort deserves a critical commentary. For Chance and John Sutter, those incomparable partners, changed the world and the people and the maps thereof in wondrous fashion.

Piedmont, California　　　　　　　　　　JULIAN DANA

CONTENTS

ILLUSTRATIONS

SUTTER *of* California

Chapter I

IN THE BEGINNING

JOHANN AUGUSTUS SUTER was forced to adventure. No personal curiosity would have driven him to sail seas, climb mountains, or cross deserts to new things. He would have been content to live within a tight, comfortable circle of familiar landmarks and faces until he died.

But the choice was not his. Necessity made him a home-seeker and chance made him a state-maker. He became an incredible fellow who changed the boundaries of a continent and added a billion dollars to the golden wealth of nations. He played the rôles of planner, wanderer, trader, diplomat, emperor, benevolent blunderer, and finally that of a rubber ball tossed into a basket-world of kittens. That his trajectory influenced human history was beyond his purpose or volition.

He was born in the closing minutes of February 23rd, 1803. The place was the village of Kandern in the Grand Duchy of Baden and only one home in the sleep-ridden town held candles that glowed into the black new day. Next morning, when the schoolmaster thought of it, he made foreboding mention that the newcomer was a child of midnight. . . .

The clan of Suter were paper-makers by trade. Hans, the infant Johann's grandfather, had lived in Basle. There he owned and operated a paper-mill. But red ink splashed its unwelcome way over the firm's ledgers. Then Hans betook himself and his family to Kandern.

There he served as foreman of another small paper factory. Students of the little university towns of Southern Germany needed something on which to scribble. Hans Suter helped supply their needs.

His two sons grew to manhood in the village—tall, strong fellows of a blue-eyed breed. Johann Jakob, the eldest, met and married Christine Wilhelmine Stoberin,

the daughter of a clergyman. As was the custom, he
pledged himself to his father's trade.

When Hans died, Johann Jakob became foreman of
the factory. It was in his home that the candles had
glowed that February midnight.

Herr Adolph Vandenburg, the spectacled schoolmaster, was the important figure of provincial Kandern.
He was not a great man or a wise man, this Herr Vandenburg; yet there is no question but that he was a good
man, intolerantly sure. He was a vehement instructor of
youth. Under his waving ferule Johann Augustus Suter
absorbed a boy's first impressions of the lands beyond
Baden's borders. The young Swiss fed, with the others,
upon the militant spirit of a sedentary falcon.

He was athletic and ambitious, a hearty normal boy
more given to wishful doing than his noisy schoolyard
companions. He was protectively fond of his younger
twin brothers, Heinrich and Friedrich: they did not often
leave his side. . . His world was bounded by the town
and the insolent iron creatures of Herr Vandenburg's
impossible alien earth.

When the United States trounced England in 1812,
Johann Augustus was nine. He warmed to the picture of
a mighty young nation twisting the tail of the British
lion—even fancied the writhings and roarings of that
dignified beast. Herr Vandenburg, who hated John Bull
with all the virulence of his small body, added occasional
deft splashes of color to the picture.

Odd moments found Johann listening to the tales of
the cobble-stoned village, pausing at gutter-shrines
oracled by oldsters. His thoughts were those of adoles-
cent magnificence; of a boy who has not seen great cities
and marching men and belching carronades. . . . A fasci-
nating, unknown land, this United States.

At fourteen, the clearest figure in his consciousness
was a man, not a distant nation. Someone to deify, to
emulate—a man whose armies had surged over Europe,
an idol who still rode gloriously in men's minds. What if

the Corsican's dream was a thing of impotency? His glittering legend would persist as long as youth had imagination.

The paper business struck the recurrent doldrums again in 1819. Young whippersnappers were not scribbling so furiously. They met in dark places, talked much and wrote little. Men were pushing war schemes faster than pens. To the elder Johann Jakob it seemed that Neufchatel offered more opportunity to one of his guild than the small Kandern. So to Neufchatel he took his family and his hopes.

Johann was sixteen then, the twins eleven. In the next four years, uniformed and bravely brass-buttoned, he attended the Military Academy. A cadet's life was the thing. Guns interested him—big guns, little guns, all kinds of guns. He liked to hear them crash and rumble; he liked to study their functions in the game of war. He never ceased to know the spell of their shining black lengths and their echoing voices. All his life their bellowing was to excite in him a peculiar ecstacy. Other men might prefer wine or wandering or wealth or women—Johann Suter loved the crash of cannon. He was always happiest when he heard guns booming in salute or anger.

When he graduated he looked more like a soldier than a purveyor of paper. His uniform gave a thrill to his heart that a ream of paper could never do; it gave a set to his shoulders that shamed the baggy hang of a clerk's apron. Yet the Suter brothers were duly apprenticed to the trade of the Suters before them. On the same day they entered the old firm of Thurneysen, book publishers and general merchants, in Basle.

Johann became a book clerk and was initiated into the glue-odored secrets of the bindery. Heinrich and Friedrich became printers.

Days shuffled into months. Johann grew restless in the dingy, staid shop. The cutting of binding, the sorting of paper, palled upon him. He detested the sight of a

bucket of glue on the fire as much as its odor nauseated
him. He longed for the open drill-ground and the black
guns and the sun-bright sky.

Man-made walls and man-made dictions fretted him.
Life was dull, without savor. He wanted wings. . . .

Then he fell in love. Her name was Anna Dubelt and
she was shy and lovely, content to be almost inarticulate in his presence. He did not rest until he married her
and carried her away to live on the income of a struggling
book clerk.

At first they were very happy with very little. He had
strong arms and warm lips and a demanding young body.
But there are demands of life which love alone cannot
alter.

The months fled into ill-paid years. The buckets of
glue grew more odorous and despicable in the prison of
trade. Fatherhood came to the laboring Johann. The
children were three sons and a daughter—Johann Augustus, Jr., Anna Elisa, Emil Victor and William
Alphonse.

Now his responsibilities were greater, towered with
an implacable bleakness. Always the funds available
were never quite enough to satisfy present needs. No
amount of stint or saving seemed to remedy the matter.
He served as an officer in the reserve corps of the Swiss
Army from 1826 on. That commission held him ready for
instant active duty. Then, for a few hours a week, he
could see the great guns and study them, hear them in
dark-mouthed thunder at parade intervals. A change
from the walled-in bindery and stodgy souls who saw
heaven and earth through a frame of wood pulp.

Then a chance for advancement came his hard-pressed
way. Abruptly he deserted the dusty offices of Thurneysen
and became associated with the publishing firm of
Weber, in Leipzig. But there, too, he found four walls
and steaming pots of glue.

Truth is, Johann Suter was contesting in a stagnant
backwash of Old World depression, of economic ebb-

tide. The debts of wars were being paid and the citizen is ever the source of the musket-carrier and the costs of conflict.

Dire days, these later ones. Johann Suter found a way to flee the walls and the glue and the pale-faced slaves of paper. When Napoleon III was a refugee in Switzerland, Suter was a captain of artillery in the Swiss Guard. The pay was poor but sure—at least his family would not starve.

The two men met. One was to found the Third Empire and make Paris the most cosmopolitan city the world has ever seen since ancient Rome; the other was to work with endless crudities to win an empire in a wild waste of wonder.

They were not intimates. Strange. For they were of the same breed and destiny. But then, this Charles Louis Bonaparte was experiencing a love affair with his first mistress, the Swiss singer Eleanore. That and writing brimstone bombast. Suter, too, was harassed by distractions—much less unsubtle ones than those facing Charles Louis.

Army life had color and camaraderie that Suter liked. But the pay was only a trifle more than the pittance of the bindery walls. Debts multiplied instead of decreasing. A growing family needs many things and Johann watched sadly as he counted their lacks and lustreless days. He was still feverishly attent for a new start, wits razor-honed.

He was never one to talk of conditions that plagued him; he knew no self-pity. To face a barrier made him only more determined to thrust it aside. If that was impossible, he leaped—not always successfully.

FRESH RUMORS came to him, at intervals, about the United States, tales of what that region offered to any man willing to work and till the virgin soil. Those yarns of fruitful conquest stirred swift hopes in his heart.

What one man had done another could do. Millions of broad acres for the taking, rumor said.

Johann Suter was thirty-one years old in 1834. Some vague phantom had begun to whisper strange things to him—that nearly half of his life lay behind him, valueless. Now was the time—if ever—to seek a land of New Beginning. . . . His talents and ability had yielded him nothing. He was tired of debts and futureless days and meagre comforts.

Resolve came to him that summer—almost the resolve of desperation. He would go to America and find land that would be his own. Somewhere he would seek out a place for his loved ones and himself in a country that offered a thousandfold more than the highly taxed, crowded continent. He had no fear that he had waited too long.

Johann Suter had a great regard for rich black soil, the mother of so much beauty and wealth. All greatness came out of it, all that a man could wisely wish. To him the possession of land was a symbol of content, the assurance of permanence to the tribe of Suter. He saw fields of grain growing golden in the sun, long rows of trees heavy with ripening fruit, sleek-coated herds grazing on emerald hillsides, a home set in a pleasant valley by a singing river. . . . and Anna and his children in that home. This was the dream that drove Johann Suter from the numbing sterility of the Old World.

One thing bothered him continually, kept his head tossing on a restless pillow. How was his family to exist while he sought a home across the sea? He had no money —only debts. Even if he had possessed funds he would have hesitated to take them with him. He did not know himself what hardships he might have to face for a time in that strange country.

Both he and Anna realized the impossible. They must wait until he prepared against their coming. A sustaining niche must be found until he could send for them.

"But Johann, my dear," said Anna fearfully, "it might be years—you might be hurt. I'm afraid. . . ."

Johann Suter put his strong arms around her.

"Don't worry, *mein Liebchen*," he said softly. "Remember, it is for you and the children I must find this new place. It will not be long. Think! A new land, new friends, no debts, broad valleys, fields of grain, great herds—a beginning again for us!"

He brushed her cheeks with his full lips. Johann had a way with him.

Still she was not content. He talked on. . . .

Johann Suter had the power to make those close to him feel the warmth of his longing. His emotional spontaneity put a radiant shimmer on every tumbling word. Some alchemy was in the man, not hidden, but vibrantly sentient. It was to stand him in good stead in his relationships with more practical people who dwelt in the far places where he was about to adventure. His matchless self-faith was to assure him boundless credit when he needed it most. He had the vision, had Johann Suter, and he made that vision superbly salable.

Even frightened little Anna Dubelt Suter, who would have four children to care for after his going, felt the pull of his dream, the surety of his promise.

For she said no more to hold him.

With passionate purpose, Johann sought out his brother Friedrich, more understanding than the plodding Heinrich.

"I'm away to America and a fresh start," he told the man who was still a printer.

"Yes?"

"I have been to see my creditors. They must wait. I will send money as soon as I can."

"What did they say?" asked Friedrich curiously.

Johann brushed the query aside with a gesture. "It is Anna and the children I think of most." His voice was very sober. "Friedrich, will you care for them—watch over them—until I send for them?"

His brother passed a weary hand over a broad forehead. "I will do the best I can for them, Johann," he said heavily.

"Good. You were ever a kind soul, Friedrich. I can repay you one day in money—but never in gratitude. Perhaps you will come, too—if I can find a home for you in America?"

"No. . . . No. This is my home, Johann. I pray that good luck will attend you."

"It will," said the other grimly. "I cannot fail."

He gripped Friedrich's hand quickly, turned away.

He wasted no time. He had barely enough money to pay his passage to New York. But that did not chill his resolve. He believed a friendly star of fortune led him, that the star would never grow black in the heavens.

It was July, 1834—a century ago—that Johann Suter's eager eyes first glimpsed New York rise above a grey sea-line, the city that was only a shabby promise of the city that was to be. But his eyes passed over the low spires and probed into the vagueness beyond. He raised his arm in military salute. Somewhere beyond this busy port lay fulfillment. . . and Johann Suter knew that he would not be denied.

Chapter II

A TALE TOLD AT TAOS

Suter stepped into bright drama from the steamer's deck. Andrew Jackson was President of the United States and Osceola and his Seminoles were plotting the massacre of the Wahoo Swamp. Tammany was no longer a tiger cub but a full-jowled killer. A spirit of speculation thralled the land—for the first time a parade of "Bulls" and "Bears" had invaded the public consciousness. Union Square was a potter's field and Fort Clinton had not yet become the Aquarium. The telegraph was a decade in the future. Madison Square was an open marshy plot of farm land. Fifth Avenue ran as far as Fourteenth Street and ended there in the woods of Lover's Lane.

The map of the United States in 1834 is an amazing legend a century after. Wisconsin was still free territory under the Ordinance of 1787. The terrain which was to be Montana, the Dakotas, Nebraska, Wyoming, Kansas, Colorado and Oklahoma was also free under the Compromise of 1820. The Republic of Texas held its borders along the waters of the Sabine, Red, and Arkansas rivers. From the historic 54th degree 40 minute parallel to the 42nd degree parallel, the Oregon Country was jointly occupied with feeble gestures by Great Britain and the United States. California and Nevada were part of the United States of Mexico. Not a large country then, the United States. But the Swiss was to aid its leap from sea to sea.

There was an electric thrill in the air of the new land. Men worked with bustle and speed and certainty. There was nothing like it in the Old World. Suter felt the magic of it—the pulse of a lusty nation on the way to great things. He wanted to be one of the busy throng—to be an American. As soon as he could trace his name in English, he became John A. Sutter—no longer Johann Augustus Suter. It seemed the thing to do.

But cities did not hold what he sought. He wanted virgin country to be had for the taking. The towns and surrounding lands belonged to men who had come before him. He wanted to push on.

Aboard ship he had met two Frenchmen and two Germans. They, too, were minded to seek fortune beyond the crowded places. So the five, held together by a common impulse, began to trek on to the then-existing Indian frontier, Missouri.

The prices of foodstuffs, real estate and stocks were rocketing daily as they went. Men were leaving the shop, the plow and the anvil to gamble on the first "get-rich-quick" scheme in America's history. Much as Sutter admired this commercial activity, it held a personal sting in it. Neither he nor his companions had the money to buy high-priced food. Often they went hungry.

At last the five came doggedly to the frontier camp that was St. Louis. There they determined to spend the winter of 1834-35. That season held a blustery bleakness which did not please John Sutter. It was not the land he sought. He was looking for more sun, more warmth, more fertility. Missouri would not do. . . .

During the long, cold weeks, the amiable Swiss met and talked with all kinds of frontiersmen and settlers. He met a merchant who was in need of a German and French-speaking clerk and was given the position. German was his native tongue and he spoke French fluently. A mastery of English was coming to him swiftly, although he was never to lose the heavy-timbred accent of his mother language. He became invaluable to his employer and the customers liked his genial smile and courteous speech.

The men who interested him most were the daring Santa Fe traders. Prosperous fellows they looked, too. They told long tales of the riches to be had from the Santa Fe Trade. Also they were indisputable proof of their own yarns. It seemed to the interested grocery clerk that here lay an easy route to acquire wealth and spy out the land which might be suitable for settlement. He determined to sink his carefully hoarded wages into just such a trading venture.

Only one of his original companions—a German— was impressed by the scheme. The five came to the parting of the ways. Sutter and his friend formed a partnership and labored most of the winter months in perfecting their plans.

INDEPENDENCE, MISSOURI, was the real point of outfitting, departure and arrival of the Santa Fe caravans. It was there that Sutter and his partner came in the early spring of 1835. The village was rough-hewn, well-defenced. The center of the town was a log cabin as formidable as a fortress. It was surrounded by a score of blockhouses, loop-holed and heavy-walled to resist attack.

Here all the Santa Fe traders foregathered for the customary May passage. It was a long, dangerous journey. Yet at the end they were assured of profitable sales, either in New Mexico or the provinces farther south or west.

In confusion and clamor Sutter, and his aide purchased their wagons, mules, oxen, supplies, and "trade." They had barely enough funds to outfit themselves properly; but Sutter's late employer had stood guaranty for such a lack. The purchasing power of each penny received earnest thought. In the end, Sutter remarked with elation that no man would move out on the barter-trail with better equipment or more well-chosen trade-goods.

They started from Independence in late May, with many others—only two men of a great company that flowed along toward the arid reaches of an alien territory. The way led through Council Grove, a strip of timber a half-mile wide with oak, ash, walnut, elm and hickory trees shading the trail. These trees wandered all along Council Grove Creek, the main branch of the Neosho River.

The usual halt was made to organize the caravan. A trail-captain was appointed. Pledges for mutual protection were exchanged for the passage through Indian country. Supplies of wood for axle-trees and other wagon parts were cut and laid in; no more suitable timber would be found until the Rockies were reached near Santa Fe.

SUTTER FOLLOWED the lure of fortune south and westward. Sounds beat against his ears: the jangle of bells; the clatter of chains; moaning of axles; snorts of animals; rattle of yokes and harness; curses of drivers; yelps of dogs. Yet he was content. In the blue haze that ever opened ahead he was sure of satisfied desire. . . . Anna and the children under fruit trees, beside a great house that sat on the banks of a broad river. . . green fields under a yellow sun. . . herds that grazed away into a placid sunset. . . . John Sutter rode for hours on the creaking castle with his dreams; a part of the scene yet apart from his fellows.

The caravan plodded past Diamond Spring and the Cottonwood Fork of the Neosho. Their route ran along prairie for nearly five hundred monotonous trail-miles. A few narrow fringes of stunted trees sat sullenly beside the margins of streams. Occasionally, scattered buffalo herds and antelope flashed by the train or fed fearlessly within view. Many were shot for food by the hunters assigned to that task.

Beyond Cottonwood Fork they came to the Arkansas River Valley. The quarter-mile-wide stream ran between yellow, sandy, wave-like ridges. Several green islets, studded with cottonwoods, rose out of the river's course. The banks were low and barren. A few dwarfed trees—cottonwoods, elm, or a lonely hackberry—huddled in an abject weariness of waiting behind sandhills or swamps.

They traced the course of the Arkansas a hundred miles through a desert country—a starkly desolate place—until they swerved left toward the Cimarron. Each day on that portion of the journey they fought back fierce Indian attacks. Like darting wasps the painted warriors plagued the ant-like column. But the wagons crawled on, slowly, without pause save for the noonday and night watches. They marched with the indifference and persistence of the sons of barter who have always broken trail for the home-seekers.

Fording the dry Cimarron—it was not always a moistureless river-bed—they passed Willow Bar and reached Upper Spring on the first day of July. They found a small fountain plashing out into a ravine which knifed into the Cimarron, three or four miles distant. To Sutter and the parched train that crystal stream seemed to burst out of Paradise. It gave new life to every man and hoof-jaded beast in the sun-seared string of canopied stores-on-wheels.

Again the rumbling wagons lumbered off southwest to the headwaters of the North Fork of the Canadian River, a territory now part of northeastern New Mexico. They wheeled and tramped an angling course past Rabbit Ear Mound, Rock Mound, and Point of Rocks to the main branch of the river at *El Vado de Piedras* (Rocky Ford).

There they met the Santa Fe customs officers, guarded by military escort. Trade-goods were examined and duties grudgingly paid. The caravan organization ceased to function; there was no longer any fear of savage forays. The wagons began to string out.

They passed the *Mora*, last trace of the Canadian, some fifty miles beyond the main stream. The road stretched away over an elevated plain without a mountain ridge until they reached the *Gallinas*, first of the *Rio del Norte* waters.

San Miguel rose languidly out of the veiled distance some twenty miles farther on. The town was a cluster of adobe huts squatting indolently in the valley of the *Rio Pecos*, a silvery river that spumed down from the Santa Fe Mountains.

The Swiss and his partner were then almost alone—
the high wagons were strung out along the home course
like laggard snails that were sure of a cabbage patch no
matter the hour of arrival.

South bent the road to find a passway through the
broken extremity of a Santa Fe Mountain spur. From
that point on, the spur was slashed into detached ridges
and flat table-lands.

The mountain trail was good. They sloped down
upon an open plain a few miles from their destination.
To the northwest, Sutter saw a valley dotted with green
corn and wheat-fields and groves of trees. Here and there,
square, block-like houses were visible. With smug precision the caravan had come at last to Santa Fe.

GREAT EXCITEMENT showed in the village. Sutter
and his partner were in the van of the snail's procession.
As they neared the *plaza publica* they heard glad voices
shouting: "*La entrada de la caravana! Los Americanos! Los
carros!*"

Crowds flocked about, eager for the bargaining.
Many of the caravaneers snapped their whips expertly
and flicked newly cut beards with an air as they grinned
covertly at laughing *señoritas* gathered to inspect their
wares. Covertly, because snapping black male eyes were
also present. It was a happy day for sleepy Santa Fe.

Sutter and his companion did well in the trading.
Little haggling was heard about any of the wagon-
stores. Yet they did not sell all their goods in that first
plaza. Two days later, in convoy with a half-dozen other
traders, they again set out. They chose the northerly
route to Taos.

It did not take them long. Every bit of trade-goods
they owned was sold in the tiny, heat-baked village
resting so tranquilly on the old Spanish Trail of the
padres and gold-seekers. Save for baskets and rugs and
other produce accepted in exchange, the wagons lay
empty. . . .

Sutter met the *alcalde* of the town, a French-Canadian named Popian. This suddenly rooted wanderer had traveled far with a pair of sharp eyes in his head. It was he who gave the Swiss his first tales of California.

They sat under the stars at night, in the semblance of a *patio* that leaned before the story-teller's rude home. Those stars were so near that Sutter could have reached up and snatched them out of the velvet sky with either hand. . . . Popian spoke of the fertile land that never knew snow or ice or bitter cold, the land that was ever golden with sun-warmth and where every fruit and tree and living thing grew with miraculous rapidity.

His visitor was a good listener. This Popian was one of the first of California's publicity agents. He was salesman enough to sell his story to the young trader who was dreaming a dream of pleasant lands.

BACK WENT SUTTER over the perilous trail to Independence. But he never forgot the tale he heard in Taos.

For three years—until 1838—he was a successful Santa Fe trader, driving himself to the limit, always planning. Twice he sent money home—small sums—and with them went vivid letters of the life that was soon to be for all of them.

Over and over again he assured Anna that it would only be a little while longer. They must be patient. Of danger, hardship and privation he said nothing.

The Panic of 1837 hastened his schemes. By then he was supremely confident that he had enough money to start the California trek. Only when he was certain did he make a definite decision.

In April, 1838, he sold out his business interests to his partner, who still wished to continue in the lucrative Santa Fe trade. He had first determined to reach California via Sonora. But Sir William Drummond Stewart, a shrewd Scot of his acquaintance, advised the Oregon Trail. Stewart believed it was a much safer route for a small party. It was this northern trail which Sutter finally chose to travel.

He organized his eight-man expedition in St. Louis—two Germans, two Americans, and three Belgians. Captain Tripp of the American Fur Company was one of the Americans who joined the party. Tripp wished to journey with them as far as the Wind River rendezvous in the Rocky Mountains.

Sutter insisted on traveling light and fast. They used horses and pack-animals only. For most of their food they had to depend on the chance offering of the trail. For safety they had to rely on speed—they were too small a command to dare pitched battle if war smoke began to waver against the skies.

They left St. Louis in late April and rode swiftly to familiar Independence. They made no halt there. Many Indians thronged the turf-cut streets as Sutter's company passed through the camp-lined outskirts. Kansans stalked about in worn and greasy blankets, dirty and miserable; intent Foxes sauntered here and there with painted faces and shaved heads; Shawnees—the Beau Brummels of red society—were present, decked out in calicoes and prints in superlative color schemes; and brooding Cheyennes sported war-bonnets of feathers and beady, calculating eyes.

Through the dust and bustle went Sutter and his men. He rode his horse as if he headed an army. Occasionally he lifted his hand and called a greeting. This happened usually when he passed the mule-pulled wagons of the Santa Fe traders here for the spring journey, men he had known and companioned with on the outland trails.

The eight went on outside the place and camped. There was no business for them to transact in Independence. They were ready for the wilderness.

At sun-up they went forward, northwest. Out through Westport, past the Shawnee Mission wound the road, to a point near the present town of Gardner, Kansas. Here the Santa Fe and Oregon Trails ceased to run together; they branched away, each dim ribbon leading to the conquest of a new land.

For the first time John Sutter turned right.

Chapter III

THUNDER IN THE EARTH

THE TRAIL led first through prairie and they crossed many little streams along whose banks wound narrow lines of elm, burr-oak, black walnut and white hickory. Then they passed over a large and rapid flood, the Little Vermilion; and came again to another branch of the Kansas, the Big Vermilion. The water was higher than in the first stream, the crossing more difficult. It took them anxious hours to reach the farther bank. That night they slept in a fragrant forest land, watered by a tiny brook, lush grasses all about.

Three days later they approached the Big Blue. Once more they breasted muddy waters and rode on north-westward, killing an antelope for meat while on the march. The Platte was reached near Grand Island, a milestone of another turning.

The eight followed the south bank to the forks, as-cended the South Platte for a few miles and then forded it. In the dry season the stream was a ghost of a river trickling among sandy shoals; but Sutter found it a boil-ing barrier of swirling silt that roistered over hidden quicksands. Yet they won their way to the north bank, mud-spattered, exhausted.

Then the North Platte glinted out of the path ahead and, following its southern bank, they began to glimpse great herds of buffalo. The Swiss had never seen such a vast army of creatures on his southern journeys and the sight stirred him to wonder. Day after day the prairies were hidden by a solid black wall of moving bodies. The myriads were drifting endlessly northward from the distant plains to sink water-hungry muzzles in the cur-rents of the Platte. They plunged in until there was no river to see. They swam across by thousands and their passing roiled and tainted the water until Sutter and his party could barely force themselves to drink it. But drink it they did; there was no other.

One day at dusk the beasts came in appalling droves. Their ranks seemed to thicken as night came down. The eight sat up, sleepless.

"We got to turn 'em," said Tripp anxiously.

They mounted at his insistence and rode some distance from the camp, wasting precious powder and lead as they went. They built what fires they could and waved make-shift torches and shouted. The packed bodies angled away almost imperceptibly. Had the riders not turned the host beyond the camp, the press of buffaloes behind would not have allowed the leaders to swerve aside. A million knife-sharp hoofs were riding the dark.

All night the passing drummed in their deadened ears. When John Sutter was very old, he still remembered that crashing thunder; and spoke of it with awe. The horses and mules stamped and cried out uneasily. If the thunderers had not been so desperately diverted both men and mounts would have been pulped under the feet of the black runners.

In the morning, the travelers saw that even the tough, curling buffalo grass had been cut and uprooted. . . .

The thirtieth day beyond Independence had a breath like an oven. In the afternoon came a terrific cloudburst followed by a biting barrage of hailstones as large as hen's eggs. Men and horses and pack-animals staggered under the frozen bullets. In ten minutes the pelting ceased. They went on.

A huge cloud-funnel came their way three days later. It raced with spiral vehemence, ever nearing, a rotary column of unguessed fury. They stopped, dismounted, huddled against their animals. The funnel veered to the right. It passed a bare four hundred yards beyond the halted cavalcade. . . . Again they rode forward to the west.

Four times they beat off sudden attacks by mounted warriors. Easy prey, the small band seemed, but many an Indian pitched from his pony to the prairie floor under steady rifle fire. The red riders always drew off and away, carrying their dead with them.

Weary, unkempt, retching at the sight of buffalo steaks as they cooked on the fire, plagued by saddle-sores, the eight rode on.

For nearly half a thousand miles they plodded, past Court House Rock, past Chimney Rock, through Mitchell Pass that bisected Scott's Bluff and had been used as an emigrant trail since Astor's men ventured through it in 1812. Sutter was passing by a graveyard of surpassing antiquity, a resting place of nightmare creatures who had trod this planet when the earth was young. In the bad lands, at the north base of the bluff, erosion had bared the fossil remains of the miocene camel, the three-toed horse and other skeletal phenomena of a lost age. But Sutter rode on, unseeing. . . . He was not a scientist; he was an adventurer driven by men and events to the vision of a home and peace and placid permanence.

Through the pass they came down to the plains and a level way. Forty-one days out of Independence they sighted Fort Laramie, surrounded by the Black Hills, sentineled by Laramie Peak.

As Sutter's party rode in they threaded among scores of lodges of friendly Indians which entirely circled the fortress. The twelve-foot-high adobe walls of the citadel enclosed a hundred and fifty-foot square. Inside were several huts which housed the chief trader and his clerks.

Savages were loitering about, gambling, trading furs, horse-racing, gorging themselves on chunks of half-cooked buffalo meat. With them could be seen white trappers dressed Indian-fashion or clad in buckskin, topped by coonskin caps. Ponies fed or roamed in restless numbers within a quarter-mile radius.

In an hour Sutter's pack-animals once more bore a full burden. From the gateway filed the eight and struck out over the barely discernible trail which led into the Black Hills—the foothills of the Rockies—and to the Great American Desert region.

At first the hills were sandy and wild peas and pears grew plentifully along the winding way. But the trail grew rough and alkaline with dismaying swiftness. They were entering upon that portion of the trek which only the stout-hearted could dare. Many who followed Sutter's trail, years later, were to be turned back by the hardships encountered—were to give up the battle after having safely crossed the plains. They set their faces once more to the east, even with the gold-fever burning in their veins. . . .

Narrowing mountain valleys made ravine and stream crossings ceaseless. Most of the springs were alkaline and the sun-heat shriveled bearded faces and cracked lips. Then, after five days, they camped on Deer Creek and broiled fresh, tasty fish, pierced by willow-wands, on the cool river bank.

Almost impassable ravines barred their way from that point. It was a test when men have no strength for speech and journey in silence. Most of the broken way they led their mounts and pack-animals. Four hundred yards an hour was good time. The world of sloping rocks and jagged path seemed endless. Yet finally they came upon the welcome waters of North Fork and found pleasant green groves on either side of the river-lane.

They rested a day and crossed over, at the present site of Casper, Wyoming. A crooked trail led them to a mineral spring and a small lake. The way was still rough and the hills about them took on height.

Ten miles beyond the spring they set foot on an alkaline plain, high bluffs on either side. Sun-tortured and heart-desolate, they pushed ahead. That night they found clear, sparkling water at Willow Springs.

A creek brought them to other gushing fountains in the early morning hours. No grass grew on the trail now and tons of saleratus lay scattered about. Most of the animals limped. The eyes of every man were swollen, pain-glazed.

With abruptness they rode in upon a open plain where the Sweetwater ran swiftly along its southern side. A thirty-foot strip of green roadway curved away beside the clear stream.

Mounts and pack-animals rushed forward, thrust white-coated noses into the river. Sutter and his men dropped stiffly out of saddles, drank from the inviting waters, lay for an hour on the thick, soft carpet. Then they went on, refreshed.

The emerald path rounded Independence Rock, a wall of gray granite rising starkly, four hundred yards long, a hundred feet broad and high. More thousands of buffalo grazed restlessly on the plains within sight; the pleasing valley was a meeting-ground for the vast herds.

Five miles beyond the rock they faced a great gap in the mountains—The Devil's Gate. Its harsh granite mouth swallowed up the river. Lofty palisades fell vertically to a foaming wildness of waters, three hundred feet at its widest part. The opening through which the river dashed was the only crack in that great barrier.

The eight found currants and gooseberries growing on the high banks—none too palatable but still acceptable to hungry men. Willows lining the way served as fuel.

More crooked and rocky grew the trackless going. They crossed boulder-choked creeks interminably, fought their way foot by foot. An occasional grove of trees worried their roots into the hindering rock-lands. One mule pushed his contrary neck into a rock crevice and snapped it with a single wild plunge. They portioned his packs on the remaining animals, went on.

AT SUNRISE one day they glimpsed the sudden sweep of the Wind River Mountains, crystal-covered, age-riven.

The region of ravine and boulder and crevasse had leveled away into a less difficult path. They were going faster now.

At noon they rode in upon the Wind River rendezvous, famous meeting-place of traders and trappers. It was a temporary post which existed only a few weeks in the year when the frontier clans gathered to exchange furs and fur garments for lead, powder, rifles and knives. It was the custom for travelers from the East to carry what extra goods they could to dispose of at the rendezvous. This spot was Captain Tripp's goal.

The half-dozen crude blockhouses and stores were the only structures dedicated to commerce for hundreds of miles. As the eight neared the short-lived place they saw thirty or more men moving about the buildings—drift of the wilderness, clad in wilderness garb.

A shout of greeting went up as the traders and trappers noticed the horsemen. A young fellow came riding in from a westerly course at almost the same instant of Sutter's arrival. A string of Indian scalps swung from the pommel of his saddle and the Swiss saw that an Indian boy clung precariously on the horse's rump.

The newcomers dismounted and fell into friendly talk with the knot of men who gathered. Sutter spoke to the lone rider who had just come in. He found that the young fellow's name was Kit Carson.

The Swiss found Carson a shrewd bargain-driver with something to sell. In thirty minutes Sutter was the owner of the Indian boy who had clung to the scout's saddle. The transaction involved a hundred-dollar beaver-order on the Hudson's Bay Company; Sutter did not know until later that the order was worth one hundred and thirty dollars at the rendezvous. But the grinning Carson did. It was a stiff price; but then the boy spoke Spanish and English.

Goods were all high in the trading-stores. Powder was $1.50 per cup; sugar and pepper $1 per cup; flour $.50 per cup; tobacco $2 per pound; good Mackinaw blankets $8 to $15 each; rifles $20 to $60; butcher knives $1 to $3;

a good gun was worth as much as a horse—a good cap-lock was preferred; caps were $1.50 per box; cotton and calico shirts ranged from $3 to $5; dressed deerskins were $3; deerskin trousers brought $10; and moccasins $1.

The gathering pounced joyfully on Sutter when they learned he was California-bound. Immediate offers of assistance came from every man at the rendezvous. They wanted to aid him in a carnival of wholesale pillage; it seemed to them an easy and profitable idea to sack the Mission churches and run off herds of horses and cattle from the unprotected ranchos. The amazed Sutter could have moved on with a small army had he chosen.

He was hard put to discourage these friendly offers without causing ill-feeling. Most of the uncouth, hardy plainsmen who surrounded him were for butchery and profit. "Them thar Mex critters can be driv' to Oregon an' sold," argued one of the bearded circle. Sutter shook his head. His plan was of settlement and not invasion. He waved aside the offers as diplomatically as he could. At that, most of his listeners were disgusted with his lack of initiative.

"Sech a good idee," muttered the circle longingly. But they could not prevail upon the stubborn Swiss.

The expedition finally rode from the redezvous without unwelcome additions. They still numbered eight; the Indian boy rode in Tripp's stead.

A beautiful valley a score of miles broad opened before them. It was South Pass. They had expected a narrow defile. It lay between the Wind River Mountains to the north and the connecting chain of the Rockies to the south. The grass was good and their lean animals champed hungrily at each brief halt.

The ascent was so gentle they did not realize their elevation. At the summit of the dividing ridge were two springs within a stone's cast of each other. The waters of one flowed west to the Pacific; the other sought out the streams wandering to the Gulf of Mexico.

Pacific Springs! It was an elementary sign-post attesting that they had crossed the continental divide. John Sutter stooped and drank from a spring whose waters would reach a sea that lapped the shores of his future empire.

JIM BRIDGER's FORT was not yet erected and Sutter made no looping turn to the left. They pushed on through South Pass to the fairly level basin of the Green River. Almost directly west they struck the headwaters of Big Sandy Creek, descended that stream to the river and rode down to Black Fork. The trail led to the source of the Green, crossed to the muddy Bear, and traced that stream to the marvel of Soda Springs.

Sutter counted more than a hundred bubbling cauldrons in a small radius. Some were bursting out on top of the ground and others along the low river bank; some gurgled up surprisingly in the bottom of the river. The spring water was strongly impregnated with soda and deposited a reddish sediment which solidified and formed large mounds of porous rock. Some of the mounds were entirely dry; their spouting column of water had been forced so high that their pressure had eventually found outlet at a lesser elevation.

In most of the springs the water was tepid; in none was it cold. Cedars grew all about the place and the country was a pleasing one. As they had ridden into the region their horses' hoofs had thudded hollowly; it was as if a cavern lay far below. . . .

Six miles beyond the springs they left Bear Valley and turned north around the point of a rocky spur. That night they camped on the banks of a mountain brook.

Next noon they reached the valley end and nosed their mounts up an ever-rising defile toward the top of the dividing ridge between the Bear and Columbia rivers. For some miles the way fell and rose abruptly. Cottonwoods and shrubby trees clutched stubbornly at the sides of the gorge.

They passed the highest point and began a precipitous descent. Evening found them still in the pass, camped by a blustering stream that sang of hardier heights.

It took them nearly all day to come out of the defile, through straggling poplar groves, and set foot on a barren plain. High mountains ringed the hilless expanse. They paused on the borders of the lazy Neuf, a day's journey from Fort Hall.

The Snake was reached next morning, a narrow bayou at that point. Grass was plentiful and so was a virulent host of mosquitoes. Dusk brought the blotch-faced company to Fort Hall.

Wyeth had erected the fort in July, 1834. Francis Ermatinger was the present commander and he experienced some difficulty in persuading his savage allies that the visitors were "King George Men" and not the hated "Boston Men." Luckily for Sutter, he succeeded.

Here the Swiss had planned to strike south and overland to California. But Ermatinger advised against it.

"So small a party is sure to meet trouble," he warned. "These savages are always on the lookout—always hostile."

"What, then, shall I do?" asked Sutter.

The commandant considered. "Keep on to Fort Vancouver and try to find a boat sailing for the California coast," he counseled. "It's a better plan. Winter is not far off, either. Snow and cold are as deadly as Indians in a strange country."

The Swiss hesitated, shrugged. "Good advice, Captain Ermatinger," he said. "I shall go to Fort Vancouver."

THE TRAIL tracked away on the south bank of the winding Snake and they crossed the river at the present Glenn's Ferry in Idaho. Onward they angled to the Boise and found Fort Boise at its mouth.

Five days they rested. "Never," wrote Sutter, years later, "had a friendly place of refuge been so welcome."

Payette, hospitable French-Canadian commander of the stronghold, pressed them to linger. Trail-worn nerves relaxed in the security of the stockade. Good food and fellowship worked their revitalizing part.

Regretfully, the eight went on. A guide, furnished by Payette, took them over the Snake and Malheur and up and over the Blue Mountains. Nine days later they sighted Fort Walla Walla, sitting close to the junction of the Walla Walla and Columbia. It was a more imposing establishment than the last post. The stockade was oblong, built of driftwood logs, with bastions holding cannon at the southwest and northeast corners. The enclosure sheltered several houses, a trading-store, a blacksmith shop and a large corral. The houses were square, thatch-roofed, single-roomed affairs with good plank floors, one glass window, and a cheery fireplace. Sutter had not seen such swanky housing accommodations before in the wilderness. It impressed him.

Monsieur Pambrun, an ex-officer of the British Army, was no less cordial than Payette. His doors and larders were flung open with zest. Bitterly he regretted that Sutter planned a swift departure. At parting he wrung the Swiss' hand warmly.

"Alas, my friend," he said sorrowfully, "how desolate I am you go so soon! We have just killed a fat mare and would have enjoyed a feast!"

The Swiss had never been accustomed to the delicacy of horse meat. He kept back a smile and thanked his host. But Pambrun's sincere invitation gave him a hearty laugh when the fort walls had fallen behind. There is so little to be merry about on wilderness trails. . . .

A guide led them on to The Dalles. They found a Methodist mission there—a few dwellings, a schoolhouse and a barn. It had been erected by Reverends Lee and Perkins on a site where the river rushed through a long, narrow rock tunnel with a white fury that no boat could conquer at high water.

Sutter noticed with his land-hungry eyes that the near-by country had been tilled and harvested—mostly by Indian labor, he learned. It gave him an idea.

He inquired the way to the Willamette Valley. Reverend David Lee agreed to guide the party himself. He was just setting out with some horses which he wished to exchange with the Willamette Valley settlers, he explained; he intended to leave on the morrow.

The eight started early with the clergyman's party. At the end of the first day the California-bound company was dubious. Lee and his Indian aides seemed to be running about the uneven country in useless circles; the course seemed to run 'round and 'round in concentric abandon—quite as if no fixed destination existed in the guide's mind.

This was too much for the trail-hardened group from Independence. The next morning, without critical comment, they deserted the Reverend Lee. They waved farewell to their puzzled pilot and struck out on what seemed a more direct course.

That was a wild, mad ride. They climbed mountains and brought their floundering animals down steep ravines by the aid of ropes; they clawed with hands and feet to secure a hold where failure meant death; and wondered dimly if perhaps ministerial guidance might have led them on an easier path.

Deep, dangerous streams had to be crossed or the entire route retraced—rushing torrents that seemed to be in as much of a hurry to get some place as the determined Swiss. Once the floods carried away his horse; only the valorous action of the Indian boy saved the animal. The hundred-dollar beaver-order—and the thirty-dollar loss —had proved a good investment.

They camped at the foot of Mt. Hood on the fourth night from The Dalles. There was no water at that point; nor any grass. Supplies were low. Nothing but dried fish remained.

Next morning, after three hours of desperate trek-king, the horses and mules scented water. They jerked away over the rough ground and jolted the breath from their riders. They halted only when their noses were deep in the stream's swiftness.

The party rested for an hour. Then they plodded on, men and horses and mules, famished, exhausted.

SUNSET OF THE sixth day they came to the reaches of the Willamette Valley. No one would have believed Sutter's tale of such a speedy passage from The Dalles but for one thing: he carried a dated letter from the Reverend David Lee. So difficult and dangerous was the route accounted that it took the clergyman from seventeen to nineteen days to make the journey under favorable conditions! The chamois-like continent-hikers had cut the usual time by at least eleven days.

For three days they paused in the pleasant valley, intent on the last leg of the Fort Vancouver trip. They found they must use canoes to make the final dash. Horses and mules and equipment—excepting personal effects—were sold to the valley settlers and beaver-orders on the Hudson's Bay Company accepted in exchange.

Down the water-lanes they went; and with an amazing suddenness saw an end to the river journey. A swift glimpse of the fort made them thrust their slender craft abruptly to the right side of the river where a low bank gave promise of an easy landing.

The fortress sat on a beautifully sloping and fertile spot a quarter-mile from the Columbia. Sixty miles away Mt. Hood jutted a white head into the cold blue. The lovely valley rolled to the southward, spacious, tillable.

Leaving their canoes on the banks and shouldering their packs, the eight took swinging strides toward the twenty-foot-high stockade. The walls covered more than eight acres and a thin stream of bartering humanity trickled in and out of the open gates. There were more people in sight than Sutter and his men had seen since passing Fort Laramie.

In the enclosure they found forty buildings grouped about the chief factor's house. Fort Vancouver was a strategically vital Hudson's Bay post and at the moment its commanding officer was the future Sir James Douglas. Neither he nor Sutter were aware that they were to duel wordily—and craftily—for the possession of Fort Ross and Bodega at a later date; or that limits of empire hung on the successful outcome of their separate schemes. . . . The Swiss sought out the governor at once. They sat in big, fur-covered chairs beside the flat-topped redwood desk in Douglas' office and discussed Sutter's plans. Sir James was amiable and unbending. His visitor hastened to present letters from Sir William Drummond Stewart, Popian, and others—those written valuations probably had something to do with the governor's affability.

The day was October 3rd, 1838. It had taken Sutter six months to come thus far; and his objective was not yet reached. He had planned to ship aboard some outbound Hudson's Bay vessel that would touch at a California port; either that or try the coastal trail. But each course seemed blocked, he ruefully discovered. No vessels were sailing to California now or in the near future; and winter was about to make the overland route impracticable.

A winter spent at the fort was unthinkable. It seemed like wasted time. The eagerness for action never left Sutter, waking or sleeping. Something must be done. . . .

He importuned Douglas repeatedly for a solution. The Hudson's Bay Company bark *Columbia* was ready for an early departure. She carried lumber for the Sandwich Islands and furs for London.

"Why not sail to the Islands?" said Douglas to his impatient guest. "You can land there and find a boat for California in a short time. Many trading ships call there and—"

"Good!" cried Sutter. "I am forever your debtor, Governor Douglas. Your plan will save time and hard riding!"

He laughed delightedly, shook the official's hand warmly, and forsook the fur-covered chair for the fever of preparation.

But his men balked at the roundabout way. They preferred to stay where they were and await the spring. Only one of the Germans—an expert cabinet-maker—decided to chance the voyage. The Indian boy went, too; he had no choice in the matter.

On October 26th, 1838, the *Columbia* sailed. Sutter walked her tiny deck and dreamed his restless dreams. He was following the most lengthy course ever attempted from Independence, Missouri, to his future empire on the Sacramento.

Chapter IV

"QUIET HAVEN"

John Sutter, striding the small deck, first glimpsed the barren promontories of Oahu, straight ahead. On the shore the surf was a feather-edged, ever-charging, ever-changing line. Makapuu was the sterile point to the east. All black the land looked, starkly stern, shrouded with cloud-barriers.

Astoundingly, the dank veil swept away before Sutter's eyes. Color that was vague but delightful came into being. He saw the intense yellow of salt grasses along the sea-edge, the less vivid green of cane-fields, the purple-blue of steep mountains where the trade-winds were harrying masses of silver-gray clouds.

The *Columbia* sailed on, rounded the point, beat westward along the southern shore. She skimmed past Koko Point. Then into view came the spacious, shallow bay of Waialae.

Coconut trees deployed along the beach. The island jutted up swiftly a short way back into ravines that sheltered narrow, fertile valleys. The ridges sped up to loftier slopes, became without substance, lost in the verdant kingdom of the mountain tops.

On went the *Columbia*, skirting the coral reef that shields the bay from the crashing swells of the open sea. Leahi—Diamond Head—loomed near. Low-hutted Waikiki leaped into view as they passed the point; and Honolulu—"Quiet Haven"—lay only a few miles distant. Slowly, the grass-dwellings and warehouses and the white-washed mariner's chapel, topped with rank vegetation, took on nearness.

Outside the reef the ocean was blue. White surf marked the sharp denture of the shoal. The wide reef beyond was pink and buff and green—a lustrous, always-changing veil that draped the place with liquid glory.

It was the loveliest land the Swiss had ever seen. Trees grouped themselves on the mile of sloping green that lifted from the beach to the mountain spurs. The green marched from the shining sea to the still more shining ridges. Softly it stood about the lower reaches of Diamond Head, surged past the two villages until it vanished in the dim purple of the Waianae Mountains.

The low-lying Koolau range stretched away to Honolulu's rear. There was a crystal-blue about them which made Sutter think they were much higher than they really were. He measured the color on their slopes—the emerald of banana trees and ohia, the yellow of kukui trees, the softer neutral shades of fern masses, all gaining in perspective with exposed splashes of brick-red earth. The air seemed to sparkle and glow under the urging trade-wind. To John Sutter, who had been born in the Grand Duchy of Baden, it was a radiant dream. . . .

The *Columbia* hoisted the English colors and fired two guns as a signal for a pilot. Out from the shore came a canoe and over the rail dropped the rheumatic Kuakini, a native who had long ago so admired an American statesman that he changed his name to John Adams. For thirty years he had been master-pilot for "Quiet Haven" and the kapa-clad ancient was a familiar sight to every mariner who touched the islands.

"Old Adams" took them skillfully in. A fort, well-equipped with ordnance, commanded the entrance. It pleased Sutter, that fort, for it had an air of being placed exactly where it was needed.

As soon as the ship was made fast at the wharf she was boarded by Pelley, head-agent of the Hudson's Bay Company in the islands. Trotting along beside the long-legged Britisher was dumpy William French, a prominent merchant. French was the proud owner of a horse-worked sugar-mill of rude construction; it had been imported from China and manufactured the amazing output of 250 pounds daily! Or so its owner claimed within the first five minutes of Sutter's arrival.

During the first small talk Pelley casually mentioned that the *Bolivar* under Captain Gorham H. Nye had sailed only six hours before for California. To Sutter's excited query the agent was uncertain as to the next departure for that coast.

"Three or four months, probably," he guessed.

"By Jupiter!" cried Sutter. "Let us hope you are mistaken, friend Pelley. I looked forward to a quick passage."

Pelley was impressed by his personable visitor in the next hour. So much so, that he invited the Swiss to share his quarters until a ship presented itself. "Accommodations in the town are very poor," he finished. "Best come up with me, Captain Sutter."

The visitor felt honored; and said so. He packed his personal traps and made hurried shore arrangements for the cabinet-maker and the Indian boy. Then he and Pelley began their journey on foot.

They passed over streets ankle-deep in light dust and sand. The thoroughfares were not clean and pigs slept undisturbed in favored siesta spots. There was only one principal avenue in the entire village of nine thousand people. Along it ran substantial two-story structures of wood, adobe, coral or stone, usually fronted with long balconies and verandahs. The rest were filthy, crooked alley trails that wandered among native huts—rough wooden frames tied together and thatched over with grass or *ti* leaves, almost windowless hovels with low, narrow doorways.

The day was Sunday. Sutter watched with interest as barefooted natives, some clad in kapa and some in silk dresses, flocked to the coral church where Lowell Smith was to preach to them. Pelley was a wordy, friendly chap who kept up a running fire of comment. His guest learned that the islands were passing through a period of swift transition in this year of 1839; that missionaries and merchants were invariably at loggerheads; that native babies, if too many of them arrived, were still strangled or buried alive by their parents; that business was brisk but that the sandalwood trade was dead.

As they walked, the Swiss noticed that many of the Hawaiians wore sweet-smelling chaplets of flowers and bright-colored feathers. Some even wore strings of orange-colored pandanus fruit on their heads or about their necks.

The two strolled up the Nuuanu Valley, where Pelley's home lay some four miles away. Usually, the Englishman rode a horse to and from his residence; but Sutter had wanted the walk. They passed fields of tall grasses, sea-like in the breeze; trailed down lines of tropical trees aslant with glitter; skirted rocks overgrown with vines. It had been warm when they began their leisurely ascent. As they came to the higher elevation of the agent's quarters it was perceptibly cooler.

The official's retreat was a snug cottage surrounded by plants and flowers and criss-crossing garden paths. The orange, lemon, fig and olive trees captivated Sutter. Limes and guavas and citrons and pomegranates and love-apples brought him to an incredulous ecstacy. Nearly all the trees were unknown to him—the prickly pears, the date-palms, the camphor-trees, the oriental lilacs.

In the garden he hung over the melons and yams and strawberries and other succulent offerings. Every new thing delighted his heart—how well the soil repaid those who worked with it! His single-purposed mind swirled with plans for California. . . .

He came to know the island well in the days that followed. Once he peered over the 1200-foot sheerness of the Pali and saw the bewildering sweep of the windward coast. He rambled in Manoa, the first valley to the east. Each step was a new adventure. He never tired of it.

Sometimes his feet lingered by great kukui trees whose leaves were like the maple; gigantic ferns cast their patterned fronds above him; the leaves and berries of the mokihana assaulted him with pungent fragrance;

Top: Governor Micheltorena
Bottom: Governor Alvarado

the yellow candles of the ie ie vine, with rings of
crimson leaves, burned exotically as he passed; clumps
of wild bananas companioned with lehua trees whose
blossoms were pink flames. There seemed no end to the
Paradise of Oahu—no magic to match the alchemy of
the warm soil.

The natives interested him. They swam or dived or
bowled with polished stones; they rode surf-boards and
ran foot-races and boxed; they darted on wooden sleds
down steep slide-slots set in the hillsides. But, to a Continental mind, they were a shiftless lot.

The full-bosomed girls had intriguing possibilities.
Distractingly acquiescent creatures of liquid movement
they were too. Yet Sutter—who had been absent from
his own hearthstone for four years—seemed blind. The
jovial Pelley was a bit miffed at such unresponsiveness at
first—couldn't understand it.

"Demmit, man," said he, "you're not giving the
islands a fair trial!" For to twinkling-eyed Pelley all
curves were dedicated to ravishment.

But Sutter was a busy man, plagued by seething plans.
One passion kept him from another. And, tucked away
in the intimate personal taboos of his mind, was an in-
stinctive aversion—only once spoken—to maids whose
skins were not the color of his own. Not that John
Sutter was a virginal soul. . . .

Most men liked the Swiss; most women approved
him with speculative glances. He had an ease of manner
that pleased and a dignity that included and never
offended. His enthusiasm lent a sparkle to drabness and
he was a deft *raconteur* who told a good story well. He
knew the art of listening, too—a more important thing
than his quick laugh and ready word. In a week he was
the most sought-after socialite in island life.

He enjoyed the round of parties and dinners. Hosts of
smart Oahu imported all the luxuries—rare foodstuffs,
vintage champagnes, liqueurs, lustrous furbishments. No

epicure could elevate eyebrows over island cuisine; there was nothing lacking, either in setting or service.

Dapper John C. Jones, the United States consul, encountered Sutter in his convivial moments. One declaration of the Swiss pleased him—that the United States would one day own California. Jones thought so himself. "A wise fellow, this Captain Sutter," said he.

They had long talks—exchanged confidences. The consul promised aid to Sutter's venture. He even wrote him several strong recommendations to smooth the way with Mexican officialdom. "You must keep me informed of your progress," he urged. "We must not lose sight of each other."

The Swiss promised.

GOVERNOR KEKUANOA heard of the visitor and his project. A message came shortly, bidding Sutter to an official banquet. Many of the influential merchants attended—Pelley, French, Jones, Reynolds and others. Sutter came down from the cottage with his host.

Kamehameha III had moved his court to Lanai and Kekuanoa was the highest ranking native official on Oahu. The gathering was chatty and colorful. All the chiefs were decoratively attired in Windsor uniforms, island royalty having imported a London tailor three years before.

When dinner was announced each of the resplendent chiefs took a guest by the arm and escorted him from the reception salon to a larger banquet room. It was European in appointment and arranged with a long mahogany dining table, buffets, chairs and sofas. Yet Sutter learned later that most of the furnishings were of native workmanship.

There was white napery and shining glass and plate and shaded lamps; there were fruits and sweetmeats and delicious entrees and wines—even fragrant tea and coffee. The Swiss was to remember the smell of that island coffee on certain bleak wilderness mornings.

Each plate held a name card. Guests and hosts were seated in that sequence. His Excellency bulked amiably between Sutter and Pelley during the banquet and commented moistly on island affairs. All the Hawaiians spoke passable English. They were courteous and unboisterous—well-poised even after the liqueurs and cigars.

The evening seemed flawless to Sutter. He noticed no lapses from conformity. But Sir George Simpson, who attended a similar function two years later, had a number of inconsistencies to report. The Englishman remarked that all evening one of the chiefs insisted upon asking, with a great show of anxiety, if Sir George thought that his (the chief's) whiskers were more than ordinarily handsome. It developed that he was on the look-out for a new wife and considered his facial shrubbery as one of his greatest physical attractions.

Personally, the whiskers left Sir George unmoved. Later, his eagle eye noticed, in a sudden entry into another apartment, the swift disappearance of a pair of shapely legs under the hangings of a bed. After this phenomenon the discreet Sir George recalls no more.

But Sutter did observe one happy habit of the governor's in the following weeks—he was never seen without an attentive escort of breast-bare, sun-brown maidens. It was quite the thing, a fashion that caused no comment on Oahu. They were used to it.

THE WAIT for passage grew tedious. Old Adams brought no vessel into the inner harbor that was bound for the California coast. The Swiss damned his luck and kept his restless eye on the sea-line.

Three months he fretted. Then an idea gripped him. Swinging on a hawser in the harbor was the English bark *Clementine*. She was open for charter and no one had made a bid for her.

Sutter made swift inquiries, and then reached a decision. He began to interest French, Greenway, Reynolds and others in a trading venture of his devising. He proposed to freight the vessel with produce and articles which could be shipped without spoilage, sail to Sitka, and barter with the Russians. Finally, he planned to sell the remaining cargo at Californian ports.

He offered to advance a share of the outfitting cost, sail with the vessel, and act as supercargo without pay. French was invited to accompany him and take over the financial management for the interested merchants when he—Sutter—left the brig in California.

The scheme appealed to the merchants. The Russians represented an exceptional market and there was little risk in the undertaking. Contracts were drawn, and the ship chartered, and freighted with the necessary supplies.

With the voyage assured, Sutter gave a thought to other matters. Three small brass cannon were purchased and stowed away for wilderness taming. The German cabinet-maker, who had been doing a prosperous business during the wait, found a countryman anxious to join them. Then the Governor offered to supply ten Kanakas—two with their wives—who were willing to go to California for a three-year period at a salary of ten dollars each a month. Sutter guaranteed them a return passage and food, clothing and shelter during the time they were pledged to his service.

In April the *Clementine* was ready. Captain John Blinn, her hard-faced Cockney master, declared her sea-worthy. She lay low in the water, her hold packed to the deck-line.

The sailing brought a bright host to the harbor. One friend brought along a huge bulldog that had been underfoot around the house and presented it to Sutter a moment before the ship cast off. Jones, Pelley, Stephen Reynolds, Abell, McClure, Cheevers and an added score of well-wishers gathered on the wharf. The smiling Kekuanoa was there to wave a quivering jelly of an arm in aloha.

The throng tossed fragrant white flowers on the deck. One slim-hipped girl threw a lei about Sutter's neck. He stood, booted feet spread wide at the rail, calling farewells. . . . His friends grew smaller and the land grew misty.

The white sails filled noisily, and the *Clementine* dug her nose into the salty glitter. She was on her course to Sitka, away from California.

Chapter V

BEAR'S LAIR

THROUGH HEAVING sea-leagues the brig slapped her bulk. Sutter was never a happy sailor man. He liked the smells of the soil, the scent of its fruitage, but the salt-tang of the briny breeze did not quiver his nostrils. It was a salt-tang to John Sutter. Nothing more.

Colder grew the passage. For only a few moments a day could the dipping deck be braved and ship-tightened muscles flexed. The Kanakas felt the change more than the others; they huddled bleakly and chattered little. . . . Summertime should have been approaching the northland latitude and Captain Blinn held that the continued cold was mystifying.

The perfect cone of Mount Edgecumbe jumped out of the sea one dawn. Still hidden under its peak lay Russian America—Sitka. It was nearing April's end, 1839.

The *Clementine* came edging into the sound and fired two guns to speed the pilot. But it was two hours before he drove a skimming kayak into view. The breeze had almost died away. Behind the canoe came the governor's barge in charge of Alexander, his secretary, who clambered aboard and gave an order to tow the *Clementine* to her anchorage. As the ship maneuvered through the channel, the secretary and Sutter found French a common tongue and made the most of it.

The way was obstructed by islands topped with slender-tipped birch. Suddenly, quite close, New Archangel lifted into vision. And, over all, a silken marker flew on the sloping *kekoor*—the smug eagles of Imperial Russia.

Sutter thought of his homeland: above the castle and the houses and the spangled flag stood Edgecumbe—the Sisters showed in the distance of Indian River, pale creatures, snow-jeweled; Mount Vestoria's arrowhead fronted the glittering glaciers in the east and a curve of mist-clad mountains sprawled to the southeast.

The *Clementine* was warped to within a cable's length of the arsenal, where a half-dozen other craft lay under the Russian batteries. Baranoff Castle was the summit of the height, a hundred feet above sea-level.

A twenty-five-foot-high stockade of picketed logs ran twenty feet from the sea-edge and a mile long to the river flanked by loopholed blockhouses lying within musketshot of each other. That barrier cut off all connection with the natives, save for a single well-policed portcullis that led into a railed yard. There the wild Kolosh, Sutter learned, brought their furs and goods for marketing.

Alexander landed with the Swiss and French, offering to guide them to the castle. As they walked, the secretary mentioned that guards paced the stockade day and night.

"They hate us," he remarked. "Hoonahs, Chilkats, Auks, Stikines, Kakes, Sitkas—all of the sly butchers. We have had one massacre here. We don't intend to have another."

At that moment a dark, feathered comet slashed down out of the sky before them, seized a half-grown grubbing chicken. It was the largest raven Sutter had ever seen. Aloft it shot, prey held fast.

"It is nothing." Alexander gestured carelessly. "We lose many such. These ravens even nip the tails off our pigs—that is why so many of our hogs are tailless in Sitka!" He laughed.

An air of commercial prosperity was evident, with an added hint of military precision. Men were passing briskly from shops to storehouses, from storerooms to stores. Furs were being carried down to the beach for consignment to waiting ships. Other shore freight was being unloaded from the vessels.

Sutter shifted his gaze to the Castle as they climbed. It was a huge, two-story wooden structure, one hundred and fifty feet long, seventy feet wide. Giant eighty-foot logs, each squaring one foot, had gone into the thick walls; there they had been dove-tailed over each other and tree-nailed together. The roof was pitched and covered with sheet-iron; in its center, on the Castle's very crest, stood a lighthouse. The light on that tower was for more than a century the only aid to navigation on the entire coast of Alaska. In the cupola were four square cups into which whale-oil was poured; wicks burned in grooves rising from them; back of the flame was a reflector that sent the gleam far out to sea among the islands.

The young secretary chatted on. He pointed out with some pride that the *kekoor* fortifications were five-sided, adequate. Forty cannon sat in thick wooden bulwarks and pointed black snouts out of open ports. They had never barked at an invader yet. . . .

GOVERNOR IVAN KOUPREANOFF, colonel in the *Garde Imperial* of the Russian Navy, received Sutter and French warmly. He was a cheerful cosmopolitan, eager for companionship, fiercely whiskered, soft-voiced. One of his imperial majesty's seventy-fours—the *Asof*—had been his late command. In the Black Sea he had fought one of the deadliest sea duels of his time. His ship had won. All Russia honored him as one of the most intrepid officers in the Czar's service.

He was pleased with Sutter's cargo list of fruits, sugar, molasses, salt, paint oil and an abundance of other acceptable stores. In the meantime, while business details were in order, he insisted that both his visitors consider themselves his guests.

"Dinner this evening, gentlemen," he requested courteously. "You must meet my friends and assistants."

Sutter bowed, thanked him.

"It is a privilege we shall not miss, your excellency," he said in parting.

The social life of Sitka was dashing, notable. The governor and his lovely lady, the Princess Maksoutoff, entertained with the patrician hand in Baranoff Castle. Sutter attended his first affair in the elaborately furnished and decorated dining room. A colorful attendance came to group themselves about the governor's board. Father Veniaminov stormed regally in, clad in his gorgeous vestments, a swift word for everyone. Naval officers scintillated in gold-lace dress uniforms. Secretaries, accountants and storekeepers wore the garb of the ministry of finance. Captains of ships in harbor paraded in their best.

The Swiss was delighted with the display; also with the cut of his own natty frock coat. That coat had been made in New York and sent to St. Louis at his order; only that afternoon Catherine, the tailor's daughter, had pressed the garment. Not a wrinkle was left in it. Sutter was a stickler in the matter of dress-up hours— something of a dandy. He believed in soap and water and clean linen and shined boots—as much as the wilderness would let him.

A hundred people were there that night. Back of the long table, at a smaller board, sat the naval cadets in bright-buttoned, youthful exclusiveness. The meal itself was delicious; but did not compare by a gourmet's eyelash with the imported viands of Oahu.

Dancing in the smooth-surfaced, high-ceilinged ballroom followed dinner. Several of the junior clerks were excellent musicians with a flair for sustained effort. Quadrilles, waltzes and Russian dances pulsed a rhythmic background for the gayety.

The Russian officers and their wives spoke French. That made the evening easier, more care-free. Sutter was soon learning difficult Russian steps, a laugh on his full lips. Who would not have proved adept with the Princess Maksoutoff as instructor?

The imperial lady was piquantly chic, intelligent. In a critical moment she had ridden horseback over barren

Siberia to Okhotsk in order to accompany her husband to his new post. Hers had been the gay, spirited life of royalty. Now, as the first lady of Sitka, she brought warmth and brilliance to a harsh land. . . .

Liqueurs and cigars were served at strategic intervals. A smoking room was convenient for those seeking a moment from the whirling scene. Sutter's straight legs never wavered or tired in the scramble of sliding boots and skipping slippers. He danced with the Princess; he danced with other scented ladies; he danced with Catherine, the tailor's daughter, who was not well-born but whose wit and loveliness captured more moon-eyed suitors than the dainty flirt could bother with. . . . Gray dawn shuffled out of the sky-line with a leaden yawn before the boots and the slippers went home to rest.

THE COLONY had men of every trade and artifice in its nine hundred population—blacksmiths, locksmiths, coppersmiths, rope-spinners, chandlers, painters, masons, sawyers. A water-powered sawmill operated steadily at *Les Sources*—Warm Springs. A shipyard turned out fine vessels fashioned of close-grained yellow cypress. There were social halls for the workers and tea houses sat on the little knoll in the center of the village where the public gardens were located.

In the next few days, while stores from the *Clementine* were being purchased and shifted ashore, the governor conducted Sutter on a tour of the town. They passed through the hospital where the sick received fresh food, tea, sugar, and medicines, free under a doctor's orders. The three-roomed apothecary shop was inspected where three Creole boys doled out the precious potions under a physician's supervision. The two-thousand-volume library presented by the scholarly Nicholas Resanov in 1806—books in English, Russian, French, German and Latin, resting on neat shelves—was viewed approvingly. They walked through the museum where all objects of interest collected in the surrounding country were placed and catalogued. Next came the observatory, equipped with the most improved magnetic and meteorological instruments, where a careful record was kept of all natural phenomena.

Later, in the arsenal, the visitor lingered over a thousand muskets and scores of pistols, rifles, sabres and cutlasses. Set apart from the others were some rare weapons: a sabre set with gems; a Persian carbine; two Persian yatighans, silver-mounted; a magnificent blade of Damascus tempered with a cunning art, and two gold-mounted Persian pistols. And, standing in the same depository, they came upon what was to Sutter the strangest sight in Sitka — four fire engines, brought from St. Petersburg to guard the remote spot from conflagration!

The magazines interested him most. They held every necessity and many a luxury carried in the general European trade with which he was familiar. There was sugar and sealing wax; Virginia and Kirghiz tobaccos; calico and broadcloth and Flemish linen; ravens-duck and frieze; *arshins* of blankets and *pouds* of yarn; butter from Yakhut, from California and from Kodiak; *vedras* of rum, cognac and gin; salt beef from the Ross Colony; and beaver hats and cotton socks.

In the next row of storehouses were astounding piles of furs. Here lay the real reason for the existence of the Russian American Fur Company. There were pelts of sea-otter, land-otter, seal, martin and the American sable with its silky *pelage*. In other storerooms lay fox-skins—thousands of them—blue, white, black, silver-gray, red and cross. Then he saw more thousands of mink, musk-rat and beaver, pile on pile. Tons of ivory from the walrus herds of Morzhovia lay heaped near great mounds of wolf and bear-skins.

A fabulous fortune stood walled in those packed places. A fair share of it would be treasured in coats and smart wraps by beautiful women in the capitals of the world; and even the beauties of the provincial towns would boast their pelted portion. This was the outpost Peter the Great had dreamed and had not lived to see— the focal point of all Russian activities in North America.

Sutter drew a long breath between the wonders of the furry lanes and thought of the wealth that would be his in that new land when next the *Clementine* came to anchor; there were thousands of fur-bearing animals in California, ready for the trapping. . . .

The chartered brig lay in the harbor for six weeks. At least once a day Sutter dined with Koupreanoff. Twice he visited the church and witnessed a ceremony ritualized by Father Veniaminov, most personable prelate ever to grace the halls of worship and Russian-ruled streets of *Novo Arkangelsk.*

The Swiss took a great liking to the steady-eyed Veniaminov. The priest was a gem of bewildering facets. He admitted Sutter into his workshop, a privilege not accorded his countrymen. In the tool-lined, compact cubicle was a barrel-organ he had made with his own hands; also a barometer and an array of useful scientific devices.

He even consented to doctor the ailing barometer of the *Clementine* and effectually cured that crotchety instrument. A man of even unsuspected qualifications, this Father Veniaminov; and one who was to become a high dignitary in the Greek Orthodox Church.

A CASTLE must have a ghost and Baranoff Castle had a charming wraith. In 1831, eight years before Sutter's visit, Governor Baron Ferdinand Wrangell made a written report to the Russian American Fur Company officials in St. Petersburg. He stated briefly that Colonel Borusof had been implicated in the tragic death of Under Officer Paul Buikof. That same year the Baron's dark-haired daughter, Mary, brooding and disconsolate, died in Sitka.

So the legend of the Lady in Blue had crept into being about the metropolis of the old fur days. Her lover was secretly murdered by an *Ober-Offitzer* who sought her hand in marriage. Much was suspected; little could be proved. But she was true to her lost love. One night she disappeared from the crashing music of the ballroom and hid herself away. After a search they found her, a pool of scarlet over her heart, dead by her own hand.

This is the legend. She walked, the old ones said, about the Castle in the dark nights when all was cold and bleak and desolate; and cried aloud the name of Paul, the slain. Poor lady, perhaps she found rest when the purifying flames razed Baranoff Castle half a century later and left a mound of black ashes where so much gayety and laughter and sorrow had been. . . .

Chapter VI

THE GOLDEN GATE

THE CLEMENTINE rode high on the day of departure. More than three-quarters of her cargo had found its way into the storehouses on the *kekoor* and few stores had been exchanged for California barter. Sutter was well-satisfied. High prices had been paid for the goods and the voyage was certain to show a profit.

His parting with the friendly officers at Sitka was merely *au revoir*. Many of them were to grasp his hand again. He was to rendezvous with Koupreanoff on board the *Nikolai* and discuss the purchase of Fort Ross and Bodega. And Governor Rotscheff, Peter Kostromitinoff and a score of others were to fête him aboard the *Helena* at Ross, after they had sold to him every Russian possession in North America below the fifty-fourth parallel.

June had reached the northland when the *Clementine* sailed out of Sitka Sound. They came to say farewell, the governor, the Princess, Veniaminov and the others. He did not see Catherine in the crowd on the beach; but he had said goodbye to her the night before, alone and magnificently. Or so the envious French sets down.

The guns on the hill boomed. Castle and town were abruptly sheared from sight by sharp shore-lines—forever for the Swiss. Mt. Edgecumbe sank lower and lower into the land and water. Then it was a blunt finger, flexed into nothingness.

John Sutter turned his eyes away and paced the slanting deck. The sting of the sea-breeze was once more with him. Shifting planks gave him no lift, no promise. He felt a restless loss in the passing from new friends. . . .

That was a dreary voyaging. Great seas hurled their curling fury against the brig. Winds tore at her wailing canvas, slashed rents, strained masts, snapped cordage. A universe of mad waters and malevolent days.

Southward she beat her lonely way. No other whiteness riding the wastes came into view. Each league was
an endless milepost to those below decks; to those above
it was a bruising battle on groaning planks and spray-
wet rigging.

Governor Koupreanoff had traced a copy of Sir Edward Belcher's Survey for Sutter; without it there is a
question whether Captain Blinn could have found the
entrance where the Golden Gate tides swirled through
the rocky headlands. Wheeling flights of gulls and
cormorants and pelicans convoyed the ship those last
few miles. It was July 1st, 1839.

Sutter glimpsed high ridges and grassy slopes as the
Clementine nosed in. Untended herds of cattle grazed on
the green cliffs. He let a hand fall to the head of the
shivering bulldog who hunched at heel, braced against
the sea-roll. . . . There was rich land beyond the heights—
for the asking. . . . The wind lost its coldness.

"We are here!" he cried to French.

The merchant, pasty-faced from sickness, was clutching the rail with the grip of a man who did not care
much what happened. He detested Sutter for his enthusiasm. . . .

Slowly they worked through the channel into the
port. They passed a dilapidated, dismantled fort to the
right. Beyond the ruin they sighted a square of huts—
the Presidio of San Francisco.

Laggardly, they entered into a huge stretch of un-
troubled harbor, sheltered from the winds by a rising
slope of hills. A littoral of open plain was dotted with a
score of dwellings. A frequent column of dark vapor
filtered placidly into the sun-bright sky from some man's
hearth. Peaceful it seemed, and pastoral. A haven after
danger.

The *Clementine* dropped her anchor close to where the
dozen buildings of Yerba Buena straggled on the shore.
Three other vessels lay swinging on hawsers in the easy

swells. Blinn pointed one out as the *Bolivar*, the craft Sutter had missed by a few hours at Honolulu.

From the *Clementine's* deck they noticed that someone had made note of their arrival. A shore-boat put off hurriedly from the beach, oars slapping raggedly.

An officer in tattered uniform and cracked boots popped over the rail. He whirled and gestured imperiously to the six men in the boat to stand by. Then he turned bear-oiled mustachios and flashing eyes on Blinn and Sutter and French.

"This is not a port of entry!" he told them. "It is forbidden that you land here! I cannot allow it, *señors*. You must sail on to Monterey for your permit!"

His listeners were dismayed. They tried to soften the dignitary. But he was firm. In halting Spanish they admitted the knowledge that Yerba Buena was a closed port. But they assured the sputtering Mexican that they had no intent to willfully disregard regulations.

"Stress of weather forced us in, my dear *Teniente*," Sutter explained. "We are willing to depart as soon as the ship—"

"It is impossible, *señor*. *Basta!*—if we allow privilege to one, all would ask," growled the functionary with his toes out.

The three tried again, intent.

Meantime, another boat had made its unnoticed way to the *Clementine*. It brought three prominent citizens of Yerba Buena—John Wilson, Gorham H. Nye and Nathan Spear, the leading merchant. They swiftly cut into the discussion. At their names being mentioned in greeting Sutter beamed, excused himself, rushed below. He returned with a sheaf of letters of introduction, two or more addressed to each of the three. Those lucky letters had been pressed upon him by well-wishers in Honolulu.

The trio moved at once to influence the officials. Captain Wilson, a brother-in-law of General Vallejo, made some pointed demands. Juan Prado Mesa, the

Monte Diablo from the Sacramento River as it looked at the time when Sutter first ascended it in 1839. Sketched by Lieutenant J. W. Revere, U.S.N.

military commander, had followed his first underling aboard. He listened courteously to explanations and requests. Then he granted a grudging forty-eight hour stay. The crew might land, make repairs and secure provisions. But, he warned, the craft must depart on or before the exact time designated.

Thankfully, Blinn ordered the carpenters and sailmakers to work. Sutter and the bilious French went ashore as Nathan Spear's guests. They stretched sea-legs and dined on fresh vegetables until the too-soon sailing hour. The Kanakas, the two Germans and the bulldog were installed with Spear until Sutter could return from Monterey.

Every American in town called in at Spear's and asked the newcomers to remain for the big Fourth of July celebration about to be given. The visitors were willing enough. But Commander Mesa would not hear of it.

"No further delay," he ordered.

The battered brig sailed on schedule. Sutter watched Yerba Buena fall away and vanish behind the ridges. Once more the Golden Gate tides parted under the keel.

Next afternoon they rounded Santa Cruz Point with Punta de Pinos to the south. Monterey Harbor curved in before them. They came abreast two ships at anchor and fired a three-gun salute to the squatting fort. Spear had advised that courtesy. With great dignity the rusty mouths of the *castillo* ordnance belched a reply; and by a miracle did not burst their ancient black lengths.

They were boarded by a smirking band of customs officers—there were six of them—who scraped and bowed and slithered their way on deck. The first request tendered by this delegation was to Captain Blinn for some powder; the welcome given the vessel had used up all the available Mexican ammunition.

While the eager gentlemen went to work, Sutter prepared to land. Armed with the usual sheaf of letters, he and French boarded the ship's-boat. He felt that here his plans were really to begin. In Yerba Buena he had been somehow a mariner in distress; here he was an *empresario de colonizacion* come to present his glowing schemes to Governor Alvarado.

The little boat hesitated on the outer edge of the surf. Then a comber rushed them into the end of the cove, at the foot of the customs house. The sailors leaped out and dragged the craft farther inland. When the wave fell away they were high on the beach.

Sutter set out swiftly, French quickening his stride to keep pace. Into the town the Swiss stamped confidently. In his mind he saw an empire beyond the ridges. . . . He had spent five years of his life on this crooked, troubled trail. But the time was now.

Chapter VII

FIGHTING BIRDS

THE CALIFORNIA of 1839 was a cockpit filled with steel-spurred roosters of every plumage. Everyone enjoyed a grievance. Native Californians were infuriated by the presence of convicts and cholo soldiers sent from Mexico. Veterans grown gray in California service railed at Mexicans who held preferred commissions. The Californians, landholders as their fathers before them, detested the interlopers—called them *de la otra banda*.

Foreigners were another troublesome group. Many had drifted in recently, by land and sea, hunters, adventurers, deserting sailors,perpetual wanderers. Mostly Americans, they were easily pledged to intrigue that promised either advancement or privilege.

Apart from these opportunists were residents of some standing, men who had attained their citizenship. They were identified with the country as landowners, husbands of native Californians or reputable merchants. Some had lived in California for years. Naturally, these men were the most pacific of the aliens.

Many of them were to aid—or plague—Sutter. Captain Henry Delano Fitch was the leading San Diego merchant. Ugly Don Abel Stearns—he of the eye for beauty—was the prominent Los Angeles figure. Lanky Captain John B. R. Cooper, staid Thomas Oliver Larkin, and David Spence—from Aberdeenshire—lived in Monterey. William Antonio Richardson, Jacob Primer Leese, William Alexander Liedesdorff and Nathan Spear were officials and traders in Yerba Buena. George C. Yount, Edward McIntosh and drink-loving Timothy Murphy had settled north of the bay. Near Monte Diablo had rooted the miserly John Marsh, in his doorless, floorless hovel.

One of the intense irritations fostered in California hearts was caused by dishonest Mexican officials who came regularly to collect and disburse provincial funds. Also, the Mission fathers were still loyal to Old Spain— spoke ceaselessly against all things Mexican. The loss of their temporal prestige in the chaos of secularization did not lessen their bitterness.

Secularization had been begun in 1831 by the close-lipped visionary, Governor Echeandia. His scheme had been to liberate the eighteen thousand Indian neophytes under padre-rule, develop their property sense by apportioning them small land-holdings, and thus avoid any possibility of foreign colonization by an adventure in citizenship.

The result was sure. The missionaries had dedicated their lives to the spiritual and physical conquest of a wilderness. A lifetime's labor was suddenly snatched from their hands. To them the plan was unspeakable, unbelievable; for the neophytes it was impractical.

The padres met the challenge with a very human reaction. They ceased to care for the gardens, the vineyards and the buildings under their charge. Swiftly they accomplished the slaughtering of Mission cattle for the hides and tallow—the quickest way to realize funds.

To feed and clothe the usual number of Indians became impossible under such conditions; much less were the establishments able to contribute food and supplies to a government that was held accountable for their present plight.

The friars were deprived of their management. *Comisionados* took their place and made inventories of all Mission property. An allocation of land was made and other supplies were presumably distributed to the amazed neophytes.

After the *comisionados* came the *mayordomos*, who began to woefully mismanage the estates under the eye of a casual government. With heaviness of heart the padres became either temporary curates or left the country.

For years the ranchos, Missions and towns had hugged the shore-line from San Diego to Yerba Buena. Men had not cared to venture more than a few miles beyond the sound of the surf. Whales spouted daily along the coast. Sea-lions, sea-elephants and seals were plentiful. Trading vessels were still few.

The central valleys and the interior were practically unmapped, unknown regions—the domain of wretched Indians and wild beasts. Great herds of elk, deer and wild horses spread over the Sacramento plain. Flocks of wild fowl darkened the surface of every inland lake and the air vibrated with their hoverings. Vultures pinioned in the heights, watchful for death. Hundreds of ferocious grizzly bears roamed about, restless food-seekers, given a wide berth even by the fierce cattle bands. Indeed, so savage and undesirable was this inland country rated by the Californians that no grant of land had ever been petitioned for prior to Sutter's coming.

The *Clementine* sailed into San Francisco Bay only a week before Mexican President Bustamante confirmed Vallejo as *comandante militar* of California and his nephew Alvarado as governor. These two had been responsible for the successful 1836 revolt. Vallejo, then only a lieutenant, had sat in prudent innocence at Sonoma and engineered the rumblings that frightened Mariano Chico, the Mexican-appointed civil leader. That mistress-ridden official took flight to Mazatlan. But he did not forget to take his faithless Dona Cruz, author of most of his troubles, on the return voyage. He left an easy-going, amorous Spanish gentleman as his successor, Colonel Nicholas Gutierrez.

At once Alvarado, Castro, Pico and Carrillo advanced on Monterey with an army of seventy-five men. They felt that now was the time to rid themselves forever of unwelcome officialdom. Thirty of their force were gathered by the reckless Tennessee rifleman, Isaac

Graham, as cantankerous a mountain-man as ever lingered
long on a plain. This crack-shot wine-bibber owned a
distillery near San Juan that became a favorite loafing
place for foreigners. He had no difficulty in raising a
nondescript party of *rifleros Americanos* at Alvarado's
request.

It was rumored that Gutierrez had been maintaining
a seraglio of Indian maids from San Gabriel in his *palacio*.
One excuse was as good as another. The dignity and
morals of all California was outraged—so said the Californians. They were determined to settle the matter
briefly.

The attackers approached the town, found the fort
undefended and occupied it. Honey-tongued Francisco
Soto was armed with several bottles of brandy and urged
forward to the Presidio, there to induce desertion in
Gutierrez' ranks.

A careful examination of the *castillo* armament was
made. One six-pounder was declared serviceable. This
gun was turned and pointed in the general direction of
the defending forces. Jose Abrego furnished a cannonball.
Cosme Pena was allowed fifteen minutes to "read up"
on artillery practice.

Great deliberation was used in elevating the gun.
Some perturbation existed as to what would occur—an
explosion or the hoped-for gunfire.

Then the courageous Pena did his duty. The pro-
jectile hurled itself weakly into the *zaguan* of Gutierrez'
house at the very moment that worried official was discussing the situation with his officers in the courtyard.

That was the only shot of the revolt. The Governor
immediately abdicated and was permitted to sail for
Mexico. Vallejo and Alvarado were proclaimed temporary leaders by the insurrectionists.

In a month there was a coolness between the new
administrators. Each held the other's authority to the
narrowest limits; each regarded himself as superior in
authority to the other. They sat back and mumbled to

mutual friends. And mutual friends rode horses to death in the happy avocation of bearing tales.

This rivalry between the pair had a two-way meaning for Sutter. It was to assure him a friend and an enemy in the high places.

MONTEREY STOOD on a pleasant plain that sloped northward. A tree-crested ridge rose to the south. Sutter saw the town as a mere collection of buildings sitting in jumbled placidity that July 4th.

There was no real street in the entire village. Some of the dwellings were two-storied adobes with overhanging eaves, an occasional rude balcony and glassless windows set in the protection of grilled embrasures. Red tiles covered the roofs of the more pretentious, white-washed homes. Cracks angled along many walls, the result of frequent temblors.

The customs house was the most imposing structure of California's capital. It had been building for three years, French informed, and was still unfinished. They noticed that a number of offices were already in use, probably for the transaction of clerical business.

The half-stone church was also unfinished—had partially begun to disintegrate. The adobe fort with its adobe wall seemed tenantless; usually its garrison of five men were enjoying a perpetual siesta because of the lack of food or powder or shot. Next to the *castillo* stood a small, windowless guardhouse of the inevitable sun-dried brick, doorless.

Two hundred yards beyond the customs house Sutter and his companion slackened their steps to inquire the way to the Governor's new mansion from a curious, ragged *soldado*. French remembered the old quarters; but had suddenly recalled a rumor heard in Yerba Buena that the Governor had recently moved.

"It is but a little distance, *señors*," said the barefooted fellow importantly. "I, myself, will conduct you."

A number of flea-bitten, sad-eyed dogs, intrigued by this courtesy, also joined the guard of honor. Thus escorted, the pair moved on.

The house was small. Without a wait they were ushered into the executive's best apartment, a room filled with an overflow of cheap chairs and a scarred table. A large Dutch clock beat its heart out on a shelf, flanked by a half-dozen inexpensive mirrors which offered astounding personal impressions if one was bold enough to dare their mottled faces. But there was one unique feature that gave the room dignity: three large glass windows, reaching down to the floor, looked out on a splendid vista of sea and sky and town. One could push them open, step out on a lengthy balcony and pause with the sweeping view and the fresh, sunny air. A saving grace, thought Sutter; one sat in ugliness and yet a glance could capture beauty. . . .

The Governor, indisposed at the moment, came in languidly. He leaned on the arm of Jimeno Casarin, his secretary. On a creaking sofa, hidden behind the table, he sank wearily. He smiled and voiced a swift apology— waved a hand in deprecation.

Juan Bautista Alvarado, one-time choir-boy and customs inspector, was thirty years old. This last breath-taking elevation was the greatest leap of his life; and his self-estimation had swooped accordingly. His father had been Sergeant Francisco Alvarado, a patient plodder who had demanded that the soldier-schoolmasters teach his son to read and write and cipher. Later, Governor Sola had given the observant boy a chance to improve his penmanship at a clerk's desk in the gubernatorial office.

Young Juan had two comrades then—Jose Castro and Guadalupe Vallejo. When they could escape the vigilant friars these three read aloud many a contraband tome. Readers, all; and bound to get ahead. Juan soon spoke English well. He was often employed as a clerk and collector by foreign traders who relied on his honesty and intelligence.

Sutter noticed, during the salutations, that marks of dissipation had begun to set unhealthy lines in the Governor's face. Aguardiente, he concluded, might have something to do with the official's illness.

Alvarado was friendly. He and his eagle-beaked secretary scanned their visitor's letters politely. William French was already favorably known to them—for a very good reason. He had supplied Alvarado with two cannon for the 1836 uprising, cannon that had arrived too late to be used in the one-shot battle of the war.

The Swiss' missives were from trustworthy sources—James Douglas, Colonel Ivan Koupreanoff, John C. Jones and a score of others. All were witness to the good character and honesty of the bearer; each urged the Governor to aid him in every way possible. It was the custom of Sutter's time for every traveler to carry such letters and he had been deluged with a commendatory flood of them.

Sutter stated his plans briefly in throaty, imperfect English. French occasionally threw in a sentence. He had come, said Sutter, with a small party of emigrants to found a colony somewhere in the interior; he wished to obtain a tract of land with His Excellency's consent, as an *empresario de colonizacion.*

Alvarado was reflective. But he shook his head.

"Your party is too small for such a venture, Captain Sutter," he said. "Perhaps we can design a better plan."

With a smile he turned to Casarin, consulted him in rapid Spanish. Then he turned back.

"Here is a better scheme," he assured. "I advise you to announce officially your intention of becoming a Mexican citizen. After that go inland, select any tract that strikes your fancy. Return to me at the end of a year. I shall then give you your naturalization papers and your grant at the same time. A little *paciencia* on your part—and it is done!"

In reality, Alvarado was pleased. That great inland territory was given over to Indians, robber-bands and wild animals. Here was a chance to establish a permanent rancho in the very heart of a savage district without personal risk or expenditure. . . . It was a clever move to have an ally in that region, reasoned the Governor. The Fox of Sonoma might be watched—possibly even checked in his autocratic rule over the northern bay area.

Sutter was quick to see the advantages of the offer. It assured him legal possession of the land. He would not be handicapped as a foreigner in a strange country.

Up he rose and, thanking the Governor, assured him of coöperation in all things. Casarin slipped a paper forward and Sutter signed. It proclaimed his official intention of adopting Mexican citizenship.

In a few moments they parted with mutual well-wishes. Back went Sutter and French toward the *Clementine*, still escorted by the patient guard of honor.

On the way they met the Scotsman, David Spence. He had come to greet them—was walking toward Alvarado's home. Sutter thumbed a letter for him out of the sheaf and he paced with them to the ship's-boat.

"Davy" was a canny soul, owner of the prosperous *Encinal y Buena Esperanza* Rancho. He was one of the most respected and influential of the early foreigners in the province. In the few minutes that they talked he offered pointed advice to Sutter.

"Na' doot it's a wise way," he said thoughtfully of Alvarado's offer. "Ye'll be treated fairly enow' here, I ken. But best tread softly wi' *all* concerned—"

Sutter nodded understandingly.

Customs duties paid and permit aboard, the *Clementine* sailed for Yerba Buena. Next afternoon they crept once more through the Golden Gate and anchored in the harbor. The Kanakas were on the beach, capering, laughing, shouting; awaiting his coming like children. Only the bulldog showed sedateness on the treeless beach.

Sutter turned over his duties as supercargo to French. Accounts were rendered and totaled. More than $3000 had been paid out to Mexican authorities as duty charges. Sutter's share of the profits were not available in cash. He was content with the knowledge that he could order supplies to the amount owed him; these necessities could be shipped to him from Honolulu as he demanded them.

The remaining cargo sold swiftly. Lists were well chosen. As was the California custom, the promise to pay in hides and tallow the following season was accepted without demurrer.

On July 10th, 1839, the *Clementine* departed, Honolulu-bound. Sutter raised a hand to Blinn and the crew from the beach-line; French was below in his cabin, ill. Then she slipped away beyond the headlands—to a deep-sea grave in the next eight months.

Chapter VIII

PALADIN OF SONOMA

SUTTER HAD schemes beyond Alvarado's imaginings.
He spoke of them to no one. Certain reservations
guided him. The land he sought *must* be distant enough
from any Mexican military post to discourage a close
watch on his undertaking—he detested the idea of interference. He would only consider a site offering a navigable river and adjacent fertile valley. Such he had heard
the Sacramento region rumored to be.

In the meantime he bought supplies and inspected
some craft open for charter. As his circle of acquaintances extended, his information about the country increased. But knowledge of the interior was vague and
unsatisfactory, he judged. Facts were lacking even if
words bubbled endlessly. He shook his head at most of
the tales.

One flying trip struck him as necessary before the inland venture. He had letters directed to Vallejo. To
establish an entente cordial with the *comandante militar*
was worth a trial. He felt that such a visit would be a
prudent gesture, especially after several chats with bluff
John Wilson and William Antonio Richardson, captain
of the port. He could ask the General's advice with a
becoming humility; whether such counsel was to be
heeded was another matter. The visit was the thing.

Only a few leagues beyond Sonoma lay Fort Ross and
Bodega. Sutter carried letters for Alejandro Rotscheff,
the Russian governor. Here was a chance to see two important men on one short expedition. Invaluable data
could be stored up by the judicious use of eyes and ears
and a courteous tongue.

Richardson and Wilson agreed to accompany him to
Sonoma. On July 15th, Wilson furnished a rowboat and

crew for the first leg of their journey. After the bay was crossed they secured horses from a small rancho.

Their path lay over a rolling country, dry under a summer sun. It was not until late afternoon that they neared Vallejo's village, the spot he had founded and named as a *Comisionado* of Missions. The church, calabozo and a dozen detached buildings flanked the central square. It was a drowsy scene, still lethargic from the lingering heat of midday.

Sutter eyed the place curiously as his horses' hoofs snapped up little firecrackers of dust behind him. Vallejo's home was the focal point of the settlement; its wings faced each other, a billiard-hall in one, Jacob Leese's house in the other. Flanking the central building stood Don Salvador Vallejo's quarters and a large barracks.

Vallejo had ordered the erection of the church, which supplanted a still larger one. The calabozo—every mission had its cage for refractory converts—had been part of the original establishment. But the church and calabozo were empty. Father Quijas, the resident friar, had chosen to move to San Rafael.

The padre was a close friend of good-natured Timothy Murphy, administrator of Mission San Rafael and owner of the *San Pedro* rancho. It had been the habit of these two cronies to associate secretly with the Russian colony —they appreciated vintage wines downed in a congenial atmosphere. The fact that such social intercourse was sternly forbidden by the authorities bothered the pair not at all—at first.

Finally Vallejo lost patience with the roving roisterers. Upon one melodic return the duo were cast into the calabozo by a half-dozen *soldados*. The memory of the next twenty-four hours convinced Father Quijas that he should remain permanently at San Rafael. Vallejo made no objection. So Sutter rode past a church that lacked a spiritual guardian.

Two cannon rumbled as the *caballada* came to within a hundred feet of the General's home. The Mexican colors dipped and rose again on the flagstaff before the square. Sutter might have visioned the Stars and Stripes on that flagstaff in a future day; but no man could have dreamed the crude insignia of the Bear Flag that was to replace the Green and Red and Blue—a banner that would not be painted on a strip of sacrificial petticoat for nearly seven years.

They rode through a gateway and into a wide court-yard, bordered by plants and flowers. Every building of the menage was constructed of adobe bricks, cemented with mud. Each residence had long verandahs and hanging eaves. The walls were four feet through and every partition was nearly as thick as the outer walls; each room of any size had its own separate roof. There were no fireplaces—no California home had such a convenience, except perhaps an occasional foreigner's house. All cooking was done in outhouses and the food transported when it was ready for the table.

In the courtyard the smiling Jacob Primer Leese greeted them. He had come to California as a trader, turned a storekeeper, and later married the General's sister, Rosalia. This Ohioan was a clever fellow of little education, mainly concerned with good food, swift trading and a monthly bear hunt.

He led the trio up a half-finished flight of steps to the principal room of the house. It was a huge place, thirty feet wide, fifty feet long. Sutter saw doors set in the walls that appeared to open on numerous smaller chambers. The room itself was indifferently furnished. Gaudy chairs such as the Swiss had seen in Oahu littered the floor, the only comfortable features in the official cavern. Rugs sprawled about but the walls were bare.

Here the General and Don Salvador joined them. Mariano Guadalupe Vallejo was the son of Sergeant Ignacio Vallejo, a pure-blooded Spanish sire, and of Maria Antonio Lugo. As a boy he had chosen the military as a profession and the patronage of the gifted Figueroa had been his. The governor had granted his protege large tracts of land north of the bay, appointed him *Comisionado* to secularize Mission San Francisco Solano and given him command of the *frontera del norte*. Success had made him autocratic and haughty, quick to make useful friends, as swift to snub those without prestige.

His brothers had fared well. Courageous, unprincipled Don Salvador was a captain of militia and grantee of the *Napa, Salvador, Lupyomi* ranchos; the popular Jose Jesus was awarded the post of *comisionado* and administrator at Mission San Jose and became grantee of *Arroyo de la Alameda* Rancho. By these tactics Vallejo was kept informed of every Alta California activity. It was even rumored that the General had married most of his sisters to influential foreigners with an eye to strengthening his position in all circumstances. A sure-thing conservative, this autocrat of Sonoma.

The six sat in a tight little circle after the punctilious amenities. Conversation was light and general. Finally, the visitor presented his letters. John C. Jones, the United States Consul, was convinced that Sutter was a "Swiss gentleman of the first class among men of honor, talent, and estimation, worthy of all confidence and support." So were the rest of the lot.

Talk centered on Sutter and his hopes. Vallejo was reservedly impressed. He advised his guest to settle somewhere near Sonoma and take full advantage of the law-abiding qualities of that territory. It was foolish, he suggested, to seek the interior where disaster in the form of Indians, floods, starvation, desperadoes and wild animals was a continual hazard.

Sutter listened; and thanked the *Comandante Militar*. He would give consideration to advice so wisely expounded; at present his plans were not clearly formed and no choice had been made; yes, he considered the counsel to be most instructive and helpful. . . . The discussion went on. . . .

Dinner was announced. The guests were escorted to the dining room with its long table, a smaller apartment than the reception hall. There the ladies of the household joined them. The poised and gracious Señora Francisca Vallejo led the feminine van. With her appeared her sister, Captain Wilson's wife; the General's sister, Mrs. John B. R. Cooper, who, it was affirmed, resided at Sonoma as a pledge for the fidelity of the one-ship provincial navy, skippered by her husband; her daughter, Anna Maria; Mrs. Leese; and an unmarried sister possessed of a provocative shyness.

Leese presided as the cheery master of culinary ceremonies while the somewhat unbent Vallejo sat among his guests. Servants placed an array of five dishes on the table—two kinds of stewed beef, fowl, rice and beans. The dishes lacked heat after being leisurely conveyed from the outhouses; in serving twenty people they became colder. But pepper and garlic almost made up for the deficiency of fire-hot food.

The observant Swiss glimpsed beef, tongue, garlic, pumpkin, cabbage, onions, potatoes in their jackets, tomatoes and the eternal peppers in the same dish. The tea was weak and tepid; the wine of an inferior vintage. Yet Sutter was to remember that meal with relish many a time in the stern work ahead.

After dinner the ladies retired and the men went for a stroll. Vallejo piloted Sutter on a tour of inspection, pointing out improvements he had begun, portions of the house yet to be completed and commenting on various conditions his visitor would face in colonization.

The General had fifteen *soldados* under his command and Sutter was discreetly amused by their equipment. None were dressed alike. The only common accoutrements were immense swords, deerskin boots, nascent mustachios and the everlasting serape with a hole slit in the middle of it to drape over one's head at night or in siesta. Several small field-pieces and carronades grouped sullenly about; Sutter rightly deduced that there was little ammunition to stuff their black tubes.

A three-hundred-foot-square vineyard drooped with ripening bunches of grapes behind the big home. Under the padre's care it had produced an annual thousand gallons of wine. Vallejo had replanted the vines with fair success. Even the once-neglected peach and pear trees were again bearing.

Later, the ladies met the assembled company for tea. They were reënforced by two more juvenile doñas. Half a dozen visitors, men and women, arrived noisily. Everyone wandered into the large reception room at Leese's request. The dashing Don Salvador and one of his troopers began to strum guitars. Soon the cotillon and waltz warmed the *valecito casaros* into full swing.

The Swiss danced and smiled and bent low over small hands. Many a calculating feminine eye followed him with interest. It was his first glimpse of California social life and one custom caught his attention: both men and women, when they were not dancing smoked continuously—as he termed it, furiously.

Among the later guests waddled a thick, paunchy little man, one whom Sutter well remembered from his first two-day stop in Yerba Buena. He was Juan Prado Mesa, commander of the Presidio of San Francisco; successor, in fact, to General Vallejo who had hurdled from the same post to his present dignity.

Mesa's life, Sutter learned in an aside from Leese, had been a succession of private brawls and blood-lettings. He had recently attended a religious festival celebrated at Mission *San Francisco de Asis*—later Mission *de los Dolores*—in honor of the patron saint. The affair had progressed in its usual sequence of mass, bullfight, supper and ball. In the course of the evening, he had interfered with Francisco Guerrero, steward of the mission, who was enjoying a public altercation with his mistress.

It proved to be an unhealthy idea. Señor Guerrero's knife found its way into Señor Mesa's expostulating body. But the corpulent commander was not so easily or permanently spitted; on this occasion his excess fat saved his bacon. Years later, Guerrero was to meet a bizarre end: he was murdered in broad daylight on a San Francisco street by a French deaf-mute armed with a slingshot and mounted on a mule.

Leese delivered a final *sotto voce* tale in regard to one of Mesa's near-sanguinary meetings. One of his enemies had come up behind his adequately padded posterior at a *baile*, drawn a knife and shouted dramatically: "What! Here's dancing and midnight and no pig stabbed yet?"

Vallejo caught his arm as it flashed down on the wheeling Mesa. It was only with the greatest difficulty that the General nipped so promising an affair in the bud. But the fat dandy refused to miss any sort of a function. It could never be said that Juan Prado Mesa was not ready for sharp steel, a brimming cup, or a ravishing—or ravished—*doncellita*.

The party wore itself out soon after midnight. Distribution of the guests was hospitably arranged. Some were quartered in the Vallejo home, some at Don Salvador's. Richardson and Sutter were escorted by Leese to his house.

It was the custom for all visitors in California to carry their own blankets. No host of that period even attempted to furnish a guest room of any pretensions. Every visitor had come, thus equipped, to spend the night. The bedding-rolls had been brought up by the servants and left for the owners to arrange as they pleased. Sutter's candle showed him that the bed was well-appointed, with embroidered sheets, coverlet and pillows; only the blankets were needed to make it comfortable.

As he drew the coverlets about him, his body still warmed by the wine and dancing, John Sutter knew one resolve. He felt with certainty that Sonoma—or its neighborhood—was the last spot in California where he wished to establish his future home.

Chapter IX

PRINCESS OF BANISHMENT

SUTTER HAD mentioned his intention to visit Fort
Ross during his evening stroll. The General had
no word of opposition and later wrote out the necessary
passport. On occasion, Mexican authorities were officious about contact with the Russians. Sutter rather
fancied this might have been one of the occasions—
without the passport.

He breakfasted early with the men of the household.
Vallejo was thoughtful enough to assign him a *vaquero* as
guide and the two rode oceanward alone. Wilson and
Richardson remained at Sonoma. Sutter promised to
rejoin them within three days.

Over plain and sloping hillside led the *vaquero*. The
sereness of the rainless summer months had stolen away
the vividness of the land. It was golden hot. They saw
deer and elk and antelope and cattle, here and there even
a roaming grizzly.

They halted at the *Estero Americano* Rancho, near
Bodega, and borrowed fresh mounts. The owners,
Edward McIntosh and James Dawson, were prompt to
assist. But the Swiss noticed that the two men were not
speaking to each other. Also, that Dawson was engaged
in the eccentric labor of sawing the community house
in half!

Later, in Yerba Buena, Sutter learned the reason for
this strange behavior. A short time previously, McIntosh
had obtained the rancho land grant and had conveniently
forgotten to include his partner's name in the deed.
Whereupon, the fiery Dawson horse-whipped the careless
Edward, sawed their home in half and moved his
portion to another rancho! The puzzled Sutter was wit-
nessing the extraordinary dissolution of a wilderness
partnership.

The trail passed by the first Russian station, midway between Ross and Bodega. It was a small farm of two wooden buildings which housed four Muscovite workers. In one of the houses a well-furnished room was set apart for the convenience of travelers. Sunset was on them and Sutter decided to stay the night.

Both food and bed were excellent. Nor was any charge made for the accommodations. One of the men spoke a few words of French and was persuaded to pilot his visitor to Fort Ross at dawn.

In the morning Vallejo's *vaquero* took his leave with a respectful salute and a "*Vaya con Dios!*" Sutter and his new guide went forward.

The squared barriers of Fort Ross were sighted before noon. It sat seventy feet above the sea on a rocky cliff that fell recklessly away to the boiling surf. To the left and rear rose wooded hills of pine and cedar and fur and laurel. Outside the enclosure were fifty redwood buildings: a large boathouse by the landing place; cooper's, carpenter's, and blacksmith's shops grouped together; a scattering of stables and granaries; a windmill, and three tiled storehouses for fishing craft.

It was an active scene; but not as impressive as the Sitka colony. Laborers were speeding from shop to shop, landing place to granary. There were less than three hundred Russians at the post, yet twice that number seemed rushing about. Some stopped and stared as the guide came onward with the stranger.

Beyond the more pretentious dwellings, on the slope of a hill, were twenty Kodiak huts, homes of the Indians employed for fur-taking. Many of their huge bidarkas, fashioned of sea-otter skins stretched tightly over wooden frames, could carry a hundred passengers and seven tons of freight. Without their assistance the Russian fur catch would have been negligible.

Just past the Kodiak village stood the huts of the native aborigines, Indians who had labored for their Russian masters since the epileptic Kuskof founded the colony in 1812. Most of them had forgotten their tribal tongue and spoke only the language of their overlords.

The rising path brought Sutter at last to the fortress. A sentry with a cutlass stood framed in the space of an open gateway that faced the sea. The citadel's enclosure was a hundred yards square and its timbered walls were eighteen feet high and eight inches thick. Each angle held a blockhouse tower, loopholed for musketry, that equaled the stockade height. Each tower mounted four twelve-pound carronades. Four six-pound brass howitzers sat grimly fronting the gate.

The guide turned his horse away and bade Sutter guttural farewell as the latter dismounted. A tall officer came through the entrance and welcomed him in flawless French.

"I have come to see Governor Rotscheff," the Swiss informed him. "I bring him greetings and documents from Sitka."

"His Excellency is honored," said the officer courteously. "If you will follow me, m'sieur?"

Sutter went through the gateway. His latest escort led him toward a three-story, eight-roomed mansion, largest of the interior structures. Window-glass was a rarity in California at that period and he noticed panes shining at the different heights of the residence—the same unique feature that had been present in Alvarado's home. Clustered about the central dwelling were buildings of lesser dignity, storehouses, officer's homes and a church, all within the walls.

They passed a polished brass nine-pounder that guarded the base of the Governor's staircase. Up broad, resounding steps they tramped and the officer thrust back a huge redwood barrier to enter on a large hallway. This corridor was the armory of the establishment: the place was bright with sun, and cutlasses gleamed in swash-buckling humor beside wooden stands which held a warlike abundance of small arms—a display to awe the unwary before reaching the official presence.

At the end of the passageway they faced another door. The guide knocked smartly, opened it, stepped back, bowed his charge inward.

A gracious giant of a man, impeccably tailored in the costume of the Ministry of Finance, stood up before a littered table. A glowing friendliness fastened itself upon Sutter. His quick eyes took in the packed bookshelves, the hangings, the carpets, the pictures on the walls, the comfortable chairs—all as the big man was leading him to a seat, greeting him easily.

Five years before, Alejandro Rotscheff had lived in the swirl of St. Petersburg. He was thirty, dashing, brilliant, author of a half-dozen books of prose and verse, famous as a translator and adaptor of French and English plays for the theatres of the pleasure-mad capital.

Then one of the loveliest women in the world had stormed her imperial way into his heart. She was the Princess Helena Gargaren, toast of the imperial court, destined to be the bride of some imperial majesty.

But love has a method of tangling ordained taboos, savage or imperial. Rotscheff stole his princess away and fled with her. They crossed Siberia by night, hunted, marked for death—or worse—under an emperor's anger.

As they waited in a peasant's hut, lost to men and days, the imperial furor died somewhat from its first white heat. Banishment was the final decree—a concession ruefully secured by Prince Gargaren, her father—banishment to one of the far-flung Russian American Fur Company colonies.

To the lovers that was no punishment, almost an act of forgiveness. Being together was all that mattered. They sailed first to Sitka; and there Rotscheff's energy won him the post of Russian governor at Fort Ross and Bodega.

If the imperial princess felt the lack of social glitter in her new home, her husband never learned it. For Helena Gargaren ruled a mind that knew no dullness. She was familiar with the sciences and the classics and music and she was master of French, Italian, English and Spanish. To her light-footed living there was no monotony.

AFTER AN INTERVAL, Sutter presented his letters. He had fresh news of mutual friends, new developments and the latest Alaskan gossip. In a scant half-hour the two men cemented a bond that was to exist as long as Rotscheff lived in America, and beyond.

At luncheon Sutter bent low with Continental grace and kissed the fingertips of the Princess. His lips were fluent with chatter and his blue eyes were alight with admiration as the three sat at the small table. For the beauty of a woman has much to do with inspiring cleverness—or imbecility—in a man.

In the afternoon they walked in the Princess' flower garden, a court of beauty set behind the fort. The fragrance of many blooms was in the tranquil air; and there was a primitive lushness about that color-crested rectangle of soil that calmed and revitalized.

It was the favorite retreat of the Governor's lady. In the very center stood a twenty-foot-square, glass-covered garden house. A crystal door led in upon a couch, sunwarmed; and walled-in flowers glowed all about and scented the air with an almost sensual sweetness.

"I spend so many happy hours here," she told her guest.

"Content in her bright wilderness," said her husband.

As John Sutter marveled, he saw Rotscheff smiling at his wife. There was a tender certainty in that caress. It made the Swiss feel, for a moment, like an alien thing, shut out from the world of warm lips and soft bodies and human passion. . . .

Later, when the two men were alone again, Sutter spoke more fully of his plans. In his company ordinary things were transfigured, took on the glamour of mystery and import. It was so easy to believe, in his presence, that one had a secret, personal revelation of those great concerns that in every-day life seem remote. With John

Sutter one adventured swiftly through portals that are usually barred, walked proudly with an eager guide and a sense of kinship into an empire of superlative dreams.

Rotscheff possessed the wit to glimpse the pattern before the shuttling of the loom was well begun.

"You have my word," he said, "that my aid is yours. Yours is a great project, M'sieur Sutter."

They gripped hands over the littered table-top.

That night an impromptu dance was given in Sutter's honor. Officers, clerks and their wives attended, some forty of them. Imported liqueurs and sandwiches and cigars were served and the entertainment lasted until midnight.

Before retiring, Sutter was initiated into the mysteries of his first steam bath, one of the civilized comforts that Rotscheff's insistence had brought to Ross. To the saddle-weary Swiss it was a laving gift, gratefully enjoyed; but through the entire experience he had a secret fear that he was being par-boiled. . . .

He rode away in a misty billow of fog. In the breaking grayness Rotscheff stood at salute in the gateway. The rider raised his hand, turned his eyes to the dim path. The man in the gateway was an ally; and a faithful one, the Swiss was soon to find.

He spent that night at *Estero Americano* Rancho, with welted McIntosh and the sawing Dawson. Wisely he made no inquiries and continued on the next day with his old mount. The stars were bright before he reached Sonoma.

His adieus were made to Vallejo next morning. Then he started for Yerba Buena with his two companions. On the sea-leg of the return, as the rowboat tossed on the bay swells, he had leisure from the jolting saddle to measure the value of his present journeyings. . . . He had met two men in authority and seen the country; both men had promised aid and given advice.

John Sutter was busy marshalling facts and hopes as they beached safely before the dozen scattered adobes of Yerba Buena.

Chapter X

FIRST ACT ENDED

Sutter chartered the *Isabel* and *Nicolas* the next morning. These two small schooners were owned by Nathan Spear and William Sturgis Hinckley. He appointed the firm as Yerba Buena agents for the colony-to-be. They agreed to supply all agricultural implements, blacksmith and carpenter tools, provisions and other gear.

A four-oared pinnace was bought outright from Captain Wilson. It was necessary to have an active carrier for the wilderness site and the pinnace was expected to make regular trips to the bay.

Sutter's choice of business associates was a fortunate one. Spear had been a sickly druggist's clerk in Boston before he made the long sea voyage to health and resurgent enterprise. His partner was a jovial sort though given to extraordinary facility in two languages when emptying a wine bottle. Both men were popular with the native Californians. While Spear was a steady, 'tend-to-knitting' fellow, Hinckley was partial to the thrills of contraband trade and practical jokes. In this last field he was somewhat of a rough-and-ready artist.

Some of Hinckley's best efforts will never be set down beyond a yellowed manuscript page. But, regardless of the scatological tendencies of his pranks, he shot many a splinter of light into drab days. Governor Alvarado recalls that while he and Hinckley were once discussing certain confidential matters, they were annoyed by an inquisitive secretary who kept pussy-footing into the room every few moments to snuff the candles. That officious nuisance was disposed of by the resourceful ruse of tapping gunpowder into the snuffers. It was William Sturgis Hinckley's idea, admits the admiring Governor.

The new agents smoothed the way for speedy inland sailing. Everything was carefully stowed aboard the little fleet. The three brass pieces freighted from Honolulu were part of the precious cargo. Sutter believed that nothing captured—or held—savage respect as much as a loud-mouthed cannon. There were other plans for those guns, too—plans where he saw their shining lengths, multiplied by twenty, looking down from high walls, ready to defy unfriendly whites as well as Indians.

William Heath Davis, Spear's nephew, commanded the *Isabel* and Jack Rainsford skippered the *Nicolas*. Both were competent seamen who, like the rest of the inhabitants, knew nothing of the interior save rumor.

A half-dozen recruits were anxious to join the expedition. Sutter accepted them dubiously. Still, he reckoned that the tools of a colonizer were usually crude; and that which comes to hand—either in implements or men—must be used.

Most of Yerba Buena joined in a farewell banquet for the expedition. Few were hopeful of their success. Others predicted disease, disaster and death. The interior valleys were terra incognita; and who but a fool wanted to brave the heaping dangers of such a region for the mere possession of land, anyway? A simpleton's journey, they said. Plenty of land near the settlements for those who wanted it. They resolved to wait impatiently for news of the worst.

But the foreigners were partisan to Sutter's scheme. The celebration was held on board Captain George Vincent's ship, the *Monsoon*, the only vessel then in harbor. It was an evening of wit and wassail and fellowship. Toasts to the venture gurgled down happy throats. Advice was given, most of it spiritous and inconsequential; yet received with smiling urbanity by the guest of honor. Many a yarn with a salacious point rocked the candle-lit cabin and vibrated the timbers overhead.

That farewell lasted until the sun splashed the east's dark wall with gold and harried away the slight mist that had crept from the sea to the bay waters. They surged unsteadily away from the long bolted table and out upon the open deck. What if a few well-wishing voices were husky and tangled? They were experiencing kinship with a stout fellow's dreams; for the moment they felt a personal partnership in his company of conquest.

Sutter went over the *Monsoon's* side to the *Isabel*. Sails rose to catch the freshening breeze. The Kanakas bent brown backs in the pinnace and oars flashed silver foam. Slowly the three craft drew away.

The Indian boy and the bulldog crouched at Sutter's feet. Voices were still raised in parting. He could still see the faces of Spear and Leese and Hinckley and Vincent and the fifty others bobbing indistinctly in the deepening brightness.

It was August 9th, 1839.

Wine-warmed against the slight chill, he kept his eyes to the vanishing scene. . . . Yet as Yerba Buena and the *Monsoon* and the revelers fell into vagueness, he turned to the dancing bow. It pointed to new lands and new waters.

That evening they reached Rancho *Pinole*, the first— and last—civilized haven touched by the expedition. The boats were tied up on the banks of Suisun Bay, near Carquinez Straits, only a short distance from the rancho.

Don Ignacio Martinez, the owner, was much interested in his visitor and his aspirations. His beautiful daughters, *Doñas* Susana, Rafaela, Francisca and Dolores, had downcast eyes and sharp ears for the newcomer. They cared little for stupid talk of *colonizacion;* but they liked the sound of John Sutter's persuasive voice.

Before retiring that night, the two men made a pact. The *ranchero* was to furnish the Swiss with horses and sheep and cattle as soon as he was informed by messenger of Sutter's permanent residence; his guest promised to pay for the animals in beaver-skins or other produce in a year's time.

Each was content with the bargain. Sutter had no more funds. Already he was indebted to Spear and Hinckley for more than half of his present equipment. But he had faith that the wilderness would pay well for its subjection.

In the morning he parted from Don Ignacio with felicitations and polite mutual hopes for another speedy meeting. Other eyes than the Don's watched Sutter stride away to the river bank.

FOR EIGHT DAYS the fleet explored all the branching bayous of that region, progressing slowly, always on the look-out for the Sacramento River entrance. But the river continued to elude them. In darkness, as they lay moored to the banks, a cloud of mosquitoes staged ceaseless assaults. The pests seeped into the cabins and the nights were split with oaths. Sleepless hours. Luckless days. Hard labor.

Side-trips were made inland to inspect the tributary territory as they went. No landing was too difficult, no terrain too rocky to go unexplored.

On the ninth morning they found the elusive entrance. Padre Presidente Narciso Duran had first voyaged the river and named it. The Catalonian zealot had come from San Jose and ascended the stream some thirty miles. He was seeking gentile Indians to bring back as Mission neophytes. These savages were usually smacked on the head, tied up, and returned to the Mission where their spiritual welfare could be attended to at the earnest padre's leisure.

Sutter's craft turned right up the channel. Now the banks were low and bare; now cliffed and wooded. Smaller streams frequently led off on bypaths to either hand. The pinnace made the side-trips, followed more cautiously by the *Isabel* and *Nicolas*.

The larger fanning waterways were patiently traced and retraced. Notes and blaze-marks on the trees pointed the path to the bigger vessels—gave instructions whether to come or wait.

Indian signs were plentiful. Sutter found bunches of white feathers hung in tufted sequence from the swaying branches of trees. These were the prayers of a primitive people to their gods and devils for an abundance of fish and food.

Hundreds of eyes watched them along the course. But they were hidden eyes. The boats went tortuously on. Every location was pondered. Sutter knew what he wanted. Too long a trail stretched behind to risk failure now through poor judgment.

On the second day up the river they approached a spot some twelve miles below the present city of Sacramento. Rounding a curve, they found two hundred warriors grouped in an open space on the right bank. The screaming savages were defiant, their bodies painted red and blue and yellow.

Sutter gave an order. The crews prepared for action. Firearms were made ready and the vessels swung in toward the shore.

They came within a few feet of the bank. "*A' Dios, amigos!*" cried the Swiss. Perhaps in the yelping ranks might be found deserters from the pillaged missions. If so, they were certain to know the Spanish tongue.

One of the aborigines stepped out of the grimacing gang and came fearlessly to the river edge. The guess had been shrewd.

"Whence come you, strangers?" he called in Spanish. "Do you come in war?"

"I come in peace," Sutter shouted. "I am your friend and I have come to live with you forever."

Then through the interpreter on the bank, the Swiss told a part of his plans to the jabbering throng. He was a kind man, he said, and carried many presents which he would soon distribute. Just as soon, in fact, as he could locate his future home. But, he warned, there must be no treachery among his new brothers. If so, death would strike swiftly out of the brass thunder tubes; the fish would turn belly-up in the streams; the wild herds would die; berries would wither away on the bushes. Sutter rather fancied himself as a spellbinder; how much of it got over to the painted yammerers through his mouth-

piece he could not tell. In conclusion, he promised friendship to all true men.

"If you will come to me when I have landed," he
said, "your presents will be given you."

At this news most of the gathering rushed off to their
rancheria to pass on the startling word. The interpreter
came off in a tule canoe and offered to accompany the
expedition. He was taken aboard the *Isabel* and given a
small gift. Ever after he was Sutter's man, a useful
friend in time of savage emergency. Homo Bono, the
Swiss named him.

Shortly the boats reached the confluence of the American River and veered right. A few miles farther on, the
country delighted Sutter. A fertile valley bordered the
stream, level and pleasing, stretching on to distant
ranges. The river itself was broad and navigable. Thick
grasses and high trees grew in the green expanse.

It filled John Sutter's land-hungry eyes. "Here! Here
is a likely spot!" he cried. "Pull in! Pull in!"

They landed, tied up the boats, pitched their tents.
The earth-firmness under his feet meant much to the man
from the Grand Duchy of Baden. It seemed a splendid
ending to a rigorous trail.

Supplies and freight began to be shifted ashore. The
three cannon were mounted and put in order; nothing
was certain or secure in the new spot.

"Vigilance," said the Swiss, "is the first order of a
lonely land."

Soon the savages swarmed. The unloading went on.
Trinkets were passed out to clutching, incredulous
brown paws. The sun began to pass beyond a western
barriacade of tinted rose.

That coming dark brought fear to the Yerba Buena
recruits. News that the vessels left at dawn unnerved
them, caused a near panic. Terror gripped them at the
idea of the *Nicolas* and *Isabel* sailing away, leaving
them surrounded by fierce primitives.

In a group they waited on Sutter. They told him that no power could hold them in this dangerous camp. They were going back when the ships departed at sunrise.

The Swiss heard them out, shrugged. "As you wish," he said in brittle fashion. "I was never sure you would care for wilderness life."

He turned away to speed an order to a passing Kanaka. Uneasily, they shuffled away. But they took no chances. They boarded the *Nicolas* immediately.

Kanaka sentries walked the circle of the camp that night, as they would for months to come. Fires burned brightly, fed by driftwood and tree-branches. Every hour Sutter roused and prowled the lighted area, bulldog at his side. He brooked no thought of disaster now. His mind was teeming with the possibilities of the land. . . . Soon he would make a fort—a high adobe-walled citadel to give him peace against all comers.

"Soon—very soon," he muttered.

Anticipation was on him. Patience would turn the trick. Only a little while now. His feverish mind saw fruit-leaning orchards and grain yellow in the sun and a tiled home sitting on the valley sward. Anna's voice in the home; young voices in the orchards. . . .

THE MORNING was gloriously clear. In the murmuring tide the two ships cast off for Yerba Buena. Young William Heath Davis stood on the *Isabel's* deck and looked back at the bright wilderness drama. He was to remember his last sight of that camp with an astonished admiration; an indelible memory of which he wrote in later years.

Sutter ordered a salute of nine rounds fired for the departing ships. The crashing cannonade—the first ever fired on the spot—echoed like the thunder of angry gods. In a moment, before Davis' amazed eyes, the camp was surrounded by a squirming, wailing wall of Indians. Herds of deer and elk fled with fluttering hoofs across the valley carpet, yawing in great tacks, repelled and yet fascinated by the mighty roars. The howling of wolves and the yammering of grizzlies came out of the woodlands. Huge clouds of wildfowl swept over the tents, the whir of their wings perceptible after each discharge. It was the first chaos that had ever come to this placid plain of the Sacramento in recorded history; it was not to be the last.

Then Davis, Rainsford and the rest—even the deserters—gave nine rousing cheers back to the now silent guns and the tingling wilderness. On sailed the *Nicolas* and *Isabel*. Soon the curve of the river curtained the scene. The first act was ended.

Chapter XI

SHADOWS IN THE NIGHT

A RISING HILL caught Sutter's fancy that first morning. It showed itself two miles from the river bank, the only near elevation on the valley floor. For two days the Swiss tramped over the plain, bulldog and cabinet-maker beside him, a scattering of curious Indians in the rear. But always his eyes came back to the grassy hill.

Late afternoon of the second day brought his steps again to the almost imperceptible crest.

"This is the place," he said.

"Ja?" said the cabinet-maker wearily. He hoped it was. The sun was westering. Elk and deer grazed within musket-shot. A herd of wild horses chewed emerald fodder beyond the nearer animals. Three grizzlies wandered out of the chaparral, four hundred yards away, and passed into a thicket as the bulldog growled thickly. Clouds lay over the distant range, mist-soft. A dozen Indians sat at Sutter's feet, stolid watchers of long days.

"I shall call it New Helvetia—New Switzerland— after my homeland," he rambled on.

The cabinet-maker made no comment. He was very tired, and wondered how long Sutter would linger on the hill. It was time to eat.

All the way back to the camp the Swiss was garrulous, elated. The savage guard trailed behind. . . .

A multitude of visitors daily besieged the tents. Beads and trinkets drew them. There seemed to be hundreds underfoot, slow of comprehension, watchful of the shiny guns, content to help if they were painstakingly instructed.

The camp was moved to the knoll on the third morning. Shelter of a permanent sort was the first concern. Sutter set a number of Indians to manufacturing adobe bricks. Hour after hour they danced on the commingled straw and mud, until it formed the proper constituency for the sun-drying.

The Kanakas scurried about and began the construction of three grass houses after the fashion of their island dwellings. More Indians were hacking a road through the chaparral to the river bank. They worked willingly, slashing away the dense undergrowth and making passable the trail to the *embarcadero*.

Grass huts rise swiftly. But roads and adobe-building take time and patience and back-bending effort. Sutter planned a three-room, forty-foot-square structure. It was to contain a blacksmith shop, a kitchen with a fireplace, and a private living-room for himself. Most of the delay was caused by the tedious process of drying the bricks in crude moulds. When the adobes were finally ready the walls rose fifteen hours a day.

Tules topped all the dwellings, a roofing that turned aside rain and took only a few hours to lash in place. Sutter watched anxiously as the work progressed; the buildings must be completed before the rainy season.

As soon as the Indians proved tractable enough under his personal eye, he ordered almost his entire force back to Rancho *Pinole*. The stock promised by Don Ignacio Martinez was needed as a herd nucleus. Two white men, the cabinet-makers, and four Kanakas took the pinnace away; only the leader, bulldog, Indian boy, and remaining islanders were left to defend New Helvetia.

That pinnace crew oared their way into official disrepute. General Vallejo detained them in an inquiry about passports, the artisans not having bothered to secure the demanded documents. This action infuriated Sutter, coming, as it did, during the most acute moments of the new colony.

As early as December 1839, he wrote a scathing letter to the General, damning his officiousness as absurd, unfriendly, and unreasonable. It was the first gun in a verbal battle between the two. Sutter's temper overbalanced

Sutter's Fort, New Helvetia. Sketched by Lieutenant J. W. Revere

his tact; doubtless his sizzling analysis of Vallejo's character was unwise—even if warranted.

Finally the men were allowed to start homeward with the animals. Two of the Kanakas rowed the pinnace and the rest guided the herd. They left Rancho *Pinole* with 500 cattle, 50 horses and a *manada* of 25 breeding mares.

ONE NIGHT, during the absence of the boat crew, Sutter lay sleeping in his tent. The adobe was not yet ready for occupancy. Indian boy and bulldog lay at his feet. A Kanaka sentry paced his rounds with a lagging step. His vigilance was less than that which guarantees life over death in a wilderness land.

For weeks the Indians had worked, willing, never unfriendly. Yet sharp eyes had hung over John Sutter's possessions. Many of the bolder Cosumnes coveted secretly, longing for the riches resting so temptingly beneath the white shelters. Schemes were made in the rancherias.

"The thunder guns cannot see to speak at night," said the chiefs. . . .

It was after midnight when shadows came seeping through the dark. The fires were low. In the flickering light the guard's head nodded and swayed, his step slow, uneven.

One shadow reached the tent flap. Others gloomed close. A naked arm thrust the flap aside. John Sutter's breathing sounded heavily . . . A form stooped to enter, knife raised.

There was a deep-throated cry—not human in its anger. The bulldog catapulted forward, gripped deep in the shadow's throat, worried savagely. The knife fell away. Both Indian and dog struck the earth, ten feet beyond the tent.

The dog loosed the squirming thing. His second leap was as sure as the first. Again his fangs cut deep into a quivering jugular. The other shadows were gone then. Again a crimson tide rolled over set jowls.

The Kanaka was wide-awake now, running forward, musket ready. The Swiss was up, cool, bootless, pistols in hand, the Indian boy beside him.

Crashing shots snarled into the night—uselessly. Two bodies lay on the turf. The dog still shook his tight jaws, sunk in the second skulker.

Sutter bent over, patted the broad head, drew him away. "Brave fellow!" said he calmly.

The other islanders were grouping, eyes rolling, lips chattering. Sutter gave a curt order to the guard, pointed to the bodies, turned away. He entered the tent, let the flap fall, dropped into slumber.

But one guard lay quietly, eyes open, a tiny rumble in his throat. No enemy could pass while the giant bulldog lay at John Sutter's feet. . . .

It took the herd-tenders eighteen days to come plodding in from Rancho *Pinole*. They crossed the Sacramento to gain the camp. The day was October 22nd, 1839. But the numbers of their trail-herd had dwindled. More than one hundred head of horses and cattle were lost in transit. Some strayed; some were drowned in the river crossing.

The Indians were more amenable—or crafty—after that first lesson. They seemed awed beyond measure by this master who was infallibly guarded by both beasts and men. At least, they lent themselves to his service.

Sutter knew nothing definite about the soil under his feet; that is, except that it had never been turned by spade or shovel or plow. But the verdure of the spot proved it fertile in his judgment. He never doubted its fecundity. He set the Indians to breaking the virgin greensward of the valley as the first rains began to fall.

Chapter XII

TEMPEST

THAT WINTER season of 1839-40 was a nightmare test. For forty days and nights a Biblical torrent fell upon New Switzerland. Trace of the scratching shovels was swept away. The river rose above the baffled barriers of low banks. The valley became a quagmire; then a lake dotted with muddy islands. Those islands sheltered shivering herds of deer and elk and wild horses, huddled there to prevent being hurled away in the surge of waters.

Only Sutter's insignificant hill held any certain refuge against the seething expanse. At his very back door a stream ran, roiling swift, that could carry the pinnace to the leaden river. And still it rained. . . rained until Sutter's herds stood belly-deep in the improvised corrals beyond the adobe and the grass huts. . . rained until it seemed as if the sky were an ocean leaping through a gargantuan, arching sieve. . . .

Work went on in a sloshing sequence. Trees were cut and dragged and floated to the blacksmith shop. Furniture was sawn and put together. Sutter's living-room held a desk and bed and chairs and the warming fireplace. Iron plows were fashioned to take the place of the rude Californian sort. The latter were only branches of trees with a fire-hardened point that barely tooth-marked the soil as it went. Other tools were sharpened or welded in entirety.

Until the great downpour the pinnace had traveled regularly to Yerba Buena for food and supplies, taking eight or ten days for the trip. For six weeks the boat could not venture out upon the raging flood-lanes. The little colony was forced to eat meat, and meat alone, for every meal.

Then, when the craft did win its way to the bay, it took twenty-seven days to return against the adverse currents and winds.

Still Sutter did not complain. "A great country for moisture," he remarked naïvely to the German cabinet-maker. But that uncomfortable artisan had another and more profane description for it.

Yet it ended. Late February brought the last offering from cloudy skies. The winds that had ripped and slashed over the débris-filled waters became less violent. The chill went out of them. Once more the sun sloped up with renascent warmth, a welcome visitor after grey days.

Spring came to the Sacramento—a fragrant spring. The waters fled back to the river or burrowed into the rich earth. An emerald glow came where the liquid expanse had been. Ground grew firm under one's feet and the quagmire waned to an impossible memory. Rough plows cut sketchily at first, then deeper, into the expectant soil. Seed was sown, seed that had come in the pinnace from Yerba Buena and Rancho *Pinole*.

Adobe-making was renewed. At nights now, by candlelight, John Sutter sat raptly before his table, a sheet of paper under his spatulate fingers. Carefully he traced a rectangular square and marked the dimensions in precise script. It was the plan of Sutter's Fort, the first stronghold of all interior California and destined to be the only refuge for Americans in that region for the next decade.

His pen drew swift, bold dreams. . . five hundred feet long, one hundred and fifty feet wide. Eighteen feet high, three feet thick, it traced. Bastions above the walls at the southeast and southwest corners, commanding the gateways in the center of each side except the western. Loopholes piercing the walls at intervals. Cannon sitting before the entrances. An inner wall with the intermediate space roofed over and partitioned promised a large number of shops and manufactories. Other detached buildings were sketched inside the enclosure—

living-rooms, granaries, workrooms. . . . While the camp slept, John Sutter drew his careful lines, full of a keen awareness.

APRIL 1840, saw the citadel begun. Detail became the daily measure of the Swiss' life. Tasks had to be assigned. Results had to be checked. Letters had to be written, supplies ordered, new plans weighed, adopted or discarded. New neighbors must be met—at least the nearest *rancheros*, leagues inland as they were, must be called that. The Indians had to be instructed; and vigilantly watched.

His letters to Anna and Friedrich and the children were buoyant. There was no money to send yet, he explained. But there could be no failure here. "Man can fashion this land into a paradise," wrote John Sutter. And believed it.

More men came journeying to New Helvetia, seeking the chance to profit through so hardy a beginning. They were welcomed and a place found for them. There was work for many hands. If the latecomers were blacksmiths or carpenters or coopers, so much the better—the more skilled the laborer, the swifter New Helvetia's rise.

Rudolph van Alstine, a Hollander, was sent with a small party to explore the Eel and Pit river regions. He was a thorough fellow and he made a careful report on the timber stand. On his return, he cut down some choice trees and rafted them twenty miles down the American to the rasping saws and ready hands of New Helvetia.

Indian tribes from the base of the ranges brought occasional news of great trees "that reach the sky with green heads." The Swiss was uninterested, too occupied with a struggle for survival to investigate. Thus, he missed the opportunity to be one of the first white men ever to see a grove of mighty redwoods—*sequoia gigantea* —oldest living things on earth. This grove of which the Indians spoke was only twenty miles from Lake Tahoe.

Sutter made horseback tours in the immediate vicinity and then rode on more extended trips seaward. He purchased more cattle from Don Antonio Suñol, owner of *Los Coches* and *San Jose del Valle* ranchos; also two *manadas* from Joaquin Gomez of Rancho *Los Verjeles*. John Marsh, grantee of Rancho *Los Medanos*, supplied some animals. Robert Ridley, who had been |entrusted with command of the pinnace in its later Yerba Buena trips, contributed a *manada*.

This Ridley was an English Cockney who had come to New Helvetia early in the spring on one of the supply boat's voyages. In Yerba Buena he was considered the wag of the town. Everybody knew him and everybody liked him. He was a news-carrier, he-gossip of the village and at home in every house. Such a wayfarer was a great boon to a remote colony—as long as he was there.

'Bob' had a limitless capacity for liquor and was ever desirous of testing his prowess with the best. He had one other accomplishment. He was the most facile, artistic, and bare-faced liar in the Californias. But Sutter liked him. Beside, he played a good game of whist.

As fast as sailings could be made the pinnace brought grain, poultry, tools and other supplies from Nathan Spear. These debts were later paid in beaver skins, tallow, hides and deer fat—the 'money' of the wilderness. Cash was scarce. Exchange was the only feasible means of carrying out any commercial transaction. Credit was cheerfully extended and a man's word was sufficient security. Notes were unknown.

Sutter's creditors—Suñol and Martinez chiefly—were not impatient during that first season; or even the next. Don Antonio dispatched corn, beans, peas, geese and turkeys whenever the Swiss ordered them. It was an admirable arrangement—at least for Sutter. He soon could afford eggs and fowl for his own table from the increasing flocks.

Beaver-trapping was poor in 1840. The colony lacked experienced hunters, traps and articles of barter suitable to exchange with the free-trapper. But an encouraging start was made. Sutter felt that the next year should bring him scores of prime pelts.

Another infant industry was given a trial, even though it was handicapped by a woeful shortage of equipment. Wild grapes were gathered in large quantities for the manufacture of brandy. The fruit grew about New Helvetia in abundance and the Indians easily picked any quantity desired. Something could be made in the venture, Sutter thought. He planned to install a distillery when credit, and availability, permitted.

In early July came the first concerted move to dislodge the colony. The neighboring tribes gathered en masse ten miles away. Insolent messengers came strutting to the knoll. The Swiss was ordered to leave at once. Otherwise he would be attacked and killed.

Regretfully the ex-captain of artillery selected six well-armed men from among his retainers. He advanced the same night he received the ultimatum. In the darkness they stole upon the hostile *rancheria*.

Withering volleys burst into the camp from a distance of ten paces. Thirty Indians died. The rest were routed in the blackness. Then the *rancheria* was fired and the victors rode back to New Helvetia.

The remaining savages retired twenty miles, terrified by such surprise tactics. No Mexican had ever made a night attack. Vermin-rife pates were shaken in council over a foe whose actions were unpredictable.

Sutter's Indian policy was a wise one. He was alert, prompt to punish for offenses, and uniformly kind to the peaceful savage. Mission-bred outcast or gentile, they came to depend upon John Sutter as an impartial, benevolent force.

Tribes in the vicinity soon discovered that he would aid them against Indian attackers from a distance. Steadily a bond grew up between Sutter and the near *rancherias* that made his task a more tranquil one.

Indians who worked for him were generously paid. A tin currency was adopted for New Helvetia use. The metal was stamped out by a blacksmith and a star-shape cut into each coin. It bore no superscription. A disc with one star meant one day's work; one with two stars meant two days' work; and so on. These were distributed to the Indians if they had no present needs. Later, if they wanted shirts or tools or food, the coins could be presented and the equivalent in goods was passed out to them.

CAPTAIN W. D. PHELPS of the Boston brig *Alert* entered the Golden Gate in late July. Up the river he came in his ship's-cutter, the American flag flying prophetically over the craft's stern. It was the first time the Stars and Stripes had flown over any vessel ascending that stream.

Phelps found a number of Indians at work near the *embarcadero*. One of them dog-trotted away to the rising walls of the fort and horses were soon sent for the visitors. On they rode to New Helvetia.

A military welcome awaited them. John Sutter was ready with his cannon. Ten guns crashed a salute. A gay display of flags flapped in the sun-bright wind. The Swiss, very much the *grand seigneur*, greeted them graciously.

The *Alert's* master and his crew were hospitably entertained for three days. They even went on an elk hunt with their host. Phelps shot a grizzly on the same outing. On the fourth day he left for a week's journey farther up the river.

In a fortnight he returned and remained another day with the Swiss. Sutter was full of questions; and Phelps was full of answers.

When the cutter departed at dawn another ten-gun chorus roared out. Sutter felt the powder was well spent. The Red, White and Blue sped proudly back to the waiting *Alert*. But the Swiss remembered its brightness.

Chapter XIII

COURIER FROM KOUPREANOFF

Josiah Spaulding, hard-headed skipper of the American brig *Lausanne*, sailed into a thundering political squall in the midsummer of 1840. On July 16th he arrived at Fort Ross, direct from Fort Vancouver. Among his passengers were the morose Peter Lassen, William Geiger, John Wright, David Dewey Dutton, "Whistling William" Wiggins and the half-dozen men who had crossed from Independence with John Sutter.

The Captain entered into brisk trading with the Russians, a stubborn glint in his Yankee eyes. He had not visited Monterey, declared his cargo, or paid customs duties. His action made him the first American to disregard Mexican authority in that manner.

Hawk-eyed Lieutenant Lazaro Pina detected the brig at anchor in her forbidden business. He boarded her with a six-man squad and ordered Spaulding to consider himself under arrest for violating customs regulations; also to proceed at once to Yerba Buena for official investigation.

Word came to Rotscheff that the Mexican officer had boarded the brig. The Russian governor came off to the ship to request a reason for the disturbance.

The situation was delicate. Officialdom of the two nationalities had never been cordial. Rotscheff resented Pina's zeal so clearly evidenced in a Russian harbor. Nor had the Mexican queried him before acting. He ordered Pina to depart in peremptory fashion; that or be fired on.

The officer dryly remarked that his force was too small to defy the Russians in their territory. "But," said he with fiery candor, "I will fight in the line of duty, come what will. These *Americanos* are under arrest."

Rotscheff was impressed by his bravery. Impulsively he patted him on the shoulder. But he insisted that the lieutenant and his squad must leave without molesting the *Lausanne* or her personnel. Even in the face of this opposition, Pina had half a mind to sail the brig to Yerba Buena himself.

Finally, he was persuaded not to try the impossible. Post-haste he departed for Sonoma to inform Vallejo of the American vessel's efforts to evade duties. Also Rotscheff's attitude in the matter.

Meantime the passengers landed and remained a week as the Governor's guests. Sutter's continental party wished to rejoin him. At their request, Rotscheff furnished them with horses, food and a guide for their inland journey. "Anything to aid my friend, Captain Sutter," he told them.

They left at night, riding warily. To avoid detection and capture they were compelled to skirt all ranchos. They had no passports, were not citizens, and might be classed as undesirable aliens if Vallejo chose. They doubted his friendliness under the present conditions.

Hiding and resting by day, it took them twelve nights to reach the Sacramento goal. They arrived August 17th. Nine men were in that group, including the guide, Wiggins and Lassen having traveled with Sutter's original company. Geiger, Wright and Dutton remained with Captain Spaulding, sailed on a later boat to Honolulu, and did not reach New Helvetia until the following year.

This *Lausanne* controversy particularly irritated Vallejo. His authority had been discounted by the Russians. No customs duties had been paid by the Americans. On hearing Pina's plaint, he issued warrants for the arrest of the offending skipper and his crew.

The unperturbed Spaulding and a number of his men went to Yerba Buena by ship's-boat in the interim and concluded some business there. Sending two sailors back with the boat, the Captain returned to Ross via Sonoma. There the exasperated Vallejo called on him to pay tonnage duties and subsequent fines. Spaulding refused.

With nasal certainty the unbluffed skipper stated that Bodega was a free port belonging to the Russians.

"I'll pay no customs," said he with sailor-man trimmings, "and be damned to ye and yer tin army!"

The General sputtered aghast. He threatened prison; even darker things.

But while he raged the Boston tar and his party mounted their borrowed nags and bumped back to Ross without a parting bullet.

This incident, and its repercussions, was a fortunate occurrence for Sutter. It hastened the end of Russian occupation and made imperative the quick sale of all Muscovite holdings in California. Certainly, it aided the Swiss in his cashless negotiations.

He went overland to Monterey at the end of August. It was time to remind Alvarado of his promise. Traveling with four armed *vaqueros*, Sutter crossed the valley and stopped at Rancho *Pozitos*, owned by Robert Livermore. Don Roberto, as the Californians called him, was an English adventurer who had served in the American navy. Later he had transferred his allegiance to Lord Cochrane and sailed in the *Esmeralda* to Callao and other ports. He deserted in order to join a trading vessel and promptly repeated the act when the ship touched on the Californian coast. An amiable fellow was Don Roberto; he liked the people, the country, and its opportunities. In 1822 he located in Livermore Valley. There he built his home and yearly marketed thousands of hides and *arrobas* of tallow. He was a thrifty soul; and it was his destiny to prosper.

After spending the night at Rancho *Pozitos*, Sutter went on to Mission San José. Next sunset his horse's hoofs were swirling dust in the capital's streets.

Alvarado proved himself as solicitous of the venture as in his first interview. The legal documents were drawn up before David Spence, justice of the peace. The date was August 29th, 1840. The successful applicant gravely proved by papers and three reputable witnesses,

Estrada, Watson and Spence, that he was a "Swiss Catholic, and of good character."

He was commissioned as a captain of the regular Mexican Army, entitled to receive the pay and emoluments accorded to that rank. The Governor authorized him to represent the departmental government at New Helvetia. He was endowed with all civil authority necessary for the local administration of justice; the prevention of robberies by "adventurers from the United States;" the repression of hostilities by savage tribes; and the checking of illegal trapping and fishing carried on by "The Company of the Columbia" for which purpose he might even resort to force of arms if his judgment so dictated. The last proviso was a canny suggestion of the new captain himself.

Michel La Framboise, agent of the Hudson's Bay Company, had for years regularly invaded the Sacramento and San Joaquin valleys with large bands of trappers. Each season they killed thousands of beaver and land otter, furs that were transported to the company warehouses in Oregon. Sutter was determined to stop such 'half-breed' poaching and quite resolved to see that all trapping rights reverted to himself.

Under his new powers, the Swiss was officially the lord of his domain—*Encargado de justica y representante del gobierno en las fronteras del Rio Sacramento*. Just why the Governor chose to accord Sutter such authority is conjectural. Perhaps, the land appeared remote and unimportant in his eyes; perhaps the titles vested in Sutter seemed only empty names that might, happy thought, disgust an officious *Comandante Militar*. Whatever the cause, the new captain's reign was absolute. He walked out of Alvarado's presence armed with all he required— citizenship and a mantle of legality. He meant to make full use of both.

Trouble had brewed in his absence—met him almost at the gateway. It was early September and the San José chieftain, Acacio, accompanied by fifteen natives, had

Sutter's Fort as it is today

come with a Mission pass to visit relatives among the Ochocumnes. The newcomers bought *coritas* and *plumeros;* also a choice number of women with the consent of all concerned—an aboriginal custom of the country.

But they did not long remain on their good behavior. Several full-breasted maids at the Yalesumne *rancheria* drew their attention, and they promptly staged a surprise attack while the Yalesumne men were working for Sutter in the fields. Several Yalesumnes were killed and all the young women and children carried off.

The news of the raid came to Pulpule, Yalesumne chief, by a messenger who fell dead at his feet. At first the excited natives blamed Sutter, shrilled curses at his treachery.

His answer was action. Joining Pulpule and his angry followers, he freed the captives as they were being dragged on board rafts in the river. Seven of the abductors were shot down. Ten of the Cosumnes were taken prisoners and herded back to New Helvetia.

That day the Swiss ordered all savages in the vicinity to speedily collect about the knoll. On the third morning, allowing time for the word to spread, the ten captives were executed by a musket-squad before five thousand speculative Indian eyes. It was the first mass execution in the Californias.

John Sutter knew savage psychology. And he was always an adequate master of ceremonies. No impressive trick was missing when he wished to secure an effect. No one was less sentimental in an emergency; no one more kind to a deserving native.

TWENTY WHITE MEN lived on the hill as 1840 drew to a close. More buildings had been erected in the summer months to house the increase. Ridley, Daylor, Burns, Altgeier, Keyser, Sinclair and the half-dozen men who had ridden the Oregon Trail with Sutter were the chief workers of the colony.

Their numbers grew steadily. The walls of the fort rose. The Indian boy died of a fever. More corrals and outhouses were built. Men worked ceaselessly in the fields and the shops and the woods. Creditors made demands. Sutter ordered more supplies and hoped for their arrival. The bulldog fell before a grizzly's deep-driven claws. So the ancient business of living and dying marched in the wilderness.

A special courier came from Ross in November. He carried an urgent request for Sutter to meet Colonel Ivan Koupreanoff on board the *Nikolai*, then anchored in Bodega Bay. Koupreanoff had lately been relieved as governor at Sitka. He had come to inspect the Russian settlements and was engaged in exchanging a torrid series of communications with Vallejo in regard to the *Lausanne*.

Sutter started without delay. On his arrival at Bodega he remained a day and a night aboard the ex-governor's craft. The Russian official was frank in his statement that Ross and Bodega must be sold or abandoned. Both establishments had operated at a loss for years. Furs were becoming scarce in the area. Now relations with the Mexicans were becoming daily more bitter.

"We prefer to discuss the sale of these properties with you, Captain Sutter," admitted the Colonel. "It was most important that I see you at once."

There was good cause for Koupreanoff's choice. He knew and liked Sutter, had more confidence in him than in any other non-Russian in California. True, James Douglas and Vallejo had been given a tentative chance to make an offer for the land and property. Both had been evasive and uncertain. Both were in the discard.

No definite pledge was made on the *Nikolai*. But the two men understood each other. Their parting handclasp was self-congratulatory. The next morning Sutter returned overland to the Sacramento.

NEARLY EVERY AMERICAN in California was thrown into prison between April 7th and 22nd, 1840. Seventy of them were on board ship by April 24, heavily-ironed, on their way to San Blas. By the end of May they lay in Tepic Prison, half-starved, dirty, vermin-tortured.

The blow was swift, unexpected. No foreigner had suspected such a move; that is, no foreigner who was not later given credit for having had a hand in the plot. With such expediency was the actual capture of the men staged that no news traveled to other regions ahead of the arresting officers.

Reason for the action was hydra-headed; and probably trivial. Alvarado and Vallejo were always unsure of the turbulent aliens. One of them, Isaac Graham, late Mexican ally in the 1836 uprising, was invariably loquacious when under the influence of his Natividad distillery product. He loved tall yarns and brave threats at such moments. It was rumored that he had made some significant statement to the effect that he had placed the Governor and the General where they were; and that he could just as easily unseat "them thar garlic-hounds."

It was enough. Secret preparations, crystallized by orders from Mexico, were perfected. Imprisonment and banishment was the result for Graham and many others.

There were exceptions. A few Americans and Englishmen who had become citizens were unmolested. Usually they were the popular, respected merchants.

One isolated spot did not enter into the scheme of arrests. The Swiss autocrat of New Helvetia experienced no interference with his plans. Even then John Sutter's sun was sweeping high. Isolation was not the chief cause of his immunity. There were guns and ammunition on the Sacramento. Captain Sutter was an imperious gentleman, commissioned in the Mexican Army, who was quite likely to protect his stronghold. It was known that he could control the Indian population and might even be able to depend on them in case of invasion. So diplomatic necessity forced Vallejo to forget that the Swiss empire-builder even existed.

As for the Tepic prisoners, their case prompted heated exchanges between the United States and Mexico. In less than six months they were released with apologies, given passports, and presented with small sums to ease their thoughts and flea-encrusted bodies. Many of the exiles returned. Most of them nursed a grievance against the men who sent them away. In six years that hatred was to have an outlet.

Chapter XIV

GREEDY EYES

JOHN SUTTER's contemporary drama conditioned him as a prompted actor. Like others of fate and history, he was essentially a man of his time. Inescapably, he had absorbed all the colorations and prejudices of the period that had preceded him. And had the Stage Director limited him to one garment for his engagement, he would have played out his rôle clad in the singlet of determination.

During the first three decades of his life the growth of the Napoleonic legend and the inflation of the Napoleonic stature was an emotional phenomenon, sired by an entire continent. Even babes were innoculated. Old men fathered incomparable tales. As a boy the Swiss knew a daily comradeship with this Corsican myth. It was thrilling; it was glorious; it was magnificent. It made hearts pound and eyes glisten. There was no adventure like it.

Every fireside was a shrine dedicated to a fabulous renascence. The harassed, haggard, bewildered figure in the careening coach at Waterloo had recovered his romance, his youth and his fire. Some supernal leaven had filtered out of old men's beards; that and the indisputable habit of mankind to create its own heroes, symbols of glitter to vary life's monotony. Every lad in Europe felt an envy of emulation, however hysterical or passive or transitory; and no mention of the Great Retreat was recalled by hoary mumblers.

John Sutter was neither peasant nor noble. The feet of his forebears tramped the middle pathway. He was a provincial Swiss, adept in graces denied so many princes. Born between two classes there was only one possible scenery in his dreams—empire, power, pomp, an earnest desire for civilization. His ambitions were social, expansive, possessive. They could be nothing else.

Later stimuli guided him. Napoleon Third, exiled from France by law, served as an officer of artillery in the Swiss Guards; with him, side by side, served Sutter as a captain. Here was a Bonaparte one could see and hear,—fiery, obsessed. A renewal of glory in the flesh.

What was more logical than, when financial stress confronted him, Sutter should turn his swift concern to a distant spot—a New World. He believed, with a fierce self-religion, in himself. He had the gift to make that belief marketable; that radiant individuality of his was equipped to convince the majority of men in the practicality of dreams. Out of a world that worshipped a bantam god came the psychological impetus of Sutter's objective; that and a driving necessity.

Events are relative. They make history. The Corsican lived to bemoan the sunken road of Ohain and pace an island cage, furious for imperial continuance. Sutter purchased the muskets thrown away by the broken ranks of the Great Retreat and lived to face an army, mad with the gold-lust, intent on overwhelming his kingdom.

Yet they met on the raceway to that common goal of all adventurers—seeking to satisfy, at Destiny's expense, the utmost appetite they felt for life. Chance aided them both. Yet each was smugly sure that his hands sped skillfully to weave the pattern. . . .

The breach between Vallejo and Sutter widened and reverberated. The *Comandante Militar* was especially piqued by Sutter's letter of December 1839. "We must not loose sight of a settlement of foreigners in the direction of the Sacramento," he wrote his brother, then commander at San José, on December 26th, "said to have been made with permission of the departmental government, yet contrary to law and the latest orders from Mexico. That establishment is very suspicious, and *respira sintomas venenosos.* . . ."

Animosity is equally divided between Sutter and Alvarado in that note. As the months went by, and as

early as 1841, the Swiss knew that he held the key to
California, that his valley would send out the tentacles
of conquest when the time was favorable. Small wonder
that Vallejo was apprehensive. The menace to Mexican
permanence from the prospering colony was plain.

For years France, England and the United States had
cast proprietary eyes on California. They hoped for a
near day when Mexico's feeble grip on her Pacific province would end. Even the Californians admitted the
necessity of change; some favored one nation, some
another. Every foreigner in the province was discreetly,
or boldly, speculative.

A visit by James Douglas to Yerba Buena was a two-
fold project, only partially concealed. In addition to
Hudson's Bay Company business, he was attent on the
possibilities of British accession. Both his party and Sir
George Simpson's later expedition were designed to
favorably shape pro-British sentiment in California.
Both men were aided by Alexander Forbes, the English
consul, and Michel La Framboise, leader of the annual
Hudson's Bay Company trappers.

Douglas had been the perfect host to Sutter at Fort
Vancouver. But conditions had changed. Now the Swiss
was a troublesome entity; the fellow's insolence was not
to be tolerated. He was actually in conflict with English
commercial dominance and territorial expansion. His
meddlesome manners irritated Douglas. Something had
to be done—at once.

Naturally, Sutter's interference with the Company
fur trade led the van of Douglas' grievances. For the
same cause one may discount Sir George Simpson's bitter
estimate of the Swiss—a man whom he never met. When
you trim the capacity of a man's pocketbook there is
little chance he will think well of you. Sir George was
no exception. Some of his adjectives must have scorched
his original manuscript pages. But then, agate-eyed Sir
George was given to facile, blustery bunkum. The most

amiable people encountered in his travels invariably discovered themselves indicted in his printed displeasure.

Douglas—when well warmed up to his task—went so far as to question Sutter's authority in the disputed section. The Swiss ignored him. That indifference pained Douglas.

Forthwith, he interviewed Vallejo on the fur disagreement. No decision was made. Sutter was well within his rights. Much as the General wished to checkmate the inland baron, he lacked the power.

Douglas was wise enough to recognize a stone wall when he faced it. He dropped the matter and turned to the easier task of establishing a trading post at Yerba Buena with Alvarado's approval. William Glen Rae was placed in charge of a site and building purchased from Jacob Leese. It was a headquarters for whatever action might occur in California, commercial or colonial. The Lion had a foothold.

France made a tentative bid the same year. M. Eugene Duflot de Mofras was a young *attaché* of the French embassy at Madrid. He was recalled by Marshal Soult, minister of foreign affairs, and attached to the Mexican legation. Within a few weeks he was dispatched, under orders of Louis Philippe, on a special mission to California "in order to ascertain, independent of political viewpoint, whatever commercial advantages might be offered us by mercantile expeditions and by the establishment of trading posts in these regions still little known to France."

De Mofras, later to hold the portfolio of *minister plenipotentaire*, reached California in May 1841. He was the choice of the shrewd monarch who had succeeded the Bourbons; and, doubtless, he had secret instructions never disclosed to history.

In the next few months he inspected every important Mission and settlement in the province. M'sieur de Mofras was tireless; also he had an eye for a pretty woman and the California variety seemed lovely and daring enough for any discerning diplomat.

August 1st brought him to New Helvetia for a four weeks' stay. He walked after breakfast in the fields, rode on elk and deer and grizzly hunts, let a sharp eye rest on mounting walls, promenaded in the twilight with the courtly Swiss under the oaks and sycamores.

The envoy was a friendly fellow. He brought light tales of city life, bright raillery and table-talk. Sutter was to regret his departure; everyone did—with possibly the exception of a few husbands. Tactful, observant, lustily sensual, de Mofras was inclined to hold forth eloquently on the future of the Pacific Coast. That sort of comment was a tonic to Sutter.

Surely they speculated on conquest. But no record remains of it, either in Sutter's memoirs or de Mofras' books. Such words were then too acute to set down in print or scribble carelessly in ink; later they had lost their significance or were lost in distortion. But Sutter must have pointed out to his guest that only two nations might be conceded a chance of seizing California; and that France was not one of them. Sutter never troubled to conceal his preference for the young republic to the east.

De Mofras' published account does seek to convey the certainty that Sutter was a Frenchman at heart and favored French domination. That was volatile enthusiasm without foundation. Sutter had made his choice; was convinced he had picked a winner. At no time did he ever waver in the belief that California would one day be a part of the Union.

A unit of the Wilkes exploring expedition was next to visit New Helvetia. It was commanded by Lieutenant Ringgold of the United States Navy and arrived at the *embarcadero* in ship's-boats on August 23rd, 1841. For a day and a night they enjoyed the food, shelter and respite of Sutter's dwellings.

Dawn of the 25th found them once more ascending the river, their errand to make a swift survey of the interior waterways and the surrounding country. Sutter provided them with whatever they lacked and sped them with his roaring cannon.

There were degrees of welcome and departure on the Sacramento—degrees of powder-punctuated dignity. Salutes were graduated: lesser personages received from three to seven guns; great travelers and officials received as many as twenty-one. And if the supply of powder and shot ever gave out in a crucial moment no record remains of it.

Ringgold and his men returned September 4th. They made another short stay and discussed their findings with Sutter. Their observations helped him. The land was still strange; news such as Ringgold brought was authentic.

Six weeks after their departure another group came overland from Oregon. Lieutenant Emmons led this second party of the Wilkes expedition. They reached Sutter's hill on October 19th. Botanists, geologists, officers, sailors and soldiers made up a company of thirty.

They remained two days and were impressed by the colony's organization. Their leader was so delighted by the apparent industry of the place that his written tributes caused Commodore Wilkes to acknowledge the kindness shown his two roving commands by Captain Sutter, who was found to be "a man of frank and prepossessing manner, of great intelligence, conversant with several languages, and withal not a little enthusiastic."

The Swiss shook hands with Emmons at parting.

"You will bring your flag back some day soon, Lieutenant," he said. "By Jupiter, no man in California will be happier than I when you do."

Americans had no doubt it was their "manifest destiny" to win the western land. Annexation was a topic of conversation and newspaper comment. At one time the United States actually proposed the cession of Alta California. Certainly, the American press had expressed inky wrath when a rumor credited England with the intent to gobble California in payment for outstanding debts due the British by Mexico.

"The location of California," summarized Commodore Wilkes, "will cause its separation from Mexico in the next few years. . . . It is evident that it will fill a large and important niche in the world's future history."

Obviously, the United States had much to gain by watchful waiting. Emigration had begun to fight its way over the plains and mountains. Each day strengthened the American position. The only present action to be feared was the armed intervention of another power.

Sir George Simpson was swift to analyze Sutter's part in the coming change. "The Americans," declared Sir George, "as soon as they become masters of the interior through Captain Sutter's establishment, will discover they have a natural right to a marine outlet. Whatever may be the fate of Monterey and the more southerly ports, San Francisco will, to a moral certainty, sooner or later fall into the possession of the Americans—*unless the English take it*."

Sutter made plans early in 1841 to survey and map the region already guaranteed to him. That record was a necessary inclusion in the formal application for his huge grant. Not a moment was lost in its production.

Jean Jacques Vioget, a Swiss civil engineer and draftsman from Yerba Buena, prepared the document. He completed his work on June 5th. Armed with the *diseno*, Sutter sped to Monterey.

His petition was granted by Alvarado on June 18th. He considered Sutter "has sufficiently accredited his laboriousness, good conduct, and other qualifications required in such cases. He has manifested great efforts in advance, shown constant firmness, and displayed patriotic zeal in favor of our institutions by already civilizing a large number of savages, natives of our frontiers."

This original grant was eleven square leagues within the tract designated on the map opposite this page. It was bounded on the north by the Three Peaks and latitude 39 degrees 41' 45"; on the east by "the margins of the Feather River;" on the south by latitude 38 degrees 49' 32"; and on the west by the Sacramento River. These eleven leagues did not include lands flooded by the two streams in overflow.

The conditions, in addition to those of the usual formalities, were that "he shall maintain the different tribes in the liberty and enjoyment of their possessions, and he shall use no other civilizing agents save those of kindness and prudence. Nor shall he make war upon them without previously obtaining permission from the government."

Thus the first seventy square miles of John Sutter's empire became his, to have and to hold. It was only an earnest of his future acres, a beginning. The Grand Duchy of Baden, where he had been born, was a child's playground compared with the lands to come.

Chapter XV

FEATHER RIVER RANCHO

THE SWISS turned to military schemes when his feet were firmly planted, his foothold secure. In 1840 he began the creation of an army. Out of the dull-eyed welter of neighboring *rancherias* he laboriously hand-picked a hundred Indians. Fifty of them he mounted on good horses—two *caponeras* of superb blacks —and taught them all the cavalry commands and evolutions.

That was a task. They were thick-headed beyond imagining. But John Sutter was patient. He had need of those slow-witted dunderheads.

The remaining fifty were trained as infantry and drilled with continental precision. He spent an hour a day with each unit. It took long months for both commands to acquire reliability and formidable equipment. If one Indian proved himself lacking, another was promptly chosen in his place. The instruction went on interminably.

In the beginning forked sticks had been their only arms. As Sutter's resources increased he issued rifles, muskets, and ammunition to his footmen and gallopers. Regardless of stupidity and trials involved, in a year and a half he had a dependable force ready for active duty. And Sutter had the knack of instilling loyalty into the mentality of even a Sacramento Valley aborigine.

Yerba Buena had begun to hum with new business activities. More traders opened stores in the village. Joseph Limantour, a Frenchman—later a land-grabber extraordinary who laid claim to nearly the entire city of San Francisco—set himself up as a purveyor of the finer imported delicacies. Dainties not carried on Spear's more practical shelves—brandies, cheeses, sweetmeats, condiments—found their way to the rough table-tops of yearning New Switzerland, paid for in deer-fat, land-otter and beaver skins. Of course, these imported goods were unusual fare. Only visiting notables were regaled with such expensive luxuries by the provident Captain.

Hiram Teal was another new merchant who in 1841 sold goods to Sutter. His stock was cheap and good. Most of it was of Mexican manufacture, lately arrived from Mazatlan. *Ponchos, serapes*, silver spurs, headstalls, hair bridle-reins, saddles and *armas de pelo*—riding robes that protected the body up to the waist—were in demand in the colony. The lisping-tongued Teal supplied most of them.

Salmon and sturgeon were plentiful in the Sacramento. The Swiss frequently shipped a catch to Nathan Spear on the pinnace. Being something of a *gourmet*, the merchant was delighted with the delicious taste of Sutter's offering.

"These fish have commercial possibilities," he wrote eagerly. "I am sure you and I could make a good thing of it. Are you agreeable?"

Sutter was. Anything that promised to expand his credit always interested him. His favorable reply so enthused Spear that the latter sailed for the *Embarcadero* on the *Isabel* without delay.

The two made a verbal contract on his arrival. Then Sutter ordered all the Indians living at the fishing *rancheria* to aid the visitor. Hundreds of fish were caught and smoked or fresh-salted. Spear camped in a tent on the river bank and watched contentedly as the *Isabel's* hold was packed with its pungent cargo.

In a week the ship sailed back, deep-laden. So low, indeed, was the slow-moving craft that her crew were apprehensive of any freshening breeze.

Safe at Yerba Buena, Spear promptly transferred the fish to kegs and barrels. He hawked his delicacies by word of mouth as the work went on. The supply did not last two weeks and customers called for more. For years the partners maintained the fishing venture. It made a snug return for both until the merchant died in 1848.

IN 1841 HOCK FARM, so called because of its nearness to the Indian village of that name, was portioned off by Sutter. That site became his great cattle rancho. The herding ground sat on high, fertile territory close to the Feather River. There the horses, sheep and cattle were guarded by *vaqueros*, safe from the terror of rising floods. Great gardens were laid out on the uplands with no fear of rushing waters destroying them.

Adobe buildings and corrals were erected. Indians from the adjacent *rancherias* worked faithfully. This *Rio de Los Plumas* Rancho was a pleasing spot and the Swiss counted it as one of his chief sources of wealth. It was to be more than that—a refuge in bewildering days. . . .

This same year emigrants were cutting ruts in parched plains and snapping axles in mountain passes on the way to the West. The hardy first ones were few. Some were to become famous. Of that number was the piercing-eyed John Bidwell, Charles Flugge, Thomes, Nye, Bartleson, Chiles, Joel P. Walker and Talbot H. Green. Most prominent to be was Bidwell, right-hand advisor to the Swiss. He was to know John Sutter better than any other man.

Bidwell was a New York boy who had tried his hand at schoolteaching and found it "monstrously tedious." To Missouri he came and began to "prove up" on a tract in Platte County. But after a temporary absence he returned one afternoon to find that a pistoled stranger had "jumped" his claim.

With great disgust the twenty-year-old youngster waved the flint-eyed gent farewell. Then he helped organize a California-bound wagon train.

His party was small, luckless and persistent. They suffered eight months of incalculable hardship before they came wearily down out of the ranges and within sight of their goal.

John Marsh's rancho, near Monte Diabolo, was their first California stopping place. Trail-jaded, skin tightened over ribs, wagonless, without animals or food, they

reached the adobe hovel. The eccentric Harvard grad-
uate received them with an initial show of good will.
But the welcome did not persist. Marsh was a creature
of undeterminable impulse and his vagaries drove the
emigrants quickly on.

Bidwell's estimate of Marsh is illuminating, written
as it was to be conveyed eastward for the information of
other travelers about to start west. He says:

"To my friends in the East who may come to California: I must speak candidly of Dr. Marsh. I speak for the
emigrant, that he may be on his guard, and not be gulled
by him, as some of us have been on first arriving here.

"He is perhaps the meanest man in California. After
our company had encamped near his house for about two
days and a small hog and bullock had been killed for
us, he began to complain of his poverty.

"'This company has already cost me a hundred
dollars,' he said. 'God knows whether I shall ever get a
real of it!'

"Yet poor as our party was we had already paid him
five fold in powder, lead, knives, gifts, etc. He charged
the company three dollars each to get their passports—
a good price for his services. There is not a person in
California who does not dislike the man. He is never admitted into a house to sleep; if rightly informed, I find he
had to sleep under his own cart in a Spanish town to
which he had taken some hides. No other foreigner
would be so insulted or obliged to do so.

"He came to this country pretending to be a physician, which he was not. He has, however, gained by his
deception—he has charged and received $25 for two
doses of salts; he has refused his assistance to a woman in
labor, not expected to live without immediate relief,
unless her husband promised to pay him fifty cattle.

"When he first came to this country he hired himself
into the family of an obliging American, during which
time he paid out 50c on one occasion for some fresh fish.

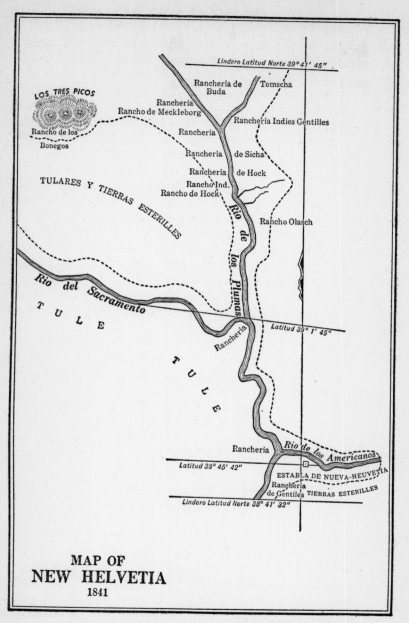

Map of New Helvetia, 1841, by Jean Jacques Vioget

After spending a whole year in the man's home without charge he dunned his host for the 50c when he left.

"I could fill fifty pages detailing similar incidents, but it is unnecessary to mention but one more. Marsh was called to administer to a child suffering with headache; he gave the child two doses of medicine and demanded fifty cattle as payment.

"The family was a poor one, not owning more than one hundred and fifty cattle in all. In order to reduce the price they charged Marsh twenty-five cattle for washing two of his shirts. Off he went, grumbling—but driving his twenty-five animals. . . ."

Bidwell and his party moved on to Sutter's Fort after leaving the crotchety pseudo doctor. One of their number, James Johns—"Jimmy Johns" he was called—had preceded them a few days. Into Sutter's sympathetic ear he gave the tale of the company's plight. Mules were packed with food and supplies and two guides were sent out with them, being instructed to lead the hungry men to New Helvetia.

On November 28th, 1841, Bidwell and his destitute friends reached the rising walls on the green hill. Sutter made shift to care for all of them. To the young schoolteacher he offered a clerkship. Young Bidwell never forgot the hospitable welcome he received from the Sacramento chieftain.

There is no doubt that John Bidwell's analysis of the Swiss is colored by his friendship for the man. But Bidwell proved himself capable of clear, critical commentary on California personalities; he prided himself that his impressions were honestly given and "little tinged by personal bitterness that is always futile." They were written with no prompting outside interest. For that reason the document has more than ordinary significance.

"Sutter was no common man," he said. "No one can fittingly appreciate his influence and services who was not acquainted with his trials and circumstances.

"He had come to the Pacific Coast without a great deal of money, but he had that which brought money—a magnificent address. He was of fine and commanding presence and courteous as a prince to all. I have never seen one more polished in his deportment. Always liberal and affable, no one could be more obliging than he, especially to needy or destitute strangers.

"He was the most generous and hospitable of men. Everybody was welcome—one man or a hundred, it was all the same. He employed men, not because he always needed and could profitably employ them, but because in the kindness of his heart he simply hired everyone who asked employment. As long as he had anything he trusted everyone who asked—responsible or otherwise, strangers or acquaintances. He employed anywhere from a hundred to five hundred men, the latter number at harvest time.

"The object of his admiration was the Republic of the United States. He was always an American at heart and longed for the day when Mexico and her revolutions would, as he believed, lose California to the United States.

"Sutter had one glaring fault; he was too outspoken in his personal admiration of the United States. Because of it the Mexicans began to early view him with suspicion. His establishment became a home to all Americans, where they could live as long as it suited them without charge.

"Sutter's attitude toward Americans was so friendly and his fort so invariably the headquarters of all Americans reaching the Pacific Coast, that his actions fostered jealousy and hatred among the native Californians.

"It is true that no such thing as open war was ever waged agaist him at New Helvetia; still, hostile rumors were numerous. To my mind the rumors were without more than petty foundation. Vallejo, Alvarado and Castro were men of too much shrewdness and influence to incite an open conflict with the American government because Sutter was already sheltering American settlers already in California."

Another arrival at New Helvetia in the last month of 1841 was to prove of much assistance to the colony. He was Charles Flugge, the clever, quick-tempered German whose glasses gave him an owl-like solemnity contrary to his swift moods. Loyal and reliable, he soon fitted into Sutter's plans. Moreover, he was a hard-headed business man and ever alert in the Swiss' interest. Given a dozen of Flugge's sort, Sutter might have owned half of California today. . . .

One unexpected reverse irritated Sutter at the year's close. He had sent John Sinclair to Honolulu on the brig *Llama* in the early spring to bring back a consignment of much-needed supplies. Arrangements had been concluded with French and Greenway to ship him anything he required in seeds and agricultural implements. Profits of the *Clementine* venture were still unpaid to him; and he was perfectly willing to accept his desired items to the amount of the debt.

Two days before Sinclair arrived in the Islands the firm of French and Greenway turned up its commercial toes. Naturally, any previously agreed-on contracts with the defunct company were worthless. Sutter's original cash investment in the Sitka-California voyage, plus his expected profit, was wiped out.

Sinclair, being at loose ends, was approached by Eliab Grimes, a prominent Honolulu merchant. He was engaged to return to California and assume management of a land grant which Grimes proposed to secure from the Mexican government.

Then Sutter's ex-agent sailed on the *Julia Ann* for Monterey. The news he later brought to New Helvetia was exasperatingly final.

"By Jupiter!" exploded Sutter, "we cannot count on anything until it is finished!"

Chapter XVI

THE COASTAL LEAGUES

THE MOST important California incident of 1841 was Sutter's purchase of Fort Ross and Bodega. That coup was a triumph for the Swiss. It meant a lavish gain of needed stores and equipment—on credit.

Offers made by the Russians to Sir James Douglas and General Vallejo had held little significance. Douglas' luke-warm British drawl had irritated Rotscheff during their interview; he detested noncommittal swank. In turn, Vallejo tried to hold off indefinitely under the mistaken idea that no buyer could be found. What was to prevent his acquiring the site and immovable fixtures for nothing after the owners departed? It seemed like a chance worth waiting for to the *Comandante Militar*.

On December 4th Rotscheff made a surprise move. At least, it was unlooked for by both Englishman and Sonoma chieftain. He anchored off Sutter's *Embarcadero* and paid the Captain a visit. He brought an offer for the sale of all Russian holdings and property; and he was prepared to make the purchase less difficult by various concessions.

The two were alone for an hour. Each man talked from the shoulder, without fencing. Sutter agreed to go to Fort Ross at once. There he could look over the situation and make a decision.

They sailed to San Rafael. In order to make swifter progress, they left the Russian schooner at that point. Servants and horses awaited them. Overland they hastened to the Russian post.

Much has been written concerning the legality of Russian land claims in America. Certainly, the Spaniards had no rights beyond that of actual occupation. San Francisco was the northern limit of such occupation in 1812 and the Russians—or any other nation—could acquire a perfect title to any port north of San Francisco Bay by settlement.

Any objection on the part of Spain or Mexico would be absurd; as well claim *all* of North America because of Columbus' discovery. A nation that has held actual possession of a territory for a third of a century without opposition by any other country is certainly entitled to a clear deed to such a region. There is no fact to disprove that Russia had the right, moral and legal, to sell such land and its improvements to anyone they chose.

At Fort Ross the party were joined in debate by Peter Kostromitinoff and the captain of the brig *Elena*, then in port. After various tours of inspection, a formal offer was made to Sutter to buy the site and the equipment. At first, he preferred to purchase the equipment only. But he finally consented to include the real estate at Rotscheff's insistence.

Terms were graduated for Sutter's benefit. The sum of $30,000 was to be paid in four years, in annual installments, beginning September 1st, 1842. The first and second payments were to be five thousand dollars each; the last two payments ten thousand dollars each; the first three payments were to be in produce, chiefly wheat, to be delivered in San Francisco free of duties and tonnage; the final payment was to be in cash. Sutter was requested to post New Helvetia as security for his good faith and to allow a company agent to occupy a small farm on the property until the debt was paid.

The Swiss accepted the terms. His agreement combined necessity as well as opportunity—he needed everything the Russians possessed. The payments were so distributed that he believed he could easily meet his obligations. The Russians also agreed to send vessels each year to collect their produce; and to ship Sutter, aboard these vessels, any supplies he might order from Sitka.

Charges that Sutter undertook contracts without an intention of fulfilling them are unfounded. He was as sure of success as a hound on a fox-trail. Certainly, his enthusiasms made him set too fast a pace in his wilderness building; but that is little indication of a dishonest purpose. He really believed that he could accomplish all— and more—than he promised; that events and conditions frequently thwarted him was quite beyond his power to prevent.

THAT NIGHT an informal gathering met on the *Elena*. The affair was in honor of the new owner of Ross and Bodega. All were there to wish Sutter luck in his venture —the clerks and their wives, the officers and their ladies, the Governor and his Princess.

The evening held laughter: even though the pall of Russ defeat must have been wrapped close in every heart —the surety of failure and departure.

During a break in the light talk, the Princess drifted close to Sutter. "I must see you tomorrow, Captain— before you leave. I have a request—"

"It is granted," laughed her guest.

"At eight, then—in the garden."

He bowed. . . .

It was a warm night. The *Elena* swayed on easy swells, her small deck lighted by stars and ship's lanterns. Four of the Russians made music that throbbed above the voice of the sea. They danced, these subjects of the Czar who were being forced back to their homeland; and with them danced the straight-legged Swiss who was to profit by their going.

At times John Sutter held the radiant Princess in his arms. . . . She was a distracting lady, Helena Gargaren: flying feet that beat a rhythm on the sometimes tilting deck; silk that contoured firm breasts and a glorious body; fragrant with some essence the Swiss could not give a name; all-desirable woman who had dared death to know life with the man she loved.

The pulse of the Captain coursed faster than the dancing demanded. . . . This woman, too, was an adventurer of chance and dreams; love had driven her to a rôle and she had not turned back.

In the morning they walked alone in her garden. The breath of the blooms and their colorings smote Sutter with some vague resentment. So soon to pass, they were; without the care of white hands; the hands of an imperial princess. Near beauty always stimulated the man from Baden. Such moments he recalled long after they had been dulled and dedicated to remoteness by age and continual struggle.

Silently, they came to a crystal-covered garden house. They paused; and the dark eyes of Helena Gargaren were, very suddenly, misted with tears.

She touched his arm, looked up. "My friend," she cried, "when you take this loved spot of mine away will you love it, too? Promise me you will carry it away so carefully! I cannot bear to think of my flower house all broken up, destroyed! Please tell me you will cherish it; it has given me so many happy hours."

The Swiss bent over her white hand with lips that lingered.

"My lady," he pledged, "it shall always be as you loved it. Some day—I hope—you may see it again."

John Sutter, like most enthusiasts, made his promises boldly. No grudging answer, his. No room for thought of failure—or accident—on his horizon.

She smiled through wet lashes. "You have the knowing heart, *m'sieur le capitaine*," she murmured. "I shall remember your kindness long after I leave this California of yours."

"Dear lady, I, too, shall not forget. Think of it always as you saw it last—with the sun on it."

The Lord of New Helvetia stood straight, saluted. "I must go now, Princess. But I shall see you both before the time of departure."

"*Au revoir, m'sieur le capitaine.*"

She watched his erect figure as he strode down the path to where his men were waiting.

Sutter made plans as he rode. The property and live-stock must be moved to the Sacramento. There were 2,000 cattle, 1,000 horses and 1,100 sheep to be driven across country; tons of supplies—tools, lumber, doors, windows, cannon and smaller arms must be transported by water.

The Russian schooner, tied up at San Rafael, was in-cluded in the sale. When Sutter stepped on its decks he proudly christened his new craft the *Sacramento*. Home he sailed to the *Embarcadero*.

One hour after his arrival he organized a party to hurry overland and bring the Ross animals to Hock Farm. Bob Livermore, Joel P. Walker, Ezekiel Merritt and thirty Indian vaqueros were chosen. Livermore was placed in command and the journey begun.

Things went well on the coastal trip. But their return to Hock was a bad trek for men and beasts. More than mere trail dangers were encountered. Forced to proceed over Vallejo's territory, they found themselves subject to various stiff-necked delays and inspections. The General's men solemnly relieved them of various animals, claiming they were Mexican cattle stolen by the Russians.

This treatment had to be stomached for fear of more serious entanglements. Finally the party were allowed to continue their journey. But they lacked 150 head of the original trail-herd.

They crossed the river just above where Sacramento now stands and moved slowly on to Hock Farm. More than 300 cattle had been confiscated, lost, died, or drowned on the way. Regardless of this ill-luck, Sutter's herds were increased by nearly 4,000 animals.

The *Sacramento*, skippered by Bob Ridley, began a series of feverish trips to Fort Ross and Bodega. Among the fire arms transported were a number of muskets thrown away by Napoleon's men in the Great Retreat; they had been picked out of the red-stained snow by the Muscovites and later shipped to this lonely imperial outpost. As weapons they were a total loss; but as drill-muskets for dusky troops they had long hours of service in their battered lengths.

On December 12th Sutter rushed back to Ross to sign the concluding documents. The Russians proposed to desert the site after these formalities, never to return. There was a heavy-footed listlessness about the place when the Swiss rode up the winding path. The preparations for departure that he noted were spiritless, discouraged.

That very night he received the deed to Ross and Bodega from Rotscheff, who was invested with full authority to do so as governor of the territory. The deed was clear and concise. It read:

"I, the undersigned, employee of the government of the Russian Empire and Commandant of Fort Ross, on the Coast of California, do by these presents certify that the establishment embracing the land on the north adjacent to Cape Mendocino, and the land on the south adjacent to Punta de los Reyes, or Cape Drake, and extending back from the shore three Spanish leagues, and of which property the Russian American Fur Company has had and held possession from the year 1812 to the year 1841, or for twenty-nine years, has been ceded by said company for the consideration of thirty thousand dollars ($30,000) to Monsieur le Capitaine Sutter and delivered into his indisputable possession, with all the lands, personal and other immovable property not here enumerated, said company relying for their power and right in the premises upon the institution and spirit of the laws sanctified by Spain and Mexico. The said transfer of the Establishment of Ross was effected during the time that I occupied the position of Commandant of the Establishment, and by my own free coöperation, this, the 12th day of December, 1841.

(Signed)   ALEJANDRO ROTSCHEFF

*Comandant la forteresio Ross,
sur les côtes de la Californie.*

The next morning—December 13th—Peter Kostromitinoff and Sutter rowed by Aleut-driven ship's-boat to
Yerba Buena. There they signed a contract in the office of
the sub-prefect; this in order to leave an accredited record with Mexican authorities. Jacob Leese, Francisco
Guerrero and Jean Jacques Vioget were witnesses. By
its terms Sutter came into immediate possession of all
the property as specified in an annexed inventory.

Both Alvarado and Vallejo in later years were inclined to accuse Sutter of acting dishonorably toward
them in making the Ross purchase. Yet there is no evidence to prove that they were displeased at the time.
But when the land took on value it also climbed importantly on their horizon. Their subsequent fulmina-
tions were doubtless occasioned by the sour-grape
knowledge that a more clever juggler of schemes had
done them out of a bargain—even if it had not resembled
a bargain at the moment.

The claim that John Sutter never bought the Russian
real estate seems rather incredible, based as it was on the
premise that Rotscheff did not have the right to sell the
land. Under date of December 19th, 1841, Peter Kostromitinoff, alleged by the doubters to be the only
accredited representative of the Russian American Fur
Company in this matter, wrote the following letter to
Governor Alvarado at Monterey:

"Your Excellency:

"On my last visit to Monterey I had the honor to state
to you that it was my intention to sell Ross *with its real
estate* and furniture to one of the private individuals in
California. Your Excellency's answer was that as far as
these affairs were concerned there would be no interference on your part. In this present letter I have the
pleasure to declare that Ross is sold to Captain John A.
Sutter, a resident and naturalized citizen of Mexico. . .
etc . . .   "(Signed)
                              "P. KOSTROMITINOFF"

IN EARLY JANUARY 1842, Governor Alejandro Rotscheff and his princess sailed away on the *Constantine*. The entire colony, with the exception of one company representative who remained on a tiny farm, accompanied them.

Sutter was present to bid them godspeed. He clasped his friend, the Governor, by the hand for the last time; bent low, for the last time, over the hand of the Governor's lady.

"You have not forgotten your promise?" she said.

"I shall not forget," he answered.

The white sails crept under the northern skyline like white birds lost in the sea. They marked the end of an adventure, those vanishing sails; the death of an empire's hopes. . . . Fate had swept the imperial eagles of Russia from California skies; and Helena Gargaren and her untitled lover were headed back to St. Petersburg and a reconciliation with her father. . . .

Sutter turned to the bright-eyed slip of a man who stood on the shore beside him. "On your way, Bob Ridley, on your way!" he ordered good-naturedly. "You're my resident agent here and I want more work out of you."

"Right-o," said the Cockney whiskey-wit. "We'll move Russia to the old Sacrament' in jigtime, eh, Cap'n?"

Sutter nodded.

Nor was Ridley wrong. Everything within the walls of Ross was rushed aboard the *Sacramento* as fast as hands could stow the heaping cargo. Even the walls themselves came crashing down to make the interior journey. Trips were as hurried as wind and weather would allow. Out of the absolute ruin of Russian hopes the Swiss was determined to raise a more impregnable empire in his stretching valley.

Chapter XVII

MERIENDA

A FESTIVE evening at the Fort had one highlight—the snapping of pasteboards on a redwood table. Stout Theodore Cordua, Charles Flugge, John Sinclair and the Swiss played many a game of whist by candle-light. There was always a crackling log fire in Sutter's quarters, a tot of brandy handy at their elbows, mayhap even a bowl of sweetmeats for those who craved them.

Sutter liked whist; that and Twenty-one. If either of the regulars were absent someone else was easily per-suaded to fill the vacant bench and carry on. Great rivalry was displayed in those games. Stakes were small and the fun itself was the thing. True, John Sutter once lost a splendid turkey-cock to Cordua on the hazard of a night's play; but such bankrupting wagers were few and far between.

Occasionally, press of business took Sutter to Yerba Buena on the pinnace. One of these flying visits brought him to Nathan Spear's headquarters when the agent was on the instant of departure for a *merienda*—a picnic.

It was not yet noon. And nothing would satisfy the vacation-minded Spear but Sutter's presence at the outing.

"Business can wait for today, Captain," he urged. "You must come with me."

Sutter reluctantly agreed.

As long as old men could remember, great patches of luscious wild strawberries had ripened in the springtime on the hills toward the ocean, between the Presidio and Fort Point, and south as far as Lake Lobos. It was the yearly habit for California families from north and south of the bay, and even from Santa Clara and Sonoma, to gather on the ocean ward slopes during the berry season. There they picked and ate the delicious fruit, camped and frolicked, leaving Yerba Buena and the outlying ranchos almost deserted for a week.

The end of the strawberry festival was nearing when Sutter's pinnace beached at the tiny town. It was the Swiss' first visit at such a time. But he was only one of the few. Everyone who could possibly get there attended the berry-picking, even the captains and officers of the ships in harbor.

The two strode up the mounting way to reach the merchant's tent-camp. They were hailed by many acquaintances and friends who were busily engaged in stuffing red fruit into eager mouths. Only infrequently did some surfeited gatherer place a few select berries in a basket for future use.

Sight of one of the most spirituously expansive merrymakers jolted Sutter into an exclamation. The fellow was in holiday mood and gushing words. He was none other than Bob Ridley, supposedly perspiring at Ross. Evidently, the convivial cockney had taken French leave of his assignment in order not to miss the celebration.

The Captain was much more chagrined than the hilarious Bob. When he saw his employer come walking over the berry-covered dunes, he waved an unembarrassed greeting. "Welcome, Cap'n Sutter," he belched blithely. "Better late than never, ol' topper!"

That Sutter's answer was coldly formal did not bother him. If the Cap'n didn't know that nobody worked at berry-time—well, that was due to personal ignorance; it wasn't his Ross' manager's fault.

Californians and foreigners were mingling in the slow-moving groups. Most of the important figures of Alta California were wandering about the crimson-splashed heights. Sutter nodded and spoke to dozens he knew: Don Ignacio Martinez, Don Juan Prado Mesa, Don Francisco Guerrero, William S. Hinckley, John Wilson, William A. Richardson, Henry Mellus, William H. Davis, W. D. M. Howard. Señoritas with bright eyes and scarlet-stained lips and slim hips were everywhere, puffily chaperoned, however, by less agile señoras.

Nobody but had a smile and a laugh and a swift word with an eye-twinkle tied to it. Good food, good wine, good humor and good fellowship formed an arm-in-arm quartet. The Swiss began to enter into the spirit of the day. It was good to hear such happy clamor on a sun-bright hill.

The pair talked as they went along. Spear was a usually silent, contained fellow. But for the moment he was positively gay. Sutter learned this was the last day of the pilgrimage. In less than an hour—twelve o'clock, high noon—all had been bidden to gather in a little windward valley that looked out to the ocean, not far from Spear's camp.

"A farewell of sorts," explained the merchant. "Don Francisco has planned it. He's been doing some such thing pretty regularly in the past few years. . . . Too bad you weren't here all week, Captain."

"There's little time for play at New Helvetia," said Sutter. "You town people are becoming idlers, Nathan."

Spear grinned. "Outside of July 4th we have little enough fun. I enjoy it, for one."

The converging parties met in the glade selected by Don Francisco. Besides wine and other delicacies, he had provided a number of calves and bullocks for the feasting. They were prepared as *carne asada*—meat roasted to a tender brownness on spits over a bed of hot coals.

At two o'clock their host rose and gestured for silence.

"My friends," he announced, "I crave your indulgence but a moment. We have come to the end of this *merienda* and what is more fitting than that we should celebrate it with dancing and music? I invite you to make a *pasear* to the Mission Dolores. There we shall dance until the cock-calls greet the day!"

A cheer sped over the rolling hills; and John Sutter's acclaim was as lusty as the rest. The tents and baggage were collected and packed on horse and muleback. Soon, the assemblage was straggling over the green-and-red crests and valleys to the Mission.

It was playtime and springtime in a golden land. The Swiss found himself as restless as a child to dance and laugh and tell stories and watch lambent-eyed girls with a glow of expectation. . . .

The *baile* of Don Francisco began to sparkle. Red wine warmed hearts that did not need warming; gayly clad California dandies danced as if they had springs in their glistening boots; the foreigners' attire was less striking but not so their spirits and antics.

Anticipative señoritas and the younger señoras had come prepared to dazzle a masculinity quite willing to be dazzled. Their loveliness was decked with finery hoarded for the occasion. Jackets of silk buttoned high at the throat were half-draped by silken *rebozos* which did not conceal the allurements of beautiful figures; high combs sat above raven hair cut square across the forehead, a lock curled distractingly along each velvet cheek; nets of gold or color held those tresses at the back; necklaces of pearls and ear-drops sparkled on creamy necks and tiny ears; trim ankles in red-stockinged silk with dainty feet shod in silver-buckled shoes peeped from beneath the embroidered hems of voluminous white skirts; broad, scarlet ribbons whose ends nearly swept the floor clung jealously about slim waists; and fans, held by soft hands, waved gracefully.

El tecolero, the master of ceremonies, organized the scene into dashing life. Dances rushed by—waltzes, *la jota*, quadrilles, *jarabe*, contra-dances. Refreshments were served frequently—champagne and other wines, poultry, cakes, ham and steaming coffee.

Shapely legs spun untiringly; firm little breasts rippled like ripe fruits under lace and nestling silks; dark eyes burned bright with life and laughter; old *rancheros* capered as lithely as youngsters with incipient mustachios; ancient señoras sat about and eyed the scene with approval, dreaming—who knows, perhaps of youth—and John Sutter whirled about the hall floor, gayest of them all, his erect figure followed by half the ravishing black eyes under the tall combs, even by ancient eyes lit by ancient visions. . . .

The pinnace went back to the *Embarcadero* two days later.

"I would like to come again next year, Nathan," called the Swiss as he saluted in farewell.

THE FIRST GREAT floods that came to New Helvetia might have meant a bumper crop. But Sutter had not been equipped to work swiftly after the downpour. He had few plows and a limited supply of seed; only the bare numbers needed in the battle for survival were present in the colony; and the Indians were not ready to obey his order faithfully or intelligently. Few green stalks of wheat came sprouting up out of the Sacramento soil in 1840.

The second season of 1840-41 was one of drought; and bitter disappointment. Skies were leaden and promising. But no rain fell from the cloudy blanket.

Then the third season of 1841-42 followed the second in arid sequence—two dry years in a row. Less patient men than the Swiss would have capitulated at such vagaries of climate. But not John Sutter. His will knew no faltering; it would come, the fruition and the glory. One must work and plan and wait. It would come.

Only enough seed was threshed that third year to replenish the seed that had been sown. The large, fat kernels that had gone into the soil were replaced by stunted, parched, flat kernels—a poor offering from a rainless earth.

There were some compensations. Trapping in 1842 was much more successful than in the preceding years. More traps were either purchased or made by Sutter's blacksmiths; more hunters were employed; a greater variety of goods was kept to tempt the free-trapper to the Fort, and Michel la Framboise and his roving company were so harassed by Sutter's commands and demands that they made little inroad on the pelts in the Sacramento region.

In increasing numbers beaver and land-otter skins flowed into the steadily rising walls of New Switzerland. From the *Embarcadero* the *Sacramento* carried them to the Captain's creditors in Yerba Buena and elsewhere.

Don Antonio Suñol supplied Sutter with the distillery equipment. Wild-grape brandy of a good quality was promptly added to the list of exports. Deer-fat and hides and tallow also went by boat to the bay region. "This valley," proclaimed Sutter to John Sinclair, "is only beginning to send out a ten-thousandth part of what this land can produce."

In March and May 1842, Sutter sent one hundred and forty beaver-skins to Don Antonio, asking that he be credited with the amount of $2.50 per pound on his account; also thirty land otter skins at $2.50 each. In the May letter the Captain is much incensed at MacVickers, recently in command of his trappers, who is declared to have stolen a large number of skins; MacVickers has sold these pelts to Dr. Marsh and others. Sutter concludes with great vehemence that something will be done about it. Which probably occurred, but no record remains.

Sutter was fast expanding the occupancy of his grant beyond Hock Farm and the Fort. He had placed Nicolas Altgeier on the north side of the Feather River at a site known as Nicolas; between the Feather and the Yuba rivers he had leased an area to Theodore Cordua, his corpulent, whist-playing crony of the long evenings. This spot was named New Mecklenburg by its lessee. John Sinclair was in charge of Eliab Grimes' rancho on the American River. William Gordon was settled on Cache Creek.

Others who had served the Swiss faithfully were given outright gifts of land. They were friendly buffers against any intervention, Mexical or aboriginal. Into Sutter's plans they dovetailed admirably; his method of binding men to his service was the common-sense one of bettering their personal fortunes. Shrewdly, he made their sense of property ownership add to the stability of New Helvetia.

John Sutter was not a greedy fellow. To have been stingy with his parcels of land would have been foolish —land was the cheapest commodity in California. The gain completely overshadowed the loss of a few square miles of his grant. Parsimonious Dr. Marsh was the only man to exclaim over Sutter's liberality. "The man's crazy as a Digger squaw," said Marsh tersely.

But Sutter's strength was the strength of numbers and group-cohesion. He was determined his aides should share in the benefits of the enterprise. "I am no stronger than the men who surround me," he confided to Flugge one night before the blazing logs. "By Jupiter, if we give a man land he's a home-owner—not a trapper! He'll fight for his home. That means he'll fight for New Helvetia. This is a common venture, Herr Flugge."

The wave of American emigration receded in 1842. Few people came over the deserts and the ranges. It was too soon for news to seep out through the men who had arrived the year before. Not for eight or ten months would letters—and a backwash of emigrants on the re-turn trek to bring their families—bear the enticing ac-counts of the golden land to the East.

But come they would. It was only a pause as the next wave curled its towering crest. That comber was to be resistless. Eyes West read the spume of the surf-lanes. America was about to storm the Sierras. . . .

Then John Bidwell, who had earned Sutter's respect and friendship through his duties as Fort clerk, was ordered to Ross as the manager. "Somebody," remarked the Captain with a smile, "must give Bob Ridley a chance to attend all the *meriendas*—the loafer!"

Bidwell was glad to go. Of his adventures he writes in lively fashion.

"At the beginning of 1842," he said, "Captain Sutter sent me to Fort Ross to care for all the property which still remained and to keep up the occupation. The man in charge when I went there was Robert T. Ridley; he remained for three months and then left, leaving me in complete command.

"During that year Sutter continued to remove lumber, iron and other equipment. Even large circular threshing floors (*eras*) in which the Russians tramped out their wheat with bands of wild horses were torn to pieces and removed. These threshing floors were made in the most substantial manner of hewn redwood planks six inches thick and perfectly matched together. They were joined so tightly and perfectly that they would hold water. The sides were planked up about eight feet high with 1½-inch redwood planks, also hewn, for there was no such thing as a sawmill in California in those days. The diameter of these *eras* varied from two to three hundred feet, according to the amount of grain to be threshed. These *eras* were fastened together with Russian nails and were very difficult to pry apart.

"Sutter tried to raft some of these around to San Francisco Bay but found it impossible; they had to be taken apart for transport. The Californians had no such provision for keeping the grain clean and ivariably threshed upon the ground in *eras* of similar size and form.

"The wild cattle which had been left by Captain Sutter when the main band was taken away the previous year were about one hundred in number. They were really the wildest brutes I ever saw. Deer were tame in comparison and often, while trying to get a shot at the wild horses between sundown and dark—which was the time they chose to leave their haunts in the impenetrable thickets near the Russian River—the deer stood between me and them, spoiling an easy shot. Antelope, elk and deer I could kill—but not those wild horses.

"After trying in vain to shoot them, I let a noted expert with the lasso, one Manuel Saez, have the contract to take them on shares. He was to have half the hides for catching them. Believing that he could drag them out of their haunts, he made the attempt with plenty of skilled help and trained horses.

"For ten days they labored with the utmost effort. In that time they lassoed nine grizzly bears, one black bear, many elk, antelope and deer—*but* they only caught five of the wild horses. One that they killed had an arrow embedded in its liver.

"Grizzly bears were very plentiful. On one occasion we succeeded in scaring away a mother bear and caught her cubs. At first nothing could be more silent than those cubs. We concluded to send them back to the rancho with one of the *vaqueros*, a distance of some three miles. Their little paws were tied together and they were made fast, one on either side of the saddle.

"The *vaquero* then started off. At once both cubs set up a most unholy discord. Their huge mother sprang wrathfully out of the bushes and charged madly to the rescue. The horse jumped about until he was both free of *vaquero*, cubs and saddle—the saddle turned bellyward on the horse and both cubs were still hanging by the ropes. Away went the frightened mount, dragging the screaming cubs along the ground. A most interesting time for all concerned was the order of the day.

"Nothing but the speed of our horses saved us from that enraged mother bear. Fortunately for the unseated *vaquero* there was a tree close at hand; up he climbed and it was too small for her to follow him.

"I remained in charge of the place fourteen months for Captain Sutter. During that period he put forth his best efforts to meet the Russian payments. He lacked almost everything in the way of proper farming implements.

"The California plow—as rude an instrument as was ever devised by man, I guess—was the main reliance at the time. It was merely a crooked tree limb with a piece of flat iron for a point and a pole for a tongue to pull by. The Russian plow was difficult to manage and very little superior to the Californian. Later, Sutter's own blacksmiths improvised a few plows of better pattern but then neither he nor anyone else had implements suitable for tilling the soil."

Chapter XVIII

CAPITAL'S CAPTURE

THAT ENIGMATIC croupier hidden in the shadows never dealt lucky cards to John Sutter. To the contrary. If winning counters ever stacked themselves in front of him it was because he was an amiable planner with genius enough to play a poor hand well. Even his exaggerations were warmly human—no stuffed shirt, this lord of New Helvetia.

Affairs political began to swirl dangerously about the valley in 1842. Mexico was determined to stick a greedy brown hand into the California fruit-basket again. She appointed the usual Mexican official—the first move to control the province. Vallejo and Alvarado had been handling departmental worries since their successful revolution; also the revenues. Such a thing had gone unnoticed long enough.

Colonel Manuel Micheltorena was the newcomer. On January 22nd he was designated as Governor, *Comandante General* and Inspector of California. His threefold dignity eliminated the two powerful native Californians from the political arena; and also disgusted them. The hated Mexican rule was returning—what was to be done? Yet no matter the turmoil beneath the surface all was serenity to the public gaze.

Micheltorena arrived in San Diego with three hundred soldiers on August 22nd on his cross-country tour of inspection to Monterey. After being fêted by the principal San Diegans he moved on to Los Angeles on September 16th. There he was greeted with a semblance of good will and the customary round of feasting.

A dust-caked messenger met him at that point. He bore a letter from General Vallejo advising the new appointee to march at once against Sutter's Fort with all his command. Sutter, reported the despot of Sonoma, was harboring a vicious foreign element. If California was to be long held, he and his colony must be driven out and his stronghold laid waste.

Before Micheltorena received that warning Captain Sutter was aware of it. Which came of being an intimate of certain foreign gentlemen very much "in the know" in regard to Vallejo's affairs.

So the wary Swiss was not caught napping. At once he wrote a letter to the approaching official. In it he pledged his personal coöperation; congratulated the new-comer upon his appointment; and declared briefly that any previous dispatches received by his excellency which might offer contrary reports were utterly infamous and without foundation. In closing, he offered to wait immediately upon the dignitary as soon as he arrived at Monterey; and also delicately hinted that news of some importance was being reserved for the Govervor's ear at a more appropriate time.

This message went by the resourceful Charles Flugge, now fluent master of the Spanish tongue, who had orders to intercept the gubernatorial party. Riding almost day and night the envoy arrived at Los Angeles before the Governor was ready to move on to Santa Barbara.

With great earnestness Flugge paid his flattering respects to Micheltorena and delivered his letter. Three days he remained with the official entourage, waiting an answer. In that time his report on Sutter's progress and aims was so well-presented that the Governor was favorably impressed with New Helvetia and its ruler.

"Don Carlos," said Micheltorena on that third day, "if your Captain Sutter is but one-tenth the man you paint him I shall be well-satisfied!"

When Flugge returned he carried a cordial message for the anxious Captain. In it was pledged Micheltorena's regard in the future; also an invitation to make a call at Monterey at his own convenience.

For Sutter it meant victory over Vallejo's barbs. Those first negotiations, too, were to lead to important decisions.

THEN CAME THE most astounding event of 1842. In September, Commodore Thomas Ap Catesby Jones of the United States Navy chanced to be in Callao with the *Cyane*, the *Dale* and the *United States*. Out of the harbor sailed an English fleet under sealed orders. In the same hour Jones came upon an item in a New Orleans newspaper, asserting that Mexico had ceded the Californias to Great Britain for $7,000,000.

It looked confoundedly certain, thought the Commodore, as if the British fleet was bound for California. It would never do. Not at all.

At once Jones put to sea. After a hurried conference with his officers, the *Dale* was dispatched to Panama with a report for Washington. Quite certain that the United States and Mexico were at war, he sailed with his remining two ships for the California coast.

For months the English and American fleets had played hide-and-seek in the Pacific, each watching the other with a swooping tenacity, each on the look-out to take possession of California upon receipt of orders. Above all things, Commodore Jones wished to forestall any designs England might have of raising the Union Jack over the disputed soil. He hoped now, grimly, that he was not too late.

The American fleet captured Monterey without firing a shot on October 20th. Terms of surrender were amicably arranged and the Stars and Strips fluttered proudly over the *castillo* at eleven o'clock in the morning.

Alvarado was still in active charge of the departmental government but had cautiously absented himself on his Alisol rancho; the new governor was reported to be at Santa Barbara and was soon due at the capital.

Upon landing in person on October 21st, Commodore Jones inspected the port archives. With some amazement he discovered late dispatches whose tenor was most pacific. In the *comisario's* office were found communications under the dateline of August 4th. These most explicitly declared that a state of war did not yet exist; nor was likely to.

With growing perturbation Jones sat in his captured town and pondered his dilemma. The situation was puzzling. . . . Most embarrassing, granted the Commodore. Here he was with a captured capital and no reason for taking it. Regretfully, he made a decision. No war, no capture, said the active gentleman in disgust.

Whereupon, with due ceremony and a hasty apology, he delivered the town back to the Mexican officials. He had held it exactly thirty-six hours. Down came the Stars and Stripes, lowered by rueful seamen. Again the Mexican banner waved over the *castillo* and its rusty cannon.

SUTTER HEARD of the capture and return of the town by the same special messenger. He shook his head. The affair seemed ill-advised. It was difficult to understand why the United States should occupy Monterey one day and retire the next. Philosophically, the Captain waited for Micheltorena's arrival.

Official visits of courtesy were now exchanged by Jones and the returned Alvarado at the capital. Micheltorena was informed of what had occurred by a conciliatory letter. Immediately, he hastened on to his post. In December he was inaugurated and took over his official duties.

Commodore Jones remained in the North until the end of the year. He still hoped for positive instructions from Washington. But when they did come he was further disgruntled. Definitely, the United States and Mexico were *not* at war.

It is significant that Jones was never officially "punished" for his hasty action. He may have been premature, from the Washington standpoint. But he had the same idea.

Chapter XIX

SWEDE AND SWISS

FEW MEN EVER achieve power in the absolute. But John Sutter did. In his valley he was the law—the lord of lonely lands. Thirty thousand inhabitants of the Sacramento acknowledged him as such, respected him for his wisdom and kindness, feared him for his vengeances swiftly executed.

True, his authority was challenged. Often and bitterly. Yet no armed force dared march against him. Remotely he ruled, impregnable now, almost disdainful of interference. He was openly aggressive with Vallejo, deftly courteous with Micheltorena. Day by day he planned and schemed and labored—watched a dream shaping into reality.

The walls of the Fort were high in 1843, formidable; yet not complete. The adobe buildings rose, brick by brick; shops and granaries were added inside the enclosures; beehive activity was ever present.

"Wheat," says Captain Sutter, "was ground in a horse-mill. Four mules would grind for four hours, and then four other mules would take their places. I had but one flour-mill at this time; this mill and the bake-oven were kept going day and night.

"We lived very simply in the main—roast beef mostly, vegetables when we had them. Many times we had neither sugar nor coffee. We found that peas were a fair substitute for coffee and acorns still better. Indeed, it was difficult to tell acorn coffee from the real beverage.

"Rations of beef and bread were given daily to the Indians, also a mush made of flour was cooked for them in a huge kettle. I paid them their regular wages in my tin money.

"The younger Indian boys were obliged to appear, well-washed, tidied and neatly clad, every Sunday

· 138 ·

morning for drill. Their uniform was blue drill pantaloons, white cotton shirts and red handkerchiefs tied
around their heads as bandeaux. The youngsters were
very proud of this uniform. After drill they spent the day
as they pleased, visiting their friends at the various
rancherias, playing games, etc.

"The adult soldiers of my infantry and cavalry personnel had regular uniforms of blue or green cloth with
red trimmings. I purchased these uniforms from the Russians and they were manufactured at Fort Ross.

"Military discipline was always strict at the Fort.
My quarters were near the guardroom; if anything of
importance occurred I was immediately notified. I had a
half-hour glass and every thirty minutes during the
night, when the sand ran out, the chief guard struck the
bell (brought from Fort Ross) and called out: "All is
well!" I made them adhere faithfully to this rule.

"At daybreak, summer and winter, this bell was the
signal for all hands to arise, eat breakfast, and begin the
day's labor. Newly arrived Americans sometimes complained of such a custom; I explained that it was wiser
to get up early, make a fair start, and then rest during
the hot noon hours.

"No work was done on Sunday, although little attention was paid to religion in a strict ritualistic way. I
always kept a physician in the establishment if I could
get one. . . ."

Sutter was experiencing great difficulty in getting his
mail from Switzerland. Sometimes it took two or three
years for the looked-for letters to reach him. His own
mail to Anna, Friedrich and the children went by devi-
ous routes. Some he sent via the Hudson's Bay Company,
over the Rocky Mountains to Canada. The company
maintained an express, guarded by fifty men, that attempted a twice-a-year schedule. Other letters traveled
by way of Sitka to be relayed to St. Petersburg and
thence to their destination. It took a year or more for
his messages to reach his anxious family.

On May 1st, 1843, Thomas Oliver Larkin was appointed United States Consul at Monterey. He was one
of the shrewdest and most farsighted Americans in the
province. Coming to California at the invitation of his
half-brother, Captain Cooper, he soon proved himself
an astute merchant. And in his new office he proved himself an able tactician—a force to be reckoned with in the
race for American accession.

Pitted against him was the new British consul, James
Alexander Forbes, who was appointed in October of the
same year. This official with the broad Scotch accent and
hidden foreign-office orders was a foe to any chance of
United States conquest, a rather bitter-tongued apostle
of British rights. Openly the two consuls were friendly;
what they chose to call each other in private is not of
record.

Larkin had begun a correspondence with Sutter as
soon as his official duties commenced. An understanding
grew up between the two men. They shared the same
beliefs and hopes. Thereafter, they worked together,
somewhat clandestinely the written documents show,
for the furtherance of American designs in California. . . .

Came Stephen Smith this same year with the first
steam engine to reach the province. After a tour of the
immediate bay area he bought a few leagues from Sutter
near Bodega. There he set up his lumber mill close to the
redwoods and went to work. With him he also brought
three pianos, the first ever seen in California. One of
those pianos was to musically acclaim the birth of California as a state, in a hall not yet quarried from a hillside.
A man of parts, this Stephen Smith.

Emigration became more brisk in 1843. The crest of
the wave was sweeping on. Lansford W. Hastings and
his party were among the first to find their way to
Sutter's Fort after the long trek. This Hastings was an
adventurer with predatory visions. "He came to California," recalls John Bidwell, "with the avowed purpose
of inciting a revolution and wresting the province from

Mexico, thus to establish an independent republic with himself as president; either that or bring about the annexation of California to Texas.

"Finding the country not ready or sufficiently populated for such a movement, he entertained, for a time, the idea of obtaining a Mexican land grant on the west side of the Sacramento and went so far as to have the place mapped out.

"Still, the region must be peopled. The thing obsessed Hastings. In order to hasten that necessary emigration he determined to return to the United States, write a book about California and its resources, and publish it as soon as possible.

"He went home the southern route through Mexico, stopped in Texas to confer with that state's president, and then went back to New York and wrote his book. He pictured California as an earthly Paradise, a land blessed with eternal verdure and sunshine. His book was published in 1845. . . ."

With Hastings came a number of men who entered Sutter's service—George Davis, Coates, Shadden, Coombs and others. While the main body of the party was encamped near New Helvetia on July 10th, the infallible Captain Sutter was called upon to exercise another of his prerogatives. Davis and Miss Sumner were married at the Fort, the Swiss reading the service and issuing the certificate. This union was but one of many which he solemnized.

Another party was commanded by Joseph B. Chiles, who had come first in 1841 and now returned. With him came many men who were later to be famous in state annals and useful to John Sutter. In this company was Pierson B. Reading, Samuel J. Hensley, Jasper O'Farrel, William Baldridge, John Gantt, Winter, Wooden, Swan, McGee, Bradley and the four Williams brothers.

Sutter found places for most of them. Reading became his bookkeeper; Hensley the supercargo of the *Sacramento*; the four Williams brothers were blacksmiths and tanners; most of the remainder fitted in as hunters, artisans or labor supervisors—a distinct addition to the colony on the Sacramento. . . .

Then Vallejo saw fit to exercise his superseded authority by sending a *teniente* and a small escort to the Fort. Their stated mission was a search for deserters and horse thieves. But the Swiss chose to give it another name. Very bluntly he mentioned his suspicion that the party had been sent out as spies by the General. The letter he sent off to Vallejo was not one that would engender an entente cordial.

At once the ex-comandante general countered by demanding passports of all Sutter's henchmen visiting or passing through Sonoma territory on their way to Fort Ross and Bodega. A merry war of words and incivilities came into play. Both growled and fumed at a distance.

It was Sutter's turn to consider a checkmate. From Micheltorena at Monterey he secured the right to issue passports himself, a detail he had somehow before overlooked. Thereafter, with great decorum, he issued passports, free of charge, to all arriving Americans who wished them.

Vallejo was outwitted. But there was nothing to be done about it. This Joseph B. Chiles party was the first to receive passports *en masse* from Sutter.

An IMPORTANT VISITOR, from a descriptive standpoint, at least, came to New Switzerland in 1843. He was Dr. G. M. Sandels, a noted Swedish scientist and naturalist, educated in London and an Oxford man. This world wanderer had been interested in a business venture in Brazil, had sold out his share for $189,000, and gone to Mexico. There he lost most of his money in mining speculation. At the time of his California visit he was practically a poor man. The articles on his trip were signed "The King's Orphan." Though a bit flowery, Dr. Sandels was a keen analyst.

"I shall never forget the morning following my departure for New Helvetia," writes the scientist in his bubbling narrative. "A landscape of beauty burst into view with an abrupt suddenness. It was a scene containing every soft and delicate tint bounded by the most superb sublimities. The mouth of the San Joaquin opened to the south, a view which reached far inland to grow dim with distance.

"Before me was the Rio Sacramento; a rich green canopy fell from the trees that lined its borders; under that canopy was shade for the traveler and the creatures of the woods. It was Sabbath morning; and I never saw temples more fit for praise and worship than those. The green grass came to the water's edge and groups of oaks stood plentifully about. Crystal dew drops glistened upon leaves and branches and grasses; a million birds sang in the glory of the morning.

"It took us the day to make our way up the river from our last camp. Occasionally, a deer would come swiftly out of a tangled patch of vines or chaparral on the bank; or cattle, wild as the deer, would rush along, bellowing, heavy-footed. There was no sign of man's occupancy in all that long quest.

"In the evening we came to the *Embarcadero*, or Port of New Helvetia, our schooner coming to anchor in a fleet of smaller craft. Here were a few huts sitting upon elevated ground, guarded by high sycamores and oaks. The colony of Captain Sutter was some two miles away, the road leading over a beautiful country, constantly and imperceptibly rising as we left the river.

"Captain John A. Sutter is a native of Switzerland and was at one time an officer in the Swiss Guards. He is the most enterprising citizen in California *and is destined to play a prominent part in the future history of this country*. By making friends, due to his engaging character and extensive travels, he was ennabled to commence an imposing establishment on a grand scale in this remote Sacramento region. . . .

"Captain Sutter's headquarters has more the appearance of a citadel than an agricultural establishment. It is protected by an incompleted wall, ten feet high, made of adobes—these are sun-dried bricks—also having a turret with embrasures and loopholes to allow accurate musket-fire. Twenty-four pieces of different sized ordnance are available for defense. Against the walls, on the inside of the Fort, are erected the storehouses of the site; also a distillery to make spirits from the wheat and wild grapes, together with shops for coopers, saddlers, black-smiths, carpenters, granaries, and quarters for laborers. An armed sentinel stands on guard at the gateway day and night.

"I arrived at the establishment early in the morning, having stayed overnight at the *Embarcadero*. The people were just being assembled for labor by the clash of a bell and the roll of Mexican drums. I found Captain Sutter busily employed in issuing orders for the day. He received me with incomparable hospitality, his delightful manners putting me perfectly at ease and at home.

"The bell and the magical sound of the drum had gathered together several hundred Indians who flocked to their morning meal preparatory to the day's routine— reaping wheat. Breakfast over, they filed off to the fields in a kind of military order, armed with a rude sickle and hook.

"By this time breakfast was announced for the white employes. It was served in an outhouse adjoining the kitchen. There was wholesome corn bread, eggs, ham, an excellent piece of venison, and coffee—surprising fare for the wilderness.

"In the rear of the Fort is a large pond, the borders of which are lined with willows and other trees, ornamental as well as valuable. This pond furnishes water for the necessary domestic uses, also for irrigating the extensive series of gardens.

"Owing to this year's drought, the vegetables, as well as the wheat have suffered, the latter proving almost a failure. Lack of rain is the greatest evil that has befallen this fertile country. In front of the Fort are corrals and enclosures for horses and cattle; also places to deposit corn and wheat.

"The raising of wheat and corn and the breeding of cattle, horses and sheep constitutes the principal business of Captain Sutter. But he has also realized considerable income from the salmon fisheries on the river, the fish being excellent in flavor and found in the greatest abundance. He has organized extensive hunting and trapping expeditions for the purpose of securing beaver, otter, elk, deer and antelope skins. In this he was greatly interfered with by paid interlopers of the Hudson's Bay Company, trappers who trespassed upon his territory without legal right.

"His complaint in the matter only made him enemies. They cunningly informed the suspicious Mexican government that Captain Sutter was fostering revolutionary plans and that he encouraged deserters and other disorderly people to make a rendezvous of his settlement. The Captain replied to these charges by stating simply that his purpose was to colonize the valley; that to do so he had encouraged all stragglers to flock to his remote outpost; that, in conclusion, these men were mostly unmarried, lawless spirits from the mountains, very independent, and—as Sutter deftly mentioned—were quite competent to defend themselves.

"Naturally, the government officials were not satisfied with Sutter's explanations. An investigation was presumed to have been ordered. But no force was sent against him, since his establishment was too strong. . . .

"Having made somewhat of a visit at Captain Sutter's citadel, I prepared for an excursion among the Indians and to see more of the interior of the country. The land around New Helvetia is open and flat, subject to annual inundation, excepting some few acres of rising ground. It is rich, virgin soil, wooded by oak, ash, sycamore, cottonwood and willow. From the great drought the soil was cracked and rough to travel on, even when the trail led over the bottom lands. Very few flowers showed along the way, ground squirrels were to be seen dashing from hole to hole, and a great area of the plains had been recently burned over by fire.

"On the east were high hills; and farther back, higher ranges. The boundary line, far inland, is a forest of pine. These clothe the hills and mountain bases and ravines; the latter are usually enriched by clear, cold brooks whose waters roll down from the slopes in a merry ripple over rough and pebbled bottoms. But this year they lie dry and desolate. . . .

"We came to an Indian village whose salmon fisheries are considered the most productive. The Indians make excellent nets from a native herb. They also build an interwoven screen of tree-branches and bushes, running them from bank to bank of the river; on the upperside of this fence is a corral into which the fish enter through a small opening. As the quarry continually head upstream no difficulty is experienced in their capture. . . .

". . . On my return, I discovered a large number of Indians assembled about Sutter's Fort. Only the chiefs present were armed with bows and arrows; their followers were weaponless.

"They went through curious evolutions in file, in square, and in flank. Then their leader made a long speech, earnest and doubtless eloquent, in his guttural language. At very last he set down his bow and arrows at Sutter's feet.

" 'Take these,' he said, 'and with them penetrate our hearts if we betray the trust you put in us. We solemnly promise to keep the peace with you and your children forever.'

"This was translated for me.

"Then, turning swiftly to me as I stood beside Captain Sutter, the chief handed me an arrow. He said: 'Take this and let it always remind you that you have witnessed this happy meeting for peace and submission.'

"Three more chiefs then came forward and made the same pledge. . . .

"I found that many of Captain Sutter's men were what was termed Rocky Mountain Men; they had come from the States—hunters, trappers, landless rovers. Much of their lives had been passed in mountain and desert fastnesses and they had nearly always been at war with neighboring aborigines.

"The predisposition of these men to have trouble with the Indians exasperated and annoyed the pacific Captain Sutter; in a measure it nullified the effect of his good and kind treatment of the natives. But gradually he brought about a better feeling between his men and the Indians; for these latter were of incalculable aid to the Captain in his plans for ultimate civilization.

"I noted that military discipline always prevailed at the Fort. By the clash of the bell and the beat of the drums the people arose and went to work; by the clash of the bell and the beat of the drums they retired at night. . . ."

ONE ANECDOTE of Sandels' visit is given us by John Bidwell. After the scientist's arrival, Captain Sutter spoke to him one evening in a jocular mood: "Doctor, why can't you find me a gold mine?"

"I never think of gold-mining," answered Sandels quietly. He looked over at the Swiss intently. "Captain Sutter, *your* best gold mine is here in this rich soil."

"True, my friend." His genial host laughed and clapped Sandels in comradely fashion on the shoulder. "This good land is all the gold mine I could ever wish."

Chapter XX

RAINLESS VALLEY

No ALIEN trappers invaded the Sacramento Valley in 1843. Sutter, delighted with the absence of the rival fur men, placed forty men in the field.

"Every year," wrote the Swiss, "the Hudson's Bay Company sent trappers to the region who annually collected a vast quantity of prime furs. Their women—squaws and half-breeds—made moccasins, shirts and pantaloons of dressed deerskin, a commodity greatly in demand. I bought large quantities of these articles from them. But they would not sell furs. This was labeled as a most heinous offence by the Hudson's Bay Company officials and all culprits were severely punished. The trappers might sell deer-skins but never beaver or land otter.

"These servants of the company used to journey down from the North, enter the Valley of California in the fall, trap during the winter, and leave in the spring with their catch. Before I settled there and assumed judicial powers, the provincial government had been unable to prevent this annual raid into the rich Mexican fur territory. These encroaching trappers were chiefly Canadians, half-breeds and Indians. In a short time the Hudson's Bay Company bought out the interests of the Northwest Company and soon the interlopers came and went in larger numbers than before. When their tents were pitched, the scene took on the look of a large, permanent tent-city.

"A leader—or agent of the company—accompanied each of these groups. To him the trappers delivered their furs and received supplies in exchange.

"When I first visited these expeditions Michel la Framboise was the commander and he came for a number of seasons.

"I did not consider it the right thing for these citizens of an alien land to carry off each year a vast fortune in furs. They came in such groups that all fur-bearing creatures would in time be exterminated. Moreover, they purchased stolen horses from the Indians under my jurisdiction and thus aided that rascality by providing a sure market for the stolen animals.

"I complained to the departmental government and advised that a heavy export duty be assessed against the furs. This was done. The duty was so high that trapping ceased to be profitable for those people. An officer was sent to collect this duty and the Hudson's Bay Company was forced to abandon the valley as a scene of operations. Soon my trappers were the sole fur-seekers in the region.

"Ever after this, the Hudson's Bay Company officials blamed me bitterly for their trade exclusion from the Sacramento territory."

So THE FUR CATCH for New Helvetia was much greater in 1843. Deer-suet, brandy, salmon, sturgeon, beaver-skins, land otter skins, and even rifles were sent to the colony's creditors; these firearms had been purchased at intervals from arriving emigrants. Three hundred cattle were sent under Robert Livermore's supervision to Don Antonio Suñol as an earnest on the amount due him. Under the conditions, it is not difficult to see why payment of all debts was not immediately made.

Yet much as Sutter sent, it did not satisfy all his creditors. There were rumblings and even detonations. As was the manner of volatile *Californios*, threats were made, hot words were spoken—at a distance—and letters flew about like dark birds which never expected to alight. For, after all, the *Californio* loves his pyrotechnics. Life is dull and all occasions must be taken advantage of to enliven it.

Sutter retained his placid courtesy; at least in ink. He assured all the interested parties that the next year would see all deficiencies wiped away in entirety. With a flair for effect he invited his creditors to feast on his bones if the future twelve-month did not entirely live up to his expectations.

On October 7th he wrote Suñol that "who ever the stranger was who said that I only write letters to you to pass the time away and that I would pay whenever it suited me, is an infamous liar and dare not make himself known."

Literally, Sutter felt assured that all would be well. The man never lost his self-faith or his belief in New Helvetia's success. . . .

RUMORS BROUGHT all the Americans in the valley to the safety of Sutter's Fort at certain periods in the early part of 1843. These fear-inspiring yarns broadly hinted a recurrence of the 1840 debacle and the possibility of arrest and deportation of all foreigners in the province. Those scares were rather groundless, it appears. No force existed that was numerically strong enough to carry out the threat even if an official order had been issued. As a matter of record, no such order was ever made; perhaps even contemplated.

Sutter made his first visit to Manuel Micheltorena after one of these disturbing rumors had disrupted the routine of the New Switzerland establishment. He found the Governor an affable handsome fellow, as cordial as his letters. These two seemed to 'click' from the beginning. Both men had California's welfare at heart; each recognized ability in the other.

Micheltorena was always to show himself a friend to Americans. He favored emigration:proof is present in the facility with which land grants were available for all those desiring them and willing to comply with the regulations. Certainly, no official fearing American domination would have been unwise enough to make land assignments of such a generous nature if he shortly expected trouble. There is no moment that Micheltorena does not show himself as a progressive, eyes-forward executive. In this he most assuredly differed from the usual run of official vulture appointed in the Mexican aerie. Sutter liked him for his personal qualities, his benevolence, his easy courtesy, his gift of humor.

Back from his visit came the Swiss with a new ally and a surety that expulsion of foreigners was a myth. His news calmed the valley, caused a wave of friendly feeling for the Governor. That official needed these new well-wishers. Dark days lay ahead.

THE DRIEST SEASON in the remembrance of man came in 1843. It was the third year of drought for New Helvetia.

Feed was scarce for the cattle—you could count their ribs at fifty yards; the hills grew barren and parched; even the mountain distances held a burnished brilliance; cracks appeared in the plain floor, uneven gashes stabbed by a searing sun; ravines and water-courses lay dry, stone-hot, verdureless; the tule marshes west of the Sacramento River were moistureless stalks, rattling in the winds, moaning thinly.

"The only rain," says John Bidwell, "came December 1st. It wet the ground only to the depth of a foot. The first plowing was then done and about one hundred and fifty bushels of wheat were sown. This was the only wheat harvested.

"There was, however, a larger acreage sown. Some two thousand bushels of wheat were put in.... All hoped for rain but it never came.

"Later on, Sutter was consoled by the promise there would soon be a heavy downpour. Mr. Preuss, I think it was, said that the change of the moon at midnight, which was to take place, was an infallible sign of rain and had never been known to fail.

"As the time approached, wind came from the southeast, clouds rolled up over the great valley. The air was warm with the promise of rain. It *did* commence to fall. . . . But the slight moisture barely wet the top of the ground, an inch or two deep. Then the wind lulled, the clouds fled away, and the skies became like brass.

"It was the same as the year before. The hundred and fifty bushels of wheat first sown was the only grain harvested and its yield was less than the quantity put in for seed. In place of the excellent plump kernels of wheat which he had sown, Captain Sutter reaped only shrunken kernels. It was a great disappointment."

So went the year. Good luck and bad. But the fort walls rose swiftly to the marked level of John Sutter's diagram. More men came to enter into his service. William Benitz was sent to Ross, and Bidwell returned to aid the New Switzerland chieftain. Wisely, he still parceled out generous bits of his valley, binding men subtly to his kingdom; he knew that the future days would make him stronger. Surety was his now. Just a little longer.

Chapter XXI

THE MAP-MAKER

THE RUSSIANS patiently sent their vessels to collect the debt installment at Yerba Buena. But John Sutter had nothing to give them in the three arid years up to 1844. Yet they came; and even brought iron, agricultural implements, and other supplies to New Helvetia.

In that third dry season the *Alexandrovitch* made her second voyage to the California Coast for the promised wheat. With her came the usual agent in charge, this time a pleasant young man named Sergei Brinikoff. By ship's-boat he made his way to Sutter's Fort.

"One evening during Brinikoff's visit," relates John Bidwell, "some dozen of us were strolling along the river after dinner—the Russian agent, Captain Sutter, Leese, myself and others. After some distance had been traversed I noticed a small skunk promenading ahead of us, his plume at a sprightly angle.

"Brinikoff ran delightedly toward the spotted animal. The rest of us said nothing—naturally, we supposed that the young Russian was familiar with the creature and its habits.

"But, to our amazement, he tried to catch it. Immediately, his eyes and ears and nose and clothing were saturated with the pungent secretion!

"Poor devil, he was very ill for several hours. His broadcloth suit was buried in some clay ground and left overnight. Some hours after his failure to catch the skunk he looked up from his bed, still glassy-eyed, and demanded feebly:

" 'What pretty bird was that which hurt me so?' "

COMMERCIALLY, THE year 1844 promised much. Rainfall was normal. Sutter made plans to seed an immense acreage, hundreds of *fanegas*—each *fanega* weighing one hundred and thirty-three pounds. Half a thousand Indians labored long hours in the fields. The Captain was determined to secure a tremendous yield to offset the arid past.

More Indians, under Sutter's direct eye, worked feverishly on the fort. Trouble loomed in the political cockpit. The walls must be finished before autumn, ordered Sutter. . . . In June the fort was completed. An imposing citadel this, well-garrisoned; a colonial bulwark equal to resist all comers.

The annual *matanza*, killing time, was held at Hock in July. With the grass green, feed was plentiful; cattle were fat and heavy. The *novillas* (steers) averaged about two hundred pounds of meat to each animal: this was made into dried meat; the rest was left to the buzzards and wild beasts. When very fat the steers produced four *arrobas* of tallow (twenty-five pounds to an arroba) to an animal; also two *arrobas* of *manteca*. This last is the delicate fat that lies between the hide and ribs of a *novilla*, much prized by the *Californios* and usually reserved to aid in the home cooking.

Bidwell was in charge that year at Hock. Under his supervision there was not the usual lost motion of a native *matanza*. Hour after hour the try-pots bubbled odorously with the melted *sebo* and *manteca*; hour after hour the sweating vaqueros worked with the hides, preparing them for market. Most of the tallow was to find its way to South America to make candles and soap. "Boston ships" would transport the hides, using San Diego as a storage base, back to their home port, carrying from thirty to forty-five thousand skins packed tightly in each hold.

Interior events moved smoothly, lucratively. More and more furs were secured in season. More good traps were being made by Sutter's blacksmiths; that meant more pelts.

Peter Lassen, under Sutter's patronage, was engaged in manufacturing some house furniture which had been ordered by Don Antonio Suñol. The *Sacramento* was wrecked on a trip to Fort Ross and required fifteen days to repair. From his hattery, Sutter exchanged hats for soap with Don Antonio; also bridles, made in the leather shops. From the tannery, built on the river bank near the spot where Captain Sutter had first landed, came an increasing amount of good leather. From Don Antonio he secured dry meat for this product. His Indians were turning out blankets and shirts from the blanket-factory. Drill went on. Brandy grew better and more plentiful. Theodore Cordua became possessed of an immense thirst —for brandy. The whist games continued, if Sutter was at home. In April, Larkin wrote and asked the Swiss to send him all data on incoming emigrants as soon as they arrived. Things were looking up.

EMIGRATION CAME in only two parties in 1844. The tribe of Kelsey led the first, two of them having previously made the trip with Hastings. This pair returned in June with all the venturesome kinsfolk they could gather. There were thirty-six people in their company.

William Bennett, Granville P. Swift, and Andrew, Benjamin, David and Samuel Kelsey were the most important of these arrivals. They were either to be in Sutter's service or take some other prominent part in Californian affairs.

The second party, one-hundred-and-fifty strong, reached the Fort on December 13th, led by patriarchal Elisha Stevens. Among these travelers were Edmund Bray, Dennis and Pat Martin, Allen Montgomery and his wife, Moses Schallenberger, Dr. John Townsend and the Murphys—fifteen of them. This last party arrived at a most opportune moment. Most of them served Sutter well until that strange, utterly incredible day on Cahuenga's battlefield. . . .

JOHN CHARLES FRÉMONT first glimpsed the California scene this same year. Born of a French father and a Virginian mother, young Frémont had been expelled from Charleston college for an indiscreet love affair. A few years later he married Jessie Benton, daughter of the politically powerful Senator Thomas H. Benton. With his father-in-law's aid he shortly became a second lieutenant in the United States Topographical Engineers.

The work appealed to him. Moreover, he cherished an ambition to be the first man to make an accurate mapping survey of the Far West.

His departmental chief was impressed by Frémont's earnestness; also by his connections. With some dispatch the young officer was given permission to carry out his project. Funds were forthcoming and he went on his way.

That first expedition did not fulfil his ambitions. The second brought him struggling through Sierra snows in February, foolishly jousting King Winter at his worst, he and his men exhausted, two of them insane, and half his horses and mules lost or used as food.

Down through the same mountain pass Bartelson had used in 1841 they fought their blundering way, battling cold, sickness and an insidious uncertainty. . . .

Finally, they came out of the drifts to the lower levels. For six days they followed the south branch of the American River, not sure of anything but that the mountains and their hindering whiteness were left behind. . . . Then, on March 8th, they came to Sutter's Fort.

The visitation was unexpected. Captain Sutter himself chanced to be superintending a bit of corral-repairing in front of his establishment. Up rode Frémont and the young hunter whom the Swiss had met at the Wind River Rendezvous—Kit Carson. They were mounted on skeleton-ribbed beasts; both men were sunken-eyed; both were reeling in the saddle, held upright by a last reserve of strength.

Sutter aided them to dismount, then almost carried them to his quarters. The main body of men had been

left some miles away, muttered the weary Frémont.
They wolfed down quantities of warm food and drink
in the next hour, relaxed for the first time in weeks.
Sutter gave immediate orders to fit up ten mules, saw
they were packed with supplies, and sent them on to
Frémont's camp.

Until March 22nd the expedition luxuriated worn
bodies and enjoyed the security and hospitality of John
Sutter's citadel. Their leader was not particularly expansive; he merely stated that he was an officer of the
United States Army on an exploring tour of the Sierra
country. If Sutter suspected other motives he did not
mention them.

During those fourteen days of recuperation he did
everything to make the newcomers comfortable and at
ease. Wheat he needed badly for seed was unhesitatingly
sacrificed that his guests might not lack bread. The
Sacramento was sent on a speedy trip to Yerba Buena for
supplies which they lacked.

Destitute and ill, they needed their wilderness
Samaritan. He gave them medicine, blankets, soap,
coffee, tea, flour, clothing, thirty horses, twenty fat
cattle, eighty mules—these last purchased from Peter
Lassen who had lately settled on Deer Creek—saddles,
bridles and countless other provisions.

In fact, the expedition had to be completely outfitted.
Without comment Sutter accepted the payment which
Frémont ungraciously tendered him—orders on the
Topographical Bureau. Later the Swiss had to dispose of
the orders at a twenty-per-cent discount. It is to be noted
that Sutter charged Frémont exactly what the goods
cost: no profit was thought of.

"No one in California but myself would have trusted
him (Frémont) for a cent," wrote Sutter at a later date.
"I thought to do the United States Government a favor
in this matter, since I sensed the tide of empire sweeping
west; and I have never yet fattened my purse on the distress of others.

"All Frémont's animals—what were left—had to be re-shod at my blacksmith shop and I had to make extra saddles and pack-saddles for him. While here, Frémont accused three of his men of stealing sugar from him. They were arraigned before me and I found them not guilty. Poor devils, if they had stolen a spoonful of sugar, it was no great crime.

"But Frémont heartily disapproved my decision, regarded it as a sign of non-coöperation with him on my part. He ordered that the men could not remain with him any longer. They seemed very pleased with their discharge and it did not displease me: for one of them, Samuel Neal, became an excellent blacksmith and lived to become rich in this new land."

THERE REMAINS a record of John Charles Frémont's recollections of Fort Sutter and his host.

"An impetus," he wrote, "was given to the active little population by our arrival, as we wanted everything. Mules, horses and cattle were to collected; the horse-mill was at work day and night to make sufficient flour; the blacksmith shop was put in requisition for horse-shoes and bridle-bits; and pack-saddles, bridles, and ropes, and all the other little equipments of the camp were to again be provided. The delay thus occasioned was one of repose and enjoyment which our situation required and, anxious as were to resume our homeward journey, was regretted by no one."

Rather pompous for a near-to-death map-maker in a strange terrain. As a topographical engineer Frémont deserves great praise; as a man he invariably displayed himself as vain, tactless, surly, incompetent as a military leader, and utterly without common sense in dealing with the native Californians. It was unfortunate that a man placed in Frémont's position should have displayed a positive genius for stirring up unnecessary ill-feeling and turmoil. It not only handicapped him as an individual but was to seriously endanger United States' chances of accession in California.

After the two-week interval he moved on, once more able to take the trail. His adieus were cold, because of the sugar incident. Not for another year does this humorless and ambitious rover again appear at Sutter's Fort.

SULLENLY FOREBODING were the last few months in the year. The apparent tranquillity showed itself as a sham—a deceptive mask of intrigue. Yet despite these signs, Micheltorena had proved himself a surprisingly popular figure with many warm personal friends. He seemed to excite no ill-feeling or opposition except in his deposed underlings and their aides. He was liberal, performed his duties with creditable tact, and bestowed a good deal of attention on the educational system; public schools were encouraged with both funds and advice. Even when the bishop needed considerable pecuniary aid he was not denied; and when that dignitary later came forward with counsel in a personal matter the Governor even consented to marry his mistress.

But certain forces were at work against him. Says Bidwell: "Thenceforth, Captain Sutter and Governor Micheltorena were fast friends. Sutter always used his influence and friendship in favor of Americans. Also, although on the surface they were submissive, the deposed native officials resented Micheltorena's arrival.

"At this period there was no such thing as taxation in California—that is, except in the payment of tithes to the church, a fee that was only infrequently collected. The revenues consisted only in duties on imported goods, mostly from the United States, and amounting possibly to one or two hundred thousand dollars per annum.

"Small as these revenues were, they were of considerable importance to those who had the disbursement of them.

"As a result of Sutter's influence and his untiring efforts in favor of Americans, many became citizens and received grants of land, usually in the Sacramento and San Joaquin valleys.

"Governor Micheltorena treated native and adopted citizens' impartially and with the same courtesy and friendliness. So far as he could, he encouraged the settlement of the state.

"Regarding his troops: they were termed 'convicts' by the native Californians; some of them may have been. I saw them all; sometimes complaints were heard at Monterey about the soldiers taking things without permission; yet I was on the march with these same soldiers for more than two months and I can truthfully state that I do *not* believe that Governor Micheltorena's men deserved the wholesale abuse heaped upon them. The real animus of the opposition to them was engendered because *no* Mexican governor or soldiers were welcome in California.

"The real causes of opposition to Micheltorena are easily enumerated: his friendship toward Americans; his granting of lands to them to encourage their settlement; the supposed character of his troops; and the eager desire of the native officials to handle all the monies derived from the provincial revenues."

That vast unrest of late 1844 held a sporadic intensity. From New Switzerland the epicentre moved temporarily to a new spot. Alvarado, Castro and their friends furnished the nucleus for the rumblings. Once more the word moved from rancho to rancho that "the despicable tyrant thus throttling all Californian liberty and honor must be driven out!" That the Governor was a somewhat uncertain target for such bombast meant little: the revolt was the thing.

John Sutter went overland to the capital in October. He wished to conclude certain land-grant business with the Governor's consent; also to convey further assurances of fealty. With him rode Bidwell, his trusted lieutenant in all important ventures.

It is evident what was in Sutter's mind. He was most concerned in New Switzerland's continuance; to preserve that surety he intended to support the legal representative of the Mexican government against any internal strife waged by native *Californios*. In the case of foreign intervention—that was another thing again. But this impending conflict, if any, would be between accredited power and revolution. John Sutter was most distinctly in favor of the accredited power. So he rode on to Monterey, discussing the eventualities with Bidwell, certain as to his course and its wisdom.

The two riders stopped at San José for a short time, an hour for food and rest. The British consul, Alexander Forbes, was present and eager to pass out information. He had married a native Californian and was always in possession of the latest details in intrigue. Sutter was told that the *Californios* were preparing to attack Micheltorena and drive him and his troops out of the country.

On went the Captain and his aide to Monterey. On his arrival, Sutter poured out his startling information to the Governor. It was the first intimation the chief official had that trouble was brewing in the department. The Swiss remained as his guest for several days and the affair was pondered with graveness.

After some consideration, the two men entered into a pact. In case the Governor was attacked, Sutter agreed to furnish military assistance; Micheltorena promised to send a special courier in case such aid was necessary.

The Governor, in turn, agreed to guarantee all land titles in the Sacramento region, a legal assignment which protected Sutter and every settler in the valley; also to pay the costs for transporting all soldiery, equipment and ordnance in the event of hostilities.

Subsequently, he sent Sutter what was designated as a general title. With this in his possession, the Swiss was empowered to strike off official copies for those who applied to him for Sacramento Valley lands and who had previously carried out the necessary regulations.

"I made out deeds in this manner under the Governor's instructions," Sutter remarks, "and signed and delivered them. But they were afterwards declared invalid. This was an act of injustice since these deeds were legal and honorable transactions.

"I had recommended that these grants be made to various Americans and the government had given me the power to confer these grants with a clear title. Surely the costs and intent alone should have respected and guaranteed such title. . . ."

Sutter's return trip was apt to be a dangerous one. It was well known that he was Micheltorena's friend; he had also been seen and reported by busy tongues—all Monterey was aware of his dinners and interviews with the Governor. No doubt the latest news had trickled out to the conspirators. What to do about it was Sutter's problem.

He decided to embark on the *Sterling*, then in harbor and bound for Yerba Buena. Bidwell was instructed to remain for some time as a possible messenger between the two allies. The sea route, Sutter reasoned, would be less perilous than a back-track by land.

THE SAVANNAH, United States man-o'-war, was also in port. Both the Governor and Sutter were bidden aboard her as guests of honor by Commodore Armstrong. Here the Swiss met Surgeon Wood who later gave his impressions of the genial visitor.

"With Micheltorena," says Wood, "came a striking personage with a marked military air. He wore a tilted cap, a blue frock coat, immaculate trousers and polished boots. His forehead was broad and fine; and he wore a mustache also. His expression was intelligent and kindly and his manners were precisely courteous. Such was Captain Sutter, a Swiss by birth. . . . He rules the Sacramento region. . . .

"The Governor himself, smiling and debonair, dressed in his richly embroidered crimson-and-green uniform, was not so imposing. . . . When Captain Sutter and Micheltorena left the ship they were saluted with fifteen guns. . . ."

So cordial was Sutter's reception that he failed to keep a weather eye on the sailing hour of the *Sterling*. Suddenly, she was seen gathering headway, his luggage aboard her. At once Commodore Armstrong gave him a ship's-boat and crew to overhaul her.

The effort failed. Oars were not equal to wind. So Sutter returned to his convival American friends and spent the night on the *Savannah*. . . .

Next morning he caught the *Don Quixote*, Captain John Paty, a craft also bound for Yerba Buena. He landed safely next day at noon and luckily found the *Sacramento* freighted for a return to the *Embarcadero*.

He gave orders to his men to secure his luggage from the anchored *Sterling* and transfer it to the schooner. Exchanging civilities with the Mexican authorities, he caught a swift word with Larkin, then in Yerba Buena, and hastened onboard his own craft, fearful lest news of his pact with Micheltorena cause his arrest.

Scarcely had the *Sacramento* nosed her seventeen tons out into the bay then an overland courier brought an order from Castro for Sutter's apprehension. By minutes he had beaten the demand. The schooner's sail could still be seen as the order was read by the capering Juan Prado Mesa. Without further trouble the Swiss reached New Helvetia.

There he made arrangements for warfare. Arms and ordnance were inspected, ammunition was carefully checked, drill was carried on with vigor. Steven's party had just arrived and on Sutter's solicitation most of the men joined his prospective field army.

THE REVOLTING FORCES made the first move on November 15th, 1844. A party of fifty Californians under Pico, Castro, Chavez and Rico drove off the government horses from Monterey to the Salinas Valley. Soon they seized arms and ammunition cached at San Juan Bautista and set about rallying the people to their cause.

Alvarado claims this was done without his conni-vance; which may be true. He was in Sonoma at the time, doubtless sounding out his wary uncle on the probabili-ties of successful revolt. At any rate, he immediately joined the insurgents. José Castro was proclaimed commander-in-chief, an exceedingly doubtful honor at the moment.

Vallejo was ever cautious. To be on the winning side in every argument requires an artistry not always fully appreciated by one's contemporaries. He hedged a bit; it was better to remain neutral and not openly join the revolution until events shaped themselves to his liking. To avoid the necessity of sending reënforcements to his superior officer—Micheltorena had already ordered him to do so—he disbanded his military forces, at least for the present. He did this on the plea he could no longer carry such a financial burden at his own expense. These men at once joined the rebels, as Vallejo knew they would.

The Governor marched from Monterey with one hundred and fifty men on November 22nd. He was with-out cavalry yet fully determined to nip this uprising at once. Ten miles southeast of San José, he camped at *Laguna Seca*.

The revolutionists, now two-hundred-and-twenty strong, rushed down from Santa Clara to meet him. They made their headquarters at Santa Teresa Rancho, less than a mile from the Governor's camp.

After forty-eight hours of scowls and skirmishings Micheltorena fell back toward his base. He was out-numbered and handicapped by his lack of cavalry. So he felt it a wise maneuver to return to Monterey and call on Sutter for aid.

As he was retreating, quite unhampered by any rebel opposition, he met the impatient Bidwell on his way back to New Helvetia. He paused for ten minutes and gave Bidwell an official order for Captain Sutter; this communication directed the Swiss to gather his forces and proceed at once to Monterey. The Governor assured Bidwell of his ability to handle the situation and sped him on his way; his parting words assured best wishes and friendship for the Americans of the Valley.

At San José Bidwell rode directly into the ranks of the rebel army, then encamped near the village. Castro and Alvarado met him with smiles and soft words. They sent their most cordial greetings on to Captain Sutter. So much for the facial conformities of all *Californio* hostilities.

Thus detained only a few minutes, the messenger pressed on. . . . In time he galloped his lathered mount through the fortress gates. Sutter read his orders and speeded his plans. He sent agents over the whole northern frontier in search of military supplies, even requisitioning some horses at Soscol and Petaluma, a procedure which drove Vallejo frantic.

THE SACRAMENTO made her appearance at Yerba Buena on December 22nd with a small cannon and other arms on board. Sutter had thought it advisable not to dispatch the craft without some means of defense at the crew's disposal. That arrival of the New Helvetia boat caused much comment, some derisive, some calculating and some stormy.

One night, Francisco Guerrero and a number of Californians captured the schooner and smuggled the armament across the bay for the use of Castro's army. They left the boat at its moorings, using the customs-house craft for the actual transfer.

Sutter had yet made no hostile move. So, for some indeterminate reason, the leaders of the revolt deemed it politic to let the New Switzerland captain commit the first overt act. Accordingly, his cannon and small arms were returned to Yerba Buena.

George Patterson regained possession of the gun and firearms. Placing them once more in the *Sacramento* he

---

[The following text appears inverted (upside-down) on the lower portion of the page:]

. . . came up with the man and lassoed him. . . . back they came. I then had handcuffs placed on the prisoner, informing him I would probably release him when we reached his home near San José.'

Perhaps Sutter was tempted to treat the fellow as his own courier had been treated. They were coming to San José; the same cottonwood on which Pablo Gutierrez had been hanged was not far off; indeed, summary action might have been wise. But Sutter set the man free. . . .

'Next morning,' the Captain continues, 'we reached Mission San José, having sent forward twenty-five riflemen as an advance guard. Accompanied by my staff, I called upon the padre in charge, who received us in a friendly manner. . . He then told me that General José Castro had visited the Mission briefly, retired from San José, and was now believed to be in the general direction of Santa Clara.

'The padre set refreshments before us. But some of my men followed the *mayordomo* as he was serving wine, discovered its abundant source, and soon drank more than they should.' . . .

Captain Sutter states the case lightly. Though he gave a swift command to move on, those orders came a bit late. For some hours after leaving the hospitable mission the infantry column may be described as staggering after the enemy; the mounted portion, though given to raucous song, were more orderly, owing to the fact that the horses had not followed the *mayordomo*.

'That night we camped five miles from San José,' reads Sutter's account. 'A strict guard was kept during the hours of darkness for fear of a surprise attack. Reports placed Castro not far distant. Here the thoughtful padre sent us provisions and I had two bullocks killed to supply my men with meat.

sailed for the *Embarcadero* to bear the news to the owner. . . .

Now Sutter was incensed by a more serious affair. Pablo Gutierrez was acting as a special courier carrying important missives between the Swiss and the Governor. Special boots had been made for him in Sutter's shoeshop; a double sole had been designed which securely held the dispatches while the rider was enroute to his destination.

One December morning Gutierrez galloped away, capital-bound, waving to Sutter as he went. That night his body swayed on a cottonwood in San José, making restless shadows in the moon glow. Alvarado and Castro had found the dispatches and made their answer.

At the time the ruler of the fort received news of the strangely burdened tree in San José, came a visitor riding boldly from that village. He was Charles W. Weber, making an unwelcome appearance to look things over. Since he was a friend of Castro and Alvarado—Bidwell had seen him in their company—the purpose of his reconnaisance was discernible.

With great abruptness he was seized and thrown into the fort calaboose, that dark chamber usually reserved for recalcitrant savages. There he stayed until released, some three months later.

ONE MORE PRIVATE conflict ends the year on the eve of dark days. Jacob Leese is reputed to have fought thirty thrilling minutes with Colonel Victor Prudon in the Sonoma public square. This contest ended with a balled fist smacking the immaculate Colonel flush on the chin-whiskers. Which ended his interest in the affair for the moment.

Reason for the disagreement: not recorded. Aftermath: Leese lost his position as alcalde; Prudon offered to renew hostilities with pistols; and both of them finally tapped fingers and made up.

head. Pierson . . .

great gate, raised his own . . .

left in command of the fortress until the . . .

Sutter's chief military threat was the company . . . hundred foreign riflemen under the leadership of John Gantt. Then came his hundred trained Indians, infantry and cavalry, under Ernst Rufus. A large brass field piece wheeled groaningly along, intent on battle, attended by a dozen pompous artillerymen. John Bidwell was Sutter's chief aide-de-camp. Jasper O'Farrell was quartermaster; Samuel J. Hensley was his assistant. A few subordinate officers completed the roster.

Past John Marsh's rancho near Monte Diablo ran the line of march. There the voluble owner insisted on joining the force, this despite his well-known sympathies for the insurgent cause. Marsh's action was unexpected. But the pseudo doctor was cunning. . . .

On hastened the troops to the Governor's support. At Don Antonio Suñol's rancho, ten miles from Mission San José, the cavalry caught a spy. The man had been sent on by Castro from his San José headquarters to report on the strength of the approaching column.

The captive was brought before Sutter. For an hour he was cross-questioned, but the fellow, evasive and clumsily contradictory, admitted nothing. Finally placed

under guard, in the night he eluded his captors and escaped.

"My corporal," wrote Sutter, "upon finding the spy missing, immediately jumped on an unsaddled . . . hotly pursued. He caught . . .

"Before proceeding next morning, I sent orders by special courier to the alcalde to close all places in San José where liquor could be obtained or sold. This precaution was necessary since I had some bad customers and hard drinkers among my riflemen.

"Then I invested the town, drums sounding, ranks deployed for action. . . . But we encountered no resistance. . . ."

Few men remained in the village. Most of them had retreated with Castro and Alvarado. Rumors were plentiful but uncertain. Halting only an hour, Sutter continued his advance.

Orders now arrived by courier from Micheltorena, naming Salinas as a rendezvous. By way of San Juan the Swiss led his men to the meeting place.

Near Salinas a small mounted troop of Sutter's command bagged another spy, a more important exhibit this time. It was Manuel Castro, brother of José, and the original leader of the revolt. Castro and a companion were apprehended near Gilroy's rancho; they were on their way to rejoin the retreating rebels and were picking up some stray information as they rambled.

A lucky series of events aided the two prisoners. They were captured by only four of Sutter's men. Almost at once the Americans and their captives were pursued by thirty mounted *Californios*. Castro and his friend, lashed to their saddles, were led toward the San Joaquin.

They were overtaken and surrounded at Pacheco Pass. The American quartet was obliged to exchange the two men for one Charles Brown, the only captive held by the pursuing party. Off rode Castro, his companion, and their rescuers. Back rode the crestfallen four to report the affair. So Sutter lost a most important hostage at the very beginning. Charles Brown seems to have been the only foreigner satisfied with the transaction.

THE TWO ALLIES joined forces January 9th at Salinas. This swelled the combined personnel to five hundred men. But the foe refused to wait and be crushed. Promptly, they retreated south, spreading rumors and threats impartially as they proceeded. Wild tales of robbery, rapine and ruthlessness were circulated about the pursuing demons of that arch-fiend, Micheltorena. Such tales bore fruit, however. The rebel force augmented, rather than lessened, as they fled.

After the insurgents went the merged forces. "At the Salinas," says the Swiss, "we arranged the order of march. The entire army was divided into two divisions, the Governor commanding one, I the other. He appointed me a colonel, and an extra company of dragoons and a trumpeter were assigned to me.

"At every evening halt the quartermaster laid out the camp in trim military fashion. Tents were pitched and orders were issued as to the night's watchword. The Mexican soldiers wished to tear down the near-by fences to supply the camp with wood. This I forbade them to do and ordered a chopping squad to the woods."

Progress was too deliberate to suit Sutter. Daily, he cautioned Micheltorena of the dangers attendant of such an unhurried pilgrimage through enemy territory. But the Governor was sick at the time—could not ride a horse; he was being transported in a "kind of buggy" where he could recline at full length. Being in no condition to pursue a vigorous campaign, he could not follow Sutter's counsel.

The rebels fell back repeatedly without any show of resistance. To the restive souls of Gantt's company it was almost unbearable. Grumblings were heard as to the loss of time and the lack of battle, both of which irked firebrands of the "foreign legion."

"We stopped at San Louis Obispo," says Sutter, "and were guests of the Mission. We also stayed briefly at the Mission of Santa Ynez. At both these places we enjoyed good food and excellent quarters.

"From Santa Ynez we were forced to construct a road along the beach to Santa Barbara for the cannons. . . . This occasioned a delay of several days.

"Then we continued on to Santa Barbara and quartered safely at the mission, being welcomed by the Bishop and three other Padres."

HERE THE ARMY rested for some time. It was the rainy season and hardships had been encountered. "We experienced supreme discomforts in that cold, wet winter," recalls Bidwell. "The transport of baggage and munitions on ox-drawn Mexican carts over muddy roads and difficult passes was a nightmare. Living most of the time on poor meat, without the luxury of bread, coffee or sugar, and performing the arduous military duties of such a march, it was not a difficult task for the traitorous Marsh to sow dissension among those of our company who had no real or personal interest in the result of the campaign. . . ."

Sutter made an effort to secure supplies for his men. At Captain Wilson's store he secured a hundred pairs of duck trousers, shirts, tobacco, sugar and other necessities. For these goods he gave Wilson orders on the government, orders which were later honored and paid. The bright-eyed lad who waited on Sutter that day in the little store was to become famous. That youthful clerk was Romualdo Pacheco, destined to be governor of California.

"While in residence here," recalls Sutter, "Captain Wilson invited me and a few of my officers to dinner. Captain Estrada burst into the room hurriedly as we were dining. He excused himself and called me aside. Governor Micheltorena had sent him with an escort of twenty-five men for my protection. He had received some information which made him fearful lest I be seized and made prisoner. I informed Captain Estrada I would make apologies to my host and return with him.

"In a few minutes we took leave of the cordial Captain Wilson and were escorted back to headquarters by Estrada.

"I found His Excellency in bed when I returned, still very sick. He earnestly asked me to exercise more caution; he felt I was needlessly running a great risk at being so far from my command. . . ."

Whether Captain Wilson's sympathies for the rebel cause had anything to do with the Governor's fear is left to inference.

Chapter XXIII

SOBRANTE GRANT

IN SANTA BARBARA the Swiss met the impeccable Don José Antonio Aguirre, owner of the *Tejon Rancho*. Don José, nicknamed *Aguirron* because of his huge bulk, was a distinguished and popular figure. Owner of the most beautiful mansion in the region, he was the perfect type of the old-style Spanish merchant, patrician *hidalgo* to the core. He was noted for his ability to keep aloof from politics yet was often employed in "delicate missions" by the government. It was one of these "delicate missions" that occasioned Sutter's presence as Don José's guest.

A courteous note came by vaquero to the mission during the waiting period before the more southern campaign began. It was an invitation for Sutter and his aide-de-camp to visit the Aguirre home and named the hour....

The Swiss was pleased to accept. Away whirled the vaquero with his answer. Then Sutter busied himself.... To be signaled out by the hospitable Don José was an honor. Don José was a personage. Out of the luggage came clean linen. An Indian boy followed Sutter's steps, polishing his boots as best it could be done as the Captain walked about his quarters donning his raiment....

At last he was ready, resplendent in fresh clothing, immaculately attired. Always a stickler for personal neatness, he was more so before attending a function of importance.

John Bidwell rode by his side, astride a black that paced the *palomino*. An escort of dragoons trotted at their heels. The day was pleasant, the scenes eye-arresting. Breath of a soft, premature spring went with them, exhilarating even as it caressed....

Don José's mansion was set in a grove of stately trees—a many-roomed, red-tiled building clothed with

the architectural charm of old Spain. . . . Clouds had
cleared away and the sun was warm upon the path and
their bodies as they passed through the entrance-way.

Their host awaited their dismounting before his
patio, a giant of a man, smiling.

"*Valedor mio!*" cried Don José, "my home is yours,
Captain Sutter! And yours, *Teniente* Bidwell! You make
the heart glad with your presence. Come, walk into your
house!"

They followed him. Where the patio lay open was
loveliness of an unordered kind. In its heart was a
fountain jeweled with ferns and orange lilies brought
from Mazatlan. Clematis and jasmine climbed pillars in
intense rivalry, curled heavenward until they could
twine their questing masses no farther. Cactus huddled
against white walls. Spanish bayonet and yucca stood
with spiked assurance. In the brilliance of sunlight and
foliage was a squirming foam of puppies and rabbits and
children and kittens. Under the patio roof sat many
people at work: Sutter glimpsed deft brown fingers
flashing on small portable looms; other women were preparing food in bowls of infinite capacity; some sewed
industriously, eyes slanted to see the master's visitors,
especially the handsome *caballero* with the broad shoulders and the twinkling blue eyes; a few nursed babies in
unembarrassed waist-nakedness. There was a hum of
light laughter and good nature about the place—"a
happy hum," John Sutter called it.

Through the great doorway leading into the *sala*
Don José ushered his guests. The room was a treasure-
house garnered out of his homeland. In tapestried chairs
they sat, sun shining on rich drapes and white embroidered napery, sipping Chianti of an ancient vintage
out of glistening goblets as they talked. . . . John Sutter
warmed to the sight of so many perfect possessions. A
bright shawl like a sunrise splashed with a rainbow
caught his roving eye. . . .

Later, their hostess—she who had been Maria del
Rosario Estudillo—sat with them through the well-
appointed meal. The talk was light, gay, invigorating;
the wines old and pleasingly potent; Don José, the lover
of good books, talked on with a low, clear, almost
hypnotic voice. . . .

Sutter was ever lustful of such creature comforts and
intelligent fellowship. . . . Somewhere unseen a sweet-
voiced boy sang softly to a guitar's accompaniment; then
he was silent and a harp joined its string-timbred sweetness to the guitar's. . . . It was gracious living such as
this that the Swiss dreamed for his New Switzerland and
Anna and the children in the soon-to-be. . . .

AT LAST CAME a three-cornered talk between Don José
and his two lulled guests. He was discreet, this son of old
Spain. Very. . . . He deprecated the present unpleasantness
in the political situation. Truly unfortunate, he murmured. Surely the time to prosecute a campaign was not
now. It was the rainy season. The sun might not return
in the morning. The roads would be almost impassable.
There was always a possibility of much sickness. . . . Perhaps some understanding might be reached with Micheltorena. . . . Perhaps the Governor's army might not find it
necessary to venture farther. . . . Don José paused, leaned
his great frame earnestly forward, waited. . . .

Sutter had been unprepared. But the thing was very
plain. As courteously as his host, he weighed the matter.
Then he drove to the point, without hedging.

"I do not believe," he said quietly, "that the Governor will turn back. The integrity of his leadership is at
stake. The situation is too critical for a backward movement." He sipped appreciatively at a half-emptied gob-
let. "As for me, Don José, I am an officer in the Mexican
Army and subject to the orders of the existing government. As such I have no recourse but to obey commands. . . ."

That was that. Clear. The talk drifted to less personal matters. If there had been a slight chill in the room more wine soon drove it forth again.

· Sutter and Bidwell rode home by midnight with their escort. Don José watched them ride away with a hint of resignation in his brilliant, clever eyes.

THE FOLLOWING MORNING Manuel Micheltorena legalized Sutter's second grant, known as the Sobrante, of twenty-two leagues. Sutter's empire was growing. More than half a thousand square miles now.

All the necessary papers were witnessed and signed at the mission. Conveyed by the governor of California there was no question as to their legality. The Swiss was impatient for this present trouble to be concluded; there was so much to do and Time, strange fellow, never lingered. John Sutter was forty-one years old. . . .

"The next day," Sutter continues, "we took breakfast at the mission with the padres. The Bishop gave us his benediction when we left and our force moved on to the Rincon.

"No horses or other equipment were stolen. I would not allow my men to rob or pillage and we respected private property rights at all times.

"We camped on the Rincon several days. It began to rain in torrents. We had very little meat, our chief staple. My Indians caught mussels and clams in order to bolster up our larder.

"Castro was at this time encamped at Buena Ventura, about twenty-five miles distant. James Coates, lieutenant in the rifle company, was sent forward with fifteen of his men to reconnoiter. He set out by way of the beach. Next day he returned saying they had been captured, treated well, fed and given wine to drink, and had finally been released on giving their word not to take up arms against the insurgents.

"I had great doubts as to the truth of these assertions but concluded it better to be rid of them rather than to be uncertain of their support on the field of action.

Sutter on horseback in 1855

"It was now determined to attack the enemy and I was selected to lead the advance with all my command, the Mexican Dragoons, and two companies of Mexican Infantry.

"I started to cross the mountains at sundown. The Governor remained with the artillery and the rest of his forces to begin their march along the beach at dawn.

"During the night it rained hard; the hills were very slippery and all footing was insecure; men and horses fell and even rolled down into the ravines. . . . When day broke I found my column in the woods, in sight of Mission San Buena Ventura.

"But not more than half of my original complement had come up. A council of war was held. Gantt affirmed he did not believe that half the guns would fire; Comandante Valdez was of the opinion that we were not strong enough to attack at the moment; Estrada said that he no longer considered it a night attack, seeing it was broad daylight; Rufus, captain of my Indian company, had the only favorable report—he said the Indians' guns were in good condition and ready for action.

"Meanwhile, the stragglers came up and we grew momentarily stronger. I reasoned that an attack after such weather would be a surprise, regardless of conditions, and so ordered it.

"Furthermore, I was aware that a *fandango* had been planned for the previous night and I expected to find Castro's command half-drunk or asleep. At all events, I determined to make the attack.

"Deploying my men—such as had arrived—we made our charge upon the town. The enemy were panic-stricken and fled as soon as we were sighted. On seeing us emerging from the woods, it was impossible for them to guess our numbers.

"I sent Bidwell post-haste to Micheltorena, asking immediate permission to pursue the rebels. But he sent back an order requesting that all our forces be joined before continuing on.

"If we had followed up this initial advantage we could easily have routed them and ended the warfare in one coup. But this is never the Latin fashion. They must first have something to eat and drink. The Governor's forces finally arrived and aided us in investing the town.

"Knowing my men to be tired and hungry, I demanded meat and *aguardiente* from the *mayordomo*. Although the priest favored us, this *mayordomo* was an enemy. He made great protest that Castro's men had taken everything with them in their retreat. Naturally convinced this was untrue, I tartly assured the official that I would break open his cellar and storehouse if he did not produce the desired supplies. Seeing our determination he finally yielded with ill-grace and easily produced a great plenty of foodstuffs and refreshments.

"We spent the next day there. Long-haired Indians dressed in short shirts came in from San Antonio Mission and played for us. They composed a regular musical band, these Indians, a most remarkable aboriginal aggregation. . . .

"A big cross was set up in this place. The inhabitants informed me that the *Californios* swore they would nail me on one side of that cross and Micheltorena on the other—if they could catch us. . . ."

THE GOVERNOR'S ARMY moved forward more briskly now, Micheltorena somewhat recovered from his illness. While passing a tiny *milpas*—an outlying cultivated garden belonging to a rancho—they were accosted by a beautiful woman and a small boy. The child carried a number of *tortillas* in a little sack, wrapped in a cloth.

This pair approached the infantry column and asked for the captain of riflemen. Gantt was pointed out and the lad presented him with the package of *tortillas*. In the middle of those interesting delicacies Gantt discovered a letter signed by Alvarado, Castro, and others allied with the rebels. In it they called upon Gantt and his company to abandon Micheltorena's cause and come over to the *Californio* banner. At once the officer presented the letter to Captain Sutter. The indignant Swiss turned it over to the Governor.

It was then found that the lovely lady was reputed to be Alvarado's mistress and the boy her son. Regardless of that possibility, it was certain she was an instrument in the present intrigue.

They camped in a large vineyard surrounded by a stone wall that night. Another woman was ushered into Sutter's presence. But hers was a different mission. With tears running down wrinkled cheeks she fell on her knees before the Swiss.

"Please do not punish my foolish sons!" she cried. "They are fighting with Castro, those blind, unwise ones. I fear you may kill them. Spare them, generous sir —spare them to a weeping mother!"

Sutter was amazed and touched.

"Señora," he said sympathetically, "your sons shall be unharmed. I promise it. They are very lucky young *caballeros* to have such a brave mother."

With a cry of joy she grasped and kissed his hand.

"Tell me, Señora," he said hurriedly, "how many sons have you?"

The woman rose, very proudly. "Nineteen, my brave Captain," she answered.

"What?" cried Sutter.

"But only nine are with Castro!" she offered pleadingly.

Sutter shook his head. "I perceive, Señora," he remarked dryly, "that I have promised to pardon half the rebel army."

THAT NIGHT SUTTER wrote two notes and sent them by courier to Los Angeles. One went to the smooth-tongued, hair-trigger Charles Flugge, then a resident there. He was instructed to prevent the government-owned schooner *California* from falling into rebel hands if she touched at San Pedro.

The other note was to Gessen, another German, in which Sutter went into detail to point out that the men under his command were not serving for pay but for patriotism. The real reason for this second letter was probably Sutter's fear that foreigners in the South might be induced to aid the insurgents if not in full possession of all the facts.

March was resumed and the Governor's troops advanced rapidly upon Los Angeles. Great preparations had been made there to aid the rebels. Pio Pico and other prominent Californians joined Castro and Alvarado. Even some recently arrived American hunters and trappers allied themselves with the insurgents; also a number of important resident foreigners—Stearns, Vignes, Workman, Wilson and others.

"It required," says Bidwell, "only the further disaffection, so adroitly instilled into our American volunteers on the long, hard march overland by the shrewd Dr. Marsh, to guarantee disaster. There is not the least doubt but that Marsh joined us to encompass our defeat. . . .

"At this moment William Fallon, the Irish trapper, commanding some forty Americans, joined the rebels. This Fallon and party had heard only one side of the question. They had been showered with hospitalities including free living, wine, and all the luxuries of the Los Angeles of that day; they believed they were doing right in aiding the revolters to save their city from pillage and the inhabitants from the outrages of the despicable Governor and his barbarous allies. . . ."

Chapter XXIV

BATTLE

THE MICHELTORENA forces passed through El Triunfo and Las Virgenes. At nightfall of February 19th they arrived at the Encino in San Fernando Valley. Only a few miles away lay Los Angeles.

From Cahuenga came the rebels; from the Encino the Governor's men moved to the attack. Friday morning, February 20th, the columns clashed.

"From the hill," says Sutter, "we could see the enemy awaiting us. The wind was blowing a half gale. During the night the blasts had beaten our tents down and sand and dust annoyed us beyond measure. A strong guard had been kept but none of us slept because of the storm. . . .

"With drums sounding we beat to arms. . . ."

John Bidwell continues the narrative: "The artillery from both sides began to fire simultaneously.

"Sutter with his American riflemen was directed to occupy a deep, winding gulch, midway between the opposing armies. They approached within rifle shot of the enemy. Then, for the first time, the Americans under Sutter could see Castro's forces clearly. To their amazement they discovered that Castro seemed to have nearly as many Americans under his banner as Micheltorena. Where had they come from?

"Dr. Marsh was now volubly in evidence and the very man to suggest what to do. An effort was made to communicate with the enemy by signaling. Soon shouted information brought the news of Fallon's men with the revolters!

"Almost every American found some acquaintance or friend on the opposing side. Many had known one another in Missouri. In the cordial parley which ensued they forgot all about fighting in their eagerness to inquire about old friends and relatives and the latest news.

"During all this time the cannon balls and grapeshot were whistling over their heads. It hardly needed a suggestion to point out that it was unwise for Americans to engage in a conflict and murder one another.

"'Let the Mexicans fight it out among themselves,' yelled the majority.

"All agreed to this except Captain Sutter and a few others. Acting in my capacity as Sutter's aide-de-camp, I was continually carrying orders between Micheltorena and Sutter. All orders sent to the riflemen in the gulch to charge were being ignored.

"The Governor ordered Sutter to join the riflemen personally and march with them to an advanced position. But the Americans under Micheltorena withdrew from the battlefield, acting with the understanding that their friends with the enemy would also retire. While they were deliberating as to the position they should occupy, volleys of grapeshot burst among them. Hurriedly, they retreated out of battery range.

"Several horses were shot but no one was killed. In the meantime the Governor advanced and occupied a high hill. From him I rode with an order to the riflemen.

"I found Captain Sutter with the men vainly trying to persuade them to rejoin Micheltorena and support him. After an interval he realized the futility of making them change their mind. Then the two of us rode desperately across country to rejoin the Governor. . . .''

As Sutter and Bidwell galloped toward the hill they were surrounded by a company of wild-riding rebel cavalry. Lassoes snaked about their horses' heads and the two were prisoners. A black moment—John Sutter was a marked man and not beloved by the insurgent leaders.

Then the Americans allied with the revolutionists broke their pledges. They rejoined Castro and fought for him while Sutter's riflemen stood off and took no part in the conflict.

Off rode Sutter's captors for the rebel headquarters, then the adobe buildings of the Cahuenga Rancho.

"Then Antonio Castro came up," says Sutter, "and recognized me. He spoke to his men. 'I will take your prisoner.'

"Then he saluted me and remarked: 'I am very glad to see you here, Captain Sutter.'

"'Doubtless you are,' I answered. 'But I am not particularly delighted.'

"Then he remembered he must send word to Alvarado and dispatched a vaquero. We had ridden forward only a short distance when Alvarado came spurring to meet us. We dismounted and he embraced me affectionately like an old friend.

"He then ordered his vaquero to pass him a bottle of *aguardiente* and we both drank. The vaquero was sent to summon General Castro.

"Soon the General came dashing up.

"'Dismount, General Castro, salute Captain Sutter and welcome him as an old friend,' ordered Alvarado.

"We dismounted and there was more affectionate embracing on the field of battle.

"Then we mounted amicably and I rode between my two cordial captors, surrounded by a hollow square of Californians. Those troops eyed me viciously. . . . Soon we came to the adobe at Cahuenga.

"There I was placed in a dark room and held prisoner. I set down my little double-rifle before the door and that splendid, well-loved piece disappeared forever.

"Many people came to gaze at me curiously. I was like a strange animal on exhibition. An under-officer then entered with a strong guard and demanded my sword. I surrendered it without objection.

"'This begins to look ominous,' I said to myself, uneasily. I paced thoughtfully about my dark cage. Then a door opened in the blackest corner of the room. In stepped a *teniente* named Montenegro, whom I knew well. We greeted each other courteously.

"'You can repay me for past favors at this moment,' I said to him meaningly. 'Please present my compliments to Governor Alvarado and say that the honorable usages of war seem to be unknown in this provincial atmosphere. An officer of my rank is never placed under a common guard or subject to the eyes of curious *cholos*.'

"He bowed and withdrew. But my words had a certain excellent effect on men who proudly wished to be known as officials aware of all the niceties of behavior.

"My sword was at once returned to me and I was escorted into another room where the officers were drinking and celebrating their victory. I was asked to join them.

"They said that at present they needed all their troops and wished to dispatch me with the alcalde to Los Angeles. Henry Rowland was present and he went surety to my captors that I would not escape. So, in the evening, I departed with the Alcalde Lugo and Rowland to Los Angeles, some twelve miles distant.

"Arriving there, I was comfortably quartered in Abel Stearn's home. A huge supper party was in progress there, including the officers of the new government—the government but newly formed by the Castro party.

"Juan Bandini, secretary of state, was a guest; Pio Pico, the new governor, was absent that night. I was invited to sit at table with the hospitable dignitaries as an honored guest.

"I declined, since I was but returned from the field, worn, soiled, jaded and without fresh linen. But they insisted and I sat down.

"Shortly after this I pleaded intense fatigue and begged them to excuse me. So Mr. Stearns escorted me to a very good room and bade me goodnight. . . ."

JOHN SUTTER was in a tight spot. At the most he could only hope to save his head by the boon of banishment. The friendly gestures did not deceive him. Luck alone could save him from a rope or a firing squad. His kingdom and all his dreams were gone—blasted out on a comic-opera battlefield where one horse formed the official casualty list.

Tired and forlorn as he was, John Sutter did not know despair. For Micheltorena he had no hope. Without Sutter's men he was doomed; in a few hours he must surrender. . . . The Swiss sat on the edge of the bed and planned. Fifteen minutes later he slept calmly. He had a scheme. . . . He was certain it would work. . . with the right stage-setting. . . .

"During the night," says Sutter, "Mr. Stearns came to my room and knocked loudly several times. So exhausted was I that I did not hear him. He was forced to enter and arouse me, a difficult task.

" 'There are two gentlemen below who wish to see you,' he informed me.

"I dressed and came down. Don Andres Pico and James McKinley, a Scotchman, were my visitors. They asked if I had any objection to writing Micheltorena and advising him to yield to superior forces as a prudent measure.

"While I was personally satisfied that what they said was true and that our cause was hopeless, still I did not wish to advise the Governor. I wished him to do as he pleased and not be influenced by my plight or suppositions.

"My visitors also wished me to write Rufus, captain of my Indians. As an excuse to this I remarked that Rufus could neither read nor write and would obey nothing but a word-of-mouth order.

"However, I said, I could write Micheltorena in French. My Spanish I deprecated as unreadable.

" 'But,' protested Pico, 'we cannot read French.'

" 'You have friends here who can,' I answered.

"It was in the middle of the night and I gambled that they would not scrutinize what I wrote too closely.

"So I wrote the letter in French, wording it in such a manner that he could readily understand my unenviable position and how I was thus forced to address him in the matter.

"At this time he was entirely surrounded by the enemy without a base of operations, and he had provisions for only forty-eight hours. He might retire and fight longer but I believed his men would desert him as the hours went on. . .

"I slept until late morning after writing my letter. After breakfast Dr. Alfred Anselin, a French surgeon who had formerly been in my employ, came to me with news of Micheltorena's capitulation.

"He remarked further: 'I have very bad news for you, Captain Sutter.'

"'What is it?'

"'There is much discussion as to what shall be done with you,' he said slowly. 'Some are for fusillading you. Others are for deportation and confiscation of all your properties.'

"'I am in their power,' I admitted. 'They can certainly do with me as they choose.'

"My luggage had been left at San Fernando in charge of Dr. Townsend. At this moment Marcos Vaca, brother of Don Juan Vaca, brought me in one of my clean shirts and my razor. This was a godsend to a soiled captive. . . .

". . . After the surrender most of the *Californios* returned to Los Angeles. They were free then from further military duty, since Micheltorena had capitulated. He asked that he might march through the Pueblo with flying colors and music. After the Treaty of San Fernando this was allowed.

"That music sounded like a dead march to me. . . .

"Among those forced to lay down their arms—my arms—were my Indians. In the terms of capitulation mutually agreed upon they had every advantage assured them which was enjoyed by the Mexican soldiers.

"Yet, while I was a prisoner, they were abominably treated and required to carry excessive burdens to San Pedro like pack-animals. These burdens were provisions for Mexican military vessels in harbor. For this work my Indians received no pay and barely sufficient rations to exist on. . . .

"I had embarked on this campaign wholly at my own expense. Naturally, with such a conclusion, no remuneration could be forthcoming.

"On the day before the night attack at Buena Ventura, I had asked Micheltorena to then hand me the deed to the Sobrante Grant, the surplus to my other survey. I made this request so that in the event I was killed in action my family would be assured of a patrimony. He thereupon executed the deed, having two secretaries with him at the time. . . .

". . . After Micheltorena's capitulation, parole was granted me. I visited a wealthy Los Angeles Frenchman, Luis Vignes, who lived in close proximity to Stearn's establishment. There I met a number of influential Mexican officers—Valdez and others—and the courtly Vignes insisted on drinking my health in excellent Burgundy imported from his homeland. . . . "

SUTTER'S SCHEME had still to work itself out. In his delicate position he had to do a great deal of tactful maneuvering. Yet his chance came.

"I returned to dinner at Stearn's home," he continues. "After dinner I walked and talked with Don Juan Bandini in the spacious yard. He presented me with a fragrant cigar and asked me to play a game of billiards. He owned a private table and I can assure you that there were few billiard tables in the country then.

"Rather grimly, I asked him to excuse me. I remarked I was in an ill-humor to play a good game of billiards.

" 'Doubtless, my friend, doubtless,' he agreed. Then he paused in our promenade. 'Would you mind telling me why you came with Micheltorena? Did you come of your own free will or did you receive orders to march with him?'

" 'Surely I received orders,' I answered, elated. 'The Governor sent me an official communication demanding that I come to him immediately.'

" 'Have you the orders?' He was surprised. 'Can you show them to me?'

" 'I had them with me,' I said. 'I believe they are in my luggage now at San Fernando. If I could send a messenger you could have the document.'

" 'It is very difficult to secure horses at this time,' he remarked. 'But I shall try. . . .'

"It was accomplished, however, and Dr. Townsend made an appearance, bringing my papers. Among them was the official summons from the Governor bidding me march to his assistance.

"I handed the order to Bandini.

"He took it swiftly, read, then exclaimed: 'Now you are safe . . . !'

This scheme to make use of the official order had germinated in Sutter's mind the night of his capture. It had been a brittle straw of a plan. To show that, as a Mexican officer, he had merely obeyed the express commands of his superior, was his aim. He knew it might not work. But it had. Bandini himself had aided him without prompting.

His only fear now was as to the extremity of punishment which might be meted out to him by an enthusiastic new gubernatorial régime. . . .

"Bandini." he relates, "then took my papers to the government house and displayed them to Pio Pico, Castro, Alvarado, and all the new officials. Then he spoke in my favor, very eloquently pleading my cause. He was a very exceptional personage, this Juan Bandini, a Chilean and not a Californian. Moreover, he was well-educated and of charming manners. . . .

". . . After breakfast the next morning, Bandini came to me and escorted me courteously to the government offices. There were gathered all the functionaries of the recently devised government. As I stood before them I felt confident.

"Pio Pico arose and said that I had done nothing but my duty to the then-legal government; that the new government intended to recognize me and assure me all my former rights; provided I would swear fealty to the new they were sure I would be faithful as I had been to the old.

"I was instructed to retain all my property and offices. I then held the post of *Comandante Militar de las fronteras del norte y encargado de la justicia*.

"So I made the promise which they required and took the oath of allegiance to the new régime. Then I received a certificate, resembling a diploma of sorts, which confirmed me in all my property and titles.

"*Aguardiente* flowed freely after this happy conclusion of what was to me a most distressing—and uncertain—position."

JOHN SUTTER had gambled on the temperament of a people he knew well; that and upon his "document" from Micheltorena. He had won. But for a week he had been a landless, futureless prisoner, his life-thread paper-thin. Now he was even more powerful than before.

Chapter XXV

WARRIOR'S RETURN

SUTTER now faced a new difficulty. He was half a thousand trail-miles from his Sacramento Valley. A practically weaponless, foodless, unmounted company of one hundred and twenty men depended on him for transport back to that base. And he was without money. . . .

At first the thing seemed simple. His credit was ample. But horses and provisions were hard to get. It would have taken a small fortune to outfit his men. He had already lost his horses and arms, also valuable time when his personal supervision was needed at the fort during the all-important planting season.

After some negotiations, he sought out a German named Mumm. The latter was a cooper who had secured staves in the Sacramento and been transported to Yerba Buena free of charge by the obliging Swiss. Mumm agreed to aid. He bought thirty horses for Sutter, a debt that was later faithfully repaid. These horses mounted the white contingent but left the Indians still on foot.

"Then Bidwell," recalls Sutter, "asked the government for supply orders which would send us back to our destination at governmental expense. This they refused to do but cordially reaffirmed that my credit was good for anything I wished to buy. . . .

"But I knew that a purchase of such equipment as we needed would mean a huge debt, quite beyond my ability to pay at the time. . . . There were my Indians, my servants, the Kanakas, vaqueros, Bidwell, Dr. Townsend, Juan Vaca—a company of one hundred and twenty men to provide for. . . . I shook my head and said no, feeling that the new government was treating us very badly. . . .

"Then the officials finally offered to give me an order on Padre Blas of the San Fernando Mission for *pinole* for

my Indians. This I accepted. We also made some shift to
secure limited provisions for the white company. . . .

"On arriving at San Fernando, Padre Blas received us
well and gave us provisions for everyone.

"While there the Padre and I ate in lonely grandeur
at his well-laid board, my officers having a table for
themselves and being well-supplied with wine. . . .

"The next day was Sunday. People came to church
from miles about and mass was solemnized by the kindly
father. After the rites a dance was held and all joined in
the merrymaking. . . .

"The following day we set out for the fort by way of
the Tulare Valley. After leaving the friendly Padre we
passed onward through a desert country. Since we had
no guide we found no water. There was nothing along
our pathway but stunted vegetation and dwarfed palm-
trees. It was fatiguing for man and beast. . . .

"To escape the desert we struck off to the mountains.
There we found a little stream where we camped. This
San Fransquito farm was our first stopping place.

"From here I sent out scouts to find a pass through
the mountains. In time this was found. So we went on
over this mountain ridge through which is now (1878)
a railroad tunnel—Tejon Pass it is called.

"It was a magnificent view we had from the mountain top down into the green and fertile Tejon Valley!
We passed over snow in spots on our descent and on our
way down it seemed like going into Italy—fine verdure
and the promise of rich lands. . . . Then we rested one
whole day so that the animals might graze plentifully.

"The native savages looked grim and not over-
friendly. My own Indians had no arms and the provisions of all ran low before we came to the wild-horse
country. Then my Indians came to me and requested that
I permit them to hurry on ahead. They said that they
could find roots and grasses to live on; they felt they
could arrive home more swiftly if they went alone. I
told them to go. . . .

"We had not entered the Tulare Valley yet. This valley was what was termed the 'Wild Horse Country'— there were no horses in the Tejon Valley. . . .

"So we traveled on, crossing streams, camping, existing on the scanty fare we had brought from San Fernando and San Fransquito. Then we reached the swollen King's River.

"The Indians of that region were saucy, although when we offered them pay they grudgingly aided us to cross over. By a great lake, Tulare Lake, we encountered another village of Indians from which we could procure no fish or other food. . . . Farther on we camped beside a stream where one of the men made fish-hooks of the kettle-vine. With these we managed to catch some fish.

"Our mounts now began to give out because of a lack of proper grazing. We were forced to travel very slowly. When at last we came to the Merced River we were compelled to build a rude raft. . . .

"With the departure of my hundred Indians, my party was reduced to eight white men, four Kanakas, and four vaqueros. After safely crossing the Merced we chanced upon a band of Indian horse thieves, four in number, who were driving twenty horses they had stolen in the San José Valley.

"I ordered an attack at once. We needed those horses. Soon we might have been on foot and in dire straits. Our charge drove off the savages and we secured the stolen animals. Now we were better mounted, since the horses were in much better condition than our own mounts.

"Then we came to the Stanislaus, worst stream of all to cross. We had no hatchet and this was the second raft we were forced to construct. So we again lassoed the dry branches, bound them together, and launched the unwieldy makeshift.

"A Kanaka swam the river with a line. Only one man and a little baggage could cross at once. The man was force to lie flat, hold on, and pull himself across by means

Ruins of Sutter's Mill, painted by R. C. Holdredge.
From the collection of Philip B. Bekeart

of the line. The raft was pulled back by a rope and thus most of us passed over.

"But not without further peril. At this moment the horse thieves returned with reënforcements and molested us from a distance. The banks were high and it was a difficult feat for the vaqueros to swim the horses across. We had to detail a squad to keep up a continuous gun-fire while the raft was being made and the horses transported.

"The original four savages had returned with their entire village. They were thus much bolder in their attack, believing us handicapped. . . .

"That night, after crossing the Stanislaus, we did not camp. On we kept through the darkness, fearing to stop because of lurking hostiles. . . .

"We had no path in the blackness and the North Star was our only guide. . . .

"Then our provisions gave out. We were compelled to halt and hunt. An antelope fell before Bidwell's rifle. . . . Finally we won our way to the Mokelumne. There we were met by vaqueros with horses and provisions sent me by Major Reading. From thence on we rode comfortably home. My Indians had arrived four days previously."

ONCE MORE the ruler of New Switzerland rode through the gateway of his stronghold. He had been absent three months to the day. It was April 1st, 1845.

"A proper Fool's Day," muttered John Sutter with a half-smile.

Chapter XXVI

VALLEY VENGEANCE

IN SUTTER's absence a small party of Walla Wallas had come down the Sacramento Valley as far as the Fort. Their young, hot-headed chief Elijah was a trouble-maker of the most insidious kind. Within a day of his arrival the Indian leader had thrust a quarrel on Grove C. Cook, a quarrel assuredly not of Cook's seeking.

Elijah was shot and killed by the white man in the altercation. Back went the slain man's tribe to Oregon, vowing reprisal. The incident created much concern at the fort. Moreover, it was to occasion grave repercussions the next year and lead to unexpected danger for John Sutter.

Two weeks after the Captain's return a terrified vaquero spurred a lathered horse through the fortress gate. An arrow, thrust through his left shoulder, splashed red drops on the turf as he rode. He almost fell from his saddle beyond the barrier.

"Indians!" he cried. "Madre Dios! Lindsay has been murdered! Captain Sutter—I must see Captain Sutter!"

Supported by John Bidwell and Juan Vaca, the wounded man was helped to the Swiss' quarters. There he poured out his story to the listening Captain.

Tom Lindsay had been killed in his hut, the place burned down, his cattle and horses stolen. Straight from the present site of Stockton had the rider ridden, seeking aid. "Two hundred warriors!" he gasped.

Sutter's fist crashed on the redwood table-top. "Ten men together at once, John!" he shouted to Bidwell. "And the cavalry! We go within the hour. Haste does it . . .!"

They rode fast, that avenging army, Vaca and Bidwell beside the law-enforcer of the Sacramento. San

Joaquin Indians had been the spoilers, the wounded
vaquero had said. So be it. The San Joaquin savages must
be taught a lesson.

Only ten miles beyond the smouldering hut Sutter's
forces flashed down upon the marauders driving the
white man's herds. The battle was short, bitter, bloody.
Juan Vaca went down beside the lord of the valley, a
dead thing in the dust, his body cushioning a score of
arrows.

The darts pierced Sutter's clothing until they hung
like ribbon streamers about him. But the arrows did not
draw blood. Relentlessly, he led his trained cavalry, forward and back, harrying. Rifles cut leaden lanes through
screaming brown ranks. In ten minutes half a hundred of
the murderous thieves lay lifeless on the valley floor.

Then they broke and scurried back toward their
distant *rancherias*. Like mad things they rode—what
was left of them—the fear of swift death in their savage
hearts.

For a short space the cavalry worried their flanks,
cut them down. Then Sutter's men returned to round up
the scattered herds. . . .

Sorrowfully, the Swiss rode home. On the horse behind him rode Juan Vaca. But not as he had proudly
come, a gay *caballero* in his burnished trappings. His
body was lashed cross wise upon his silver-mounted
saddle. He was riding home to sleep the warrior's sleep
beside the walls of the white fort.

MORE INDIAN TROUBLE came two months after
Sutter's return. Raphero, commanding three hundred
braves, made known his intention to attack and sack
New Switzerland. This ungrateful Mokelumne chieftain
had once been presented with a fine saddle, horse and
bridle as a token of esteem by the Swiss. Now the savage
leader chose to march against his benefactor.

Sutter resolved on prompt action. "If confronted
with sure hostilities, attack first," was always his

slogan. By the light of a sickled moon he went secretly, with a picked band, to where the Indians were holding preparatory rites before the threatened attack.

The ambuscaders closed in from an ever-narrowing circle. Then Sutter gave the clipped word. Rifles spat viciously like momentary stars in the blackness; shrill cries began to drown out the snarl of the guns. Many men fell. But not one of the swift attackers. Then the Indians fled beyond their fires, sought the uncertain refuge of the darkness. . . .

Raphero was captured and brought back to the fort. His army was dispersed or dead; his cause was lost.

Sutter the absolute, pronounced solemn sentence upon him. The same day he was led out to death. The rifles of five men lifted and pointed at his breast.

Then a mule walked calmly in front of him. Up went Raphero's bare foot and kicked the parading beast in the buttocks.

"Out of the way!" shouted Raphero in his own language "A chief is about to die. He does not desire your companionship."

The surprised mule lumbered aside.

The rifles crashed.

LATER IN THE YEAR, Rufino, another Mokelumne leader, was arrested for murder. His case is disposed of in the following brief sentence in Sutter's Diary: "September 16th, 1845. Rufino, chief of the Mokelumnes, was today tried for murder, found guilty, and executed."

Justice was swift at Sutter's Fort.

Two hundred and fifty more Americans—one hundred and fifty of them men—came to California in 1845. The McMahon-Clyman party arrived in July. With them came William Northgrave, J. D. Perkey, James Wilson Marshall and others, many of whom drifted into Sutter's service.

The expectant Swiss, who was in continual correspondence with many in the East, notably Hastings, was certain that more emigrants were coming than really came.

Second to reach the fort that year was the Swasey-Todd company. The convivial George McDougall, Dr. William B. Gildea, William F. Swasey, and William L. Todd, a relative of President Lincoln, were some of its more important members.

William Sublette led the third group of fifteen men. One of them, Harry Trow, became one of Sutter's most faithful helpers. Another, Charles Savage, in his declining years wrote a scathing denunciation of John Sutter's adventures in the Sante Fe trade, a denunciation without foundation or factual backing.

Next came the John Grigsby-William B. Ide company. The dashing Truman Bonney, James Gregson, George Williams, Joseph Wood and others were of that group. As usual, this contingent swelled the artisan forces of progressive New Switzerland.

THEN BACK SURGED Lansford W. Hastings, the voluble gentleman of indecisive destiny, his book a reality, his suppositions a flood of rising grandeur. With him adventured the lean William N. Loker, gangling Robert Semple, Napoleon B. Smith and others. Some stayed at the fort; others trekked on.

On December 10th came another visitor, one who had been a guest of the wilderness stronghold before. He was John C. Frémont, who deigned to linger only four days this time. He had divided his "topographical expedition" and was in a hurry to push on south where he could rejoin his lost company, the wandering portion of which, under Edward M. Kern, was as vainly seeking to contact him. As usual, Frémont needed supplies.

"At the time of Frémont's arrival," writes Bidwell, "Captain Sutter was absent from the fort and I was in command during his absence. Having failed for several years to raise wheat and make his annual installments to the Russians, Sutter was at this time making a desperate effort to seed large tracts of land for a huge yield. Because of the 1845 war which resulted in Micheltorena's expulsion and also because of the recurrent crop failures, Captain Sutter was in somewhat straitened circumstances. Through it all his faith did not waver.

"It was at such a time as this that Frémont arrived and expected to get a huge amount of supplies as soon as he requested them—an impossible thing. Pack-horses, mules and provisions were his principal demands.

"My first notice of Frémont's coming was when he and Kit Carson entered the fort. When I stated Sutter's present embarrassed condition, that he had no mules which could possibly be spared, and offered to substitute horses and such supplies as Sutter had, Frémont showed evident disappointment and anger. He unsmilingly attributed my truthful explanation as merely being unwillingness to accommodate him.

"He inferred it was due to the growing differences between the United States and Mexico; that Sutter, being a Mexican officer and official, and I, Sutter's agent, were merely acting in accordance with our sympathies.

"This was crazy talk, as far as I was concerned. As for Captain Sutter, he was most friendly to Frémont—more so than Frémont had any right to expect—and Sutter had always been friendly to the American government and to every American at all times.

"In fact, Sutter had proved his friendship on a thousand occasions. Never once had he refused an American anything he had in the fort. Sutter's hope and desire was that the United States would acquire California as soon as possible.

"As evidence of my statement, when Sutter returned from the bay he immediately offered to supply everything Frémont demanded as far as lay in his power.

"But he could do no more than I had previously promised in his absence. Sutter treated Frémont with much attention and distinctive courtesy, visited him in camp, fired all his ordnance in a salute of welcome, and feasted him at a grand dinner."

THEN FRÉMONT pushed on to join Kern's party to the south. Sutter had given him fourteen mules much needed at the fort but its master was amiable enough to inconvenience himself for the surly official.

The always-obliging Swiss was also determined to see that a fitting farewell speeded the parting guest, no matter what his antagonistic mood. Seven pieces of ordnance crashed a salvo as Frémont rode away. But one of the guns was old; a scrap of iron chipped under the force of a heavy powder charge and neatly removed the amazed Frémont's headgear. Into the dust sailed that gentleman's chapeau. With many apologies the hat was returned to him.

"Almost blew his head off," declares Bidwell, not without some personal satisfaction. At any rate, one cannot blame the roving mapper for wanting distance between himself and Sutter's cannon, whether he stood in front or behind them.

IN THE SOUTH, at the very end of the ill-fated campaign Bidwell had viewed an historic scene. "The first gold discovery in California," he relates, "was made in 1841 by Juan Baptiste Ruelle. This French-Canadian had lived in New Mexico, had worked placer mines there, and it was he who made the find in the mountains some thirty miles northeast of Mission San Fernando.

"His discovery caused no excitement. When I visited the place in 1845 only about thirty people were working there. The average earnings were small, not more than twenty-five cents a day—although it might run up to an ounce on occasion.

"Though the mine had been worked for nearly four years and consisted merely of a bank of gravel, the progress was very slow. The cut washed into the hill did not exceed thirty feet.

"An old, wise-looking patriarch of a miner whom all seemed to venerate, had more to say than his fellow-workers. He was scraping the ground out with a scoop or spoon fashioned from a bullock's horn. He was so clever that he could tell ground that contained gold from ground which did not. For myself, I could detect no difference. Yet he would select the valuable ground, place it in a basket, and invariably reject the poor ground with a casual inspection.

"In the course of a half-hour or so—frequently interrupted by stopping to light an everlasting cigarette—the basket would be filled. Then it was placed on a platform. This resembled a table covered by a tablecloth. It was erected by driving posts into the ground until they approximated a three-foot height; poles were laid across them, leveled off with a little grass and then covered with a cotton cloth. This platform was about eight feet by four feet.

"In the center of the cloth was piled up all the earth to be washed. After four or five bushels of the golden soil had been selected by the ancient, the washing began.

"Water was drawn from a near-by pool in a basket and thrown on the pile of earth. The muddy water drained off the table, lessening by degrees the size of the pile. But the manner of applyyng the water required much skill.

"The old man would becomei almost frantic when it was thrown too speedily. He would seize the basket ostentatiously and demand that all watch closely and attempt to emulate an adept.

"After some time the golden earth was so far reduced that the gravel could be discarded by hand. The skilled miner always examined the pebbles carefully to see that no gold adhered to them before they were thrown away.

"It took from one to three hours to complete a washing of this kind. The gold would be found in small quantities adhering to the cloth after the gravel and earth had been painstakingly removed. The precious residue was then carefully gathered up and placed in a quill.

"I learned of the existence of that mine in the spring of 1845 and visited it, seeing some of the gold, at the time of Micheltorena's capitulation in Los Angeles. . . .

"In the fall of 1843 Ruelle had come to Sutter's Fort from the southern part of the state. While there he showed Captain Sutter a few particles of gold and told him that he had found it on the banks of the American River. He had this gold in an old quill. Judging from this quill's appearance, one would have said that it had been owned or used for a long, long time.

"Owing to further incidents this looked somewhat suspicious. He requested Sutter to furnish him with two pack-animals loaded with provisions so that he might go prospecting for a few weeks, also an Indian boy to act as guide. Suspicion grew stronger as to his good faith—he might have filled that quill any place *but* in the vicinity of the American River.

"Then another fact damned him. A company of Canadian trappers were in the neighborhood of the fort on the way to Oregon with pelts for the Hudson's Bay Company. There was little to prevent Ruelle from carrying his prospecting venture on into Oregon—and forget to return.

"So Sutter declined to aid him and Ruelle refused to set out without food or pack-animals."

DURING SUTTER's absence in the South a strange and tragic event ended the Hudson's Bay Company venture in Yerba Buena. The convivial William Glen Rae, agent in charge, was discovered to be carrying on an affair with an amorous and lovely Californian woman. Their supposedly clandestine assignations became public property. In time they reached Mrs. Rae's ears.

With dramatic intensity she charged her husband with his peccadillo. Thunderstruck at her knowledge and finding his "secret" on every tongue, the prideful Rae went wild. He swallowed a large dose of paregoric as a starter; then, fearing its lack of potency, blew his brains out with a pistol. That was on January 19th, 1845.

With his death the Hudson's Bay Company decided to retire from California. Another manager was sent down to Yerba Buena, the business was closed, outstanding debts collected, and the property sold. Auspiciously begun, the venture had fizzled out. Why another agent was not appointed to carry on in Rae's stead was never determined. Perhaps the attendant scandal was a factor in their decision. Doubtless, the great fur corporation had adequate reasons for the withdrawal but they are not of record.

Sutter remarks that Rae had been occasionally morose. At one time, during a visit of the Swiss to Yerba Buena, the two were talking.

"A fine day to cut one's throat," the Scotchman had remarked gloomily.

"He did not smile as he said it," recalls Sutter.

Chapter XXVII

THE REAPING

NEW SWITZERLAND crops of 1845 gladdened John Sutter's heart, put warmth into his soul, vigor into his stride. Reading had followed instructions. Much seed had been planted in the rich soil, despite the owner's absence.

In June the wheat was high, golden, well-headed, swaying with a symphony all its own in the valley breeze. The Captain stamped delightedly about, directing, encouraging. Half-a-thousand strong, his motley crew bent to the reaping. Even his infantry and cavalry Indians fell from military dignity to perspiring labor.

Some of the scythes they used were heavy enough for the colter of a breaking-up plow. Sickles were so massive that a strong man could barely swish the blade with one muscular arm. Some had butcher-knives; others had only cutters which resembled sickles, wrought from iron barrel hoops by the Indians themselves. A few without implements merely pulled the wheat out by the roots; others broke the dry, brittle straw with their hands. When those hands grew tortured and mutilated by the sharp stalks, willows were laboriously split and the keen sides of the wands used to slash off the standing grain.

Laban was an old Indian harvester who served John Sutter for long years. Six feet and a half high he stood, a giant—grave, superbly muscled, impressively patriarchal. He worked solemnly with a colossal scythe of Teutonic origin. To this he had attached a snath, cut from the undergrowth of the Sacramento's banks.

The old fellow amused John Sutter, was one of his favorites. So untiring, so faithful, so grimly bent upon his task, the ancient was.

"Father Time himself," chuckled the Swiss. "Laban works just as persistently as that eternal reaper."

And, ever after, Laban was Father Time to all.

AFTER THE GRAIN was cut it was borne from the fields by groaning *carretas*—two-wheeled carts—to the *eras*. These threshing floors of redwood planks were the best in the state; in fact, the only ones. All the Mexicans threshed their crops on hard-packed clay ground. Not so the lord of New Helvetia.

These *eras* were bulwarked by an eight-foot-high fence of redwood planks. A gate led inward upon the wooden floor. From the carts the grain was thrown to a two-foot depth on the smooth-planked surface.

Then a *manada* of breeding mares was turned into the soft-carpeted area. Indian vaqueros drove the animals in a dashing circle over the grain. Sharp, drumming hoofs slashed and beat at the straw beneath. Around and around rushed the plunging *manada*, dizzy, snorting, clamorous, the cloud of straw-dust above the *eras* shimmering like a golden mist in the sun.

After a five-minute period the riders cut in front of the galloping mares. Discordant yowls came out of their throats. The equine threshing machines tried to halt, almost trampling the vaqueros underfoot. Velvet ears laid back, teeth were bared, churning legs stiffened, the entire herd skated. Bottom-side up turned the straw in that sliding progress.

Eyes wild, the mares turned, began to run madly in the opposite circle. Again and again, at intervals, the maneuver was repeated.

In an hour the grain was threshed, the straw shredded into chaff.

Then came the tedious winnowing process. No fanning mills existed in California. Only when a strong wind was blowing could this winnowing be done. Sometimes it took a month's time to winnow an hour's threshing.

The operation was simple. Shovelfuls of the flattened mixture were thrown as high as brown arms could toss them into the breeze. Away whipped the chaff in the wind; the heavier kernels fell more vertically downward. Fortunately for Sutter, a reversible breeze occurred with some regularity during the threshing season.

After the separation the kernels were placed in granaries near the mule-driven flour-mill. Out of the crude mill finally came a well-ground flour. From flour to ovens was a speedy sequence; from ovens to hungry mouths was an even swifter one. . . .

But enough grain was left over to send a sizeable cargo back on the Russian brig *Baikal* in October. It was the first shipment of any magnitude that Sutter had found possible to make.

The gardens were treasure-troves of luscious berries and swift-growing vegetables. Indian squaws labored each day, tending the long rows and loamy beds with placid patience, listening heavy-lidded to the white gardener's instructions. Continually, they irrigated the growing things with water carried from the near-by pond at the fort's rear; long files of water-laden natives could be seen, hour after hour in the summer months, going from bayou to garden, from garden to bayou. Lettuce, carrots, potatoes, peas, cabbage, parsnips, beans, melons —every succulent offering in season came out of the valley floor to present its sustenance to John Sutter's empire.

THERE EXISTS an unpublished, day-to-day chronicle of events which occurred in New Helvetia from September 9th, 1845, to May 25th, 1848. It is the so-called Sutter Diary. From the certificate at the end, written by John Bidwell and William F. Swasey, one reads that the Diary was kept by John Bidwell from September 9th to 27th, 1845; by Swasey from September 27th to October 5th, 1845; by both men from October 26th to December 10th, 1845; by Bidwell and William N. Loker from

December 11th, 1845, to December 9th, 1846; and by Captain John A. Sutter exclusively from May 20th, 1847 to May 25th, 1848.

Almost sternly pastoral, this record; brief, without comment. Stained and discolored with much thumbing, the document tells its story. Here run a few excerpts from the year 1845:

October 1st. Harry Trow's wife was delivered of a girl. A large party left for the mountains. Baptiste Ruelle and a number of Spaniards arrive from Sonoma with cattle.

October 3rd. Victor Prudon left for Sonoma. Pierson B. Reading left with the hunters on their trapping excursion. The wind continues from the north, quite cold.

October 7th. William Sublette of St. Louis and party arrived from the United States. They report sixty wagons in the mountains bound for this place. This evening a wagonload of lumber arrived from the Pine Woods.

October 13th. This morning the weather is cold, cloudy. Looks very much like rain. Have laid foundation of new house before the east gate of the fort. Commenced laying out a ditch to enclose a pasture, adjoining the Sacramento River. Arrived the launch and Captain Liedesdorff from Yerba Buena bringing letters from below.

October 15th. The Russians came today. They brought one of Mr. Reading's trappers with them as a pilot. Commenced Perry McCoon in service. He started for Hock Farm to mark cattle and attend to other duties. He is to receive $2 a day. The Russians started below and took letters, etc.

October 17th. The Lanchero Tokotchi was severely wounded by a blow on the head. It was delivered by a passenger who left in the launch.

October 20th. Arrived five wagons of the unfortunate emigrants. Engaged a number of them to work at the fort.

October 23rd. A meeting of the emigrants was called to discuss and consider the late news from the seat of government concerning the exclusion of foreigners from the country.

October 26th. Rained nearly all day, first rain of the year. Parota Berreyessa and Alviso left for their homes.

October 27th. Commenced Brown as cook. Commenced Dutton to take bread with Davis. Arrived the vaquero Luis from Hock Farm with a letter.

October 28th. Arrived two Russian boats. Bake oven fell down. White-washed the doctor's room.

October 29th. Wagons were hauling wheat to the landing for the Russians. Arrived an Indian and for misconduct was flung into the calaboose. Started a wagon with ploughs for Hock Farm. Among the arrivals were Peter Lassen, Ezekiel Merritt and William C. Moon with grindstones.

October 30th. Started the Russian launches for Yerba Buena. Started Dennis Martin for Peralta's Redwoods. He takes with him three boys, Olel, Sholsia and Tomcha and is to pay them $12 per month each.

October 31st. Received of F. Davis one horse lent him. Delivered one hundred sheep to Peter Lassen. Skinner and Tustin were shingling the hatter-shop.

November 1st. Peter Lassen passed the sheep which he received yesterday over the American Fork. Bonney moved to the tannery. Arrived M. Myers, an apothecary, from below.

November 6th. Measured 118 *fanegas* of wheat for the Russians. Arrived Shadden and Frazier from Santa Cruz.

November 7th. Started the boat for Feather River. Launch is freighted and ready for sailing. Weather pleasant and warm. Quite a bustle in the fort today measuring out wheat for the Russians.

November 8th. The launch was incorrectly freighted. She grounded and the cargo had to come out of her. This has delayed her departure until tomorrow.

November 9th. Arrived General José Castro, Victor Prudon, Jacob Leese and Captain Castillero, Mexican

Commissioner, with an escort of fifteen men. Fired a salute of seven cannon in their welcome.

November 10th. Departed General José Castro and party. Arrived the whaleboat with Maintop (Kanaka).

November 18th. Measured 95 *fanegas* of wheat for the Russians. James Smith whipped one of the vaqueros this morning.

November 22nd. Commenced loading launch with wheat, 250 *fanegas* for the Russians, also 584 pounds of ship's bread. Launch left at 6 P. M.

November 24th. Arrived a whaleboat from Yerba Buena with a letter from Larkin to the emigrants. Started William Johnson, commanding the launch *Lady Drinkwater*, for Feather River with four lancheros.

November 28th. Started Captain Sutter to meet the whaleboat at the old *rancheria*, bound for Yerba Buena. Mill broke today and was repaired. Samuel Neal was at work all day on C. Heath's auger. A. Sanders was at work all day making bridle-bits. Two carts were hauling wood. Sent for shingles that were detained at Allen Montgomery's.

November 29th. Collected the mares and horses. Sent a vaquero to sleep out and bring in the horses and mules. Sent for the milperos (millstones). Mr. Block brought two hats. Sanders made an iron for himself; also a wagon tire for Briant and fixed a shovel plough for Marshall. Samuel Neal finally finished Heath's auger. Then he worked on buckles for Perkey the rest of the forenoon.

December 2nd. Removed 68 sides of sole leather from the tannery; also 45 sides of saddle leather. Sent one cart to bring timbers for pump cylinders and gate posts. George Davis being sick, Dutton commenced to make bread in his stead. Wilson was picking mill-stones. Arrived Mr. McKenzie from the Cosumne.

December 3rd. Arrived the schooner *Sacramento* from Yerba Buena. She brought one barrel of oil. Wagons busy all day freighting the launch. Sent the boat to Hock Farm with 1000 pounds of dried meat.

December 4th. Sent the launch with 289½ *fanegas* of wheat, this being the remainder of the wheat assigned to the Russians.

December 5th. H. O. Briant and McDonald commenced digging out the well. Dixon and Ide continued to work on the fence. Skinner hung the door to the cooper shop.

December 6th. Continued to clear out the well. Three blankets were finished. Seven ploughs going all day. Sent two carts for firewood. The mill was idle all day because the bands broke. McDowell stocked a gun for Samuel Neal. Lehy made a barrel for O. Beaulieu.

December 8th. James Smith sowed wheat. Stanley continued ploughing. Neal made a crank for J. L. De Schwartz and commenced making an iron for Bird. Skinner finished the wooden frame for the grindstone. Briant and McDonald worked at the well. The Indians did not come to work today.

December 9th. Went to tannery and divided leather. Arrived Wolfskill and McMahon from the Pueblo de Los Angeles. Samuel Neal was making hinges.

December 10th. Arrived Captain Frémont.

December 11th. Dixon and Briant finished the fence. Sent to get the horses and mules together to see if some could be found for Captain Frémont.

December 12th. Delivered 14 mules to Captain J. C. Frémont. Briant went chopping wood by the cord. Very dusty, disagreeable weather.

December 13th. Finished sowing the large field with wheat. Started Captain Frémont to the south. Commenced making a pen for the pigs. A. Bruheim was occupied in castrating a few hogs.

December 15th. MacVickers and George Davis fought. The Kanakas made a hog pen. A. Briant was hauling wood for the coalpit. Homo Bono went to the Mokelumnes to call in the shoemakers.

December 16th. Neal and Sanders hard at work on the pump-irons.

December 21st. Rained today. William Lewis and Miss Casey were married by Captain Sutter.

December 22nd. Sent thirty sides of sole leather to John C. Davis by the launch; 10 sides of sole leather and three sides of upper leather for John Williams; and four sides for Mr. Thomes.

December 23rd. Neal, Buzzell and others were sent to chase the Indians who stole cattle last night.

December 24th. C. Heath finished the pump.

December 25th. Captain Lansford W. Hastings arrived from the United States. The people were enjoying a happy Christmas. Buzzell was back and busy trying to raise some volunteers to go against the Indians.

December 26th. Buzzell started again with 8 more men after the cattle thieves.

December 28th. George Cook was today married to Miss Rebecca Kelsey by Captain Sutter.

December 29th. Perry McCoon moved and took possession of his fine new place at the Hog Farm. He received his title to the above-mentioned tract.

December 30th. Captain Sutter and Hastings went up to John Sinclair's.

December 31st. Mr. William F. Swasey received his discharge. Arrived Samuel F. Hensley and Robert Semple as passengers on Cordua's boat.

So ENDS THE Diary entries for 1845—the unembellished, skeletonized synopsis of a wilderness outpost passing into empire.

Chapter XXVIII

THE COMING OF CASTILLERO

T
HE REVOLUTION of 1845 brought no tranquillity
to California. With Pio Pico as Governor and
Castro as *comandante general*, Alvarado was backwashed
into the post of administrator of customs at Monterey.
This was bitter brew for the ex-governor. Another in-
novation incensed the northern Californians—the capital
was moved to Los Angeles.

Conditions were summed up by John C. Jones, United
States consul at Honolulu, in a letter to Larkin: "I have
just returned from the Pueblo (Los Angeles). They are
all at loggerheads there. Pio Pico is most unpopular.
José Antonio Carrillo, in my opinion, is endeavoring to
supplant him. The present government of California
cannot exist six months; it will explode through spontaneous combustion."

Waddy Thompson, former United States Minister to
Mexico, was uncertain as to what was about to happen.
"I have been asked," he wrote, "as to what would
occur after a successful foreign revolution in California.
. . . California is literally a waif and belongs to the first
occupant. Captain Sutter is the real sovereign of the
country, if anyone is. I have no doubt that his force
would be more than a match for any Mexican army sent
against him. . . ."

John Sutter made a crucial decision in the latter part
of the year. It meant much to his personal fortunes; and
much more to the Americans who were his friends and
associates.

"Late in 1845," relates Bidwell, "Andres Castillero,
a commissioner from Mexico, arrived in California. He
came on a peaceful mission after Micheltorena's expulsion, a contemporaneous revolution in Mexico having
similarly swept a new administration into power. This

same envoy had been in the province on previous peaceful missions; this time he had come to reconcile and cement the new order in California with the new order in Mexico.

"Castillero was a happy choice of the Mexican government for his task. He was intelligent, kind, dignified, and so conciliatingly cordial that he held the confidence of everyone.

"He first visited Pio Pico at Los Angeles, then came up the coast through Santa Barbara, Monterey, Yerba Buena and finally coming to Sutter's Fort on November 11th.

"It was while General Castro was guiding Castillero north with a small military escort that a rumor swiftly spread asserting Castro's real purpose to be a march on New Helvetia. That sent me post-haste from Yerba Buena to warn Sutter of his danger.

"In fact, Sutter did not learn of the Castillero party's arrival until they approached within a short distance of the fort. Jacob Leese, Victor Prudon, Salvador Vallejo and a dozen soldiers made up the escort.

"When the visitors were first sighted a runner came breathless to the fort and cried that Castro had come at last to attack. There was great excitement at the moment.

"Men were sent down at once to make observations. Discovering the small force and friendly intentions of the visitors, word was sent back to Captain Sutter.

"Canoes were sent to ferry the visitors across the river. . . . All were very cordial with Captain Sutter. . . .

"It was almost impossible for Castillero to discuss anything with Sutter in private. Castro was so jealous of the Commissioner that it was very hard for the latter to see Sutter without an additional listener. . . . He did, however, catch a moment now and then. . . and in undertones signified to Sutter that he had done right in his efforts to sustain Micheltorena; Castillero also counseled him to support the party in power during any future revolutions. . . ."

But the officials had a mission beyond that of a mere friendly inspection of the Swiss' domain. If Mexico was not strong enough to acquire Sutter's empire by force of arms there were always other plans. Yet even Sutter was to be surprised by this one.

An hour after their arrival the party gathered formally in Sutter's quarters—Castillero, Castro, Leese, Prudon, Salvador Vallejo and the curious Captain. Something was in the air. Its nature their host was unable to determine.

Finally, Castillero set his half-emptied brandy-glass upon the table. His voice took on vibrancy. "Captain Sutter," he said enthusiastically, "I have a very advantageous offer to place before you—a magnificent offer." Mexican heads nodded approvingly in the circle.

The Swiss bowed his head amiably as he sat in the chair; and said nothing.

Closer the envoy leaned with a bright assurance. "I am authorized by the Mexican government to offer you the sum of *one hundred thousand dollars* for New Helvetia or" —he paused slightly— "the Mission lands of San José in their entirety in exchange for your grant."

He sat back, a smile of surety on his face.

Now Sutter had absolutely no idea of selling New Helvetia. The offer itself was an amazing thing. All of John Sutter's hopes were concentrated in those lands. Nor did he wish to exchange the site for that of another.

Well he read the reason for the honey-voiced Castillero's presence. John Sutter held the key to California in his wilderness stronghold. The nation which possessed Sutter's Fort would in time possess all the golden province. And John Sutter wanted the American flag to fly over all this land. . . .

He shook his head. "No, gentlemen, New Helvetia is not for sale. . . . Too much energy has gone into its building. . . . This is excellent brandy, Don Andres. May I fill your glass again?"

Don Andres' face lost its sureness. The circle lost its collective smile. . . . But the talk of purchase persisted. Surely this gringo-lover would not refuse such a sum. It was incredible—not to be understood. *Basta!* the man must be *loco!*

Still the talk did not budge the single-purposed Swiss. He smiled and soothed and deprecated; and filled the brandy glasses. But never did he speak an affirmative. . . .

Hours later his guests were escorted to their quarters, unsatisfied, volubly astounded. But they had made no impression on the obstinate ruler of the fort.

AFTER THE OFFICIALS had retired, Sutter gathered his principal retainers about him—Bidwell, Reading, Hensley, and Loker. In a few brief sentences he told them of the offer; but not his decision.

Concern grew on all four faces in the candlelight. A magnificent offer, yes—it *was* a colossal sum for those days—but these Americans were fearful of another issue. With Sutter's Fort in Mexican hands what would it mean to all Americans—all foreigners in the valley?

"What will become of us?" they finally asked.

"Do not be alarmed," said John Sutter. "I have no urge to accept the offer. We are bound together for a common purpose and protection here. Gold will never be the price of this land. . . . But their offer is astounding, is it not?"

Into the black hours they talked. . . . Then each went his separate way, his mind secure against a doubt.

"Gold will never be the price of this land," the Swiss had said. And believed it.

In the morning he fired a salute of seven guns as his guests departed. He even consented to ride with them as far as the Cosumne, a distance of some twenty miles.

"We had not proceeded a mile from the fort," relates Sutter, "before we saw a great troop of horsemen galloping swiftly after us. They were fifty men in all, under Hensley's command.

" 'What is all this?' cried Castro uneasily.

" 'Only some of my men,' I replied casually. 'They would have followed us sooner had they been able to get their horses ready.'

"The fact was that Hensley and the others were much alarmed to see me ride away, seemingly in the hands of my enemies. Their fear was that I might be kidnapped and carried off into Mexico, thus giving the Mexican government a chance to occupy the fort on their own terms.

"I had no such apprehensions; neither had Bidwell. We understood the Spanish temperament better than the others.

"I returned home in the afternoon and my late guests continued on to their destination. . . .

" . . . That same evening, while I was sitting alone in my quarters, I had a visitor. A surprising visitor. It was Victor Prudon—returned.

" 'Consider,' said he eagerly, 'our new offer. I am authorized by General Castro and Don Andres Castillero to guarantee you, in addition to the hundred thousand dollars, all the lands and herds belonging to the Mission San José—all for New Helvetia!'

"I knew well why Prudon was sent. He was regarded as an old friend who had much influence with me.

"He asked me further if I was afraid I would not get my money. The Mexican government was poor pay, he admitted; but in this instance my remuneration was sure. They would tender me a good sum down and orders on the customs house for the balance.

"All this they would have done—even to giving me more—had I asked it. For they were most anxious to secure possession. But I again declined. . . ."

His scheme defeated, Victor Prudon followed his companions at dawn. Within a week at San José, Castillero was shown a heavy, reddish rock, a mineral that had been known to the Indians and long used by them to paint their faces for warlike expeditions. The Californians had often tried to smelt this rock in a blacksmith's fire, believing it to be silver or some other precious metal. But Don Andres recognized it as quicksilver, noting its resemblance to the cinnabar of the Almaden mines in Old Spain.

At once a company was formed to exploit the mine. It was named New Almaden and was principally owned by Alexander Forbes, Castro and Castillero. The first man to work the mine for them was W. G. Chard. . . .

So 1845 drew to a stormy close. Uncertain days loomed. Yet Sutter was content. He was master of the Sacramento, and meant to remain so.

Chapter XXIX

THE PRINCE OF BLUNDERERS

Tʜᴇ ʏᴇᴀʀs had fled past John Sutter like scud whipped by a hurricane. For more than a half-decade he had sought this site of empire; now he had lived there nearly seven years. Twelve years now since he had left his loved ones to quest in the New Land. . . .

One night in January, 1846, the Swiss sat alone in his quarters, alone with thoughts that even come to self-sure adventurers. Another month and he would be forty-three years old. . . . Anna and the children. . . . Young Johann must be—why, he must be nineteen years old now.

"My son a man grown," muttered John Sutter.

The fire crackled in the fireplace and gave him body-warmth against the night chill. . . . It was incredible, this passing of Time, this coming of Change. . . . Anna, too, must be older. . . . And Anna Elisa must be eighteen—a woman.

"She was like her mother," he murmured, blue eyes on the leaping orange flames. . . . Emil Victor sixteen. . . . The baby, William Alphonse, fourteen. . . .

To the man in the redwood chair came a sudden savageness of hunger. That hunger had always been there. But the fierceness of struggle for survival had blanketed it; that and the lack of funds to satisfy it. More than anything he wished to have his family with him. . . . He needed them, wanted them to share in this empire that was now so surely his.

"Only the money stands in the way," he groaned. "*Ach Gott*, but for that—"

Long he sat, hunched forward, eyes sombre. He was adventuring back old paths which all adventurers tread when the years have stolen away the fires of youth.

With swiftness he stood up, snatched up a candle-holder, lit its tallow column in the flames. Then he set it down on the table and feverishly placed a sheet of paper under its glow. He began to write swiftly. The ink traced its message with smoothness and precision. John Sutter was writing an important letter.

JOHN CHARLES FRÉMONT was not long to remain away from New Helvetia. "In January," writes Sutter, "I was visited by Captain Liedesdorff, U. S. Vice-Consul, and William A. Hinckley, Captain of the Port, the latter in his provincial uniform.

"They wished to make a personal survey of a certain spot on the American River where Liedesdorff wished to select a grant. Dressed in my Mexican Colonel's uniform, I escorted them at their request.

"Proceeding only a mile or so beyond the fort, we came upon a new camp. My eyes fell first upon Kit Carson.

" 'Where is Captain Frémont?' I asked him in great surprise.

" 'In the tent, there,' he replied. 'He is very tired and not yet up.'

"I ordered him called. After greetings, I introduced my two companions and remarked that we were on a little expedition up the river. I also invited him to dine with me upon our return.

"He told me he had arrived late the previous evening, camped in the darkness, and would move his camp nearer the fort at once.

"This he did. On our return I ordered a salute fired and had a very excellent meal served in his honor. That night Frémont returned to his camp. In the morning my other two guests left for Yerba Buena."

THIS VISIT OF THE wandering topographer was on January 15th, 1846. Four days later he sailed with eight of his men to Yerba Buena on Sutter's launch. On the 24th he returned from the bay with the Vice-Consul Liedesdorff.

That same afternoon they left overland via San José for Monterey to consult with Larkin and reached the capital village three days later.

The Diary annals give an intimate glimpse into the pastoral tenor of John Sutter's valley in the first few months of 1846:

January 3rd. The son of Truman Bonney died last night. Started A. Bruheim with Theodore Cordua's boat for the Feather River. Also started Mr. Hayes to take charge at Mimal.

January 4th. S. F. Hensley started for Hock Farm, Wm. Johnson for Bear Creek. The funeral of the deceased young man, son of Truman Bonney, was held.

January 5th. James Murphy arrived with a few horses from the Cosumnes. Mrs. Allen Montgomery came to the fort. Dr. Robert Semple made a redwood chest for himself. An attempt was made to make up a school for Mrs. Nash.

January 6th. James Gilbert entered service guarding the pasture lands. Kampt, the blacksmith, made new hinges for the gate.

January 7th. The boat started for Feather River. Sanders and Briggs are making ploughs. Dr. Semple was at work on the mill but was taken sick in the afternoon.

January 9th. Went to the tannery and divided the last of the leather. The fourteen-year-old daughter of F. Scott died today. Vero started for Feather River and C. Heath for the mountains. The carpenter, Crosby, was discharged.

January 10th. C. Heath returned from the Cosumne, forced back by the high waters. Mr. Scott's daughter was buried. Chombidain bought spurs from John Bidwell. Kampt and Daylor had a fist fight. A business settlement was made with Grove C. Cook.

January 11th. James Smith, late *mayordomo*, married the widow Marshall today. The Kanakas and a number of Indians were imprisoned in the calaboose for fighting. The whaleboat came in from Feather River.

January 13th. Rained. The whaleboat started for Yerba Buena. Her crew, the *lancheros*, did not come. So she was detained at the Embarcadero.

January 27th. Captain Frémont arrived from below, being unsuccessful in his attempt to find the rest of his command. Captain Sutter, Liedesdorff and Hinckley rode up the American Fork. A salute was fired in Frémont's honor.

January 16th. Captain Hinckley and Liedesdorff departed for Yerba Buena. The evening is very stormy and Don Gildea is very sick.

January 17th. Last night a terrific gale blew the roof off the buildings in the southeast corner of the fort. Provisions were sent to Captain Frémont.

January 19th. Dr. Semple started in the whaleboat to Feather River. The launch started for Yerba Buena with Frémont and eight of his men.

January 22nd. Davis and Wm. Johnson were cutting poles for the fence. Captain Sutter and Lansford Hastings rode to the river. Macario, a vaquero, was thrown from his horse and severely injured. The child of Harry, the Kanaka, died. . . .

January 23rd. The child that died was buried today. Kampt, the blacksmith, did not work.

January 24th. Don W. B. Gildea died and was buried. The former at three o'clock A.M.; the latter at four o'clock P.M.

January 25th. Wm. L. Todd came from Cash Creek. Also three yoke of oxen from Daylor's. Pablino, an Indian, was put in prison. Samuel Neal was removing coal from the pit which fuel he burned.

January 26th. John Chamberlain was married to Miss Nancy Hess.

January 28th. William O'Fallon came from Feather River. Harry Trow went down the river to prepare stakes for laying out a town and marking the street boundaries.

January 29th. All the people attended the quilting bee at Mrs. Allen Montgomery's. Loker delivered 100 sheep to Captain Liedesdorff.

February 5th. Perry McCoon was married to Miss Lewis.

February 6th. Perry McCoon and his youthful bride retired to the banks of the Sacramento to spend their honeymoon.

February 7th. Captain Hastings and Bidwell finished laying out the townsite.

February 8th. A cold, windy day. Sumner came and got flour and squashes from George Davis.

February 9th. An invoice was taken of the personal effects and property of the deceased Don Gildea. Sent Daylor's oxen home.

February 13th. The boat left for Feather River. Baptiste Ruelle and F. Dupos went to prune the vines.

February 14th. Canuto, an Indian servant, broke into the room and took liquor without leave.

February 19th. Hubbard started below to trap. Boat came from Yerba Buena, H. Hoover master. Pulaski came to get wheat ground. Owens and McDonald finished the ditch which encloses the pasture. Reports say that no troops have arrived and that the country is about to be delivered up to the United States.

February 20th. Measured the ditch made by Owens and McDonald. The Indian boys who ran away were found and punished.

February 22nd. R. K. Payne married the widow Payne, daughter of O. Sumner.

February 23rd. Rainy. A. Sanders married Miss Bonney.

February 27th. Rained all day. Distillery was stopped.

February 28th. Measured the ditch which was repaired by Smith, Stebbins, and Company. The day was fair. The streams were high and the slough which passes the house was running from the American Fork to the Sacramento. Allen Montgomery came and took away his anvil.

March 5th. Received from the hatters all of the hats they have made to this date. Received of James Black 26 hats at $4 each, cash.

March 13th. Captain Sutter rode up the American Fork on important business.

March 21st. Arrived Captain Frémont and camped on the American Fork.

So RUNS THE RECORD. So went the daily grind of kingdom-building. Hard toil. Never-faltering persistency. Birth. Marriage. Death. And through it all, the promise of great events soon to fashion history. . . .

Frémont's movements are briefly interesting. Not until February 15th did he contact Kern and his missing party. With a combined force of sixty men he casually proceeded to saunter through the Santa Clara Valley without permission. Finally, he marched inland to Alisal and camped. By doing this he broke a definite pledge he had made to the authorities; he had assured them he would do no such thing.

Naturally, a military force parading about the interior under command of a United States Army officer occasioned stormy comment. Frémont's action oozes stupidity. At the same time he directed an insolent note to the governor in regard to a horse-stealing charge preferred against his men. To further add to the tumult, three of his men got drunk, forced their way into Don Angel Castro's rancho, behaved abominably with the lovely daughter of the house, and insisted upon her drinking with them. The natives became hourly more incensed at these interlopers on the provincial territory.

General Castro sent an order to the rambling mapmaker to leave the country. Frémont sent back a verbal refusal that was a challenge. After this hasty retort he scampered swiftly up the sides of Gavilan Peak, raised the Stars and Stripes, and thumbed his nose at the surrounding countryside.

Then Castro regretfully led a force of two hundred men against the holders of the Peak. But on the night of March 9th Frémont fled in the darkness. Back to Sutter's Fort he raced, arriving exhausted on March 21st. It was thus Sutter, Liedesdorff and Hinckley discovered him the next morning. . . .

For some days he moved restlessly about the valley, disgruntled because of his retreat, never staying long in one spot.

"No war had yet been declared," observed Sutter, "and Frémont acted most strangely with me, as if guilty of some crime or possessed of some secret beyond my knowledge.

"Every few days he would move his camp farther and farther up the valley.

"It was my earnest wish to befriend Frémont in every way at that time. . . . True, during his first visit I had made certain confidential admissions to him: I informed him that before Micheltorena's arrival I had been hindered and troubled persistently by the Californians and that I was determined, when the strength of my position warranted, to declare the independence of New Helvetia. I also informed him that if such a project were successful I immediately wished to annex this territory to the United States. . . . He said that he believed it could be done but that it must be decided by Congress. . . .

"Now Frémont's present conduct was mysterious. Flitting about the country with an armed body of men, he was an object of intense suspicion to everyone. While encamped at Peter Lassen's rancho he bought stolen horses from the Indians, giving five yards of calico or a few beads for each animal.

"Before Frémont left the valley this time, while he was still camped at Lassen's, I wrote him requesting that he return the stolen horses and not drive away property belonging to the valley settlers. He made no reply to this letter. I was an officer of the existing government at the time, a magistrate responsible for the welfare of the region, and I deemed it my duty to the men who rightfully owned the horses in question to enter this protest. This act Frémont never forgave me, after the manner of a child caught in some petty misdeed. . . ."

THE BEAR FLAG

Frémont started for Oregon on April 14th, 1846. Then Lieut. Archibald H. Gillespie was reported nearing the fort following hotly in his wake.

"One day," writes Sutter, "came a note by Indian messenger from Lieutenant Gillespie, then some ten miles away at an Indian *rancheria*, saying he would be with me at sunset. He arrived on schedule and eagerly inquired if I was aware of Frémont's present camp.

"I gave him directions and he then asked me for horses and a guide that would enable him to reach Frémont as soon as possible. He said he carried important dispatches from the United States Government. I gave him my favorite mule to ride, an animal I had paid $300 for, and this mule came back wind-broken and in pitiable physical condition. This was all the thanks or pay I received for my aid."

Sutter also sent Neal and Sigler ahead to locate Frémont and report to Gillespie. On May 1st the pursuing officer reached Lassen's. Then he pressed forward with five men. On the 9th he rode into Frémont's camp at high noon.

That night the merged parties were surrounded by hostile natives and barely escaped with their lives. The savages seemed friendly and no guard had been set. Leaving three men dead behind them, the topographer's company returned to Lassen's. On May 24th they camped at the Buttes.

A packet containing private correspondence from Senator Benton, Frémont's father-in-law, was one of the secret charges of Gillespie. What instructions Frémont received—if any—have never been ascertained. Evidently, his previous Washington instructions "to act at your own discretion" were amplified. At all events he hurried back to the Sacramento.

Top: James W. Marshall
Bottom: John Bidwell

DIARY ENTRIES for April, May and June are few:

April 7th. Daylor was fined $5 for assaulting Hess.

April 8th. L. W. Hastings was appointed executor of Don B. Gildea's estate.

April 13th. Arrived Pierson B. Reading and trappers from below.

April 22nd. Governor Don Pio Pico arrived from the Pueblo de Los Angeles.

April 23rd. Departed Pico and his escort for the Pueblo.

May 6th. Arrived Wm. O'Fallon and T. Breckenbridge from the Pueblo de Los Angeles.

May 11th. Perry McCoon and wife arrived from the Cosumne.

May 12th. Perry McCoon and wife to Hock Farm.

May 14th. Captain Sutter to Hock on business.

May 17th. Captain Sutter returned at midnight last night.

May 21st. James Wilson Marshall arrived from Hock.

June 3rd. Captain Sutter started on a campaign against the Mokelumnes. John Bidwell came from Hock.

June 5th. Began cutting barley.

June 7th. Captain Sutter returned with his party from a successful campaign.

June 24th. The young wife of Perry McCoon died at sunrise and was buried at sunset.

SUTTER PONDERED each phase of the speeding drama. Beyond New Helvetia a chaotic disintegration threatened always. Political dog-fights offered spacious battle grounds. Quarrels were continual and pointless. Pico and Castro invited trouble with puppish enthusiasm; there was strife between military and civil dignitaries; North and South transfixed each other with cobra-eyes; Castro squabbled with Alvarado about the treasury and customs-house receipts; the Governor wrestled all comers in the provincial assembly at Los Angeles. Besides this internal bickering the ever-active threat of foreign invasion was present. "A very hot stew," said Sutter, in summation. And it was.

In the midst of the uproar came a swift blast that rocked the Californian landscape. It was the investing of Sonoma and the capture of four important men—General Vallejo, his brother Salvador, Colonel Victor Prudon and Jacob Leese. This was accomplished by a group of American filibusterers under Frémont's control, if not under his actual orders.

This blunder would not have occurred but for Frémont's meddling. The so-called Bear Flag Revolt was ill-advised, as were nearly all of Frémont's actions. It achieved nothing. Without the capture of Sonoma it is logical to presume that the American flag would have waved over California without bloodshed. As long as personal safety and property rights were guaranteed most of the natives would have accepted United States rule with equanimity, even gladness. The great majority of the *Californios* were fed up with the constant Roman candle display; a change with permanence assured was to be welcomed and not defied. But the high-handed Sonoma incident was to cost the United States dear; save for that senseless seizure the province might have been annexed peaceably and without military effort.

"The floating population about the fort," writes Bidwell, "outnumbered the settlers three to one. This floating element consisted of trappers and hunters. They had no intention of settling permanently in the region; they were just camping about the Sacramento Valley. These floaters had all to gain and nothing to lose if war came. It was no uncommon thing to hear an imprudent man express a longing for hostilities so they might have a chance to plunder the Mexican ranchos and drive off the stock to Oregon.

"Seeing Gillespie in pursuit of Frémont made this gentry curious as to his message. When Frémont returned, members of the floating population were always in his camp on the look-out for news.

"Frémont reached the Butte Mountains, then known as Sutter's Buttes (now called the Marysville Buttes), early in June. Soon the curious hunters and trappers found their way to him. There may have been some few permanent settlers in that first number who went under Frémont's orders to Sonoma. But I doubt it. The great majority were floaters and trouble-makers.

"While Frémont was camping at the Buttes a band of one hundred and fifty horses was sent from the north side of the bay by way of Sacramento on their way to the south side. There was, in fact, no other way to transport the animals without crossing the bay or the Straits of Carquinez. There wasn't a ferry boat in California at this period. Team horses in small numbers—or even cattle—might have been ferried in launches; but the procedure would have been slow, perilous, and expensive. . . . It was said that most of the horses belonged to the Mexican government. At any rate, Lieutenant Francisco Arce was in charge of the *caballada*.

"Arce brought his horses past Wm. Knight's place and rode up the western bank of the Sacramento to Sutter's Fort. Knight at once went to Frémont's camp with news of Arce's passing, Sutter, as usual, entertained Don Francisco and his men with the same courtesy he showed to all.

"The next morning Arce left Sutter's Fort and reached the Cosumne River, some fifteen miles distant. Frémont, without sending men of his immediate command, dispatched a number of the floating population to capture the horses. This was accomplished, including the seizure of Arce and his escort. This was in reality the first act of war. Arce and his companions were shortly released and allowed to depart. They spread their tale with great vigor.

"Captain Sutter was amazed to hear of the event. He thought some irresponsible individuals—judging from those who had taken part in it—had been responsible on their own account, possibly to secure horses to take into Oregon.

"Being the chief authority, both civil and military in the region, Sutter denounced the theft of the horses in no uncertain terms. This was reported to Frémont's ears by one of Sutter's enemies.

"For Captain Sutter, kindest and most generous of men, still had enemies. There were those about him who had lived for years on his bounty, without charge; men who had incurred debts with him until he had little more to give. Then, when he was in no present condition to aid them further, they turned against him like venomous snakes.

"It was men of this despicable sort who carried word of Captain Sutter's indignation to Frémont. . . ."

THE AFTERMATH of Arce's loss was the end of the Mexican flag at New Helvetia. "The day after seizing the horses," relates Sutter, "Frémont and his entire force made their appearance before the gates of the fort. Merritt and Kit Carson were with him, also many of the hunters and trappers.

"They came and went at their pleasure, Frémont camping a mile or so up the American River. Naturally, he regarded me as an ally. By the simple act of throwing open my gates I renounced my allegiance to the Mexican government and declared myself for the United States.

"Frémont knew that I was loyal to him. And every-one else knew it. Yet despite this, he appeared somewhat shy of me, although we had no words.

"Seeing his actions, I remarked to Kit Carson in a wondering manner: 'Captain Frémont seems decidedly unfriendly.'

" 'Remember your letter about his buying stolen horses from the Indians,' answered Carson meaningly. After which he said no more.

AFTER THE MEXICAN *caballada* was despoiled and the mounts apportioned among his men, Frémont counseled the trouble to a head. Without his personal leadership, he dispatched the original Bear Party to Sonoma. Thirty-three men made the attack, led by Ezekiel Merritt. They reached Sonoma at dawn, June 14th, 1846.

Vallejo was aroused to discover his home surrounded by a band of leather-shirted trappers, raucous in the sunrise. Uncouth, unkempt, they were, blatantly begging for trouble—or so Semple, one of their number, himself describes them. "We were as rough a lot of men as you could imagine," he confesses.

The General, Salvador, Prudon and Leese were made prisoners. William B. Ide remained with twenty-four men to garrison the place. Then Semple, Knight, Merritt, Hargrave and Grigsby left with the bound quartet, all riding on horses selected from Vallejo's corrals.

In three days they delivered their charges to Frémont on the Sacramento. The unsmiling map-maker ordered their detention in Sutter's Fort.

"When the prisoners arrived at the fort," wrote Sutter, "I placed them in my best rooms and treated them with every consideration. I did not approve of these arrests; they savored to me of a futile show of impolitic force. I could see nothing to be gained. . . . I thought it undiplomatic, to say the least. . . . They took their meals at my table and walked out with me in the coolness of the evening. . . .

"Their rooms were not guarded night or day, nor did any guard accompany us when we strolled. They were, however, secretly and closely watched by the handful of men whom Frémont had left in the fort as a military garrison. . .

"I deemed it wholly unnecessary to be severe in my treatment of these personages. I appreciated them as gentlemen under stress of misfortune. Also, they were men of property and substance; there was no danger of their attempting to escape. . . .

"A few days later, Frémont returned with an augmented military force, nearly two hundred in all. He complained I was treating the prisoners too courteously. His men recounted how I strolled with them and fed them at my table.

"He cried harshly: 'Don't you know how to treat prisoners, Captain Sutter?'

" 'Captain Frémont,' I answered calmly, 'I believe that I do. This is not a war of petty reprisal and these men have done you no personal hurt. I have been a prisoner of war myself and believe my conduct both wise and humane. Take charge of these men yourself—I wash my hands of their custody!'

" 'To whom shall I give them in charge?' he asked in a more moderate tone. 'Would your clerk be the man?'

" 'Mr. Loker is a gentleman,' I observed pointedly. 'You can trust him in any matter.'

"Shortly after this, Loker left and joined the newly formed California Battalion, since he did not like his job. Bidwell was next placed in charge of the prisoners. They had as much liberty under his care as under mine. In fact, Bidwell instructed Victor Prudon in the English language and Prudon taught Bidwell Spanish.

"It was my custom to visit the captives often and sit and talk with them. One day, Dr. Townsend warned me privately that if I continued associating with them on such friendly terms that my castle might become my prison. So I visited them no more until the American flag waved over New Helvetia. . . ."

ABOUT THIS TIME came a new and colorful personality to the Sacramento, destined to be a friend and associate of Sutter in the next few troublesome years. He was Lieutenant Warren Joseph Revere, an officer of the *Cyane*, and a grandson of Paul Revere. Talented, dashing, daring, he was the ideal military man of the moment. Montgomery sent him, in company with Dr. Henderson, on his first visit to Sutter's Fort. That was on June 26th, 1846.

With force and fervor young Revere wrote that same year of the wilderness stronghold and its master. "Emerging from the woods lining the banks of the river," he said, "we stood upon a plain of immense extent. It was bounded on the west by the heavy timber which marks the winding Sacramento, the dim purple of the Sierra Nevada appearing in the distance. Then we came to some extensive fields of wheat in full bearing, waving in the valley breeze like sea billows. For the first time we glimpsed the white-washed walls of the famous fort. It stood alone, in solitary state, on an eminence commanding the approaches on all sides.

"We were met and welcomed by Captain Sutter and the officer in charge of the military garrison. . . .

"Our approach and entry was arresting: crenulated walls, bastioned angles, fortified gateway loomed; all about were thick-bearded, fierce-looking trappers and hunters armed with rifles, bowie-knives, and pistols; their ornamented hunting-shirts and gartered leggings clung to steel-hard muscles; savage and dauntless they were, their long hair turbaned with colored handkerchiefs or coonskin caps. Wagons were creaking in, filled with golden grain and luscious fruits and vegetables. The arid yet fertile plains stretched away. *Caballadas* were continually driven across it by shouting Indian vaqueros, enveloped in clouds of dust; the swift horsemen darted helter-skelter in seemingly every direction. All these physical stimuli conspired to carry me back to the romantic East. I could fancy I was once again the guest of a powerful Arab overlord in his remote stronghold. . . .

"Everything bore the impress of vigilance and preparation; and not without reason. Castro was reported at Pueblo San José with a force of several hundred men, cavalry, artillery, and infantry; rumor had it that he intended to march upon the valley of the Sacramento.

"The fame of Captain Sutter and his fort is so extended that some account of that distinguished personage is in order. . . . With adventurous daring he resolved to take up his abode, alone and unsupported, in the midst of the savages of this frontier. At that time not a single white man inhabited the interior of California.

"I doubt if a more remarkable instance of individual energy, perseverance, and heroism has ever been displayed under similar circumstances. This unceremonious way of conquering a strange country and founding a sort of independent empire on one's 'own hook' is one of those feats which should stimulate the admiration and respect of posterity. In times past men have been deified on slighter grounds. . . .

". . . He was made military commandant of the frontier with full authority and absolute power—extending to life itself—within the limits of his jurisdiction. . . . He always had a most decided leaning toward his adopted country, the United States. Invariably, he hospitably received and entertained, even to his own detriment, such parties of Americans who came to his domain. I regret to add that many of our countrymen made but a poor return for his kindness and liberality.

"Finally, the Mexicans, seeing the Americans were settling the valley almost exclusively under his patronage—and being jealous of his great influence—endeavored to remove him peaceably. As an inducement to give up his border fortress he was offered the beautiful and improved mission lands of San José, near the Pueblo of that name, and the sum of $100,000; and proving their eagerness to get rid of him by actually providing security for the payment, a practice unknown in Mexican financiering, which generally consists of large promises conveniently forgotten. . . . But not an inch would Sutter budge from his stronghold, sagaciously looking forward with the eye of faith to the time when the United States would acquire possession of the province—a consummation which he devoutly hoped for and hailed with delight when it came to pass. . . .

"The fort consists of a parallelogram enclosed by adobe walls, eighteen feet high and a yard thick, with bastions at the angles. The walls of these towers are four feet thick and their embrasures are so arranged as to flank the terrain on all sides. . . . A good house sits in the center of the area, serving as officer's quarters, armory, guard and state rooms; also for a kind of interior citadel. There is a second wall on the inner face, the space between it and the outer wall being roofed and divided into workshops, quarters, etc. The usual offices are present; also a well of good water.

"Corrals for the cattle and horses of the garrison are conveniently placed where they are under the eye of the guard. Cannon frown—an inveterate habit of cannon—from the various embrasures. The ensemble presents the dreamer's ideal of a romantic border fortress. It must have astonished the natives as their hands, guided by the white man's skill, made the white walls rise out of the lovely virgin plain. . . .

". . . I found during this visit that General Vallejo and his companions were rigorously guarded by the 'patriots.' But I saw and had some conversation with him which, it was easy to see, excited a very ridiculous amount of suspicion on the part of his vigilant jailers. Their position, however, as revolutionists who yet lacked actual United States approval, was a little ticklish. It engendered in them that distrust which is inseparable from low and ignorant minds in dangerous days. . . . Indeed, they carried their doubts so far as to threaten to shoot Sutter for the capital crime of being polite to the captives."

MEANWHILE, FRÉMONT marched to Sonoma with ninety men, reaching that still-astounded hamlet on June 26th. Three days later, at Frémont's order, three Californians were shot down in cold blood. They were the de Haro twins, Ramon and Francisco, and the older José de los Reyes Berreyessa, owner of the Santa Clara Rancho. All were unarmed and approaching the Mission San Rafael, having lately landed from a small boat—

another instance of unnecessary cruelty and stupidity in a man one day destined to be a nominee for the Presidency of the United States. . . .

The fast-flying rumors of Castro's preparations to attack Sonoma were unfounded. He had fallen back to Santa Clara.

On July 1st the topographical expert and twenty of his men made a move upon San Francisco. Across to the old *castillo* they rowed in a ship's boat. Boldly wading through the surf they entered the garrisonless fort. Valiantly they proceeded to spike the rusty and useless ordnance discarded there. It is of record that not one of the mouldy cannon rose up and coughed even the slightest resistance.

Independence Day found the ravishers of the *castillo* burning gunpowder at Sonoma and dancing at a *fandago* in the evening. The next morning an agreement, written by John Bidwell who had recently arrived, was signed by all present. It was a simply worded document binding the signers to render military service until independence from Mexico was secured.

A California Battalion was formed from members of the Bear Flag Party and Frémont's men. It was continually augmented, also, by others trickling in from the Sacramento Valley. Some two hundred men were mustered. Divided into three companies under Captains Swift, Ford and Grigsby, all were subject to Frémont's command.

Grigsby, with fifty men, was left to garrison Sonoma. On July 6th, Frémont advanced to the Sacramento with the remainder, planning to sweep forward after Castro through the valley. Three days later the battalion reached Sutter's Fort.

Sutter placed all the supplies he could spare in Frémont's hands, even to turning over the famous "Sutter Gun" for the proposed campaign.

Robert Semple was one of Frémont's principal aides at the moment. The first time the jovial master of the fort had 'seen the six-foot eight-inch giant had been while Semple was in company with Bill Johnson, a four-foot ten-inch red-headed bantam. Sutter had surveyed the strange pair for a moment and then burst into laughter.

"By Jupiter!" he cried, "here's a man so tall that if he spread his legs apart Bill could run between them like a scared rooster!"

Semple was a "lanky, Kentucky-looking chap, dressed in greasy deer-skin hunting-shirt with trousers to match. These last ended just below the knee. They were fastened about his moccasins by a buckskin strap. He wore a coonskin cap and usually a grin. His long rifle was his treasure and he slept with it always beside him. . . ."

He was a remarkable fellow. More than ordinarily intelligent, he was an amiable soul. He could preach a sermon, edit a paper, preside at a justice's court, play a fiddle at a *fandango*, pull a tooth, smooth political squabbles, conduct a business equably, and was a fair lawyer, historian, physician and all-around tactician. While not busied by these varied accomplishments he was hunting a wife—a quest, by the way, which was never successfully concluded.

With Walter Colton he was to establish California's first newspaper on August 15th, 1846. His partner describes him "as sure with the rifle, ready with his pen, and quick at the type case." The idea of the publication was Semple's; the equipment was the primitive old press once owned by August Zamorano and sold by him years before to the Mexican government.

Sir Robert Peel, son of the then prime minister of England, visited California some months later in the *Collingwood*, a war vessel famous for its having on board so many scions of the English nobility. This young lord had heard so much of the famous frontiersmen that he made a special visit to Frémont's camp when that officer was present at Monterey for a few days.

There the Englishman fell into conversation with the ungainly Semple. After listening open-mouthed to an eloquent dissertation on English history he turned to an American bystander.

"If this man is a fair specimen of mountaineer you will soon own both the Americas," said young Lord Peel dazedly.

Chapter XXXI

YELLOW SERPENT

CAME COMMODORE SLOAT to the port of Monterey. For an entire week—from July 1st to July 7th— he dawdled in unhappy indecision. Where Jones had shown initiative, Sloat displayed spinsterlike uncertainty. He wished to act; yet feared to blunder.

The American and British squadrons had made faces at each other for months in every South American sea-city, hawk-alert in their efforts to see that the enemy fleet did not make the first move for California possession. The irresolute Sloat hoped to outthink and outact peppery Admiral Sir George Seymour. . . . Yet still he hesitated.

Finally, on July 7th, 1846, he occupied the town. But not until most of his junior officers had entered into a state of premature baldness over the delay. At 10:15 o'clock in the morning Old Glory floated over Monterey for the second time.

Forty-eight hours later Montgomery raised the same bright banner in San Francisco, its folds snapping proudly in the breeze above the public square before the customs house. No opposition was encountered in either town.

To the Sacramento came news of Sloat's act on July 10th. Next morning Captain Sutter raised the Stars and Stripes over the fort with window-crashing cannonading. Lieutenant Misroon had hoisted the United States colors over Sonoma, lowering the crude Bear Flag, on July 9th. America and Mexico were at war. The Bear Flag Revolt had come to an obscure end.

Frémont and the Battalion marched from Sutter's Fort against Castro on July 12th. Fauntelroy and a squad of dragoons were encountered at San Juan, having been sped on by Sloat. Above the ex-Mission Pueblo leaped the Stars and Stripes and Sloat's proclamation was read in Spanish and English.

A paragraph of that proclamation should be remembered. It read: "All persons holding titles, or in quiet possession of lands under the color of right, shall have these titles and lands guaranteed to them under the United States flag." Here an accredited representative of a nation made a pledge. . . .

Thus the last "town" in northern California came under United States domination.

FRÉMONT THEN MOVED on to Monterey. The energetic Commodore Stockton arrived on July 15th to supersede Sloat, who sailed for home two weeks later. A man of action, this Stockton. At once he made his plans to conquer the province.

The American situation was a precarious one. The conquest was in full stride; its prosecution had nearly exhausted every land force avilable; even the warships had been stripped of personnel until only skeleton crews remained. A possible clash with Great Britain loomed over the Oregon country. Captain Neil M. Howison and the *Shark* sailed for the Columbia River to better observe events and protect American interests in that quarter.

To acquaint Howison with the latest Washington intelligence on the acuteness of the Oregon wrangle and with news of California events was important. One of Stockton's first acts was to order an express sent to the officer in Oregon waters. Since no ship of the small fleet was available it was decided to send the message by land.

The duty of organizing the necessary post was given to Sutter and the garrison officer at the fort. Louis Rondeau and a small group were hired to carry the dispatches to Howison.

That expedition never reached the Columbia. Had they done so, they would have found the *Shark* a sunken wreck with the flag from her unsubmerged mast floating to the wind as the first American ensign raised in the Oregon country.

CASTRO AND PICO were finding the going a bit rough. With mutual accord they took flight from Los Angeles on August 10th and fled by separate routes to Sonora. Stockton and Frémont joined forces and wandered unhindered into the town. Not a shot was fired.

Stockton immediately put his ideas of organization into effect. Frémont was made military commandant of California. Monterey was chosen as the capital, an affront calculated to wound every southern Californian heart. Gillespie was stationed in Los Angeles with fifty men. Then Stockton sailed back to Monterey, arriving September 15th, well satisfied that his work was done.

Reorganization also took place in the north. Washington Bartlett was appointed alcalde at Yerba Buena. An election was held there which brought out an unbelievable voting strength of ninety-nine people!

During this period Frémont was returning overland to Sutter's Fort. One the way he stationed Lieutenant Talbot and nine men as a temporary squad to hold Santa Barbara. The conquest was over. Only a show of force was necessary. So thought the American leaders.

Then, out of what seemed surety, leaped disaster. A group of hot-heads among the southern Californians staged a revolt and drove out the overmatched Gillespie. Forced to evacuate Los Angeles, that dismayed officer embarked with all his men on the merchant ship *Vandalia* on October 4th.

Nearly every male Californian in the south now joined the new defection. The wildfire movement took on purpose—something new in *Californio* wars.

Back raced Frémont and Stockton to the lost area. As they sailed in haste, an old threat came to New Helvetia.

The gallant young Revere, lately appointed commander at Sonoma, tells a vivid story of that threat. "Upon reaching my quarters in Sonoma," he wrote, "I received a letter stating that the Sacramento Valley had been invaded by a force of one thousand Walla Walla warriors led by Yellow Serpent. The advance guard of two hundred warriors was reported encamped on the Rio de Los Plumas, within a day's march of the fort. . . .

"Starting without delay with my own troops of 'regulars,' I bivouacked that night after hard riding in the western *serrania* of the threatened valley. The next afternoon I arrived with my *caballada* and men on the banks of the great river.

"There we hurriedly fashioned pontoon rafts of the tule bulrushes, lashed together with horse-ropes. We crossed without difficulty and rode swiftly on.

"We reached the fort without meeting the hostiles. We were warmly received amid a preparatory bustle of defense. . . . Captain Sutter had called in all his savage Indians. By way of caution to evil-disposed persons the gateway of the fort had been ornamented with an Indian scalp, the long black hair hanging dejectedly down as if in deep mourning for the skull of its late proprietor.

"I speak lightly of this scalp because it had been the top-knot of an Indian who had been sent since my last visit —some said by Castro—to burn the wheat crops of New Helvetia and, if possible, to kill Captain Sutter himself..

"In trying to carry out his orders the warrior had met his death. That scalp flapped as a warning to deter similar planners.

"The hostile visitation had been expected for nearly a year. Elijah, a young Walla Walla chief, protégeé of the Oregon missionaries, had united in himself the vices of the white man and the Indian. He met his death while at Sutter's Fort. It was proven to my satisfaction that he was killed by Grove C. Cook, an American, in a private quarrel in which the savage was the aggressor; I also learned he had previously put to death one of his own tribe for some trifling offence.

". . . Yellow Serpent and his party rode up to the fort on fast horses. They were unarmed. The chief had

Mormon Island, the second place of gold discovery after the first strike at Coloma

come to have a talk. Dismounting, he entered alone through the gateway.

"He stood before Captain Sutter, Lieutenant Kern, and myself.

"'I have come,' he said, 'from the forests of Oregon with no hostile thoughts. You see I speak the truth. I am unarmed. With me are only forty warriors. With us are our squaws and children.

"'We have come to hunt the beasts of the fields and to trade our horses for fat cattle. I have yet another mission. It is the custom of my people to visit the grave of a warrior if he dies in a distant land. I have come to gaze upon the grave of my son Elijah—slain by a white man!

"'I have not traveled thus far to only mourn. Oh, Captain Sutter, I demand justice! The blood of my son calls for vengeance. You alone have the power to punish his murderer.

"'My purpose is now plain to you. When all my missions are accomplished I shall return to my own country, an old man full of sorrow. . . .'

"With a gloomy gesture Yellow Serpent turned, mounted his horse, and rode away.

". . . Although I was inclined to believe that the chief was peaceful, the occasion seemed favorable for a show of force to impress the neighboring tribes. Accordingly, I captained a party and rode as far as Sutter's Buttes. From there I went to Yellow Serpent's camp on the Feather River.

"He received us courteously and was evidently planning no mischief. In fact, half his party were ill with fever. . . .

"Most of my men, both white and Indian, including myself, caught the ague and fever from this visit up the Sacramento Valley. I think that this meanest of all diseases may be caught wherever the tule lands border the river. The decomposition of the short-lived tule upon these lands, during the overflow period, generates an infectious miasma which produces this malady. . . . "

So ENDED YELLOW SERPENT's heralded invasion. For a short time he lingered and then started back to his home. But on the march he attacked and killed a number of Oregon missionaries at a settlement. The reason given was Elijah's murder. So, if the brooding chieftain had chanced to catch Sutter's domain unprepared, white men would have died on the Sacramento plain. . . .

In August the four important Bear Flag prisoners were released by Stockton's order. Finis to a senseless incident. Back went Vallejo to Sonoma, accompanied by his friends. The only thing that the ex-general now wished was a speedy peace.

Young Edward M. Kern had been left in military charge of the fort's garrison. He was a young Philadelphia artist who had joined Frémont's third expedition and had been chosen to oversee the wilderness post during the conquest. Kern frequently begged Sutter to accept a commission under the United States flag and assume a military co-leadership with him.

Captain John Sutter had many reasons for being cautious in the matter. He was busy in guiding the commercial destinies of his valley: to accept a commission was to render himself liable to military duty during the entire campaign. He was but recently returned from such a venture. Now he was heartily—yet diplomatically— in favor of staying at New Helvetia and dedicating all his energies to the stretching leagues of empire. His presence was demanded every moment, his counsel given, his decisions made. He hesitated to place himself in the position of being ready for instant call from his work. There was much to be done.

Finally he bowed his head before Kern's persuasions. From Commodore Stockton he accepted a lieutenant's commission, the same rank as Kern's. Both men were working feverishly to keep the fort in order and drill the garrison.

UNCLE SAM'S FIRST MAILMAN in California was given his contract at Sutter's Fort in September 1846. It was necessary for official mail to be carried regularly between Sonoma and the Sacramento fortress during this stressful period of conquest; each post must be acquainted with the latest warlike news.

For that important service Adolph Bruheim was interviewed. For four years he had served the Swiss faithfully. He was twenty-five years old, dependable, a superb horseman, and he possessed an exact trail knowledge of the route to be traveled. At Sutter's insistence he was entrusted with the perilous task.

Bruheim agreed to accept $20 for the round trip. One night Sutter, Kern and the young German sat in the Swiss' quarters about the redwood table. A document lay before them.

With a flourish, Kern signed it for the United States Government. Bruheim traced his name slowly and carefully. No wafered seals of an ordered civilization were there. They sanctioned the historic contract with tiny seals fashioned with pen marks. The bargain was complete.

Up rose tall Adolph, dispatches ready in his hands for the waiting saddle-bags. The three shook hands. Sutter and Kern wished their courier good luck and a safe journey. The door closed behind him. Soon a horses's hoofs pounded out of the gateway into the darkness. It was September 10th, and it lacked an hour of midnight.

Uncle Sam's mailman was carrying the first official mail in California.

ON SEPTEMBER 23rd, Revere wrote to Kern from Sonoma:

"Dear Kern:

"I feel for your situation. Here we have been half drowned for the past few weeks. Impossible to stir out of the house on account of mud and rain.

"Please tell Captain Sutter that Olimpio did not know what to do with the money which he sent him. I advised him to give it to Don Guadalupe Vallejo for safe-keeping. He did so, I believe.

"I want your man—Sergeant James Smith, Captain Sutter's late *mayordomo*—to go out to my land. I will give him part of it, perhaps a section, if we can arrange his supervision.

"I have seen late Philadelphia papers of August and July. All right there—theatres, concerts, everyone amusing themselves. Ah! poor Californians that we are.

"Yours, & c
"Revere"

On October 17th, he wrote again, quite in a different tenor:

"E. M. Kern
"Fort Sutter.

"My Dear Sir:

"All lower California is in arms and Gillespie closely beseiged in Los Angeles. You will therefore, on the receipt of this order, immediately call *All Americans* to arms.

"The enemy threaten the lives of every United States citizen in this country. You must enlist as many men as offer themselves, ordering as many to Sonoma as you can spare from the sure defense of Sutter's Fort.

"The danger is imminent as a rising in the north is most seriously apprehended. Enroll all for the common defense since the enemy threaten our extermination.

"Disarm all Californians within your reach. Allow none to leave on journeys.

"Enlist all recruits for three to six months. Send, if possible, all who are willing to go to Pueblo San José. A garrison there is imperative.

"In haste, dear Sir

"Yours

"J. W. Revere

"Lieut. U. S. Navy

"Comdg. at Sonoma."

This letter was the first intimation Sutter or Kern received of the more serious resistance offered American occupation in the South. . . .

ONCE MORE the disillusioned Stockton reached San Pedro and sought to control the conflagration.

On December 4th came that hard-bitten campaigner, General Kearney, moving swiftly from Santa Fe, who reached the Santa Isabel Valley on that date. There Gillespie and thirty-five men joined him. These reënforcements trundled with them the "Sutter Gun," one of the Sacramento leader's contributions to the southern invasion.

Kearney came on even more swiftly with his new guides. At San Pascual, forty-eight hours later, he charged headlong into the army of Don Andres Pico.

That was the deadliest battle of the war. Twenty of Kearney's best men died with Mexican lances in their bodies; eighteen more were seriously wounded. Even Kearney and Gillespie were slashed deep by the vicious spear-heads. Captain Turner was forced to take temporary command.

It was a week before Kearney's column came winding down into San Diego streets. Not until the last day of the year was the commander physically able to march on Los Angeles. The Mexicans were developing an astounding stubbornness. . . .

Meanwhile, Frémont could find no horses at San Pedro or Santa Barbara. Back he sailed with the battalion to Monterey, arriving October 28th. Three weeks later he reached San Juan, reorganized his forces, and marched to Stockton's aid.

Mid-December found him at San Luis. Disdaining the easier Gaviota, he climbed the lofty Cuesta de Santa Ines by a difficult pass. Always a champion blunderer, Frémont. A storm caught his men in the defile; many sickened; some died. . . . It was after Christmas before his exhausted force sighted Santa Barbara. There he remained for a week to rest his troops. . . .

IN NOVEMBER an official report was rendered on John Sutter's empire of more than two hundred square miles in the Sacramento region:

Males, white	. . . . .	160	Females	. 47	Total	207
Males, Negroes	. . . . .	1	Females	. 0	Total	1
Males, Tame Indians	. . .	50	Females	. 15	Total	65
Males, Half-breed children	.	3	Females	. 7	Total	10

Grand Total		283

Cattle . . . . . . 20,000 head.
Horses . . . . . 2,500 head.
Sheep . . . . . . 2,000 head.
Hogs . . . . . . 1,000 head.
Mules . . . . . 70 head.
3 horse-mills; 2 water-mills; 1 saw-mill; 1 tannery; 60 houses; and Fort Sutter.

NEAR THE CLOSE of the year a young fellow named Bob Evans, hailing from Pike County, Missouri, was a resident of the fort. Glowing reports had been given him of the Willamette Valley, so favorable indeed that he had made up his mind to go to Oregon and settle.

He confided his plans to Isaac Spiker, a jokester of some pretensions, who had previously been in Oregon.

"Bob," said Spiker solemnly, placing his hands on Evan's shoulder, "I don't want you to go to Oregon and live with them Webfeet, no-how. I tried it wonst and I'm tellin' you, son, you better take some cheap advice and let well enough alone." He shook his head dubiously.

Bob was skeptical but interested. "I say," he queried, "why do you call them thar as lives in Oregon, Webfeet?"

Now Spiker, as a boy, had scalded one of his feet badly; when the foot healed his toes had grown together. Before him was now presented a rare opportunity.

"Bob," he said seriously, "after a man lives in Oregon a while his toes grow together from foot to nail. That's why he's called a Webfoot."

"I don't believe that thar yarn no-how," answered the stubborn Evans. "No, sir!"

Spiker drew off one of his boots. There was no illusion as to the genuineness of the exposed phenomenon.

"My God!" cried the aghast Bob Evans. "My God, I'll never go to that thar damned country no-how!"

DECEMBER 1846, brought an unsolvable mystery into being somewhere between Yerba Buena and John Sutter's *Embarcadero*. Captain Montgomery of the *Warren* dispatched a launch carrying cash to pay off the Fort Sutter garrison. On board were his two sons, John and William, and ten other men.

They never arrived. After several weeks, Robert Ridley was sent in another launch to explore both the Sacramento and San Joaquin. He found no traces of boat or men. It was his final opinion that crew and craft had been lost in a swift gale soon after setting out; other rumors said that the men had been killed by savages; some even suggested that the officers had been murdered by the crew and the money stolen.

Years later a report was current in newspapers that one of the missing men, Ladd by name, had been seen in New York. While intoxicated he had boasted that he and his companions murdered the officers, destroyed the boat, and fled with the money. But no definite proof was ever established.

A mystery it still is. One thing only is certain: Somewhere on the voyage disaster struck with fatal surety, whether by storm or human hands no living man may say.

Chapter XXXII

HUNGER

A PLENTIFUL rainfall tokened great things for John Sutter's kingdom at the beginning of 1847. Under the Swiss' eager eyes the dream was surely growing. Only the period of flux worried him. From day to day fresh dispatches brought contrary reports from the south. . . .

But Stockton's forces beat their way through the Californian defense. On January 10th he reoccupied Los Angeles. Gillespie raised the flag over his old quarters after a four months' absence. Bands played and colors fluttered. The hills were covered with curious spectators to view the pageant. Not a shot was fired during the investment.

Both Kearney and Stockton sent letters to the resting Frémont, informing him of the city's recapture. On January 14th Frémont and his battalion made their appearence in the pueblo.

All resistance ceased. A treaty was immediately drawn up and approved by both factions. The *Californios* were pardoned for all past hostilities, were free to go home after giving up their public arms—two cannon and six muskets, as it proved—and their pledge was given not to take up arms against the United States again. They were guaranteed protection and all the privileges of American citizenship.

Such generous terms were wise. The conquest of California was completed. It remained only for the new rulers to preserve order, regulate details of civil and military administration, quarrel among themselves, and await the completion of a national treaty.

JAMES F. REED first brought John Sutter news of the stricken Donner Party. Trapped in Sierra snows only a short distance eastward of the fort, Reed, who had come on ahead, carried the message of their dire necessity.

At once the Swiss packed ten mules with provisions and sent them with two of his best Indian vaqueros to their succor. This was in late January 1847. At this time Sutter and his aides believed that the emigrants would slaughter their oxen and ".hole-in" without undue hardships.

But ill-luck and lack of trail wisdom made a different tale of it. Halted at Truckee Lake, a terrific snowstorm had buried their oxen beyond recovery. Food was low and starvation came to the eighty-seven people of the blundering party—thirty-six men, twenty-one women, and thirty children.

On December 16th, 1846, a small group of the desperate emigrants made a last effort to break through to safety. They are known as The Fifteen. It was thirty-two days before their seven survivors finally descended into the valley and reached Johnson's rancho.

All their comrades who died on the fierce pilgrimage were eaten. Even Sutter's two Indians, Luis and Salvador, who brought them provisions shared the same fate. These vaqueros had run away when they suspected they might be harmed. Later the staggering ghosts of The Fifteen found the two weakened guides dying on the snow. At once they were shot to death and eaten.

When the survivors reached Johnson's rancho, they could not go onward to the fort. They were animals, glassy-eyed, bags of bones without a soul in them. Hunger had forced them to the half-world of the beast. . . . The Bear River was in flood and the whole Sacramento plain was a vast quagmire, forty miles wide. They huddled closely together, these pitiful seven, and clutched wolfishly at all food the heart-sick Johnson gave them. . . .

Meantime, Sutter had sent out a second expedition to aid the trapped unfortunates. The third day after the second party sloshed away with their pack-laden animals floundering in the ooze, Sutter received his first news of The Fifteen.

John Rhodes crossed the icy-cold stream of the Bear on two logs bound together with rawhides, struggled through the mucky quagmire of the valley on foot, sometimes waist-deep in the death-chilling floods. Looking like a child-made creature fashioned of mud he staggered slowly into the fort, bringing his bleak tidings.

In swift succession three more relief expeditions fought their way to the dying Donner band. Wiry Adolph Bruheim, Uncle Sam's first postman, led one; Kern another; William O'Fallon, the Irish trapper, the last.

Aquila Glover, one of the heroic Second Relief, kept a Journal of his company's daily progress to reach the emigrants:

February 13th, 1847. Today our party arrived at the Bear River Valley.

February 14th. Remained in camp, preparing packs and provisions.

February 15th. Left Bear River, traveled 15 miles, camped on the Yuba River.

February 16th. Traveled 3 miles, stopped to make snowshoes, camped on Yuba River. Snow 15 feet deep, dry and soft.

February 17th. Traveled 5 miles in 14 hours.

February 18th. Traveled 8 miles, camped head of Yuba River.

February 19th. Traveled 9 miles, crossed the summit of the California Mts. Reached part of the suffering company about sundown, in camp near Truckee Lake.

February 20th. People in terrible condition. Ten already dead. Others will die here in camp. Too weak to eat. Reached second camp, George Donner's 8 miles below first camp.

February 21st. Departed with 21 people, men, women, and children, for Sutter's Fort. All food we could spare left with the 29 remaining sufferers. We will return to them at once."

AN EXTRACT from a letter by George McKinstry, Jr. to Edwin Bryant gives a brief resume:
"The rescuers were successful in bringing all safely over the mountains. Four of the children were carried on their rescuer's backs; the rest walked. On arrival at Bear River Valley they met a small party with provisions, under Edward M. Kern, sent from this fort for their relief. The same day they met James Reed, with 15 men, on foot, packed with food, who ere this have reached the remaining sufferers.

"Lieutenant Wentworth was going ahead with an adequate force; he will visit the emigrants in their camp and bring them all out. Greenwood was three days behind Reed with horses.

"Kern will remain in camp, with the soldiers, to guard the provisions and horses. When the unfortunates arrive at this post they will be received by Captain J. A. Sutter with all the generous hospitality for which he is so justly celebrated. In the meantime Captain Sutter will keep up a communication with Kern's camp and will stand ready to assist in all emergencies.

"Mr. Glover informs me that the wagons belonging to the emigrants are buried fifteen feet deep under the snows. He thinks it will be some weeks before Lieutenant Wentworth can return to this fort."

Finally, on March 4th, the survivors came to the haven of John Sutter's citadel. There the *grand seigneur* saw to their comfort. They were tenderly cared for and housed in the best quarters available. In time they won their way back to sanity and health.

Thirty-nine of the Donner Party died; forty-eight survived. Their's is one of the most gruesome, tragic annals in the winning of the West. Many heroic deeds marked their rescue. William Thompson bore little Francis Donner every mile of the weary way in his arms; part of that way led through a raging blizzard. John Stark, he of the incredible strength and fortitude, carried the giant John Graves to safety on his back—every step

through the white drifts and quagmire leagues to Sutter's
Fort. Mark a star for these two brave men in your Book
of Memory. We do not breed their like a century after.

MONTHS LATER, Edwin Bryant came to the scene near
Truckee Lake. The white curtain had fallen away from
the grim drama. "When General Kearney's return party.
which I accompanied, reached the scene of these hor-
rible and tragic events on June 22nd, 1847," relates
Bryant, "a halt was ordered for the purpose of collecting
and interring the remains.

"Near the principal cabins I saw two bodies, entire,
with the exception that the abdomens had been cut open
and the entrails extracted. . . .

". . . Strewn around the cabins were dislocated and
broken bones—skulls (in some instances sawn asunder
with care to extract the brains), human skeletons—in
short, human remains in every variety of revolting mutilation. A more appalling spectacle I never
witnessed. . . ."

So ends an episode in the creation of a new empire.

NOT MANY MOONS silvered the newly acquired province before Kearney and Stockton disagreed. That personal bitterness never was discarded.

Stockton had commissioned John C. Frémont as civil
governor and Colonel William H. Russell as secretary of
state on January 16th, 1847. A week later Commodore
Stockton succeeded Shubrick as commander of the
Pacific Squadron. During this period of swift progression
the name of Yerba Buena was changed permanently to
its original form—San Francisco.

Colonel Richard B. Mason arrived in San Francisco
in February with instructions from Washington. His
dispatches were positive in their orders that the senior
officer of the land forces was to be made civil governor.
Brigadier General Kearney was the high-ranking man.
Also included, was the announcement that the military

and naval chiefs should hold frequent and harmonious conferences.

Kearney and Shubrick issued a joint circular on March 1st. Kearney assumed the governorship and named Monterey as the capital. Frémont was definitely erased from the political picture.

At once he waited on Kearney at Monterey. The interview was unsatisfactory. Pointed words were used. Back went Frémont to Los Angeles, quite stubborn about the matter. He continued to sign documents and act as if he were still the highest-appointed official in the territory—all of which raised the very devil of a rumpus.

Colonel Mason charged militantly down upon Los Angeles in April. Frémont and he met in a series of interviews; each session grew more sulphurous. In one altercation Frémont chose to use some rough language.

"None of your insolence, sir," cried the enraged Colonel, "or I'll put you in irons!"

The offended Frémont demanded an apology. It was refused. Then Frémont ordered Major Pierson B. Reading —one of Sutter's late right-hand men who had joined the California Battalion—to convey his challenge to Colonel Mason.

That challenge was accepted. Double-barreled shotguns were chosen as the weapons. A date was arranged. But orders reached Mason in mid-April demanding his presence in Monterey. The duel was regretfully postponed until both men could meet at the capital.

But some word of the proposed affair reached Kearney's ear. Positive orders were issued to prevent such a meeting.

"Damned idiots!" said the General testily.

This appears to have ended the matter. At least the pair never looked down shotgun sights at each other's middles in a Monterey dawn.

GENERAL KEARNEY left Monterey with his escort on the last day of May, bound overland for the East. Colo-

nel Mason had been appointed to both the civil and
military leadership of the territory. A muchly chagrined
Frémont left with his mapping party the same day; he
was under galling orders to accompany the General.
Each night the two contingents camped near each other,
great dignity in evidence, and very little cordiality.

The route wandered through the San Juan, San
Joaquin and Sacramento valleys. Both parties arrived near
Sutter's Fort on June 13th. For three days Kearney and his
escort spent a leisurely time in the wilderness stronghold,
both as guests and as purchasers of needed supplies.

Frémont held himself aloof and waited impatiently
for marching orders. At Kearney's invitation, Sutter rode
over to his camp on the 16th and wished the company
godspeed. Frémont's band moved off in the column's rear.

While near the fort, the map-maker had written a
note to Kearney requesting permission to move on with
his men in advance to the States. He was refused.

When both parties reached Fort Leavenworth in
August, Kearney ordered Frémont to consider himself
under arrest, prepare himself for court-martial, and at
once report to the adjutant general in Washington.

At the nation's capital in November, Frémont stood
trial on three charges—mutiny, disobedience of the law-
ful command of a superior officer, and conduct to the
prejudice of good order and military discipline. He was
found guilty by the court and dismissed from the
service.

Stockton followed Kearney overland in July, riding
by way of Sonoma and through the Sacramento Valley.
He did not reach St. Joseph, Mo., until November.

THE DIARY ANNALS of 1847 read with the usual brief
candor, no personal comment being made. Some few of
the entries are definitely vital:

New Helvetia, May 20th, 1847. Cool weather. All
the Indian chiefs who presented themselves left here today. Carding and spinning wool. Other work as usual....

SUTTER HAD CONSENTED to serve as Indian agent early in the year, a post which Stockton had insisted he assume. His duties were of the arduous patriarchal type he had employed from the beginning. More and more of the savages had come to depend upon his kindly rule. Each Indian knew the sure penalty for misdeeds and, as General Kearney remarked, "Captain Sutter, you have more *good* Indians than I thought existed in the world." Here is Sutter's report as Indian Agent for 1847:

Statistics of population of the District which includes the region east of the San Joaquin and Sacramento rivers, Upper California.

Whites, Males	218	Females	71	Total	289
Indians, Tame, Male	306	Females	173	Total	479
Indians, Wild, Male	11,224	Females	10,649	Total	21,873
Half-breed Indian children	3	Females	7	Total	10
Sandwich Islanders, Male	4	Females	1	Total	5
Negroes, Male	1	Females	0	Total	1
Males	11,756	Females	10,901	22,657	Total

Signed
Capt. J. A. Sutter
Indian Agent.

THE DIARY for May 22nd reads: The thieves who stole Mr. Hardy's boy, 2 horses, pistols, etc. have been apprehended, tried by the Justice of the Peace, and found guilty. Constable Wood has brought them here to board the launch on their way to prison in San Francisco. A good many volunteers arrived from below. Charles Burch and Couten Myers are going to the great salt lake with a band of horses where their newly established trading post is situated. A great many men are accompanying them.

Cornelio and Carlos, Tuolumne chiefs, and Florio and Raymundo, Lakissimney chiefs, presented themselves

with ten men today at this Agency. All are living on the
Stanislaus River.

May 23rd. The launch arrived this morning with 25
men of the New York Volunteers under command of
Lieut. Anderson. Came Dr. Ward of the same regiment.
They are encamped on the American Fork. Mr. Norris
arrived with a good assortment of store-goods and will
use the tannery as his place of business.

THE NEW YORK Volunteers mentioned here had been
enlisted for the duration of the war in June 1846. These
men were to be later disbanded in California and were
expected to aid the United States in settling the country.

They sailed from New York in September aboard
three transports, under Colonel Stevenson's command.
But the war was history when they docked in San
Francisco. The first boat came in March 1847; the last
in April. Little action was offered the men save in serving
as temporary garrisons at different posts.

So a detachment of the Volunteers found its way to
Sutter's Fort in June. Still, one bit of warlike action
was indulged in by the latecomers. In December an
overzealous Volunteer, stationed at Los Angeles, fired his
gun in the darkness at an approaching cow which failed
to enunciate the countersign clearly. A great commotion
resulted. The garrison leaped to arms. Guns were
made ready.

In the excitement a lighted fuse was dropped into the
ammunition chest.

The explosion dismembered seven men fatally. It was
the one moment of bogus military action seen by the
luckless Volunteers in California before their disband-
ment, an event delayed until August 1848.

Chapter XXXIII

THE SQUAW-MEN

THE TRAPPERS and settlers of early California were squaw-men almost to a man. That condition was normal. A white woman was a rarity in the wilderness until after 1850; and a restless mountain man inevitably carried in his wake a squaw and an assortment of tousle-topped half-breed children. Such a procession occasioned no comment—it was the customary thing. And no fierce fellow of the plains and the ranges cared to point the finger of scorn at his roving neighbor when his own meals were prepared by dirty brown hands.

John Sutter was a full-blooded, vigorous male. He liked friendship, gay talk, good music, warming wine, the stimulating presence of women, the laughter of living; but he carried in his single-purposed mind an occasionally spoken taboo against skins that were not the color of his own. It was not in his nature to accept the semblance of physical passion through a savage stop-gap; there was something revolting to the Swiss in such an association. Besides, he was the busiest man in California. . . .

As for his men, he made no protest—thought little of it. On only one occasion is there any record of his remonstrance in the matter.

In the early forties William Geiger had taken unto himself an Indian wife who proceeded to present him with a swiftly accumulating sequence of small Geigers. The German insisted upon living in the fort with his family. His offspring were always underfoot when important guests were present; sometimes they caused comment.

Sutter finally took the complacent Geiger to task. In conclusion he made some caustic remarks about Geiger's living with a common squaw.

"That may all be, Cap," said the placid Geiger, "but I ain't like the rest o' you poor fools. I sleep warm at night."

THE CHRONICLE of events at New Helvetia continues to march forward in the Diary. Sutter himself sets down the record from this point on.

May 26th, 1847. Visited Mr. Norris at the tanyard and purchased some goods. Piopio Max Max, the Walla Walla chieftain, and a great number of his people were here. Dispatched two vaqueros with the *Louis Anthony* to the Mokelumne River.

May 27th. The launch left with two deserters from the United States Army; Keseberg, Master. A visit from Piopio Max Max after which he and his people crossed to the other side of the American Fork.

May 28th. Schultz, a cooper, arrived. Marshall and Gingery laid out the mill-race.

May 29th. Visit of Lieut. Anderson. Many neighbors here today. Everyone returned from Sinclair's without holding the planned Rodeo.

May 31st. Reed left with Baptiste (Ruelle) in pursuit of a horse thief to the San Joaquin. Started the tannery today after invoicing everything. James Coates took charge of it and promises to put everything in repair which will be needful. A very warm day.

June 1st, 1847. Sent Kyburz to inspect the scraping business. Bray went with six hands to cut poles for the *eras* (threshing floors). The detachment of the New York Volunteers entered into the fort this evening to take their permanent quarters as a garrison. James Reed and Baptiste (Ruelle) arrived with their prisoner, William Harris, and put him in prison. Perry McCoon married Miss Donner this evening.

June 2nd. There was an auction at Rancho del Paso of some goads (ox-whips) belonging to the Donner children. Some of the Walla Wallas dropped in to trade.

June 5th. Sent my vaqueros to slaughter some cattle at Rancho del Paso. The prisoner escaped but was recaptured by Baptiste, put in irons, and once more put in the calaboose.

June 6th. This morning Don Pepe de la Rosa left with Harris, the prisoner. The soldiers accompanied them as far as the Rancho del Paso where Baptiste received $5 cash from Mr. Reed for recapturing Harris. From thence they proceeded to Sonoma.

The chiefs and alcaldes—Petok, Mayan, Nerio, and Hincoy brought thirty men to work for a fortnight. A violent north wind after sundown.

June 7th. A most violent north wind. Using the Indians to dig out a most pestilent kind of weed from amongst the wheat. Shulule arrived with 8 more Lapototomney workers. Carding, spinning, weaving going on apace. Am breaking the partition walls of the penitentiary down to make a granary of it. Work on the mill-race with the scrapers. No more wind after sundown.

June 8th. Dr. Ward commenced to cure the sick at an early hour. Received 21 blankets from the factory.

June 9th. Making a lime-kiln. Cleaning the places for the *eras*. The waters are falling considerably.

June 10th. An accident occurred to a Volunteer of the garrison, a German named Konig. He was bathing in the river, was attacked by cramps, and drowned. We buried him in the evening with all military honors.

June 11th. The Walla Wallas left. Burgep arrived from the Pine Woods. I dispatched Kyburz, the vaquero John, and a half-dozen soldiers to return a number of stray horses. I sent Comack to secure Indians to repair the Pine Woods road. Two boys—Chino and Valentin—ran away and deserted the sheep. James Wilson Marshall came this night to report to me and left again for the mill-run.

June 12th. Jim Crow (Kanaka) left for Hock. Toiko and Hutchhumney brought in some cattle. Marshall returned with all his helpers from the scraping job on the mill-run. Loker arrived and announced General Kearney's arrival at Daylor's, also Colonel Frémont and escort at Murphy's.

June 13th. Received a visit from General Kearney, Major Sinard, Colonel Cooke, Lieut. Radford of the Navy, Dr. Sanderson, and Congressman Hall. At my order 11 guns fired a salute. The garrison paraded

June 14th. Harvest has begun with 50 reapers. Cleaning the places for the *eras* and building one. Setting fire in the lime kiln. Some of General Kearney's officers made purchases for the journey. A great number of people present from the neighborhood. At three o'clock General Kearney and staff dined with me at the fort as my guests. Late in the evening they left again for their camp.

June 15th. A visit from Dr. Sanderson and Congressman Hall of Missouri. The Walla Wallas arrived and left post-haste for Frémont's camp. Mr. McKinstry went on business to Frémont's camp. Comack and Wubul arrived with 14 more men to cut wheat.

June 16th. General Kearney came with his staff and escort to pay his departing respects today. They visited with me until the time came for their departure. The Walla Wallas came from Frémont's camp. Ex-commander Kern delivered government horses to the Walla Wallas as their pay for aiding Frémont in the conquest campaign on an order written by Colonel Frémont.

June 17th. I have paid Piopio Max Max what I thought due him on his personal demands. I also gave him many extra things since it was because I went surety for his payment that he had embarked at all in his campaign to aid Frémont. He left well-content and started homeward.

Many neighbors here. Ten of the Votumne people left last night because their chief, Wubul, had not remained. Twelve Liclimnes and five Memshaws arrived today to work. We are slow in cutting wheat since other work must be completed first. Making a granary and *eras*.

June 18th. Perry McCoon and Murphy arrived. Getting bricks up here from Sutterville. Cutting and binding wheat.

June 19th. Pollo with 22 Indians to work. Mr. Hartburg, a naturalist, came in company with Nye, Foster, and Charles Roether. I have sent a courier to overtake General Kearney with letters of importance. Repairing the corral.

June 20th. Senor Antonio M. Armijo arrived. Bidwell also. The express dispatched yesterday returned to report he could not overtake Kearney's column. Hensley, Kern, King and Jones left today. Mr. Zins married Miss Wolfinger.

June 21st. Sent Hardy's runaway boy back to him. James Smith's mare drowned while attempting to swim the Sacramento. Marshall, Wittmer, and Northgrave occupied the boys by making a large coal-pit.

June 22nd. Came a canoe from Mimal with fresh vegetables, etc. Fred Paulhaus and Hulueige began to cradle wheat today. Chulte left for Sagayack and Zlua took over his duty of caring for the fields. The masons are laboring on the granary.

June 23rd. Neal arrived with news that the Walla Wallas have committed some depredations. Justice Sinclair and Lieut. Anderson tried to raise an armed force ready for duty tomorrow. Cutting wheat and binding. Continued cradling wheat. General repair work about the fort. Homo Bono sick.

June 24th. None of the inhabitants showed an inclination to go on a campaign against the Walla Wallas and Lieut. Anderson cannot prosecute such an action without aid. Mill going all night to accommodate near-by settlers.

June 25th. A strong gale all day. Nye married Mrs. Pike and Johnson married Miss Murphy. Stopped cradling wheat because of the high wind. Schmidt and Brunner have gone to the Pine Woods to bring out the frame for the mill.

June 26th. Some Indians deserted last night. Dr. Ward has been called out to Johnson's to attend a sick man. Samuel Neal arrived in a great rush to get medicine for the same man. (For a time cathartic pills of an inferior quality—but astounding results—were $30 a box, $1 each, at the fort.) A ride around the wheat field today showed me that nearly all the wheat is ripe. The Skyuse chief arrived with letters from John Williams and Hardy today; he has also returned three horses stolen by three bad Indians without Piopio Max Max' knowledge. He left again immediately to overtake the Walla Walla camp. Three of the Volunteers went on an elk hunt. I called upon Chupuhu and Renufio to order all the neighboring Indians to report for work on Monday. Mistressey, Lenox and Gregson moved down to the Hatter-house. Ritchie and the other young men cut about 7 acres—32 rows—and have managed it so poorly that I have been forced to discharge them. Masons are repairing the fort walls.

Sunday, June 27th. After having cleaned the place all hands went *pasear*. Witash has returned with the crosscut saw. More Indians arrived for work.

June 28th. A Mormon from the San Joaquin arrived to assist in cradling wheat, which business he understands admirably. We are cutting wheat, erecting *eras*, making a new bake oven, and working on the new granary. Dr. Ward returned from Johnson's.

EARLY IN 1846 a Mormon battalion of 500 men had been enlisted in the East for a year's duty in California. The battalion was officered by regular army men and its personnel believed with canny purpose that their next home would be in the new territory. The exodus from Nauvoo had already begun. Brigham Young consented to the battalion's mission and it seemed a simple way in which to secure free transportation from the government. At the same time this company began its march, the shrewd Elder Samuel Brannan captained 250 more Latter-Day Saints who sailed in the *Brooklyn* for San Francisco.

So, by land and sea, the Mormon invasion had begun. Sickness took toll of 150 men in the overland ranks; these faltering ones were left behind and eventually made their way to Salt Lake City. The others marched on. They reached Los Angeles the last of January 1847, and found the conquest completed. The battalion was mustered out in mid-July.

Some of the footloose aggregation passed Sutter's Fort on the way to Salt Lake. But more than one hundred of them stayed to work for John Sutter during the winter, taking full advantage of the Swiss' generous wage. Elder Brannan, who led his flock by water, was to become a prominent figure in the Californian scene during the next few months. . . .

It was on August 21st that the main body of Saints decided to stay and labor in New Helvetia—at least for that year. "Never," said John Sutter positively, "did a man have more faithful or reliable helpers."

THE DIARY reads on:

June 29th. Schmidt, Paulhaus and Brunner left for the Pine Woods on the American Fork to get the entire mill frame out. Schultz, Heinrich and Schmidt—all coopers—left also for the Pine Woods to secure staves for 1000 flour barrels, etc.

June 30th. Five cradles in active use. Building on the new bake oven; work on the granary and 5th *era*.

July 1st, 1847. Savage arrived with two teams of lumber from the Mts. Many here for flour and supplies. We are gathering and threshing the peas. Half the labor were cutting wheat with sickles. Bake oven nearly completed. Schultz came back from the Mts; his party lost their horses. I loaned him further mounts and he departed with medicine for his partners. Thunder, lightning and rain until midnight.

July 2nd. Cool day. Cutting wheat. Threshing peas. Nine cradles in use.

July 3rd. Hardy's boy broke out of the calaboose. The coopers returned from the Mts. They did not find suitable wood for stave-making.

July 4th. Up by sunrise, firing guns and hoisting the flag. The garrison and others went *pasear*.

July 5th. Nerio arrived with 13 hands for work. Five Moquelumne men and one woman arrived for weaving work. Finished with the peas—101½ *fanegas*.

July 6th. Arrived the launch from San Francisco. Passengers were Dr. Bates, Vicente, Vital, etc. Getting the goods up from the launch. Savage brought two loads of shingles and planks from the Pine Woods. Three wagons began to unload wheat into the *eras*.

July 7th. The bake oven fell in yesterday. Was repaired today. Making shirts for the Indians.

July 9th. Cutting wheat. Filling 2nd *era*. Much curing of the sick and their treatment today. Pat (Murphy) had a quarrel with Ossissipo which I settled amicably.

Sunday, July 11th. Punished Multe for immoral conduct by cutting her hair. Cured the sick.

July 12th. The Spaniards—Altamirano, Higuera, etc.—left this morning without calling at my office to pay their respects; this after having spitefully abused my friend Shulule, the Yusumney chief, a very gentle man. Curing the sick. Coopers off to the mountains once more. Savage took their tools for them.

July 13th. Sent John and the vaqueros to Hock after the mares. Harry Trow arrived with the *manadas* some time after I sent them. Homo Bono sick. Also Augustin.

July 14th. McLellan, ship's carpenter, missed the launch this morning. His chest was already aboard. Receiving notice that the launch was awaiting him, I sent him in haste on horseback. Dispatched the canoes to Hock with cargoes for Major Reading. I sent two boys with the new canoe to Wollock, with orders to await Commodore Stockton. They were supplied with provisions. Also sent the regular Hock canoe with 2 iron cannon, flour for the farm, and a wall-piece for

Major Reading. Redshed and Chucut were sent to assist in my new gardens.

Mayan's wife died on the *Embarcadero*. Great mourning and wailing by the relatives. I sent John and the trappers to Hock in order to get 30 horses and 6 mules. A great many Indians are ill and Dr. Bates is attending them.

Cutting wheat by cradle and sickle, getting it into the *eras*.

July 15th. Otuh Bushoney died; also Asanag's mother. I ministered all day to the sick in the *rancheria* with Dr. Bates. James Smith arrived from Sonoma for the purpose of attending to my *eras*, etc. Hensley arrived with notice from Commodore Stockton that he will cross at Hardy's tomorrow and will proceed as far as Johnson's

July 16th. Pasquale, wife of Leandro, died last night. Mr. Rumshottel is employed as hospital steward. News comes that many are dying at the *Rancherias* on the Feather River. More and more sick people here. Consequently, work with the wheat proceeds slowly.

July 17th, 18th, 19th. Many ill. Little work.

July 20th. Charles Brunner's party returned from the Mts. again, having successfully brought out the mill frame. I paid off many of the sick people who desired it and sent them home. The boy Antonio has died and been buried. Appointed Olimpio *mayordomo* for my vaqueros.

July 21st. Schmidt, the cooper, dropped in from the Mts., borrowed a white horse and departed with provisions. Marshall and Nerio left for the Mts. on the American Fork to select the site for the saw-mill. Dispatched a number of native alcaldes to secure laborers for the coming week.

July 22nd. Homo Bono has been taken home by his brother to the Cosumne River.

July 23rd. Visited the sick with the Doctor. Every day more people ill. Threshing wheat and cleaning in the 1st *era*. Brought in 70 *fanegas*.

July 24th. Cady arrived as a courier from San Francisco and to get a subscription for the weekly service. I have paid off a great many of the Indians and allowed them to return home, the wisest course under the present conditions. The canoe arrived from Hock Farm laden with fresh fruits. Visiting the sick. Many ill yet, some recovering.

Sunday, July 25th. More Indians paid off that they may return to their *rancherias* because they wish it. I made a visit to the Mill Site. Natomo is sick. Hardy's boy Benz arrived here. Then he ran away again. Keyser is divorced. John McCracken arrived with a load of white clay. Schultz came in from the Mts. Also Marshall. Cady, our new courier, departed this morning with many letters and two mules.

July 26th. Work slow. No men. I visited the *rancherias* in the afternoon with Dr. Bates to see all the sick people and took them all the fresh fruits on hand.

July 27th. Many visitors. Marshall and Gingery have been busy examining the site where the Dam will be built. Huffner, a N. Y. Volunteer, took over the duties of hospital steward. Cleaned 104 *fanegas* of wheat. Schultz the cooper left for the Mts. again this morning; lent him a horse.

July 28th. Perry McCoon prepared his launch for tomorrow's sailing. Five wagons transported wheat to the *eras*. The sick increase in numbers. Many go the *rancherias* and refuse to take medicine—say it tastes very bitter! Captain Grimes finally got his lumber rafted up the American River.

July 29th. From Feather River came the launch with fruit and vegetables. McCracken came with another load of white clay. Visited the sick with Dr. Bates and Huffner. More ill yet some getting better. Old Merritt arrived—not dead yet. Casiano arrived from Hock asking medicines for Manaiki and Sam (Kanakas), both very ill. So I concluded the Doctor must visit my men and so dispatched him.

July 29th. Sent wheat to the *Embarcadero* for Dedmund consigned on the *Loadrep*. Bushba, my field-keeper, left for his *rancheria* today. Sent Samuel Kyburz to examine the sheep and shepherds. Chupuhu sent me the sad tidings that he is dying.

July 31st. Sebastian Keyser sent McDowell to his wife this morning with a letter about their affairs. Delivered 550 *fanegas* of wheat today consigned to Dedmund. Delivered back to Tolebau his mare, the animal having been stolen by Hardy's boy Benz. A U. S. launch arrived with provisions for the garrison. I presented Sixto and Pompeyo with small blankets for their sick boys.

August 1st, 1847. This morning I sent two wagons to bring in the garrison's provisions. Kern and King arrived from Bear Valley. They have been too ill to travel by land with the Commodore. Keyser went back to Bear Creek.

Last night Dr. Bates returned from Hock with Thomas Baquero whom I immediately returned with needed medicines. Messrs. Kern and King sold their horses to me and left for the *Embarcadero* to board the government launch. It will depart for San Francisco tomorrow morning at six o'clock. Pinego being ill, I sent Gutche, Hulvem and Chomile to care for the sheep. I have busied the few working hands with cleaning the wheat, also a few hours' labor, on the *era*. Lorenzo, his sister Marceline, and Ignacio left for the Moquelumne *Rancheria*.

August 2nd. Arrived Dr. Ward, Major Cloud (Paymaster), and Captain Folsom. Also John Bidwell. Flugge announced the death of Gayuik. A canoe came from Hock with melons and potatoes. The U. S. launch sailed on schedule.

August 3rd. Lieut. Anderson left with six men to capture some malcontents. Also to take an Indian woman away from Thomas Hardy. I made a promenade to the *Embarcadero* with Major Cloud and Captain Folsom.

August 4th. This morning Major Cloud and Captain Folsom started out on horseback. About one half mile beyond the fort, Major Cloud was thrown from his mount and severely injured. The two doctors have been called and the Major has been taken in a wagon to Wimmer's. Every assistance possible has been rendered him. He has lain senseless from high noon on. . . .

I sent the canoe to Hock with 25 bags of salt for John Williams. Sent up the large red canoe to Harry Trow. Major Cloud died at sunset. A very sad accident—a gentleman whom we regret very much. The government loses in him an able and efficient officer. Visited the sick with Dr. Bates.

August 5th. Theodore Cordua arrived here. I rode around the large wheat field with Bidwell, Ward and Captain Folsom; also made a short visit to Rancho del Paso. Threshing and cleaning as usual. Some of the sick recovering. I had the coffin made for Major Cloud and the grave dug.

August 6th. Captain Folsom drummed the garrison to arms. At half-past eleven the bells began to toll. Captain Folsom, as senior officer, assumed command of the cortege. A wagon was ready to receive the body of Major Cloud.

The troops and citizenry marched solemnly to the graveyard. There he was buried with military honors.

Captain Folsom left this afternoon for below; he intends to camp on the Cosumne River and examine the government horses. Olimpio accompanies Folsom as far as the Calaveras; there a Moquelumne will guide him on to San José. Theodore Cordua left for home.

August 7th. Arrived José Jesus, Felipe, Raymundo, with their people to work. Raymundo's daughter, who speaks Spanish well, came on a visit—she is called Maria Francisca.

Shulule brought 11 men. I now have 60, which assures me a fair prospect of getting the wheat safely in. Visiting the sick people in company with Dr. Bates.

Sunday, August 8th. Harry Trow very ill at Hock. The coopers arrived back from the Mts. this morning.

Nearly all the people went *pasear*. A warm day. Ramon Arce brought me letters from General Vallejo. I dispatched him with answers almost at once.

August 9th. Launch from Hock with melons and vegetables. Now 120 men at work. Getting wheat in the *eras*. More Indians placed in the weaving extablishment. Auction of the effects of J. J. Hostetter, deceased. Received cargo of melons from Mayan. Cada arrived with ten more men. A very warm day. In the evening the thermometer stood at 80.

August 10th. The 11 men whom Shulule brought ran away last night. Received a cargo of watermelons from Juan el Cosumne. Olimpio asked permission to marry Maria Francisca, the chief's daughter; but she doesn't like him. Dr. Bates with good news from Hock—Harry Trow and Manaiki out of danger. Lieut. Anderson arrived with one prisoner, Growling Smith.

August 11th. I have used up all my remaining medicines. The express arrived from San Francisco at nine o'clock. After breakfast the Doctor and I visited the sick Indians in the *rancherias*.

August 12th. Dr. Bates fell ill at midday while visiting the sick.

August 14th. Launch arrived with George McKinstry, Jr., Lansford W. Hastings, Buchanan, etc. Dr. Bates still ill. A large number of people arrived here to settle their accounts.

August 16th. Three Mormons arrived from the lower country. The soldiery and others went on a spree. Hastings, McKinstry and Buchanan left for Feather River to hunt for a saw-mile site. Fernando arrived from Hock with news that nearly everyone is ill there. A great amount of barter all day. Dr. Bates has nearly recovered and is once more attending the sick.

August 18th. Launch sailed. Sergeant Norris and Gerard Smith took a prisoner—Growling Smith. Lennox is preparing the mill-stones from the Pueblo for the mill in the fort. The three Mormons began work on my granary. Canoes from Hock with melons.

August 19th. John Bidwell arrived with news of numerous deaths among the Indians in the Upper Part of the Valley and especially on the Sacramento. John C. Stark accused the crew of the small launch of stealing a log and ox-chain from him.

August 20th. Finished transporting the oak bark from the *Embarcadero* to the tanyard. Cutting wheat. Visiting the sick. Five women have been taken prisoners for stealing wheat.

August 21st. Received leather from the tanyard. José Jesus arrived with news that the Tuolumne *Rancheria* has been attacked by enemies. Marshall, Gingery and Paulhaus returned from the upper country. Olimpio has apprehended and brought in some more of the wheat-stealing women. Visited the sick.

August 23rd. Four more Mormons from below. Messrs. Smith and Hundsacker arrived from the Emigration reporting that 1500 wagons are on the road for Oregon and here; also 500 Mormons bound for Salt Lake.

August 24th. Six more Mormons arrived. It has been found necessary to discharge Benito Lena, the shepherd.

August 25th. Captain Hunt of the *Marmion* arrived. With him came Harrison, Quartermaster Clerk. Gordon, Davis and Charles Heath came from Benicia City. Work progresses slowly on the wheat.

August 26th. Harrison left to secure the government horses now grazing in the Cosumne region. Captain Hunt and some of the Mormon officers purchased provisions and other supplies here. Also had their mounts shod in my shops. It was discovered that Salinas took a horse from Hock Malla on which he had no legal claim.

THUS ENDS ONE PHASE of the Diary. The next entry begins with a pact that was to herald incredible change. . . .

Chapter XXXIV

HISTORY: DAY BY DAY

AUGUST 27th., 1847. A host of Mormons here to
buy provisions and have blacksmith work done.
*Made a contract with James Wilson Marshall for a saw-mill
to be erected on the American Fork.*

THIS AGREEMENT was drawn up by John Bidwell and
signed by both Sutter and Marshall on that Friday evening in 1847. The contract provided that Sutter was to
furnish building materials, all supplies and board and
pay the men employed on the project; Marshall was to
build and manage the mill, receiving one quarter of the
lumber as compensation for his supervision.

THE DIARY continues:

August 28th. Horses shod of many more Mormons.
Employed nearly all of them to work here since they
seem to be uniformly honest, honorable, and hard-
working. James Wilson Marshall and Peter Wimmer
departed early for the Mts. to determine a proper saw-
mill site. Perry McCoon arrived with his launch.
Visited the sick in the *Rancherias*. Warm day. Cutting
wheat. George Wimmer departed with heavily freighted
wagons of provisions for the mill-site on the American
Fork. I visited Grimes and Sinclair on the American Fork;
also the sick Indians in that locality. Last night a heavy
shower fell for one hour. Little damage to the wheat.

August 30th. Norris left for San Francisco via Bodega.
General Vallejo and Ramon Arce arrived from Sonoma.
The government launch arrived in charge of Lieut. Hub-
bard, bringing two prisoners, John W. Egger and Smith.
Armijo did not come, being very ill.

August 31st. The court has been this day established
to try the murder case of Armijo, Egger, Smith, etc. I

· 272 ·

The Town of Sutterville, about 1849

have postponed the trial until October 18th because of Armijo's indisposition; also because of the great distances which witnesses must traverse. The government launch left with General Vallejo, etc. His escort under Ramon Arce left by land; also 3 yoke of oxen and 20 sheep. The following persons left for the Mts. or the saw-mill site: Stevens, Brown, Willis.

ARMIJO, SMITH and EGGER were accused of killing twelve Indians while attempting to secure forty men for labor against their wishes. A special court was appointed, Sutter and Vallejo serving as judges, and a jury of twelve men selected. In order to secure an impartial jury a change of venue took the case from Sacramento to Sonoma. Finally, in October, the case was tried. Captain Brackett acted as prosecutor; Captain Sutter was absent because of a painful eye infection. After a week's wrangling the men were acquitted—a verdict that angered Sutter not a little when he was informed of it.

"There is no justice for the Indians beyond the Sacramento Valley," he observed heatedly. But the affair was over. . . .

THE DIARY continues:

September 1st, 1847. Dr. Bates recovering very slowly. I engaged a hospital assistant, Mr. Burns, to aid him. Dr. Ward came home in a wagon, having injured his leg in a fall from his horse. Work on the horse-mill, putting in new stones and a new spindle.

September 2nd. Threshing out wheat with the mares. Transporting the large iron post to the tanyard, also adobes, hides, etc. Arrived three Cosumne Indians with passports from their employer, Don José de Jesus Vallejo (the General's brother).

September 5th. Marshall returned from the mill-site. Left again for the Mts. I sent Charles and Kong with a wagon of provisions to the saw-mill site. Keyser has been here and left again; he has his wife back and will be happy. Casiano came from Hock with heartening news—soon all the sick will be well again.

September 7th. I sent Casiano and Bruno for a two weeks' rest to their Moquelumne *Rancheria* and lent them horses. Dr. Bates ill again; is not able to attend his patients.

September 9th. Leandro Bushoney, former Corporal in my Indian Infantry, died today. The three Mormons, Woodworth, Frazer and Douglas, went up to the American Fork to the mill-site under my orders. Olimpio arrived with 38 Yalesumnes to work.

September 10th. Put a full cargo of 300 *fanegas* of wheat in the launch; she sailed with Tokatchi, Master. Passengers: Bidwell, Firefield and Dr. Bates. Sent the new canoe to Mimal with Burnes to replace Lienhard as manager. Augustin brought 22 wild Indians to work. Sam Brannan arrived in the evening with news that the emigrants are coming shortly. A warm day.

September 11th. Sam Brannan left this morning for the San Joaquin. I lent him Mr. C. W. McKenzie's gray mule. I rented my cottage today on the American Fork to Mr. Coates for $200 a year. He will use it as a store.

September 12th. A good many of my Indians drunk; it appears they secured the grog from the Shepherd. Olimpio was thrown into the calaboose. Arrived Captain Brown, late of the Mormon Battalion. Also Abeck, a Swiss from Canton Schurjtz.

September 13th. Capt. Brown, Fowler and company left for Monterey. Many neighbors here every day.

September 14th. Some Mormons returned. I employed them to work on the mill-race, now under active construction. Finished cutting the wheat.

September 15th. Engaged more Mormons for mill-race labor. Dr. Moore visited Olimpio at my request to try and round him into shape. Plastering and whitewashing the fort. Charles Flugge and his wife returned from the saw-mill to recover their health.

September 16th. Scott and Todd arrived from Sonoma peddling ox-goads. I engaged 8 more Mormons for the mill-race and a like number as wagon-loaders in the wheat-fields. In the night a wagon arrived from Homo Bono bringing melons and corn. Warm day, calm.

September 17th. Scott and Todd have a wagonload of grog also. I took a ride up the American River to see how the work on the mill-race was progressing. A suffocatingly warm day.

September 18th. Lienhard took over Mr. Samuel Kyburz' duties and keys in my establishment today. Peter Wimmer arrived and held an auction of the estate of Ames, deceased.

September 19th. The U. S. launch arrived at high noon under Lieut. Per Lee. He has orders to remove the garrison to Sonoma. Perry McCoon's boat arrived also.

September 20th. The garrison spent the entire day moving to the *Embarcadero*. After dinner, Lieutenant Per Lee, Dr. Ward and Kyburz left with the last wagon. All the prisoners and sick have also been transported. Sergeant Crosby left by land with government horses. Receiving cattle at Rancho del Paso. Cleaning and getting wheat from the fields.

September 21st. Brouett, the carpenter, moved with all his tools, etc. to the mill-site under my order. Also sent a wagonload of provisions to the same place. Lucinda the Widow arrived. (A lady or a boat? Me thinks a lady. If so, these four words usher her in our consciousness from the cradle to the grave. No other record contains her name.)

For more than a week Olimpio is sick of a fever. Ildefanso arrived with Guitep's wife.

September 22nd. Four steers killed for dried meat. Many boys ill with the fever. Sent provisions to Natomo.

September 23rd. Getting wheat in the *eras*.

September 24th. Mayan with 11 hands to work.

September 25th. By dawn I sent a wagonload of wheat to the launch at the *Embarcadero*. By sunset she sailed with 300 *fanegas*. I sent five vaqueros to Shadden's to receive the Frémont cattle; these animals he had wrongly marked for himself and the U. S. government returned them to General Vallejo. He, in turn, sold them to me.

September 26th. Marshall and Willis returned from the saw-mill site. McKinstry came from Montezuma. Vaqueros arrived with the Frémont cattle.

September 27th. I dispatched a wagon with provisions and 3 yoke of oxen to the saw-mill site; also six men whom I have engaged to manufacture shingles, clapboards, etc. Also sent supplies for another company who are securing lumber for flatboats. Shulule, a kind and faithful chief, has died. I received the Frémont cattle from Thomas D. Savage, 150 head in all. Taking clay to the tanyard to repair the tan-vats. Pollo reports 11 of his people lately dead.

September 28th. Shinube broke out of the prison. Marshall, Bennett, Ezekiel Smith, Brouett and Wm. Kelley started for the mill-site. Gingery, Sidney Willis, Brouett and William Kelly are to build two large flatboats. Allen, Thomas, Dunn and three others departed to build the dam. I sent thirty men to the mountains to aid in making the necessary shingles, clapboards, etc. Another wagon of provision to the mill-site.

September 29th. Sent Harry Trow, my Hock *mayordomo*, to Hock with his fleet of canoes. George McKinstry, Jr. returned from the Mts. adjacent to the American Fork. Sent clay, planks, etc. to the tannery. Carrying wheat from fields to *eras*. Other work as usual.

September 30th. McKinstry curing the sick, both white and Indian.

October 1st, 1847. Sheriff Page arrived from Sonoma to consult me in regard to the Armijo case.

October 2nd. McKinstry left for the Cosumne River. The Sheriff returned to Sonoma. Many of the Mormons are ill because they worked too hard. Mares threshing out the wheat.

October 3rd. Emigrants arrived, a small party.

October 4th. Capt. Brown arrived from below with an express to receive the mail from the Emigrants. After dining with me, Capt. Brown returned to his camp. The Mill was out of order.

October 5th. Capt. Brown left. I sent 40 sheep to the saw-mill site; also a wagonload of provisions. Many emigrants arrived and came to pay their respects to me at the fort. Repairing the mill. I sent Wota with a canoe to Schwartz and Charles Burch to collect the potatoes due. Poltack departed with all the sick Indians and I paid them off.

October 6th. Gingery returned and left to survey the mill-race. I visited the tan-yard and found all the shoemakers and one tanner ill. Some of the emigrants came here; some moved on to the *Embarcadero* and San José.

October 7th. Mill in order. Three canoes from Hock with pumpkins, vegetables, melons, etc. Finished threshing one *era* of wheat and filled another in.

October 8th. Sent the 3 canoes back to Hock with Maria Francisca as passenger. Last night, little Ycott, a-ten-year old girl of the Willi tribe, died. She suffered much. Ashei and Obla's wives died last night.

October 9th. Dr. Long from Bear Creek to Sonoma. Launch arrived at sunset. Passengers: Dr. Bates, Glover, Kyburz, Smith, Charles Heath, etc.

October 10th. Mr. Davis arrived in a flatboat from Benicia. She was freighted and departed this evening.

October 14th. Sent provisions to mill-race.

October 15th. A U. S. launch arrived to secure all remaining equipment and government property belonging to the late N. Y. Volunteers stationed here.

October 16th. Freighted the launch. Sheley, a consumptive, died. Threshing out with the mares.

October 17th. I visited the mill-race. Seven wagons bringing wheat into the *eras*.

October 18th. Sidney Willis and Hudson arrived from the Mts. and began to construct the flatboats at the location of the proposed dam. John Smith, the new carpenter, went up to Natomo (the other mill-site). Perry McCoon and launch arrived; also Major Pierson B. Reading.

October 19th. A good many loafers hereabout. Employed T. D. Perkey to make a new mill band at once.

October 20th. The wind is so extreme that the wagons cannot bring wheat from the fields. Swift, Gibson and Dutton left. Hardy is still loafing. The mill is not in order yet—the band would not suffice.

October 21st. I prepared to depart for Sonoma for the Armijo trial but was prevented by an inflammation in my eyes—very painful and exasperating. Hardy left for good, the loafer. The mechanics must work by candle-light long past their regular hour because of the press of labor. Two wagonloads of provisions to the Mts. They carried no flour because of the mill failure.

October 25th. The flour-mill is going again.

October 26th. Sent wagons to the Mts. to transport lumber to the mill. Also provisions. Hired a competent miller to attend to the flour-mill.

October 27th. Eighty-one hides came to the tanyard from Grimes and Sinclair. Two wagons are bringing Olimpio's and Uquerio's crops here to the fort granaries. Finished threshing wheat with the mares. Launch arrived. Came Marshall from the saw-mill.

October 28th. Provisions to shingle-camp. Marshall to saw-mill. The mill is running day and night to supply flour to all who demand it. A great many people from all quarters to barter with me.

October 29th. I dispatched the launch in Major Reading's charge. Four teams arrived with timber for the grist-mill. Showers tonight. The Moquelumne River is very high. Still grinding wheat day and night to feed my hungry people.

October 30th. A frost in the morning. North wind. The Mts. are covered with snow. Plenty of geese are passing overhead from Oregon. A wagon took nails, tar, and other materials to the flatboat builders.

October 31st. I called in all the people so that the wheat might be speedily cleaned. Very heavy rain tonight.

November 1st, 1847. Rain and gale all night. Only a few hands to clean wheat.

November 2nd. Good weather until evening. Then rain. Some wheat was cleaned but left in the *era*. Not dry enough. Started seven teams to Murphy's to get the remainder of his wheat. A load of staves came from the Mts.

November 3rd. Rain all night and this morning. Making oakum, repairing houses. Took a chimney down in one of the former soldier barracks to get adobes to make a new fireplace in the Blacksmith Shop. Sent provisions to millrace—a wagonload. Employed two men from below to cut firewood.

November 4th. Fine weather this morning. Getting firewood. Harry Trow is getting the mares together. Dispatched the sawyers to Natomo (the other millsite). After noon I started all hands out to the *eras* and worked hard myself to separate the dry wheat from the rest. Came a good drying breeze from the north. Harry got the *manadas* together. Sent four vaqueros to assist Sinclair at his Rodeo tomorrow. Murphy's wheat coming in.

November 5th. Cleaned 182½ *fanegas* of wheat with only a few hands. Worked all day myself. Dr. Bates ill again. I sent Uquerio with 208 spikes and some oakum to the flatboat builders. I received saddle leather from the tanyard.

November 6th. Cleaning wheat in the *eras*. Finished one. Worked hard myself.

Sunday, November 7th. Worked with few helpers today. Harry Trow left for Hock with the vaqueros and *manadas*.

November 8th. Cleaned wheat with more hands. Received 29 novillas (steers) from Mr. Sinclair.

November 9th. Ten novillas killed to salt in.

November 10th. Sent Basilio and Watei with 20 sheep to the Mts.

November 11th. Getting timber to repair the wagons which will transport the mill stones. Salting beef. Four wagons arrived with wheat, peas, etc. Cleaning wheat.

November 12th. A Spaniard arrived with a *manada* owned by Don Roberto Livermore charged with the duty of delivery to Captain Fitch. I sent Wittmer with the four best drivers, best wagons, and best 12 yoke of oxen to get two of the four pairs of mill stones at Memshaw. Achilles helped them. Cleaning wheat with the winnowing machine.

November 13th. Stevens came from the saw-mill with a letter from James Wilson Marshall. I visited the mill, the mill-race, and the Dam. I read the marriage service for Teronimo and his bride.

November 14th. A beautiful day. Captain Fitch's Spaniard come back from the Cosumne and crossed the river with his *manadas* safely. I visited the fishing *rancheria* to inquire for the launch.

November 15th. Heavy fog. I sent Wetza with 11 men to aid at the Dam. McKinstry and Bidwell arrived, having left the launch above Sutterville.

November 16th. The launch arrived and discharged her cargo. I sent 5 wagons of food to the shingle-camp. In the night came the mill-stone expedition with Wittmer and Monet. Only three stones arrived. One wagon struck a huge rock and broke down. Rain all night.

November 17th. Sent the mill-stone to the mill. The vaqueros repairing the *potrero*. Matthews repaired the pumps. A wagon with food to supply the various companies at work on the mill.

November 19th. Sent Wittmer with 5 teams to get the remaining mill stones.

November 24th. Sent the vaqueros with 20 oxen to Rancho del Paso to receive novillas (steers); they have been delivered this evening and marked. The teams arrived from Bear Creek with 4 mill stones. The fifth wagon broke down ten miles from Sicard's and had to be left behind. Four wagons with shingles and clapboards from the Mts. I paid a visit to the Natomo mill which they have begun to raise.

November 25th. Olimpio went down the river in a canoe, seeking runaways.

November 26th. I sent a team with four yoke of oxen to secure the remaining mill stones. In the afternoon I followed them on horseback. Rogers went to Natomo to haul the heavy frame pieces to the site.

November 27th. Delivered some *manadas* to Robert Livermore. Wittmer, Frazer and Woodworth returned, having finally loaded the mill stone on another wagon. The foundation of the upper building at the mill site was laid. I finished cleaning the wheat this evening and brought it all into the storage granary. Discharged and paid the Indians. Cleaned up the fort in general fashion.

November 28th. It was necessary to repair the flour-mill. The last of the mill stones arrived at the mill.

November 29th. The tules on the left bank of the Sacramento are on fire.

November 30th. I rode to Natomo on a tour of inspection and to see how they were progressing in raising the mill frame. Thirty-four hands have been continuously employed on it. No accident has occurred and all is going well.

December 1st, 1847. Finished raising mill-house at Natomo. Olimpio arrived with the runaways. The cattle and horses strayed through an open corral gate. A beautiful day.

December 2nd. Sent 2 wagons of flour and salf beef to the Mts. John Bidwell returned from Sonoma.

December 3rd. Sent 4 wagons of provisions to the Saw-mill; also 4 wagons direct to the shingle-camp. I concluded a contract with Kelly and Brouett to secure the needful lumber saw for the saw-mill. John Bidwell surveyed a road for me leading directly to the saw-mill at Natomo. I purchased forty ducks. A fine day.

WITH THE NEXT ENTRY the vital ghost of Robert Fulton comes to the Sacramento.

Chapter XXXV

THE SAILING OF THE *SITKA*

DECEMBER 4th, 1847. In the afternoon the little steamboat *Sitka* arrived here from the San Francisco region, having made the passage in seven days. Passengers were McKinstry, Petit, Ide, Stevens, Scott, Mrs. Gregson and baby, etc.

GEORGE MCKINSTRY, JR., one of Captain Sutter's employees at the time, gives an account of this vessel, the first steam-propelled craft to ever enter California waters. "The Russian steamer referred to," wrote McKinstry, "was brought from Sitka in the spring of 1847 to Yerba Buena, lashed atop one of the decks of a Russian American Fur Company ship. This craft was consigned to William A. Liedesdorff and was put in order on Yerba Buena Island.

"She was built in Sitka by an American and was designed as a pleasure yacht for the Russian Governor at that port. Her dimensions were: length 37 feet; beam 9 feet; depth of hold 3½ feet; locomotive engine; side wheels. From Yerba Buena Island she was brought over to the city. There Captain William A. Liedesdorff invited a number of gentlemen to take a ride on the first steamer that ever spumed the waters of San Francisco Harbor.

". . . The first trip was made to Santa Clara; the next to Sonoma. I chanced to be down from Captain Sutter's Fort at the time of the *Sitka's* return from Sonoma.

"As agent for Captain Sutter, Liedesdorff requested me to take one of the Indian crew of Capt. Sutter's schooner *Sacramento* (then lying in that port loading with an assorted cargo for the *Embarcadero*, New Helvetia) as a pilot and take her to Sutter's Fort.

"This I agreed to do. The crew consisted of a man who pretended to be an engineer and another jack-of-all-trades who acted as cook, deck-hand and fireman. Her cabin was the size of an ordinary omnibus; it contained seats which would accommodate nine persons; there was a stairway leading down with benches placed around the sides, somewhat similar to an omnibus. Everyone's knees touched in the cramped space and there was no lounging room.

"One bright day we left with flood-tide for the great Sacramento. A full complement of passengers was aboard including Judge Lansford W. Hastings and Mrs. Gregson and baby.

"The *Sitka* was a cranky pygmy of a craft and rolled badly every minute. It was the most uncomfortable journey I had ever made.

"We left San Francisco on November 28th and arrived at New Helvetia December 4th—six days and seven hours out.

". . . The day after the *Sitka's* safe return to San Francisco she was sunk by a southeaster in what is now Battery Street. She was laboriously raised and hauled by ox-team into Bush Street, above Montgomery. Here her engine was removed and she was turned into a schooner yacht. She was renamed the *Rainbow* and ran for years thereafter as a packet on the Sacramento River."

THE DIARY continues:

December 7th, 1847. The launch arrived at the landing place and the little steamboat departed. I visited the tanyard. There are great tule fires on the other side of the river. A cold, cloudy, smoky day.

December 9th. Marshall, Woodworth and Frazer arrived with four teams. Five wagons from the Mts. in charge of Wittmer and White. Sent a wagon with Brouett, Kelly, Pixton and Cox to the Mts. to get 10,000 feet of lumber sawn. Supplied the mill-race and Dam companies with provisions.

December 10th. Got the cargo to the landing place. But the launch was high and dry—they must wait until midnight for the turn of the tide.

December 11th. The launch could not be freighted until dawn. . . . She is finally underway. Dr. Edward T. Bale, the English surgeon, departed with his wagon for Napa Valley.

December 12th. John Bidwell took his team and started for his farm on the Upper Sacramento. With him went Frazer and Wade, who have also been in my employ. I took a long ride to the Fishing *Rancheria.*

December 14th. Major Pierson B. Reading left this morning with Chave for his new establishment on the Upper Sacramento. I sent Wittmer with seven wagons to carry shingles and lumber to the mill.

December 15th. A large number of working hands here from the mill-race, preparing for scraping. In company with Dr. Bates I visited both Mill-race and Dam. A pleasant day.

December 19th. Delivered 10 yoke of oxen with the yokes to the men at work on the Mill-race; also lent them chains, scrapers, ploughs, etc. I visited Anashe's daughter with the Doctor. She was dying and the Doctor bled her. We then left to bring her some remedies. The boys had a dance last night.

December 20th. Repairing wagons. Commencing on the Mill Irons for the Saw-mill. Sent ten men to the Dam. Mayan married Doloshey's mother. The Doctor again attended Anashe's daughter. She is improved. A very beautiful, mild day.

THE FIRST AMERICAN CENSUS was taken that year by John Sutter and the statistical data has already been noted. The following letter was forwarded with that information:

"Fort Sutter, Dec. 20th, 1847

"To the Hon. H. W. Halleck

"Lieut. of Engineering and Sec. of State.

"Sir:

"In compliance with the request contained in your circular to me, dated September 18th, 1847, I have the honor to transmit herewith the enclosed statistical information which I have been able to gather with much difficulty from different sources in this district, comprising the region east of the San Joaquin and Sacramento rivers.

"It would have been sent ere this but for the fact that we have no regular mail in this district and it is therefore extremely difficult to communicate with the interior. Great pains have been taken with the census and I believe it to be correct. The "tame" Indians are the Christian Indians who have been civilized since the white occupation of this valley. They are employed in the shops of the fort, as vaqueros, and as laborers on the different farms. Many of the wild Indians also come into the settlements at harvest times and assist in gathering the crops and threshing. These wild Indians live in the *Rancherias*; and those living as far as the base of the California Mountains are listed in this census.

"The western side of the California Mountains are thickly populated with uncivilized savages who are generally at war with other small tribes and do not frequent this valley. Their number I cannot give.

"The number of cattle, horses, sheep, mules, hogs, etc., may be relied upon as being correct. Also the mills and dwelling houses. We have as yet established no schools in this district, since the white population is scattered over a region some two or three hundred miles in extent.

"One of the flour-mills—driven by water-power—is now in operation; the other and the saw-mill are erected and will be in operation within thirty days. The horse-mills and tannery have been in operation for some years.

The dwellings are principally adobe structures occupied by my aides. Indians of this census comprise seventy small tribes speaking some twenty dialects.

"The quantity of wheat raised in the region last season was approximately 14,000 *fanegas*. I possess no data on barley, corn, peas, beans, melons, etc. to make an estimate, being familiar only with my own production.

"Very respectfully
"Your obedient servant
"J. A. Sutter
"Indian Agent."

THE DIARY ENTRIES continue briefly:

December 21st, 1847. One wagon of provisions to the Sawmill. Marshall has made the Mill Iron models and Firefield is at work duplicating them. The Doctor rode to Anashe's daughter who is recovering.

December 22nd. William McGloane arrived in his canoe from Yuba River on his way to San Francisco. Brown and the Wimmer brothers arrived with my 2000 fruit trees, shrubs, etc. Dr. Bates to see Anashe's daughter. Anashe came himself for flour and I gave him all the tasty things I had saved from my own table. A beautiful day.

December 23rd. Wagon with provisions to Upper House, Mill and Dam. Put the fruit trees in water and ploughed the garden to set them out. Dr. Bates visited Anashe's daughter again.

December 24th. A canoe with vegetables from Mimal. The women are washing. Livermore's delayed *manadas* are crossing today at the Bushune *Rancheria*—the most practicable place to cross. Lienhard has pruned the fruit trees, taken the new ones out of water and put them in trenches. Gingery came here with the welcome news that they were making first-rate progress in scraping and building the Dam.

Saturday, December 25th, 1847. Dolosea and Boyle arrived in a canoe from Nicolas (Altgeier's town) with pumpkins and fowls. Sent the canoe to Hock with seed potatoes. A great Christmas Dinner in the Hatter-House, given by the tanners and shoemakers. McKinstry arrived. Yanti came in the night with the news that Anashe's daughter is dead.

December 26th. A great disturbance last night by a prowling band of drunkards. It continued until dawn. The launch arrived at the landing place. A perfect day.

December 27th. Getting the launch unloaded and freighting her with wheat. Doctor Gitt arrived. Harry Trow came and left—but he got deadly drunk at Coate's.

December 28th. Many people here to trade. Rain this evening. The *Sacramento* left, Dr. Bates on board.

December 29th. The launch *Sarmiento* was also freighted and left late.

December 30th. The launch *Dice mi Nana* arrived this morning, received a full cargo of wheat, and left at once. Paid many Indians off. A fine day. Canoes from Hock with vegetables.

December 31st. Sent two large teams to haul logs to the coalpit. Getting coals here. Work on the Saw-mill irons. Wagons with provisions to Mill, Dam and Upper House. I ordered the gates to be locked. We are in the closing hours of the year 1847.

So passed John Sutter into a New Year. A Year of Destiny. It has been set down in the unpolished, day-to-day account of events in a wilderness. It has been inserted at the risk that it might prove tedious fare. For it clearly envisions the monotony and remote hours of a lonely land. In it is written the price John Sutter paid for daring to build an Empire of the Soil. Building it surely was. . . .

To his brother, Friedrich, he wrote in these last few moments of the old year:

"My beloved brother:

". . . I have received after much delay your letter bringing the sad news of our father's death. Alas, his decease comes so soon after that of our beloved mother. May they rest in peace. . . .

"You know by previous letters of my wanderings. . . .

"My holdings are extensive. In truth, I have not yet beheld them in their entirety. I named my new home New Helvetia, in honor of the ancient Roman title of our fatherland.

"A crude stockade and fort were my first concern, since the savages were at times none too friendly. The venture improves steadily now and *Sutter's Fort may still live in history*. . . . The Lord has prospered me in this new country and I now possess great herds, the measure by which a man's wealth is determined here.

". . . I can see your eyes grow large and you question who there is in this new land to care for the milk and make the cheese of such huge herds. But it is not with us as it is with you in the Alps. Our cattle are raised for the hides and tallow and we scarcely know the taste of butter. . . .

"Tell my nephews, John and Joshua, that if they were with me each would have a fine horse to race with. Horse racing is one of the diversions of this people, who, on the whole, I find to be kindly and hospitable. Withal, they carry pride to a foolish issue and have not our racial ideas of industry and frugality. . . .

"Bear my love to Christine and Barbara. They would enjoy the gay *fandangos* and feasts we have here, though the cock-fighting and bull-baiting would shock their gentle souls.

"I shall plan to send all of you remembrances of your far distant relative as well as more substantial help when opportunity affords in the finding of a trustworthy messenger.

"May the Lord preserve and prosper you all, is the wish of

"Your loving brother
"John A. Sutter"

View of Sacramento City from the river in 1849

Chapter XXXVI

CURTAIN!

JOHN SUTTER's empire was the last great fertile valley of earth to be occupied by civilized man. The whole domain was rimmed and barricaded on every hand. Coastal ranges rolled up in stony waves that buttressed the seaward edge. In the interior, the crumpled folds of an upheaved, primeval ocean floor towered loftily, high regions men called the Sierra. Within the terrain bounded by the heights spread a plain that opened toward the setting sun. There, in the first month of 1848, occurred an event that presaged swift change—an event that was to make a lusty, lustful young nation invincible, capable of sustaining its entity in civil war.

The heart of the great valley was John Sutter's Fort. It was the focal point of all valley life, laughter, labor and adjustment. On a hill it stood, bordered by the creek which vanished in the American River near its junction with the Sacramento, overlooking a huge expanse of ditch-enclosed fields and park-green grazing ranges, dotted and shaded by groves and belts of sycamores, elm, cottonwoods, ash and live-oaks.

Horses, cattle and sheep wandered on the lush plains, tended by Indian vaqueros. Boats freighted and discharged cargoes almost daily at the *Embarcadero*. Near the fort lay the ten-acre garden, skillfully laid out and cared for. Peach, apple, pear, olive, almond and fig trees marched in rows that squared the great vegetable patches. Two acres of Roses of Castile were being 'cut back' by gardeners for the glory of April and May.

Three miles below, on the river, lay Sutterville. A tiny collection of homes named for New Helvetia's founder. Sutter had built the first house there; soon some of his employees had followed suit. Zin's house was the first real brick structure erected in the country.

The *Amelia*, Sutter's twenty-ton sloop, carried on most of this settlement's river traffic with San Francisco. During the busy season two other smaller craft aided her. At the fort landing, a canoe and Indian paddler acted as a ferry. But that tenure of office was to be brief; a big boat was being rapidly constructed to take over the business and furnish a more satisfactory service.

There was no town or habitation on Sacramento's present site with the exception of one nondescript adobe, east of the fort, dignified as a hospital. The citadel itself was the great wilderness marvel. In it sat the Swiss, priest, patron, patriarch, judge, friend and father to all his people. All things to all men.

The interiors of the fortress houses were rough, with rafters and unpaneled walls; their furnishings were benches and deal tables and wilderness-fashioned knickknacks. Only the audience room and chambers of New Helvetia's chieftain differed from the rest. He owned a redwood table and some chairs and benches made in his own shops by Lassen and Neal; scattered about among these luxuries was a crude set of California laurel furniture that had been a part of the Fort Ross purchase. A few serapes hung about the walls; here and there an Indian blanket, fashioned in Sutter's looms, draped the chairs and benches. A meagre stack of precious paper sat on a little redwood stand, ready for the master's hand; a wooden candelabra, candle-filled, stood over the papers. The fireplace crackled and chuckled and glowed through every January hour that the Swiss kept to his quarters. Warm there, and scented with the fragrance of resinous wood smoke.

In front of the Captain's snug quarters stood a brass gun, sentinel-guarded. In the daily hum the sentinel's pace was lost. But at night his measured stride marked the stillness. Alone, rain or moon or stars, he chimed each passing hour beneath the belfry-post.

Daylight brought eager traders, bustling laborers, diligent mechanics. The shrill voices of the barterers cut the chorus clang of the smithy and the lesser beats of the carpenters; it won its shrillness above the clashing hoof-beats of horses. Riders dashed in and out of the gates, duty-or pleasure-bound. Wagons creaked along upon the gravelly roadbed. Mexican oxcarts complained moaningly from greater or lessening distances.

This was the valley capital, home of John Sutter and his resolute dreams, pregnant with approaching importance.

Upon the benevolent overlord of the place the people of the plain depended for permanent or temporary employment, for food and clothing, for aid and justice, for wise counsel and parcels of land. Most of the population were rough, hardy backwoodsmen. Occasionally, their buckskin garb and coonskin caps were enlivened by Hispano-Californian finery—bright sashes, wide sombreros, jingling silver spurs, astounding bandannas.

The natives were the best cared for in California. Sutter's trained cavalry and infantry were still present, dressed with military exactness; his personal staff of servants had acquired both skill and neatness under a kindly yet demanding eye.

About the fort enclosure and beyond the gates other Indians swarmed, swarthy, half-naked. They were tillers, field-hands, herders, garden-tenders. All of them huddled in Sutter-made blankets and coarse shirts, robed against the January chill, either assigned for duty, laboring, or expertly shirking. They wore strings of beads, gaudy handkerchiefs, and other ornaments. They were sure of food for the winter now; the "Father of the Fort" saw to it that they were fed, clothed, and attended in sickness. For this they were content to serve him.

Six miles up the American River the Mormons were constructing a flour mill (Natomo) for Sutter. Another party, under James Wilson Marshall's supervision, were erecting a saw-mill and race, forty miles above the fort on the south fork. Opposite the citadel, on the north bank of the American, Sutter's one-time Honolulu envoy, John Sinclair—now newly appointed alcalde—held the spacious *El Paso Rancho*. Above him stretched Joel Dedmund's *San Juan Rancho*, facing the Liedesdorff grant on the southern side.

The leagues belonging to New Helvetia's *grand seigneur* seemed to run without end. East of Hock Farm on Feather River lay the tract of Nicolas Altgeier—Le Grand Nicolas, who once, in his cups, tried to kill Sutter. Along the north bank of the Bear River, the wife-troubled Sebastain Keyser and the bantam-sized William Johnson had located. Opposite them were two reticent Frenchmen, Claude Chanon and Theodore Sicard.

The south bank of the Yuba was occupied by the trigger-tempered Michael C. Nye, John Smith and the Irish sailor, George Patterson. Facing them, along Feather River, lay the home and trading-post of the hard-drinking, whist-playing Theodore Cordua. Charles Roether was near Honcut Creek. Edward A. Farwell, the Boston printer, and Thomas Fallon, the capitalist-to-be, were his neighbors.

The lands of the perpetual bachelor, Samuel Neal, and Sutter's ex-cook, David Dutton, were on Butte Creek. William Northgrave, the fort charcoal burner, lived on Little Butte. Dickey, Sanders and the venturesome English sailor, John Yates, had recently yielded up the Arroyo Chico tract to John Bidwell.

Peter Lassen, the famous Danish trapper, had erected a mill and smithy on Deer Creek. The grindstone ''miner,'' William Moon and the quarrelsome, loud-mouthed, unprincipled Bear Flag leader, Ezekiel Merritt, held Moon's Rancho. North of the creek the amiable Albert G. Toomes occupied a tract. Job Francis Dye, the Kentucky trapper and trader, lived on Antelope Creek. Major Pierson B. Reading, on Cottonwood Creek, was the most northern settler in the valley.

On the west bank of the Sacramento lay the rancho of William B. Ide, also a Bear Flag leader. Below him, on Elder Creek, was William G. Chard, first man to work the New Almaden Mine. The peace-loving and respected Missourian, Robert Hasty Thomes, lived on the creek named for him.

On Stoney Creek, where Sutter obtained his grindstones, lived the crack-shot, Apollo-like Indian-killer, Franklin Sears, and his partner, William Bryant. Below them was settled the tanner, John S. Williams, and his wife—the first white woman in that region.

Walter Anderson lived on Sycamore Slough. On the north side of Cache Creek was honest, hospitable "Uncle Billy" Gordon, his place a rendezvous for hunters and trappers. Eastward lay the rancho of the stubborn, easily offended William Knight, exponent of the mailed fist on all occasions. Below him, facing the mouth of the Feather River, was the home of Thomas H. Hardy— Sutter's "loafer."

In a tule hut, facing the Sutter's Fort grant, lived the secretive John Schwartz. He was a taciturn soul, a builder of mind-fashioned castles. It was said of him that, having forgotten his native tongue, he learned no other. A northern slice of his land he sold to the unlucky gunsmith, James McDowell, who would be murdered within the year.

On Putah Creek lay the four-league grant of the placid Kentuckian, John R. Wolfskill. Adjoining on Ulatti's Creek, were the Vaca and Pena grants. At its mouth lived Miller, Berry, and the popular, enterprising Jacob Hoppe, fated to meet his death in the explosion of the steamer *Jenny Lind*.

Hence, down the Sacramento, were two towns sealed to disaster. Ulpinos represented Bidwell's failure. Lansford W. Hastings founded Montezuma at the junction of the Sacramento and the San Joaquin, at Suisun Bay. It failed, despite its founder's almost bizarre efforts at resuscitation.

At the Straits of Carquinez, however, sat a thriving village, one year old. Benecia it was called, in honor of Señora Vallejo. Robert Semple and Thomas Oliver

Larkin began the project after General Vallejo had donated the site. It had nearly a score of buildings and was causing a flutter of alarm in the hearts of the sanguine real estate holders at the Golden Gate.

This was the Sacramento domain, and its tributary territory, in 1848. All things seemed to favor the Swiss and the men who buttressed upon his empire. The United States flag now flew over the fort and the stretching leagues; law and order would shortly turn the plain into Paradise. It was merely a matter of months, of waiting.

So John Sutter worked and feverishly planned, never idle, not yet content. "So much to do, so little time left to do it in," the Swiss had often remarked to John Bidwell. . . . The work must go on. If ever a man saw the fulfillment of a dream in view it was this resolutely rooted adventurer, the lord of lonely lands.

SOFTLY ROUNDED HILLS covered with balsam, oak and pine stood near the south branch of the American, some two score miles beyond John Sutter's citadel. To the north were cracked, rocky slopes, patched with greasewood and *chemisal*, streaked with the deepening shades of narrow gulches. Between these boundaries slept a tiny valley, four miles in circumference. Its red soil was splattered with a thin verdure and shaded here and there by low bushes and trees. Coloma, "the beautiful vale," it was called.

Isolated it was, tranquil. In and about its confines lived an Indian tribe. They bore the name of the valley and camped nomadically on the banks of the stream which traversed the few square miles of plain.

Here, in the last six months, had come John Sutter's men, intent on rearing a saw-mill in the wilderness. They marked their course, these first white invaders, by a tree-blazed path. They had no intimation that they were laying the "props" for the first scene of a spectacular drama which would boast a world as audience. . . .

Since 1845 James Wilson Marshall, an American from New Jersey, had been employed by Sutter. Though eccentric he was an excellent mechanic. Free and easy with his fellow-workers, he was always surly, ill-tempered, and morose with strangers and superiors. Sutter's most pressing need of the moment was a saw-mill and Marshall had agreed to explore and decide upon a suitable site. After his agreement with the Swiss, Marshall began his surveys. After months of searching he had found and chosen Coloma.

On his return, Sutter fitted him out with an expedition to establish a permanent camp. Tools and supplies were loaded into Mexican oxcarts and a flock of sheep were driven with the wagons to serve as food. It took exactly one week for the ponderous vehicles and the meals-on-hoof to reach Coloma from the fort.

Shelter was the first necessity. A double log-house was erected four hundred yards from the mill-site. Later, two more log dwellings were to be added.

New Year's Day, 1848, beheld the risen mill-frame. Two weeks later the brush dam was completed. Then came a flood that nearly swept away the whole structure. But. Sutter's aide, with the Mormons and Indians, worked on.

Trouble arose with the tail-race. In order to save labor a dry channel fifty rods long had been selected; this had to be widened and deepened. It involved blasting at the upper end; otherwise it was easy to loosen the earth in the dry bed, throw out the larger stones, and allow the water to pass through the sluice-gate during the night to carry off the débris.

Marshall and Peter Wimmer, a wheelwright, supervised the Indians digging in the race; the Virginian Mormon, Henry W. Bigler, was drilling at its head; Charles Bennett and William Scott—who will "swear off" liquor for murdering a man this same year—were working at the bench; Alec Stevens and crotchety Jim

Barger were hewing lumber; Azariah Smith and bantam Bill Johnson were felling trees; and Jim Brown was profanely whip-sawing with an Indian. This was the order of labor as the mill drew onward to its completion. . . .

AT DAWN, on Monday, January 24th, 1848, the eccentric Marshall was sauntering along the rail-race, inspecting the channel. It was his habit to rise early and do this before the daily toil was begun.

As he walked, he casually noticed some yellow particles mingled with the excavated earth which had been washed by the late downpour. He gave them no heed at first. Then, somewhere in his imaginative mind, an amazing idea came into being. What if the gleaming substance was gold?

He stooped and began to gather up some particles. Then he called an Indian and impatiently ordered him to go to the cabin and fetch a tin plate. When the man returned Marshall washed out some of the dirt, separating about a half-ounce of the yellow flakes.

Then he went about the day's business. Occasionally, he pondered over his find.

"Boys," he finally remarked, that evening, "I believe I've found a gold mine."

"I reckon not," was his answer. "No such luck."

He shrugged and said no more.

The following morning he arose at the usual hour. Alone, he walked down by the race to see the effects of last night's sluicing; his first duty had been to close the headgate and shut out the rushing current.

Alertly slow, he reached the end of the race. His eye caught a glitter beneath a half-foot of water. Bending down, he picked up a larger piece of the substance than he had yet seen, a golden flake that lay against a protection of soft granite. In his palm it glittered like a tiny flame in the slanting rays of the new sun.

James Marshall's heart began to throb with an age-old excitement. The Scythians had felt it when they

mined the Ural; the dwellers on the Indus had known it
in the Gobi; in Ophir, goal of the sea-spurning Phœni-
cians, those ancient mariners had felt the self same
pulsing; men knew it as they came upon the yellow
splendor of Apulia; Cortez and Pizzaro felt the fierceness
of it as they fought for the magic metal. James Marshall
was but the latest of a vast succession. And this throb-
bing which he knew was to communicate itself to a half-
billion hearts. . . .

Could it be gold? Or was it mica or fool's gold? Marshall was no metallurgist. But he knew gold was heavy
and malleable. He weighed the heavy stuff in either hand;
then he bit it almost savagely; then he hammered it
furiously between two stones.

"Gold!" he cried thickly. "Gold!"

He set to work collecting the substance. In a half
hour he had some three ounces of it, flakes and tiny
grains. His men came down to work. Frankly they did
not share his enthusiasm about the yellow stuff. They
were skeptical.

Two DAYS LATER, Marshall mounted his horse and
rode swiftly toward Sutter's Fort. Half of his golden
find lay in a white rag in his pouch. The rain was falling
in torrents. But James Wilson Marshall took no heed
of unimportant storm gods.

John Sutter's man was bringing strange, disturbing
news to an empire-builder who visioned only trees and
fruits and crops and happiness coming out of the black
earth.

Chapter XXXVII

THE SHADOW

ON FRIDAY, January 28th, 1848, the Diary of John Sutter records: "Mr. Marshall arrived from the Mts. on very important business."

Just that. Nothing more. For John Sutter realized dimly the force of the thing that might be unleashed; the potentialities of the gleaming stuff that was filtering down through the tail-race of his remote saw-mill.

"One rainy afternoon," he wrote, "James Marshall entered my office at the fort, soaked to the skin and dripping water. He was very much excited and asked to see me alone at once in the 'big house.'

"I was surprised to see him. Only the day before I had sent him all the supplies he could possibly need—a completely cast mill-iron and provisions. I could not fathom the purpose in this unexpected visit.

"Yet I conducted him from my office to my private rooms—parlor and bed room—where we shut the door.

" 'Is the door locked?' said Marshall.

" 'No,' I answered, 'but I will lock it if you wish.' He was a singularly queer fellow and I only supposed he took this way of telling me some secret.

"Then he said distinctly: 'Are we alone?'

" 'Surely,' I answered.

" 'I want two bowls of water,' he demanded abruptly.

"I rang the bell for a servant. It chanced that I used six different signals for certain clerks and servants. The bowls of water were brought, the door relocked.

" 'Now I want a stick of redwood,' ordered Marshall, 'and some twine and some sheet copper.'

" 'What do you want of all these things, Marshall?' I cried impatiently. 'Come to your message, man!'

" 'I want to make some scales,' he replied.

" 'But I have scales enough in the apothecary shop,' I told him curtly. 'I need no more scales.'

" 'I did not think of that,' said he sullenly.

"Shrugging, and thinking to humor him, I went myself and fetched the scales. On my return I failed to lock the door. Then Marshall dug feverishly into his pantaloon pockets and pulled forth a white cotton rag which had something rolled up in it.

"Just as he was unfolding it to show me the contents, the door was opened by a clerk who was merely passing through on some business and was not aware we were in the room at all.

" 'There!' screamed Marshall, 'did I not tell you we had listeners!' Quickly he thrust the rag back into his pocket.

"I appeased him, my curiosity aroused. Ordering the surprised clerk to retire, I locked the door.

"Then he drew out the dripping rag again. Opening the cloth carefully, he held it before me in his hand. It contained what might have been an ounce and a half of gold dust—dust, flakes and grains. The biggest piece was not as large as a pea and varied from that down to less than a pinhead in size.

" 'I believe it is gold!' whispered Marshall, his eyes wild and restless. 'But the people at the mill laughed at me—said I was crazy!'

"I examined his find closely.

" 'Yes, it looks like gold,' I admitted slowly. 'Come let us test it. . . . .' "

So CAPTAIN JOHN SUTTER and James Wilson Marshall applied their wilderness wits to determine if the glittering particles were really the precious metal. After an hour's careful work, aided by an acid test in the apthecary shop, the Swiss declared the substance gold.

Marshall was overjoyed. "Let us ride to Coloma now!" he cried.

It was nearly dark; outside the rain was falling heavily and a wild wind was whipping the drops into liquid missles.

The blue-eyed man touched Marshall's wet shoulder. "Stay at the fort tonight," he urged. "We can go on in the morning. You must have food and rest."

But Marshall was obdurate. It was as if he did not hear. Without a further word he flung his serape over him, marched out the door, mounted his exhausted horse, rode off into the rain-swept gloom. John Sutter watched him vanish through the open gateway.

Then the Swiss returned to his quarters and his disquieting thoughts. . . . A new problem was upon him, a problem that set persistent creditors in the background. He must plan well. Far into the night he paced his room, his feet leaden, the firelight dancing on his thoughtful face. John Sutter was fey in those dark dawn hours, filled with nameless forebodings. He could not sleep. He could not sit. It was as if a dread presence, inexplicably menacing, had suddenly ceased its hoverings—was swooping down, talons wide.

FOR SEVENTY-TWO HOURS John Sutter pondered his new dilemma. What would happen if the news became generally known? Would his men still stay and labor for him as before? Or would they cut away from him swiftly, eager for the hidden metal? Would the saw-mill be completed under such conditions? Or the flour-mill? Could he and Marshall hold the thing secret until the mill *was* finished? A host of questions hurled themselves at the harassed Swiss. . . . .

At dawn of February 1st, Captain John Sutter started for the saw-mill, an Indian vaquero attending him. He rode swiftly, his mind preoccupied. The sun was a golden ball that adventured up into a now-cloudless sky. Through freshets and puddles their horses' hoofs splashed; there was the freshness in the air that comes after rain.

Halfway to the saw-mill his attention was attracted by a strange, half-crouching object in some bushes, ahead and to the right of the trail.

"What is it—grizzly?" he demanded of his companion.

"It is the same man who came to you in the rain three days ago," said the Indian.

"So?" said the Captain.

They came up to the hunched figure. Marshall straightened up.

"I've been watching for you!" he cried. "What kept you so long?"

"Business," said Sutter crisply. "Come, man, you haven't been waiting here for three days!"

"No, I slept at the mill. But I've come every day to meet you. Let us hurry!"

They rode on, Marshall mounting his horse that had been standing dejectedly near the bushes.

The rest of the way he babbled ceaselessly. Gold! The gravel was full of it! The whole valley was a great gold mine! . . . Sutter sat silent, a moodiness upon him.

They came at last to Coloma, "the beautiful vale." Darkness was not far off. Methodically, Sutter ordered his vaquero to unload the pack-horse and put his bags in a cabin which Marshall had lately built for himself. It stood only a little way up the mountain, not far from the mill-site.

All night the water churned and dashed its way through the race. In the beginning, experimentation had shown that the tail-race was incapable of conveying the water from the wheel. To rectify this, the water was turned into the race from the river, being diverted from the river channel by a wing-dam, and during the hours of darkness the current deepened the channel and cut away its margins.

MORNING BROUGHT the entire Coloma colony to the now waterless race, the headgate having closed off the river. Led by the expectant Sutter, everyone walked down the channel. Here and there lay the yellow flakes. Sutter stooped often, picking them up. In fifteen minutes he had an ounce and a half of gold. Later a goldsmith fashioned that metal into a ring. On it was inscribed: *The first gold discovered in California, January, 1848.* That ring never left John Sutter's finger in life. . . .

For five days the ruler of New Helvetia lingered at Coloma. He took the exuberant Marshall and went up the river on a tour of private seeking. They found gold all along the river course; even in the tributary ravines and creeks.

The truth was evident. The metal was surely gold. And another six weeks must elapse before the mill could be called finished! The flour-mill incomplete, also. . . . Sutter felt as if he was being drawn into a fathomless vortex. Without men to work for him, he could see ruin and disintegration facing this kingdom he had fought for. . . .

He called the laborers together. He doubled their wages. Then he bound them to solemn secrecy for six weeks. They, in turn, assured him they would complete the mill.

"No word—you understand—must creep out about this—happening," warned John Sutter earnestly.

The circled group about him nodded, gave their pledge. With that he was forced to be content. Indeed, his men were not yet ready to desert good wages for the uncertainty of gold-gathering.

Another plan thrust itself into his astuteness. If only the land could be secured on which this golden trove was so lavishly scattered! Perhaps the mining could be controlled to his own profit, interloping prevented; perhaps this gold might even be a blessing to New Switzerland's future. Any scheme was worth trying. The one which presented itself seemed a sane, workable one.

Mexican grants were no longer possible. But John Sutter sent out peremptory orders by his vaquero for all the native Colomans to gather in the little valley without delay. In two days they came, sixty-nine of them, and camped near the mill. They were ready to hear what the "Father of the Fort" wished of them.

Promptly, the Swiss began the same negotiations with the savages that the English colonists had made on the other side of the continent. Only he did not seek to buy the land. From the lords aboriginal of the tiny vale he obtained a three years' lease of a tract some twelve miles square. In payment he gave shirts, hats, handkerchiefs, shoes, flour, food and other articles. The document provided that the natives were not to be molested and were guaranteed the right to live on the land during the entire period of the contract.

At the parley's conclusion everyone seemed satisfied. With the sign-marked paper in his saddle-bags, Sutter went back to his fort. It seemed as if he had done all that was possible to avert a threat which held, somewhat subtly, the Known and the Unknown.

As he rode his silver *palomino* homeward, a shadow companioned him, stirrup to stirrup.

Chapter XXXVIII

THE MESSENGER

Exactly twenty-four hours after his return to the fort John Sutter sent a messenger to Monterey. He chose Charles Bennett to carry the Indian-signed lease to Governor Mason for official confirmation. He reasoned he was overlooking no loopholes by such a procedure. Before he dispatched Bennett in the launch for San Francisco, he patiently instructed the envoy in his rôle.

"No word must be spoken of gold," the Swiss drilled into Bennett. "You will merely state to Colonel Mason that I wish to legally lease the land with mill, pasture and mineral privileges. You may explain this last provision by saying that there is an appearance of lead and silver in the soil. Is all this clear to you?"

"All clear as day, Cap," said Bennett.

The Diary records this entry: "Sent launch to San Francisco, Charles Bennett, passenger. A good many people here pretty well 'corned'."

John Sutter's messenger was in Benicia for an hour when the launch tied up to unload some cargo. He wandered into Pfister's store and heard the news that coal had been found near Monte Diablo.

"Californy's bound to be a great state!" concluded the fat proprietor importantly.

"Coal, hell!" exploded Bennett. "Gather round, boys, and see this!"

He flung a buckskin bag down on the rude counter. It held six ounces of yellow flakes. The loungers crowded about him, eyes brightly curious.

When the launch left for San Francisco, a few minutes later, Sutter's envoy had destroyed the peace of Benicia.

He lingered even at the Golden Gate. There he encountered a man named Isaac Humphrey who claimed to know something of mining. Out leaped Bennet's pouch for further inspection.

"Gold," said Humphrey briefly.

On went the happy Bennett to Monterey.

On the same day the loquacious intermediary sailed for the capital, the Swiss Wittmer took two wagon-loads of provisions to the saw-mill. He arrived there on schedule and began to unload his freight.

One of the Wimmer children—Mrs. Wimmer was the camp cook—was playing about the wagons as Wittmer worked. Up marched the lad to the toiling teamster and thrust up a dirty paw clutching some glittering grains.

"Gold," said the youngster proudly. "My pap done found it. We got lots." He waited for a surprised word.

"Get out of the way with you!" grunted Wittmer. "I'm busy. Gold, your gran'ther! That ain't no gold. You're crazy."

"It is, too!" yelped the Wimmer lad. "You ask my ma! Oh, Ma—ma-a-a-a! Ma-a-a-a! This man says this ain't gold!"

Mrs. Wimmer appeared in the cabin door.

"Who says it ain't gold?" she demanded. "You needn't laugh. Of course it's gold. The earth here is full of it. You can ask my husband."

The wondering Wittmer was finally persuaded. When he departed he carried some two ounces of the flakes with him. . . .

On Sunday, February 13th, he arrived back at the fort. Without preliminary, he sought out Samuel Brannan's establishment.

"Whiskey," he demanded over the counter.

Brannan eyed him coldly. "You know our rule here, Wittmer," he said, "No liquor without cash."

He turned to wait on another customer.

"Hey, wait!" Wittmer flung out his pouch. "Here's money! Pony up that drink."

Brannan was unmoved. He picked up the pouch, looked at its contents.

"What's this?" he asked without interest. He threw it down again. "This isn't money, Wittmer. You're daffy." He turned his shoulder again.

"Not money, eh?" cried Wittmer, seeing his liquor chance vanishing. "Why, that's gold, you fool! That's gold!"

"Gold? . . . What do you mean, gold?" The store-keeper turned back to him.

"The mill-race is full of it up to Coloma," the teamster rambled on. "Ask anybody. Ask Cap Sutter!" he concluded triumphantly.

Silently, Brannan set out his drink.

Then he took Wittmer's pouch and walked swiftly to John Sutter's quarters. He knocked at the door, went in.

The Swiss sat writing at his table, blue eyes clouded.

Over walked the Mormon elder, threw down the receptacle and its golden particles on the scarred redwood surface.

"What's this I hear, Captain Sutter?" he said smoothly. "This talk about a gold mine at your sawmill?"

The man on the chair started; then relaxed. He looked at Brannan strangely.

"What have you heard, Mr. Brannan?" he questioned in clipped, brittle fashion.

"That you have a rich gold mine at Coloma," said the other bluntly. He touched the pouch. "Wittmer presented this pouch at my store for whiskey. He says this is some of the stuff here. Is it a fool's tale, Captain Sutter. What *are* these yellow flakes?" He bent nearer.

The Swiss picked up the bag, hefted it, a coldness upon him.

"It is gold, right enough," he said.

Brannan's eyes glowed. "What great news, Captain Sutter! Is there much of it?"

"A great deal—I think."

"I'm sure that those of us who take advantage of this may be very rich men," said Samuel Brannan slowly. He was a shrewd soul, was the Mormon elder.

"Perhaps so."

"It is great news for you, though," went on the other heartily. "Let me shake your hand, Captain. You will be the richest man in California!"

"So?" said John Sutter.

THE DIARY for that day, February 13th, 1848, reads: Rain until midday. Wittmer returned with two wagons from the mountains and told everyone of the gold mines there. He brought a few samples with him. . . .

The mischief was done. It was the kind of news that when you tried to bottle it up you set a fire under it. Gold! Gold! Gold! There was a magic about it that loosened human tongues and set them wagging fabulously. No one individual could have averted it. . . .

John Sutter sat speculatively in the night hours. But he worked even more feverishly by day. "So much work to be done—so little time to do it in. . . ."

THE DIARY reads on:

February 15th, 1848. Showers in the night; began to plow and sow wheat with six ploughs. Lienhard moved to the new garden.

February 16th. Rains and heavy gales till sunset. Then the sun appeared and a beautiful rainbow.

February 17th. The waters did not rise as high as anticipated. Sowed wheat and peas. Kyburz went to inspect the mill-works.

February 21st. Six ploughs sowing wheat and peas. Planted sycamore and poplar trees in the yard. William Johnson arrived with two prisoners who had killed one of his bullocks. However, they escaped in the night. Sent four square-pointed picks to the saw-mill.

February 26th. Rode to the fishing rancheria.

February 27th. A great dance at the Cosumne Rancheria.

February 28th. Provisions to Dam and Mill-race.

March 2nd, 1848. Received a load of salmon and sturgeon from the rancheria. Plowing and sowing wheat. Pachatu and a few Sagayacumnes came to me, complaining of three Chisseros (Sorcerers).

March 4th. More salmon and sturgeon from the Rancheria.

March 5th. Major Reading arrived.

March 6th. News that my launch has been buffeted severely by a heavy northeaster and is leaking. Mr. Long arrived in Liedesdorff's launch to secure some wheat. He has lost one of my Kanakas (Harry's brother) who was presumably drowned while swimming after the boat in Suisun Bay. Dr. Bates arrived again. Thirty-five Indians harrowing in the wheat field this week.

March 7th. Six men employed in repairing the small potrero. Provisions sent to mill-race and dam. Hudson and Willis started for the Mts. with intentions to be gold miners. The boys expect to have a big dance tonight.

March 9th. Many people here and drink being sold lavishly. Mr. Coates fell from his horse yesterday, had to remain with the Doctor, and has been robbed of three hundred dollars in the night. A fine day.

March 10th. I rode to the garden and the *Embarcadero*.

March 12th. All hands to the Mill and Upper House. rode with Thompson and Reading to dine with Mr. Sinclair. Beautiful but sultry day. Dances in the Cosumne Rancheria.

March 13th. Many Indians working but exhausted from their celebration. At nine I rode with Kyburz and Wittmer to the Cosumne Rancheria and burned their Temescal (sweat-houses) for having disobeyed my orders. *Mr. Charles Bennett arrived from Monterey.* Marshall and Wimmer came from the mountains.

A CRESTFALLEN MESSENGER was Bennett. He brought a direct refusal to make any promises or guarantees in regard to the land in question.

Said Mason: "California is yet a Mexican province, held by us simply as a conquest. No laws of the United States apply to it, much less the land laws or preëmption laws, which can only apply after a public survey."

It was a blow to the Swiss. More than ever he believed the find an unfortunate one for his personal fortunes. The land could be mined by anyone unless he could secure a title or lease which would be recognized. . . .

The Treaty of Guadalupe Hidalgo would not be ratified until the last of May—would not be known in California until August. By that time no legal acknowledgement could have held the land for Sutter. Yet that treaty formally ended the war and provided that all Mexican-made land grants were to be recognized; all legitimate titles in California were to be such as were legitimate under Mexican rule prior to May 13th, 1846. This treaty thereby guaranteed John Sutter's claims to both the New Helvetia and Sobrante Grants; without question it should also have assured the validity of the Fort Ross area purchase.

THE DIARY—so soon to be concluded—reads on:

March 21st, 1848. Shadden came with news that in a short time the robber bands now near San Francisco intend to raid our valley and drive off all livestock. Smith and Dr. Bates are boarding themselves from this date on.

March 22nd. Stormy, rainy day. A wagonload of provisions to the Mill-race. Major Hastings arrived from Montezuma. The wagons returned from the mountains and brought a few new-sawn planks as samples from my Coloma Saw-mill.

March 23rd. I had Wyme and Skekebe flogged for killing cattle. Two Mormons arrived with horses and mules from below; also welcome newspapers. Getting firewood. Ploughing for corn.

March 24th. Hastings departed for Sonoma.

March 25th. Finished the garden fence today.

March 26th. Last night Illameye was delivered of a still-born child. Caluge also gave birth to a girl.

March 27th. Six ploughs at work. Bidwell came in the evening.

March 28th. Thirty men working at ditching. Launch arrived. Loele brought six men to labor on the race.

March 29th. Shearing sheep. Bidwell left. Many visitors trading.

March 30th. A trial. Salinas stole Cadel's horse. I was a witness.

March 31st. Mild day. Shearing sheep. Sent launch to Hock Farm.

April 1st, 1848. Marshall and Wimmer from Coloma.

April 2nd. Rode to the Natomo Mills.

April 3rd. Marshall left for the Mts. Nearly all hands from the mill here—work progressing very slowly. Shearing sheep. Repairing horse-mill again.

April 4th. Dr. Bates and John Sinclair went to the Mts. to take a look at the gold mines.

April 6th. Sent some sick boys to the Doctor at Sutterville for treatment. Work as usual. Launch *Dice mi Nana* returned from San Francisco with Samuel Brannan. Came Mr. Hawk, the express mail carrier.

April 10th. A very busy day. Settled accounts with some of the Mormons. The launch with Brannan again a passenger left for San Francisco. A hundred hides were freighted in her.

April 13th. Finished shearing sheep. Only 1025 sheared. About a thousand remaining. The young lambs will amount to only four or five hundred. Ploughing.

April 14th. Two wagons with provisions to the Coloma Saw-mill. Willis and Jesse Martin arrived from the Mts. with a great deal of gold which they have brought to the store. Dr. Bates and Sinclair returned.

April 15th. Mr. Gray of Virginia departed this morning to carry the express overland to the United States.

Sent three wagons to Coloma. A canoe arrived from Feather River with Baptiste Ruelle and his family.

April 17th. Launch *Rainbow* (the reconverted *Sitka*) arrived. Reading, Kemble and Glidden, passengers. Planting corn. Ploughing. Beginning with the Telaria.

April 18th, 19th, 20, 21st. Absent to Coloma.

April 22nd. Pleasant day. Many people here. Bidwell, Hardy and Dickey in the evening.

April 23rd. A quiet day. Intermittent showers. Major Reading returned from the Mts.

April 24th. Launch *Rainbow* left. Started for the mountains Bidwell, Dickey and Coates. Last night a dance at the Cosumne Rancheria. This morning many of the boys arrived late. Some even remained home asleep. All were punished. A wagonload of salmon from the Fishing Rancheria.

April 25th. Wagon to Mts. with provisions.

April 26th. Rain all day. Getting cargo from the launch. All mill hands here. Refuse to work because of the weather.

April 29th. Knight and Nash left for the gold mines. Many men passing through to the gold mines.

April 30th. Gendron and Sicard left; also my excellent French baker. Marshall and Johnson returned from Coloma. Bidwell and Dickey came back from the gold regions. A great host of people here today, white and Indians; paid many off and they left.

May 1st, 1848. Sent two wagons to Coloma with provisions. Many men went up to the gold mines. Nash and Knight returned. A good many loafers have left. Getting coal and repairing potrero.

May 3rd. Harry and Manaiki (Kanakas) set out another garden.

May 4th. Sent a wagon to get salted salmon from the fishery. Bidwell and McKinstry returned from the Cosumne River region. Dr. Bates left with Linn for the Mts. Many others also.

May 5th. Nultu scalded himself with boiling water. Cockran, Chanon, Hewett left for the Mts. Brannan and Smith left for the gold mines.

May 6th. Brannan and Smith returned.

May 7th. Many people here. Brannan visited Sutterville, where he intends to build a new store and warehouse. Baptist died suddenly in the Fishing Rancheria and Butchi died at sundown in Chupuhu's Rancheria. This evening four suspicious-looking fellows camped near the fort. Delivered to the Mormons two small brass field-pieces to take with them on their journey to Salt Lake City.

May 8th. Sent two wagons with food to Coloma. Mr. Bidwell is surveying the town of Sutterville. Evans and Seibert returned from the Mts. Spinning, carding and weaving going on industriously. Beautiful day. Couvilland and Monet arrived having done well at gold digging.

May 9th. The exploring party of the Mormons to whom I sold the ordnance returned. They could not yet pass over the Sierra snows. Dr. Bates returned, saying he has discovered quicksilver, silver and gold.

May 10th. Came Thomas M. Hardy. Thomas J. Shadden, and three young men from the quicksilver mines (New Almaden) who now intend to go and wash gold. Canoe from Nicolas with cheese, butter and eggs. Sent Olimpio and Hella to Sonoma this evening with $214.20 worth of gold. A very warm day. More reports of gold and silver.

May 11th. John Bidwell went to survey again. I took a ride up to the mill at Natomo, race and Dam. Every hand who has been scraping left and went to the gold mines. Four men came from the quicksilver mines, bound for the gold mines.

May 12th. Many Mormons here. They purchased cows, mules and horses for $800 in gold. White-washed the fort. Cut ten blankets in the factory. A sultry day.

May 13th. Repaired the scraper. Verro arrived from the gold mines. Bidwell returned from his surveying work at Sutterville.

May 15th. Scores of people going and coming from the Mts. Putting a cargo of hides and wheat aboard the launch. Charles, the wagon-driver, fell from a bridge last night; his brothers and others insisted the devil had pushed him off.

May 17th. Many left for the Mts. Cleaned and white-washed the *Magasin* (penitentiary) and rented it to C. C. Smith as a store.

May 18th. Sent the *Sacramento* to San Francisco. Getting foods from the *Embarcadero* for C. C. Smith and Co. Many rushing to the Mts.

May 19th. Sent three wagons to the Mts. with planks secured from the landing place for Mr. Samuel Brannan. Many bound for the mines.

May 20th. Continual new arrivals from Sonoma, San Francisco, Peublo de San José. Sent 2 wagons to Brannan in the Mts. Dr. Bates returned from the gold region. Frost in the morning.

May 21st. Very busy. Continual stream of people going by to the Mts. C. C. Smith and Co. moved the store into my large granary in order to allow Kyburz to establish a muchly needed Boarding-House.

May 22nd. Bidwell left for the Upper Sacramento. Kyburz left my service and started his Boarding-House. I purchased Lienhard's share of the small garden for $1000. Cool weather. Boutschi died.

May 23rd. Hosts arriving by water and land for Mts. Fine day.

May 24th. Sent boat to Hock for wheat. Dr. Bates moving to give Kyburz room. Received news of the sad death of my friend William A. Liedesdorff. More and more people flocking to the gold mines. Loaned to Mr. Harlan three horses and two saddles to go to the Mts.

Thursday, May 25th, 1848. *Great hosts continue to the Mts*.

So ends the Sutter Diary. Events set so swift a pace thereafter that New Helvetia's ruler found no time to scratch a pen across paper. An ancient pilgrimage was finding renascence over a new trail. . . .

Chapter XXXIX

BRANNAN, PSYCHOLOGIST

Now CAME a transitional period between unbelief and certainty about the gold in Sutter's mill-race. It was, strangely enough, not a short one. Men usually scoff when swift fortune is assured by a few enthusiasts. "There may be gold," admitted the majority without great interest. "Not enough to bother your dad-blamed head about, though."

Some few were eager. But their eagerness was the transient kind, an eagerness which some men feel for all impossible tales. A fundamental emotional weakness for drama. When Vallejo heard the yarn from John Bidwell's lips, he made a gracious wish; no longer did a deadly feud exist between the men. "As the water flows through Sutter's mill-race, so may the gold flow into Sutter's purse," wished the adaptable Sonoman.

Most of the Californian inhabitants who did not live in the valley were as casually well-wishing. "Just a few flakes of it, anyway," they said. "Let Cap Sutter have it." The thing took time to generate its future frenzy.

Even at Coloma, the point of discovery, the change was slow, insidious. Only occasionally the workers brought out a sheath- or pocket-knife and cut away a shining flake; or took the trouble to wash out some of the gleaming gravel. But even that haphazard gold-gathering yielded them from three to eight dollars a day—much more than their wage from Sutter. The idea began to take hold. Still, they weren't sure there was so very *much* gold.

At off times they began to "prospect"—went up the river and searched farther for the bright grains. Success was theirs; some of the seams and gravel held larger and more abundant flakes than the tail-race. The golden area expanded, spread out. It was the beginning.

The Mormons working on the Natomo flour-mill took 'time out' to look for the precious stuff, advised to do so by their Coloma brethren. They found it easy to ferret out quantities of the yellow substance.

In the towns, only the eager few were at all impressed. Men of prominence laughed at the ridiculous story. "I would give more for a good coal mine," observed Robert Semple at Benicia, "than for all the gold mines in the Universe." Which was a tall statement from the tallest man in the territory.

On March 15th, 1848, the *Californian*, one of the two weekly papers in San Francisco, printed a brief paragraph mentioning that gold had been discovered in considerable quantities at Captain Sutter's saw-mill. On the following Saturday the other weekly, the *California Star*, added without editorial comment that gold had been discovered forty miles above Sutter's Fort.

The items created no excitement. Everyone regarded the possibilities of coal, quicksilver or silver as being beyond the golden chance. More speculative thought was centering on fruit-growing and agriculture. . . .

In April the editor of the *Californian Star* made a journey to the so-called gold regions to "ruralize among the rustics of the country for a few weeks." He hastened there and hastened back. His editorial read: "Great country, fine climate. Visit this great valley, we advise all who have not yet done so. See it now. Full-flowing streams, mighty timber, large crops, luxuriant clover, fragrant flowers, gold and silver."

This is all E. C. Kemble has to say about his trip. Whether he was a dissembler of the rarest vintage or merely saw nothing significant in the valley is unimportant now. But if the latter is true, Editor Kemble was a blind-eyed gentlemen in his reportorial dotage, unworthily consecrated to the Fourth Estate.

There were men in San Francisco, however, who were determined to see for themselves what these astonishing rumors might portend. They said little, for fear of ridicule. But they crossed quietly to Sausalito and thence struck out, via Sonoma, to Sutter's Fort. The trek was on, a meagre trickle of the flood tide.

Then, in May, came a frequent visitor to San Francisco from the Sacramento. He was that determined merchant-trader, Elder Samuel Brannan, a multitude of ideas whirling about under his broad-brimmed black hat. From Sutter's launch he landed and came striding confidently, blatantly up from the waterfront.

In his right hand he carried a bottle of glittering yellow grains. In his left hand he began to swing his huge hat in cyclonic circles.

' Gold! Gold!'' he cried. "Gold from the American River!''

Followed by a gathering crowd he stormed his way about, shrewdly cajoling, triumphantly sure. Samuel Brannan owned a well-stocked establishment on the Sacramento; it was probably the one item he did not dwell upon. The clever Elder was not so certain there was a golden fortune in the valley for every man he spoke to; but he was clandestinely sure that he would gather a goodly portion for himself if many men sought the yellow flakes. Was he not already collecting, as church tithes, ten per cent of all the magic metal discovered by the devout Mormon lads of the disbanded Battalion? To swell the gold-seekers thin column would be to swell Samuel Brannan's pocketbook. Which was all that interested that scheming worthy.

The drama of the market-place fulfilled itself beyond the expectations of its star performer. Every available sloop, lighter and nondescript craft in the harbor was quickly chartered for passage to the mines. They were loaded with human freight until a breath of wind might mean disaster. Many could not even obtain passage on the larger boats. Little rowboats and every rickety cockleshell in the bay region came into demand. Into these craft were stowed personal effects and equipment, a sail was put up, and the race was on.

Still others went by launch to Sausalito and thence by foot, mule or mustang into the valley by way of San Rafael and Sonoma. Some skirted the southern end of the bay and hurried forward through Livermore Pass. The Great Madness was begun.

But there were dissenters. "I doubt, sir," exclaimed one, to the editor of the *Californian*, "if ever the sun shone upon such a farce as is now being enacted in California. I fear it may prove a bitter tragedy before the curtain drops. I consider it your duty, Mr. Editor, as a conservator of the public morals and welfare, to raise your voice against this thing. It is to be hoped that General Mason will dispatch the Volunteers to the scene of action and send these unfortunate, demented people back to their homes. Yes, and prevent others from going."

The editor himself burst into tirade. "Fleets of launches left this place Sunday and Monday," he complained, "closely stowed with human beings. . . . Was there ever anything so superlatively silly?"

MEANTIME, A THOUSAND letters had gone forth to friends in the East and elsewhere, the first news of the abundant yellow flakes to reach the outside world. Incoherent, almost, some of those missives. But sufficient. . . .

Roads to the valley there were none. Only rough trails. With the sun for compass and mountain peaks for finger-posts new paths were marked across trackless plains and woodlands. Some of the seekers had horses and even pack-animals; these lucky ones proceeded swiftly. Others with ox-teams and Mexican carts travelled with heart-breaking deliberateness. Some lone plodders marched on foot with huge shoulder-packs. Only at rare points were ferries of any sort. Many a man swam a river with the gold fever in his veins; or, if lucky, had a horse's tail to cling to.

Personal comfort was non-existent. Few provisions and blankets were taken, a costly error. "Get there first," was the cry. The towns were stripped of shovels, axes, hoes, bottles, vials, snuff-boxes and brass-tubes, the latter to hold the yellow treasure.

By mid-June San Francisco was a deserted village. Seventy-five percent of the male population were mining the Sacramento Valley. "But now," moans the *California Star*, "stores are closed and offices vacated, a large number of homes are tenantless, various kinds of mechanical labor is suspended or given up entirely, and nowhere the pleasant hum of industry salutes the ear as of late. It is as if a curse had arrested enterprise. Everything wears a desolate and sombre look; everywhere all is dull, monotonous, dead."

Real estate dropped one-half. Labor rose tenfold. Merchandise not used in the mines was declined by the merchants. And now the two weekly sheets sang their swan song.

"The whole country from San Francisco to Los Angeles and from the seashore to the base of the Sierra Nevada, resounds to the sordid cry of Gold! G O L D ! G O L D !" wrote the saddened Kemble. "The fields are left half-planted, the houses half-built. Everything is neglected but the manufacture of shovels and pick-axes and the means of transportation to Captain Sutter's valley."

Whereupon the worthy editor shut up shop, paid a high price for a shovel, and started for the same place.

The town council sittings came to an end since no one came to sit. In the Plaza the little church was silent seven days in the week. Alcalde Townsend's office was locked, deserted. Shipping stood in the harbor, crews and officers gone. Judges abandoned their benches, doctors their patients. Prisoners slipped their fetters and fled inland; jailers followed hotly—as far as the gold-fields. Valuable land grants were untenanted; fertile farms were surrendered to idleness; waving fields of slowly searing grain stood uncut, oftimes open to roaming cattle; even gardens lay in untended waste.

"Bullock teams began to be more valuable," wrote J. A. Swan, one of the first miners. "Pack animals and pack saddles took a steep rise in the local markets. Blacksmiths worked eighteen hours a day to make picks and shovels—or sharpen old ones. Uncle Sam's soldiers grumbled among themselves about the hardships of standing guard, polishing muskets and pipe-claying belts when they might be busy in the mines putting gold into leather bags.

"The tars howled about the evils of holystoning dirty decks and about being forced out of dry hammocks on stormy nights to trim sail—all when they could be swinging a lazy pick and drinking as much grog as a sailorman could hold without having their backs clawed by the 'cat' for doing it.

"As the furore increased some of the soldiers commenced their march for the gold placers without official announcement or asking leave-of-absence. Some of the sailors got their land-itchy legs ashore and put on all sail for the 'diggings.' They preferred flapjacks and the musical jingle of nuggets in a poke to hard biscuits and a bos'n's whistle on a man-o'-war.

"Desert these hardy tars did, even in broad daylight and in spite of their officer's leaden objections. A party of sailors from the *Warren*, United States sloop of war, calmly took a ship's-boat and went ashore, led by the master-at-arms. Abandoning their craft on the beach they stowed themselves in a pinewood until dark.

"Then they went into town and bought provisions for their next land cruise to the mines. Instead of starting out at once they all got drunk. When they finally up-anchored from the tavern they had such a potent cargo on board that all harbors looked the same to them.

"Down to the beach they blundered boisterously, near the Monterey customs house, directly opposite their own ship. Then they all went to sleep on the sand.

"Had the *Warren's* officers known where they were, the entire company could have been recaptured and dumped aboard ship. As it was, just before daylight one of the deserters awoke. A ship's bell came clearly to his ears—a familiar ship's bell. At once he aroused his companions. With great speed they proceeded on to a less dangerous anchorage. It was a close squeak but they finally cast anchor at the mines. . . ."

ONLY A FEW remained calm in chaos. The centenarian Don Luis Peralta, called to his sons and grandsons. They gathered about him. His quavering old voice rang out in warning.

"My sons," he said, "God has given this gold to the Americans. Had He desired us to have it, He would have given it to us ere now. Therefore, go not after it, but let others go. Plant your lands, and reap; these be your best gold-fields, for all must eat while they live."

So spoke the patriarch Peralta, in whose slowing veins ran the blood of men who have always followed gold over the earth and fought for it to the death. . . Luis Peralta, the Spaniard. . . .

THE OUTSIDE WORLD—what of it when the news came? Navigation companies began an exploitation not equaled in history. Steamship lines were formed for both the Cape Horn and Panama routes to San Francisco. Every old tub of a craft that could be kept afloat by bailing was thrown into dry-dock; keels were caulked and daubed, the vessels were skimmed over with a perfunctory paint brush and renamed. Presto!—she had become one of the staunch new steamers of the reputable Pacific line. The Isthmus itself, *if* reached, was crossed by foot or on burros.

The enterprising boat owners also hired publishers and newspapers to print and circulate the most fabulous untruths about the quantity of gold actually taken from the mines. Huge pieces of iron were gilded and placed in show-cases and windows in every principal city and village in Europe and America. These exhibits bore the intriguing sign "FROM CALIFORNIA." Crowds pushed their way closer to gaze upon the fabled riches. No man could pass by such a display without knowing discontent and determination in the same breath. . . .

Newspapers presented only the glowing side of the picture. It was painted with startling yellow ochre and lacked nothing from a publicity angle. Men gathered and made plans to organize caravans of covered wagons for the overland trip. Speed was the idea. Get there before the other fellow.

In the commercial centers of the world could be seen mountain-high heaps of baggage labeled or tagged "SUTTER'S FORT, CALIFORNIA." It was the lodestone, the most suddenly famous spot on the habitable globe.

As John Sutter fought and pledged and planned and schemed the tide was gathering force, was already upon him.

Chapter XL

VISITOR EXTRAORDINARY

JOHN SUTTER's fort no longer sat in a remote wilderness. Hundreds of men were reaping a golden metal harvest out of the gravel, streams, fissures and "pockets." Over expanding square miles of foothills the diggings extended. Gold became miraculously plentiful in a land that had known only hides and tallow as the chief currency. The wilderness voices had given way to curses, drunken songs, cries of joy, the sound of pick and axe and shovel—this was the feverish heritage that gold had brought to the Sacramento.

As ever, the fortress stood supreme as the center of trade and distribution. Near it numerous shanties and log-huts rose up out of nothingness to serve as stores, hotels and saloons. Several new craft were beating up and down the river with passengers and goods, unloading regularly at the *Embarcadero*.

The ferry, now a large barge, was in constant operation. Along the roads freight caravans were rolling, their frantic oxen goaded on by merciless teamsters, great clouds of incandescent dust swirling in their wake. Parties of horsemen, heavy packs hanging from their saddles, curled out and around the slower-moving vehicles; they even passed the mule-driven wagons which were making much swifter progress than the straining bullocks.

But more numerous than all toiled the foot-weary ones, on their bent backs a roll of blankets; in the packs were flour, bacon, coffee, tobacco, a little whisky and ammunition; suspended to the straps was a frying-pan, shovel, pick and rifle; in every belt was a brace of pistols and a dirk. Up steep hills and over parched plains they came, striding beneath a hot sun; at night they were so weary that they dropped and slept wherever that sun dipped away and left them.

Bustle ruled the fort. Miners, traders, Indians came and departed ceaselessly: bronze-faced stalwarts in red and blue woolen shirts; men in deerskin suits and fishermen's boots; men with sombreros, Mexican sashes and silver spurs; and frequently arrived some ragged, unkempt soul whose fat pouches gave the lie to his woe-begone appearance.

Even then the unlucky ones outnumbered the successful seekers. It was the kind of labor that destroyed men's bodies and withered men's minds. They worked under a searing sun, often knee-deep in water and silt, usually in moist ground; continual expectation of a big strike took its subtle toll of nerves and wits and strength as backs bent to the unaccustomed task; mostly the shelterless men slept all night on hard ground. Food was scarce. Scurvy attacked with swiftness because of a lack of vegetables. Out of it all came fever and dysentery; weak men died and were buried—if their friends found time to raise their shovels from the golden gravel. . . .

Every storehouse in Sutter's citadel was jammed to the ceiling with merchandise; provisions, hardware, drygoods, whisky, tobacco, salt, sugar—these and a hundred other commodities were heaped about awaiting purchasers.

John Sutter's quarters were crowded with visitors. They had taken the appearance of a tavern rather than private rooms. The cheerful Swiss had a kind word for everyone; and a helping hand. From dawn till late at night he supervised and devised and assisted and suggested and commanded. The guard-house was deserted now. Most of the buildings had been rented to traders and hotel-keepers. A rushing, prosperous business was the order of the long days. Workshops were as busy as ever; the places of deserting artisans could be instantly filled from passers-by in temporary need.

Ready gold was streaming into John Sutter's coffers, a pleasing thing. But he had a place for it. The patience of the Russian American Fur Company was almost at an end. They cared nothing for tales of three-year droughts or wars—not more than one half of the $30,000 debt had been paid, they complained. The last installment had been due in September 1846; it was now nearly two years in arrears. The company was moving legally now, through their agents, to attach the entire New Helvetian property, including the later Sobrante Grant.

Their action came at an inopportune time. Yet if he could hang on a few months longer this steady stream of gold coming into his hands would wipe away the debt— every debt—without trouble. To make them wait was the problem. . . . It was another acute phase of his battle for continuance. "It can be managed," said the Swiss confidently. Not once did he surrender his surety in the moiling midst of change. . . .

True, he had paid $30,000 dollars alone into the Natomo mill; now it lay idle. No man would work a mill when he could dig for gold. The $10,000 saw-mill at Coloma was turning out no more lumber; the Mormons, too, had deserted to prospect the incredibly rich finds at Mormon Island. Sutter had sent some of his Indians out to bring in gold; but their efforts were inexperienced and unavailing. Moreover, he could hire no trustworthy person to go with them and instruct them. No one was willing to be hired when a personal fortune beckoned with the quick turn of a shovel or the rhythmic sway of a rocker.

In desperation, Sutter finally sold out his share of the saw-mill for $6,000; let the new owners work it for themselves, reasoned the Swiss. For him it was an impossible venture. He needed the money badly to stave off the Russian court action. Now was the time to pay off all his debts.

ON AUGUST 17th, 1848, Governor Mason wrote out his famous report. "We arrived at Sutter's Fort the second of July," he set down. "All along the whole route mills were lying idle. Fields of wheat were being trampled by horses, cattle and heedless men. Houses were vacant and farms going to waste.

"Launches were discharging their cargoes at the *Embarcadero*. Carts were hauling goods to the fort, where several stores and a hotel were already established. . . .

"Merchants paid Captain Sutter a monthly rent of $100 a room. While I was present a two-story house in the fort was rented at $500 a month as a hotel. . . .

"At Captain Sutter's urgent solicitation, General Sherman and I remained to take part in the first celebration of our national anniversary, July 4th, at Sutter's Fort. . ."

CAPTAIN SUTTER himself gives a few detail of that occasion. "The day began," he recalled, "with the hoisting of flags and the firing of cannon. It was a Valley Holiday and no work of any sort was contenanced. At this time there were four excellent cooks at the fort— Mrs. Montgomery, Mrs. Lehigh, Mrs. McDowell and one other.

"The table was laid in my old armory hall and dinner was served in the afternoon. Sitting at table were invited guests only. We were attended by my trained Indian boys.

"The dinner passed off very well. Excellent food covered the long board. I had recently been lucky enough to purchase many delicacies from a French vessel— sauterne, brandy, cheeses and other imported foods. The Captain had freighted it up to me aboard his launch. We also had sugar, fowl, game, beef and many luxuries beyond the station of frontier existence.

"This was the first July 4th in the country under the American flag and all of us were in festive mood at such a happy circumstance. We rejoiced, for we expected good government and a rapid settlement of the territory. Many toasts were proposed and numerous healths drunk. Philosopher Pickett—he who later shot down a man for differing with him politically—was orator of the day. . . ."

The fortress chieftain cast aside all personal worries and embarrassments, played the host as only John Sutter could play the rôle. Food, drink, and fellowship ringed the table round during that fleeting hour; and it is said by some oldsters that the cannons still echo down the wind on a bluff day in the Sacramento Valley. Sherman and Mason ever remembered the wit and kindliness and courtesy they were accorded by the Swiss on that roving inspection.

It is true that, years later, Sherman wrote into his book a remark anent the excellence and abundance of Sutter's wines and liqueurs on that occasion; also that the host of the affair was a bit "tight." Which was the exact condition, also, of every guest present.

IN LATE AUGUST 1848, a tall young man disembarked from the *Sacramento* at the *Embarcadero*. It was three o'clock in the afternoon of a sultry day. Ordering his luggage to be brought up by Indians, the youth began a solitary walk to the fort.

Huge wagons overloaded with freight passed him, enveloped him in clouds of dust; horsemen darted by in either direction; footwalkers like himself were many. He strode on, his eyes curious, troubled, speculative.

At very last he came to the gates. In and out surged the traders, miners, Indians and vehicles. No one paid any attention to his arrival. Hesitantly, he surveyed the busy scene for a full five minutes.

Then he went into the enclosure. The sight seemed to fascinate him. He edged up against a shop-wall to the left and stood silent. All about was confusion, shouting, hammering, hauling of goods, clangor of steel on anvil.

After a time the tall young man walked forward, toward the central building. A rough teamster passed him.

"Do you know whether Captain John Sutter is in his office?" asked the youth.

"Cap Sutter's up Coloma way—jest left this mornin'," answered the man.

"When will he be back?" questioned the stranger. "Dunno," said the man, walking on. "Yuh kin ask o' the clerk thar." He was gone.

The young fellow turned back and came to the open door of the quarters. A trickle of roughly dressed miners was streaming in and out. He waited; then went in.

A red-eyed man was sitting at a redwood table, writing. A half-filled glass stood convenient to his right elbow. He glanced up.

"Yes?" he said importantly.

"Is it true that Captain Sutter is away?" said the visitor.

"Yes, be back in a week," said the man. "What can I do for you?"

"A week?" repeated the youth, slowly.

"Yes."

"No way I can reach him?"

"Not unless you're bound up Coloma way," said the clerk.

"You see," said the young man, "I must see him on very important business—"

"Can't it wait?" observed the man at the table.

"Perhaps," the boy answered. "I'm his son, you see."

The clerk came to life. "The hell you are," he exclaimed, frankly startled. "I did know Cap was married, too." He rose up, shook the youth's hand. "Lang's my name. Sit down. We'll see what we can do. . . ."

So John Sutter, Jr., came to New Helvetia. His father's letter of three years past had finally brought one member of the family to his side. The boy was twenty-one years old—a man grown. . . .

SEVEN YEARS LATER, John Sutter, Jr., wrote an analytical story of his arrival and experiences. It is presented here for the first time in print—a vivid document that explains much.

"I arrived in California in the month of August 1848," he wrote. "The gold had been discovered only a few months previously. I had already heard many strange reports in San Francisco, altogether contradictory rumors about my father and the state of his affairs.

"Some said he was the richest man on earth and did not know his own wealth himself. Others, to the contrary, told me confidentially that because of his loose and careless manner of transacting business, he was on the brink of ruin. Instead of being associated with honorable and trustworthy men he was surrounded by a parcel of immoral rogues; instead of aiding him, said these last informants, the rascals would only accelerate and accomplish his utter moral, physical and financial ruin.

"Some acquaintances even went further: on the first day I landed in San Francisco certain individuals sought me out and advised me to interfere immediately in my father's behalf, discharge all rascals in his employ, attend to his business myself in person—all this if I wished to save a penny for my father and my family.

"Some even presented themselves with claims against my father, asserting the length of time they had patiently waited for payment, and remarking that they now looked to me for an early accounting.

"My father's agent in San Francisco was then Mr. Peter Shenibuk, a Dane. I waited upon this gentleman and acquainted myself with as much of my father's business as was possible.

"It is impossible for anyone to imagine with what contradictory feelings I set out for Sacramento in my father's schooner, that craft then happening to be in port. All the rumors made a very definite impression on my disturbed mind. Having never heard that my father was a drunkard and a victim of disorderly habits, I could not and would not believe it without proof.

"Arriving at Sacramento the first people I met were George McDougall's men—the crew of his schooner— Robert Ridley, a German named Hahn and an American named Lang. These last three men were pointed out to me as my father's business servants. Ridley was ill and left for San Francisco two days later. I never saw him again.

"But I observed Hahn and Lang drunk in my first day at the fort. My father had gone to the mines on business and was not expected back for some days. So I was left alone with my reflections. Some of my worst fears had been confirmed.

"Now I saw with my own eyes how business was conducted. Anything belonging to my father was at every man's disposal. The traders in the fort (Brannan, Ellis, Pettit, Dr. McKic, Capt. Dring, Pickett, etc.) furnished everybody with anything they desired and billed it on my father's account.

"Indians, negroes, Kanakas, white men—all indiscriminately applied to my father and easily obtained letters of credit from him which entitled them to any amount of provender or stores in and about the fort.

"Straightway every man in his employ wanted to acquire my confidence and friendship. Every man had a different tale; each blackened the other fellow with hearty zest.

"At this moment Major Hensley and Mr. McKinstry arrived at the fort. Hensley I had known slightly in Washington City before my arrival; both men had been in my father's service and were well acquainted with his affairs. Both these gentlemen informed me that my father owed the Russian American Fur Company $30,000 with interest, a sum due from his purchase of Bodega and Ross; also that William A. Liedesdorff, the company-appointed agent, had sued my father for this amount and that the sheriff of San Francisco had levied an attachment on the entire properties of my father.

"Major Hensley then departed for Major Reading's place, having heard that Reading was dangerously injured as the result of an accidental shooting affair. Mr. McKinstry stayed with me in order to urge a plan upon my father when he returned. This plan was to have my father transfer all his property and real estate temporarily to me, both Hensley and McKinstry having come to the conclusion that this was the only loophole by which to stop the execution of the attachment for the time being. Given a short time, means could be procured to pay the $30,000 debt; also all the remaining indebtedness, the total being some $80,000.

"From the books turned over to me by Hahn, I could never clearly ascertain the state of affairs, so confusing were the entries. Moreover, they had been neglected for some six months. As a proof of the reality of the confusion existing there I may state that I found the now (1855) so important original survey map of Captain Vioget in an open drawer; also the signed contracts with the Russian American Fur Company and the acknowledged bills and accounts of Captain Frémont.

"At last, after a week of terrific anguish and uncertainty, the father who I had not seen for fifteen years rode into the fort. Our first meeting after such a long separation was as affectionate and sincere as ever meeting ought to be between father and son on such an occasion. Both of us wept. Seeing my father so kind, so affectionate, I soon forgot all I had heard, and was unreservedly happy to be with him at last.

"We spoke a long time of my mother, my brothers and my sister; of family matters; of times gone by. Then we came by graduation to the present stressful period. He soothed all my fears, telling me of his splendid plans for the days to come, when we would all be united again; of his certainty to be soon out of all difficulties. I was quite happy. . . .

"Then Mr. McKinstry proposed to him the plan for the transference of everything to me. After consideration my father agreed, seeing the necessity for some such action for a short period.

"Two days later, Myron Norton and Mr. Gilbert arrived at the fort. Norton had been a fellow passenger with me on the voyage from New York, having come as a Lieutenant to join the New York Volunteers under Colonel Stevenson; the other was also an officer in the same regiment. Both men were lawyers and on their way to the mines.

"I informed my father of their arrival, asserted their civil profession, and told him that they were able to draw up a legal document of the sort which we desired. Both men were presented to my father and he requested their assistance in the matter.

"They went to work and drew up two documents, my father signing over all his property and real estate to me. These documents were recorded in the records of Sacramento City. I also pledged to my father that I would pay all his debts as soon as possible, as he was insistent on this point.

"This was my only way of saving the family fortune from utter ruin. . . ."

IN OCTOBER the rains began to fall. Cold weather made mining difficult, almost impossible. Back went the tide of seekers to the coast. Still, some hardy ones remained; nearly a thousand wintered at Dry Diggings—those of them that lived.

The wisest of the miners devoted a little time to erecting log cabins and ensuring comfort for that winter season; less prudent men could not resist laboring with pick and shovel until it was too late. The weakest of them died in their cloth and brushwood shanties before the spring floods came.

But many made the seaward trek, some sick, more disappointed, a few successful. They were a ragged, sunburned, grimy, shoeless, feet-blistered lot; their beards were unshorn; their hair fell over their shoulders; their eyes were bloodshot, filled with a fathomless restlessness. . . . Some of the lucky venturers kept their golden flakes; but most of them squandered all their earnings in the long winter debauches in the towns.

So passed 1848, a year of stress and opportunity and uncertainty for all. Yet it mattered more to the Lord of New Helvetia than all the others. He had more to lose!

CHANGE

CAME the most incredible year in John Sutter's life—1849. It was also to be the most incredible year in the history of California. In its twelve months was to be portioned drama of a sort which knew a daily climax. All the world seemed to be beating a path to John Sutter's door. Which proves a gold mine as potent a lure as a better mousetrap.

Events swirled by with stormy rapidity after Sutter passed over his real estate and property to his son. Early in January the Swiss engaged Peter Burnett—destined to be first governor of California under her statehood—as counsel. Reading, Hensley and James King of William all advised the appointment of Judge Burnett. He was a clever, honest, far-seeing man and Sutter's interests were admirably represented in his hands.

At once he took over the business in detail—a hodge-podge of accounts it was, too. During this period Sutter-ville was to contest supremacy with the Sacramento City tract—a project begun in the first days of the new year. Burnett agreed to oversee the Sacramento venture and accept as his salary one fourth of the proceeds made from the sale of all town lots.

Henry Schoolcraft was employed as bookkeeper. Captain Warner of the Topographical Engineers was also present at the fort.

Some months before, Samuel Brannan and others had approached Captain Sutter with a plan to lay out a city on the plain surrounding the citadel. Sutter had refused since he favored Sutterville as a more practicable site for swift building. Now, with Sutter usually absent and his son in control, Brannan returned to the persuasive wars. He brought pressure to bear on the younger Swiss. A cunning fellow was Elder Samuel Brannan.

Because squatters had already begun to settle about the *Embarcadero* without permission, young Sutter was all for action. He agreed to Brannan's scheme. Captain Warner was engaged to survey the Sacramento City site, having secured a leave of absence to take over the task.

Sales began to go briskly. Lots near the river sold at $500; in the vicinity of the fort for $250. Then George McDougall began a determined effort to secure the entire waterfront for himself for an insignificant sum; he threatened John Sutter, Jr., that he would attempt to establish a preëmption claim to the land unless he secured the river frontage. Merely another highbinding assault on the landholding Swiss.

"WHEN I BEGAN to sell lots in Sacramento City early in January, 1849, for J. A. Sutter, Jr.," wrote Governor Burnett, "all business was transacted at the fort. There were then only two houses near the *Embarcadero*. One was a rude long cabin turned into a saloon; the other log cabin was occupied by a fine old man named Stewart and his family.

"Nearly all the first sales of lots were made near the the fort. But toward the end of January the lots near the river began to sell more rapidly. The price of lots in the same locality was fixed and uniform; I made it an inflexible rule not to lower the price for speculators. This prevented a monopoly of the lots. I discouraged the purchase of more than four lots by any one person. . . . The terms were part cash and part on time."

THERE IS NO QUESTION but that John Sutter was attempting to pay his debts as soon as possible. At no time were his actions those of premeditated dishonesty. The transfer to his son was only temporary—was to exist only eight months. . . .

"Captain John A. Sutter, the original grantee," continues Governor Burnett, "conveyed his property, real and personal, to his son, John A. Sutter, Jr., in October 1848. This was done to prevent one creditor, who threatened to attach the property, from sacrificing the estate, to the injury of other creditors and the useless ruin of Captain Sutter and his family.

"There was absolutely no design to defraud the creditors; on the contrary, time proved that the course adopted was the wisest and most just, under the circumstances, toward all creditors.

"John A. Sutter, Jr., at once informed me he was bound, under the agreement with his father, to pay all Captain Sutter's just debts; all this at the earliest practicable period. I saw both the justice and expediency of this purpose and set energetically to work to accomplish the end intended. *By the middle of August 1849, the last debt that ever came to my knowledge had been paid.*

"It is not at all surprising that Sutter could not save up money enough to pay off his debts until after the finding of the gold. There was practically *no* money present before that time. I am somewhat of a pioneer and business man myself and I do not hesitate to state my opinion that no man could, under the exact circumstances in which Captain Sutter was placed, have paid those debts before the discovery of the precious metal.

"That great event was entirely due to an act of Captain Sutter's. But for his mill the golden treasure might have remained undiscovered for a half-century to come. No one can tell. We only know the fact that he was the direct cause of the discovery. . . .

"In his treatment of the Indians Captain Sutter was humane, firm and just. I remember well that in the winter of 1848-49, the Indians would often call at the fort and anxiously inquire for him when he was absent on his busy trading ventures, crying for him to protect them from wrong. They evidently had the greatest confidence in his justice. He had been their friend and protector for years; but his great power was even then entered into its twilight. . . ."

THEN CAME THE MEN OF '49. The *California*, carrying four hundred gold seekers, entered the Golden Gate on February 28th. She was the first vessel to bring treasure hunters from the eastern seaboard. Over the side went everyone—passengers, captain and crew; she was an abandoned ship thirty minutes after she made harbor. Some of her complement left San Francisco on their way to the mines before nightfall. From then on the sea-lanes brought them ceaselessly; thirty-two thousand of them that year.

White-covered caravans were hastening overland to Sutter's Fort, as imposing as the sea-migration. From all the states they came to Independence—or its vicinity—to organize and start in May 1848. From that month on, one long line of wagons and pack-trains was strung out as far as Fort Laramie. Cholera, fever, scurvy, hunger, exhaustion—all took their toll. A nation was on the march for John Sutter's gold. Forty-two thousand of them came to New Helvetia in 1849. . . .

The men of '48 and the men of '49 differed. Those of the first year were acquainted with their neighbors, had trafficked with them, were original settlers or trappers or hunters; they were a rough-and-ready sort with the wilderness code still strong in a majority of buckskin-covered breasts, just in the matter of personal property rights. Again, they were only a handful compared to the later arrivals. It remained for the men of '49 to really usher in the astounding phenomena of The Great Madness.

SLOWLY THEY DESERTED John Sutter's shops—the men who had worked because of temporary need. When the spring came and the winter floods died away under the sun, the exodus became more pronounced. With furrowed brow the Swiss watched his remaining aides vanish. Beside him now stood his son. He did not feel so alone. . . . It was a comforting thing, this having the flesh of one's flesh beside one; this being able to discuss problems that beat upon one's mind.

And still the laborers departed. In April, only two remained—a blacksmith and a wagon-maker. Then they, too, were gone. He had been paying them in daily graduating wages.

Leather lay rotting in the tannery vats. Anvils gave out no hearty clang. Saws lay with silent teeth and hammers sat voiceless on benches. No wandering needy ones applied to work for even a few hours. Spring was on the land and men sought yellow flakes of fortune. . . .

It was more confusing than ever. True, the Indians still labored in the fields and tended the herds; but even their numbers had dwindled. The looms still sang and brown fingers still traced a rude pattern. But John Sutter did not know when the pattern would cease to be.

His flour-mill, too, was quiet; the hoofs of the grinders did not clatter at the circling task. Whenever his boats went freighted to San Francisco now they returned, sunk to the gunwales with eager hordes, the Indian crew beaten, cowed, ununderstanding. A little while before almost everyone trusted his neighbor. Now, overnight, no one's property was safe.

The right of the strongest and the most ruthless had come to rule over the gold-lands. All very disturbing, very; the unexpected is ever that. One planned, and a torrent swept one's plans away as if they had not been; one schemed, and one's schemes were nullified and discarded by a pack of crazed interlopers who knew no law or sanctity. Respect for legal possession was swallowed up; lust for the yellow flakes had eaten away the codes by which men lived, laid a corrosive finger on the Ten Commandments.

If a miner needed a horse he took the first one his eyes rested on; more often than not it was John Sutter's horse. If a passer-by needed a bullock for food, he butchered a bullock; quite often it was John Sutter's bullock. New Helvetia sheep met the same fate as the horses and cattle. Supplies began to disappear mysteriously from the fort—nothing movable or usable was safe from pilfering hands.

Hock Farm, Sutter's Feather River rancho

One went to sleep at night and woke to find that some nocturnal wayfarer had walked off with something which fitted his necessity or caught his fancy. . . .

But all clouds were not black. The Swiss was receiving tremendous rentals for his fort rooms and store-houses. Even with the tools idle from their business of fashioning, the stores did a rushing business. Men flocked to buy food and clothing and mining supplies. But all those commodities were brought in by boat, now. John Sutter's men and shops did not produce them. . . .

Not one white retainer now remained to the Captain and his son. Bewildering. Such was the power of the golden flakes. One could only fight, resolutely.

"It can't go on!" stormed Sutter. "Some change must come!"

But a fortunate progression seemed as remote as New Helvetia once had been.

THE SWISS thought of one way to turn an ever-increasing flow of gold into his pockets; a scheme of certainty. Men must eat, wear clothing, own shovels and rockers and pick-axes. Straightway John Sutter opened trading-stores at Coloma and Sutterville, bent his energies to the task of supplying and supervising them. He chose, of necessity, partners who seemed to him trustworthy, reputable. He had known men like Bidwell and Reading and Hensley and Burnett, all honorable men; but some of these newcomers were of another breed, cunning, smooth-spoken, avaricious. They insinuated themselves with the generous Captain, became his aides.

Wagonloads of provisions now went almost daily from the fort to Sutter's posts—posts which during his absences were ruled over by his new asscoiates. These foodstuffs and supplies were bought by Sutter at enormous prices from other merchants at the fort.

The result was foregone. Every agent stole from the genial Swiss; his gold flowed out for the wagonloads of goods and did not flow back from their sale. All the rents of the citadel—some $3,000 monthly—were always over-drawn in advance.

Numerous destitute men sought him out and beseeched him to enter into mining contracts with them on shares; to all such hard-luck tales he listened and furnished provisions, Indians for labor, and tools of all sorts to carry out the projects. Naturally the only ones who profited were his self-styled 'partners.' If a strike was made the partner vanished in the general direction of San Francisco and outbound points. If a strike was not made, he called again for more provisions and mining supplies.

John Sutter was not emotionally equipped to refuse aid to anyone. "A fool," said some briefly. A weakness, surely. But then, the Swiss was a human, friendly personage; had he been ruthless, harsh and militantly acquisitive, he might have been the richest man in the world. . . .

Then again, people were ceaselessly calling at the fort to settle accounts. There was hardly a man in the gold-fields who did not owe John Sutter; and nearly every one of his debtors presented bills *against* him. It would have been ludicrous had it not carried an element of tragedy.

Each trip the *Sacramento* now made up the river and back realized an amazing profit for her owner—no matter how many miners commandeered a 'free ride' on the return voyage. The recently established ferry-boat service was also another source of prosperous returns. Most of the money found its way into the greedy hands of George McDougall, in payment for goods furnished Sutter at exorbitant prices.

In January 1849, Colonel Stuart of the United States Army arrived at the fort. He had been appointed by the Russian American Fur Company to receive the final and overdue payment for Fort Ross and Bodega. Full payment was made at that time.

Captain Sutter turned over ten thousand dollars in gold dust and the rest in notes which had been collected from Sacramento City lots; these notes were afterward equably collected by the company. Sir James Douglas arrived with a $7,000 bill presented by the Hudson's Bay Company, a debt which Sutter knew to be utterly preposterous but which he paid without demurrer. William French hunted up a $3,000 debt in the Sandwich Islands and was paid in gold dust; French had been a member of the bankrupt firm of French and Greenway, Sutter's companion on the *Clementine's* voyage, and the man chiefly responsible for the Swiss being bilked out of the sea-venture's profits. Other claims advanced by Antonio Suñol, Martinez, Messrs. Starkey, Tannion and Co., and others were paid in yellow flakes.

Sutter fretted continually against a lack of funds to bring the rest of his family across the sea. Judge Burnett advised him to satisfy all creditors before sending a penny for their transportation. It was a bitter struggle for the Swiss and his son; but, finally, everything that resembled a debt was wiped away.

In April 1849, John Sutter raised $6,000 in cash for a purpose he had dreamed for years. He engaged Hienrich Lienhard to act as his agent and take passage at once for Switzerland; there he was to pay what small debts were outstanding—$1,700 in all—and bring Anna and the three remaining children to New Helvetia. An extra $4,000 was paid Lienhard for making the trip; also his traveling expenses. In June, Lienhard sailed from San Francisco on his mission.

Then Sutter moved from his citadel to Hock Farm. That was in March 1849, and he leased his fort quarters at $200 a month. It was baffled retreat; but not defeat. He considered it the strategic thing to do. There his stock was far safer than about the fort. Provisions, farming equipment, goods for the Indians, furniture, hogs, sheep, chickens—everything was sent up before his arrival. He also sent orders for a new home to be begun;

he hoped to have it completed and well-furnished before his loved ones came.

"We have at least one happy event to look forward to," he often said to his son.

THE SWISS was not beaten. He was still planning. "Law will not come to us until we bring law," he said. "We must make a state out of California. We must make and enforce our own orders. . . ." So, with his other plaguing distractions, he gave thought to such a creation.

Squatters had already begun to claim his land, settling themselves wherever they wished. No attention whatever was paid to his protestations; he could have reasoned as well with deaf men.

In the *Placerville Times* of May 5th, 1849, the following notice was addressed to the gold-squatters who were unlawfully pitching tents and even building homes on Sutter's holdings:

"All persons are hereby cautioned not to settle, without my permission, on any land in the following designated territory: Said land is bounded as follows: Commencing on the north, in Latitude 39 degrees 33' 45", at a point on the east bank of the Sacramento River, running thence east three leagues beyond the Feather River; thence south to Latitude 38 degrees 41' 32"; thence west to said Sacramento River; thence up and across the said Sacramento River to the source, excepting a certain tract, included in the above, granted by the Republic of Mexico to one Eliab Grimes. It lies on the east side of the Sacramento, is bounded on the north by Latitude 39 degrees 1' 45" and on the south by the American Fork.

"(Signed)
"John A. Sutter, Jr."

But mere notice was not enough. The controversy went on. A few months was to bring it to militant magnitude.

"I HAD BEEN AT THE FORT only a short time," wrote Governor Burnett, "when the question arose as to some governmental organization. The great majority of people then in California were gathered in our Sacramento district. Business was remarkably brisk and continually increasing. Lots were selling rapidly; but who should take the acknowledgement and record the deeds?

"The war between the United States and Mexico had terminated with the cession of California to the United States. We, as citizens, were quite satisfied that the military government, existing during the war period, had ceased to function adequately. We knew little of Mexican laws and had no means or inclination to learn them. In the meantime, business must go on.

"We were of the opinion that we had the right to establish a *de-facto* government, which could be continued until superseded by some legitimate organization. This *de-facto* government was to be fashioned in its essentials after the existing provisional government in Oregon.

"Accordingly, we held a public meeting at Sacramento City early in January 1849. There Henry A. Schoolcraft was elected First Magistrate and Recorder for the District of Sacramento.

"Our necessity was simple and merely designed to allow us to proceed with ordinary business for the time being. In fact, meetings of the same sort were being held all over California. The advisability of some such action was apparent to all. It was the beginning of California's attempt to organize a provisional government with the express purpose of sanctioning a permanent and stable organization. . . ."

John Sutter was one of the moving spirits in this agitation for electoral and continuing government. He saw and faced clearly the present crisis: unless some law was established quickly and a new state brought into being he stood a very fair chance of losing everything. It was a recurrent specter in front of Sutter's eyes, this holocaust of change. Action—swift action—was the only solution.

So he sent letters to prominent men in Los Angeles, San Diego, Santa Barbara, Monterey and San Francisco —such men, at least, who had not come to the mines. Each missive bore his urgent wish for all to gather at some central spot and discuss the situation.

All were concerned and interested in the need for action. Comment and plans were made daily wherever men met and talked.

Brigadier General Bennett Riley—he of the astounding multi-syllabled oaths—relieved Colonel Mason in April 1849, as military governor of the province. The bluff Riley sensed the tenseness. He immediately issued a proclamation setting August 1st as the date for the election of municipal officers and convention representatives for each district; he also chose September 1st as the time for the electorate to assemble at Monterey and begin their business of creating a state.

Each district—ten of them—agreed to send duly-elected representatives as the new military chief had requested. The elections were held and the various men chosen.

The hopeful Swiss was the elector selected to head the Sacramento delegation; with him went Lansford W. Hastings and four others. Peter H. Burnett, Sutter's counsel, was elected chief justice of the Sacramento district on the same day. Up and down the length of California forty-eight men were chosen to draw up a constitution.

At last the "Father of the Fort" felt that something was about to be done that would revitalize the old sureties.

"We must become the thirty-first state in the Union," said John Sutter to his son.

Chapter XLII

THE BREEZE-WHIPPED SAILS

FROM THE ORDERLESS confusion of his valley John Sutter sailed for San Francisco in late August 1849. Changed from the village of a year ago it was now, reaching out, taking on growth. Ships lay at anchor in the harbor, deserted. "Nearly fifty of them!" muttered the Swiss wonderingly.

Then he and his five elected comrades left the *Sacramento* and boarded the Monterey-bound brig *Frémont*. Sutter's mind was sealed to security; he saw it assured through the birth of a commonwealth, through the laws to be so shortly enacted when they reached their objective. In a few months justice would be his. . . . Along the course he glimpsed other deep-laden craft beating their way toward the Golden Gate.

The last day of August brought them to port. They were the first of the delegates to arrive, the southern contingents having been wrecked enroute on the *Edith*. Not for three more days would they arrive, safe but somewhat dampened by a boisterous sea. Certain that a quorum would not be present on the morrow, Sutter and his companions began a hunt for suitable quarters.

Monterey and its twelve hundred inhabitants were poorly equipped to entertain forty-eight strangers for a month or more. There was no hotel—not even a reputable restaurant in the entire village. So the task of entertaining was to fall upon the most hospitable citizens. Despite handicaps, they managed admirably.

The most spacious and comfortable homes in the town were those of Thomas O. Larkin, Don José Abrego, Dona Augustias Jimeno, and Don José Soberanes. Larkin made it a rule to invite a different delegate to luncheon and dinner every day during the convention, this despite the fact that Mrs. Larkin was an invalid. Señor

Abrego, one-time treasurer under Governor Pio Pico, frequently entertained a number of guests in the evenings. Of all the Monterey socialites he alone boasted a piano, one of those imported by Stephen Smith some years before. Don José Soberanes, too, was a gracious welcomer of law-makers, ever alert to offer ease, good food and moments of relaxation.

Most popular of all the hostesses was the beautiful Dona Augustias Jimeno, daughter of Captain José de la Guerra of Santa Barbara. Witty, gay, accomplished, never at a loss for a charming word, she made her home the center of social life. Richard Henry Dana had praised her twelve years before in his famous book. Now, at thirty-five, the lovely lady had a daughter as incomparable as herself. For years her home had been "open house" to all American officers entering the port; there had never been a time—whether in war or peace—when Americans had not been welcome there. It was due to such saving graces that Monterey was made livable for the gathering visitors.

The convention itself was to be somewhat of a commercial awakener to the sleepy capital. During its course several houses were built, four hotels were erected and a half-dozen stores opened. A Chinaman was the smiling-faced proprietor of one hostelry. Another was built by an Italian tinsmith who had invaded the province five years before without a penny in his trousers-pockets. This mustachioed opportunist had borrowed a few sheets of tin and manufactured some tin cups. These found a ready market and brought a good profit. Rumor now rated him as worth fifty thousand American dollars; his hotel, as soon as it was habitable, rented for $1,200 a month. Washington House it was called and some of the guests paid as high as $200 per month for a single room, the place being managed by an ex-private in the Stevenson Regiment.

Several restaurants came into being under the impetus of state-making. The chefs were Indians and the shrewd proprietors were usually Mexicans. Meals were a dollar each; the quantity of food served was abundant but the variety of dishes soon palled, even on feverish delegates. An *olla* of dried beef with cucumbers and corn, an *asado* of beef and red pepper, a *grisado* of beef and potatoes, execrable coffee—this was the unchanging menu offered the convention members.

Other smaller drawbacks were sometimes noticeable. Truth is, several delegates were flatly accused of sleeping under the pines of Point Pinos, in their blankets and Mexican serapes, to escape the crawling pests.

Captain Sutter was Larkin's only permanent guest during the session; the others took their "turns" at the luncheon and dinner hours. The remaining Sacramentans were installed at various other homes; some may even have patronized the starlit "Point Pinos Hotel."

On Monday, September 3rd, 1849, a quorum was present for business in Colton Hall, first capitol building of California. This structure had been erected by Walter Colton, a chaplain of the frigate *Congress*, who served as alcalde from 1846. In March of 1849 he wrote:"The town hall, on which I have been at work for more than a year, is at last finished. It is built of white stone quarried from a neighboring hillside. The lower apartments are designed for schools; the hall over them, seventy by eighty feet, is for public assemblies.

"The front boasts a portico, which you enter from the hall. It is not an edifice that would attract any attention among public buildings in the United States; but in California it is without a rival. It has been raised out of the slender proceeds of town lots, the labor of convicts, the taxes on liquor shops, and the fines levied on gamblers' banks. . . ."

Across the great upper assembly room a temporary railing had been thrown to divide members and spectators. Inside this railing the delegates were seated at four long tables. The presiding officer occupied a rostrum at the farther end. Over this daïs were suspended two

American flags aslope above a picture of the nation's first President. An extraordinary picture, that; had the artist not thought to designate his subject no man but himself could have puzzled out the likeness as being that of the Father of His Country.

Evening sessions were held with some regularity. Lights were furnished by tallow-candles set in candlesticks and chandeliers of no elaborate pretensions. In the middle of the hall a door opened on a small, square balcony; here the delegates could occasionally retire, get a breath of fresh air, and enjoy the marine view.

In the first meeting Sutter declined the chairmanship. Put to a vote, the lanky Robert Semple was chosen for the honor. Rapidly the convention got under way and discussion began.

It was a picturesque gathering. The loose-jointed, blatant, unkempt McCarver sat with the fiery, observant Lansford W. Hastings; the grasping John McDougall companioned with Henry W. Halleck and Thomas O. Larkin; Joel P. Walker talked rapidly with the astute William M. Gwin, the politician who had adventured purposely from Washington to be California's first United States senator; the immaculate Sutter sat with Vallejo, Carrillo and de la Guerra; the convivial Benjamin F. Moore carried a huge bowie-knife and a full complement of grog for each deliberative session. When awake, he was the noisiest of the assemblage.

They were all notably young men. Six of the forty-eight were native Californians. Abel Stearns, Thomas Larkin, Hugo Reid and John Sutter had all been in the province from ten to twenty years. Fourteen were lawyers, twelve were *rancheros*, seven were merchants; the remainder were engineers, bankers, physicians and printers.

Only infrequently did controversy become heated. Some were brief in speech—Sutter, Halleck, Larkin and Stearns were of that number; many, like Gwin and Betts, were continually voluble. Most of the Californians sat together at one table; usually they voted together.

No attempt was made to formulate a new Bill of Rights. The existing constitutions of various states were studied intensively and their best points adopted. Committees were appointed and went to work; amendments were suggested and revised.

One amendment was unanimously adopted "that neither slavery nor involuntary servitude, unless for punishment for crimes, shall ever be tolerated in this state." The silver-tongued, moody-eyed young Irishman, William E. Shannon, was responsible for first entering that particular section which thus declared California forever a "free" commonwealth.

The location of a new capital brought hot debate. Finally San José was chosen. The limits of suffrage took some days for its discussion. Then the section prohibiting the sale of lottery tickets met with opposition. Sutter and others favored their sale as a means of financing the infant—and penniless—state; opponents were equally set against the measure. Sixty years earlier, all sorts of enterprises—both public and private—had been financed by lotteries. Schoolhouses, bridges, churches, public structures, even those first erected at the new national capital on the Potomac, had been built by such means. In fact, as late as 1832, as many as four hundred lottery schemes with prizes aggregating $47,000,000 had been promoted in the United States. However, the amendment was defeated.

A special committee prepared a design for a state seal. Drawn by Major Robert S. Garnett, it is the Great Seal of California today.

Humor entered into the convention hall when the seal was presented for official acceptance. General Vallejo surveyed the bear and wrinkled his nose. It suggested the Bear Flag episode, a memory of some embarrassment to the Sonoman. At once he rose to object.

"If the bear is to appear at all, Mr. Chairman," he cried excitedly, "I suggest the beast be shown as being held in check by a lasso in the hands of a vaquero!"

A ripple of polite mirth came from members and spectators. Semple's long face took on a grin.

He put the matter to a vote. Only the Californians backed Vallejo for a change. So the unsatisfied General had to accept the seal without alteration. . . .

Ten minutes later, he misunderstood another verbal passage-at-arms. He jumped up and demanded instant enlightenment. Another wave of laughter swept the gathering. This time the General had mistaken the word free-holders to mean *frijoles*; and querulously wondered why food had suddenly leaped, out of nowhere, into the discussion.

At very last came the report which was to occasion the warmest debate of the convention—the boundary question. Sutter had been appointed chairman of that special committee, his aides being Hastings, de la Guerra, Reid and Rodriguez. These five were impanelled because they possessed a wide and general knowledge of the territory. For weeks they worked on the important issue.

Then John Sutter presented his findings and opinions to the assembly. The present-day boundary of California was his choice. Bitter words raced about before the suggestion was officially adopted.

After the boundary dispute was settled the convention swept to conclusion. A few regulations providing for the submission of the constitution to the people and for organizing and installing the new government were approved in the form of a schedule. The document was then rushed to a copyist for engrossment.

On Saturday morning, October 13th, a short session was held. An address to the citizens of California was approved, submitting the results of the convention; a resolution of thanks to General Riley for his coöperation was also included, after which the delegates adjourned until two o'clock in the afternoon, reassembling then for the last time.

To all it was an historic moment. The entire assembly demanded that John Sutter sit as chairman of the convention in that last session. All the preceding night the copyist had labored to prepare the document for signature. It was completed exactly one half hour before the assembly met.

This closing act in the birth of a new state was signalized with due ceremony. All vessels in harbor displayed their colors; irrespective of nationality, the Stars and Stripes were hoisted above them all. Captain Burton, commanding the fort, was ready to fire a national salute.

John Sutter rose and set his hand to the document, a hush upon everyone. Then the flag sprang proudly up to the flagstaff peak of Colton Hall, carrying its glad message to the fort that the signing had begun.

A crashing roar reëchoed over the sea and land. It was the first gun. One by one the members filed forward to sign the momentous scroll.

The guns were booming in measured intervals. Every spectator and every signer found voice; cheer after cheer bade the infant stateling welcome and a long life.

John Sutter leaped upon the rostrum and waved his arms above his head. "Gentlemen," he cried, "this is the happiest moment of my life! It thrills my heart to hear these cannon salute our new state! . . . Gentlemen, the new State of California has just been born! God grant her honor and eternity!"

With tears of joy streaming down his face, the Swiss resumed his rostrum seat. Cheer after cheer beat out over the town.

Came the thirtieth great roar—a gun for every state of the Union. There was a pause and again every human voice was hushed.

Then it came, gloriously, the thirty-first gun. Over the sea it sang and followed its fellows over the hills and away.

Up went a great shout that drowned the mighty detonation. "That gun is for California!" cried everyone. The rafters of Colton Hall shook in the uproar.

The last delegate had written his name boldly in that last moment. . . . Semple, the lanky giant, so soon to die. . . .

A CONVENTION BALL was decided on for that evening —a farewell tendered by the delegates to their friends and hosts in Monterey. Each member had contributed $25 toward the festivities and immediately after the signatory ceremony the hall was turned over to the decorators.

Tables, chairs and rostrum were removed by a busy crew. Large and small American banners were placed along the walls, set between fragrant young pines that scented the air. Over came Don José Abrego's piano—a six-octave instrument made by Beitkopt and Hartel, Leipzig—and was installed with due care in the hall. Two violinists and a harpist were engaged to aid the pianist.

Came eight o'clock and every soul who could crowd into the confines of the assembly room. It was a great affair. Spanish dances and American dances followed each other in rhythmic sequence. Bright eyes and bright dresses and small slippers got down to business. Masculine attire was not nearly as impressive as the brave feminine show; not even if one nameless dandy did pay $50 for a pair of patent-leather pumps—cracked a bit, but a bargain.

John Sutter, a little heavier now, hair gray about his temples, danced with the zest of youth. He believed the confusion of the valley would soon be a memory. . . .

"A happy, happy night," he said to all.

Toasts were drunk to the new state and its magnificent future; refreshments were delicious and inexhaustable; the music was quite the sweetest and most lilting the old town had ever heard. . . .

Not until a fresh rose-color came flooding into the east did the state-makers and their friends go home to rest. More than the wine warmed their hearts that historic night; each man who had written his name that day felt a little like a Master of Creation.

NEXT MORNING, led by Sutter, the forty-eight strode to General Riley's quarters. Out came that officer to wait upon them, surprised at the visitation.

As chairman, the Swiss delivered the letter of thanks and made a short speech of appreciation of Riley's efforts to assure good government in a disordered wilderness. The crotchety officer was touched by the sincere show of gratitude.

He thanked them simply for their good wishes. In conclusion, he remarked that he was allowing them $16 a day each from the civil fund; also $16 for every twenty miles they would travel, coming and return, which information brought him a parting tiger on the end of three lusty cheers.

That afternoon most of the delegates made plans to sail or start overland on the morrow. Sutter was especially anxious for a swift journey home. The unsettled condition of the New Helvetia plain claimed his presence without delay. . . .

Semple and a half-dozen others came to see him that evening at Larkin's. Their request surprised him.

"We want you for our first governor, Captain Sutter," they said.

He shook his head slowly. "You do me a great honor, gentlemen," he observed. "But I am a busy man—too busy to mix affairs of state with my present—er—difficulties."

His blue eyes swept the circle. "There are many among you more qualified for the post than myself. Again I thank you." He touched Semple lightly on the arm. "But I must refuse. My work is in the Valley."

The delegation was obstinate. But he was single-purposed always, this resolute Swiss. "It is impossible, my friends," he repeated. "My time and my efforts are bounded by New Helvetia."

He sailed for San Francisco in the morning. In that short journey a portentous vision came to those aboard the brig *Frémont*. The horizon became studded with white canvas, tilted by sharp winds, driving a sea of caravels to the Golden Gate. With a magical swiftness John Sutter's ship seemed to lose its individuality, become one of the rushing argosy. . . . It seemed to the rail-bound Swiss as if all the ships in all the oceans had begun to seek out the land of the yellow flakes. Deep in his heart he suddenly felt a tiny ghost of fear parading; the men aboard these ships would know no law save that of might and opportunity.

"When will peace come to the valley again?" said John Sutter. But he asked the question of himself and not of the deckload of chatterers who cheered and watched the breeze-whipped sails. . . .

Mrs. John A. Sutter from a photograph of an oil painting

Chapter XLIII

THE FOREST OF MASTS

WHEN THE *Frémont* swept into the bay, after less than a two months' absence. A collective gasp rose from her decks. More than half a thousand vessels swung on their hawsers in the tide, deserted; they had reached journey's end and been abandoned for the treasure of John Sutter's Valley. Their masts were like swaying, unsure fingers that pointed to ever-changing ports; and never meant to leave the last one they had found.

Sutter and his companions landed on Clark Point. Once again the city had taken on distance and breadth. On Telegraph Hill a huge signal mast pierced the blue; the angle at which its arms were set indicated to the waiting crowds what class of vessel was surging hopefully into the roadstead. Already squatters' huts perched on the rugged spurs of the signal hill and tents dotted the ravines. Corrugated-iron stores reared themselves along Sansome Street. Auctions flourished along Montgomery, raucous and inviting. On the mud flats in their rear lay barges unloading merchandise. Clay Street above Montgomery was a drygoods center. Long Wharf, the water extension of Commercial Street, unfolded into a colorful peddlers' avenue and Jew's quarter; there Cheap Johns with sonorous voices and sharpened wits hourly attracted groups of idlers. The levee eastward— Liedesdorff Street—held the Pacific Mail Steamship office. California Street boasted express offices, places of amusement, and the customs house. The city did not go beyond Bush Street save along the shore line of Happy Valley.

Portsmouth Square was still a bare spot, occasionally serving as a cow-pen, pierced in the center by its liberty flag pole. Gambling houses lined the Plaza, picturesque streamers ruffling in the wind to attract idlers whose pockets were heavy; tawdry in the day, they took on the brilliance and glitter of palaces at dusk.

The migratory city hall stood on the corner of Pacific, playfully waiting to move on to other quarters and vestments. At present it was a four-story structure combining prison-room and courtroom. The opposite block, stretching toward Montgomery and at the base of Telegraph Hill, held shabby, murderous dives of the lowest strata; brothels where crime and violence were bred or enacted every hour. The ancient partners—pimp and prostitute—were hawking their virulent wares in a land of gold.

Sydney Town wound its lecherous way northeastward around the hill, favorite haunt of the British convict class where cockney, Limey and Australian met and plotted dark schemes. Many a whisky-bemused miner was being sandbagged, robbed and tossed into the bay in that region during the night hours. West of this unhealthy morass, up Vallejo and Broadway, was the Catholic church and the bull-ring. Northward along the hill was Little Chile, rendezvous of the South and Central Americans. The French lived along Jackson Street, two hotels offering significant—and intriguing— accommodations at Clark Point.

Little China was a soft-footed reality on Sacramento Street. Even the Germans had a favorite resort at the end of Montgomery where a hearty "Hock!" and a heavy mug of lager might tickle the palate and exercise the elbow muscles.

Dupont Street was a mixture of shops and restaurants. Powell was the abode of churches. Mason Street was the western limit of the ribald city; Green Street was the northern. Beyond Mason the trail ribboned away to find the Presidio.

The infamous Hounds, mongrels mostly recruited from Stevenson's regiment, bayed nightly on the rapine trail. Lotteries flourished. Everything, from San Francisco City lots to the Pacific Theatre in Sacramento, was offered for the lucky pasteboards. Street lamps were still of the future. Velvet-voiced gamblers kept open house for miners with jingling pockets or nugget-fat pokes. Their potent lures were faro, roulette, rouge-et-noir, rondo, vingt-et-un, paire-ou-non, trente-et-quarante, and the popular chuck-a-luck. Even street corners were beset by thimble-rig, shell and other delusive "guess" games. Faro dealers covered bags of gold dust worth $16,000 without a murmur; as high as $45,000 changed hands on the flip of a single card. Four bull-rings held regular bull-fights in the town; the spectacle of a bull and bear meeting in a battle to the death was common; cock-fighting, horse- and foot-racing, and prize-fighting drew numerous patrons.

This was San Francisco in 1849, a tumbled tangle of rocketing speculation and stratosphere prices, a city growing like a naughty, dirty-pawed child, lustily sensual, flimsy-souled, blatantly bawdy, reaching for hell and heaven with either soiled hand. . . .

John Sutter and his men were lucky to find the little *Sacramento* ready for a return to the Valley. In haste they sped aboard her and the Swiss gave an order to Tokatchi to sail at once.

Moodily, he watched the Yerba Buena of a twelve-year growth dip away into vagueness. He had seen her first with a scant half-dozen huts on her hills, remotely secure, tranquil. . . . Now she was to know seven great conflagrations in the next eighteen months, was to be ravaged by flames that would destroy $20,000,000 with red-tongued ecstacy. But always the yellow flakes of John Sutter's valley rebuilt her—miraculously—in a few days. For the flimsy walls of her flimsy living could be reared almost in a night.

THE FRIENDS of the Father of the Fort did not rest satisfied with his refusal. They merely continued with their plans. When the five names chosen to be balloted upon for the governorship became known—lo, John

Sutter's name led all the rest. Following him was Ptere H. Burnett, William M. Steuart, John W. Geary and Winfield S. Sherwood.

The Swiss was bewildered. He sought out Burnett and explained the situation; that his name had been listed without his sanction. As it was, he was placed in the unenviable position of running against his own legal representative for the governorship of California.

Despite further expostulation on his part, Sutter's name remained on the lists. On a stormy, inclement day—November 13th, 1849—the citizens of California went to the various designated polls to vote for the first governor of their state. Because of the weather, only 12,064 cast ballots out of an estimated 107,000 voters.

At the end of the tally the votes ran: Burnett 6,717; Sherwood 3,188; Sutter 2,201; Geary 1,475; Steuart 619. The calculating John McDougall became lieutenant governor. For a man whose unwillingness to serve was well known, the Swiss ran surprisingly well. John Sutter was not insensible to the honor of the post; but to him the future of New Helvetia came first. With California now a state he felt the battle nearly won. . . .

On December 20th, 1849, Peter H. Burnett became the first executive of the new state. Thus John Sutter lost his ablest adviser when he needed him most. For conditions were even more acute than when he journeyed hopefully to Monterey.

Once more he took up the personal struggle with a will. It is easier to fight when one is sure of victory. If the ghost of the white-sailed argosy had touched him with a chill finger of warning, it was forgotten. And John Sutter fought every battle of a long life, convinced in his heart that he could not be beaten.

Chapter XLIV

PAGEANT

IN THE ARITHMETIC of adventure one and one never make two. Nothing is clearly proven, set down indelibly. Fate has a habit of using an eraser on a seemingly fixed total. Adventurers never live—or die—bounded by certainties; the moment they begin to conform they cease to be adventurers and become one with the herd. And, doing that, they cease to hold the herd in thrall.

Before John Sutter conquered his empire he had been a true adventurer, neither chaste nor despicable, not interested in any law save a mantled semblance, holding his fort by force of arms, yearning on a dream. Now, with the wilderness his, had come a flood-tide of strangers streaming across his broad plain, backwashing pugnaciously upon his acres, thumb-on-nose and hand-on-pistol.

Chance and Metal Majesty had brought them. Each human comber mounted like a ninth wave. Faced with that engulfing presence John Sutter fought with every weapon, sharp or dulled, in his armory. It was a phenomenon beyond his experience; or calculations. Some dim foreboding had been his; but not this. From his altitude of the absolute he had plummeted to futility.

His last and greatest bludgeon was the law; and in his dependence on law he lost his adventurer's status. We are confronted with the sight of one of his breed coming at last to the refuge which the herd has created—the code by which man lives with man; the pledge by which man respects that which is his neighbor's. To hold his valley the Swiss was forced to hold the banner of the law above it.

"One man cannot fight an army," he reasoned.

No MAN's LIFE was secure in the new disorder. The installation of law-enforcement organization was a lengthy and complicated process. Men came into public office for the express purpose of lining their pockets with gold. Judges were appointed whose honesty and probity were non-existent. Decisions were favorable to the man able to pay the most money to the right people. Nothing new in it. The thing was as old as history. Hot lead, coarse hemp, or sharp steel settled most of the personal disputes anyway.

Meantime, Governor Burnett and his first legislature were struggling somewhat vaguely in San José to allay the situation. That band of legislators has been accused of every depredation and crime imaginable, not excluding murder; certainly it held its full quota of thieves and scoundrels, for when a new state is born the fat pickings attract such unscrupulous gentry. California did not differ from the past in her beginnings; nor will the tale be anything but recurrent in future states.

The new capital was to move with great regularity in the next few years. Every town that seemingly offered better accommodations than its fellows was given a trial; the opening of a new hotel or the arrival of an un-acknowledged subsidy usually meant the moving of the legislature, bag and baggage and bowie-knives. A great game, but one not conducive to reducing confusion. . . .

Came another great day in California history—news that Congress had swiftly admitted the province as the thirty-first state in the Union. The steamer *Oregon* came dashing through the Golden Gate, a smoke screen in her wake, every voice aboard her hoarse with the great news.

Business ceased. Courts adjourned. Newspapers from Washington setting forth the glorious message sold for $5 each. Guns boomed hysterically from the heights. Bonfires blazed when the dusk came down. Bands played. Processions came out of nowhere and wound themselves about the town in spirituous circles.

Crandall's stage, powered by six frantic mustangs, rushed out for San José. All the way to his destination the driver shouted his tidings:

"California is admitted!"

His stage was but one of a clattering host. The news came post-haste to the Sacramento. Men cried and laughed and cheered. A new star was added in the blue field of all the banners that flew so proudly over the valley.

John Sutter fired his two cannon at Hock Farm until ammunition gave out. "It will change now," he said. "The law will surely come! . . ."

BUT TO THE VALLEY INVASION there was to be no end. The multitudes came on, each wave more reckless, more lawless than the last. It was a case of dogged fighting now, of persistence until the coils of order could bind the raw plain into placid permanence.

In that first part of 1850 John Sutter worked with his Indians, ploughing and tilling and sowing. "Before the crops come up we shall know better times," observed the Swiss.

So he labored ceaselessly. The Indians were not so numerous now. They had been cuffed and beaten and mercilessly shot down by the arriving hordes. When they worked now, it was with eyes wide for sudden danger. Many a drunken miner had murdered an Indian for the thrill of seeing warm flesh take on nothingness. They would work for the Father of the Fort, yes; but they must run if strangers came striding down the fields. More than ever they were hunted things; John Sutter cursed sulphurously at pot-shooting miners and made stern threats. But the thing went on. . . .

Now something new came to plague the expectant Swiss. Gradually, the new city of Sacramento took on growth and importance; no longer did men come to the fort to buy. Stores cut in swiftly on the post trade. One by one the merchants gave up the shops and storerooms in the huge rectangle; one by one they transferred their goods to the rushing city marts.

By mid-June the thing was done. No storekeeper lived within the adobe walls. All life had trekked on to trade where men's feet rumbled loudest. Thieves came at night to prowl and pillage. No longer did the monthly gold come to John Sutter for the rentals.

From Hock he came, riding the silver horse, eyes sombre blue. The Indians still faithfully tended the garden acres. Grain was ripening with a golden promise under the warm sun. But the fort was a white ghost looking out on the valley.

It was a thing that throttled imagination, deadened the great desires, bewildered and distressed. John Sutter reined his *palomino* four hundred yards away, looked moodily upon the place.

"Only eleven years," he muttered. "Eleven years." A vision came back to him of that first landing, the search, the ecstacy of struggle and fulfillment. . . . Now an Indian came out of the gateless citadel and began to walk toward the green gardens. John Sutter did not see him. For his blue eyes were suddenly misty, sightless.

Then he rode on and the silver horse carried him into the desolation beyond the entrance way.

To SAVE WHAT HE COULD, John Sutter sold the usable remnants of his stronghold. That was better than letting strangers sack the place. Planks and tools and equipment —what were left—were carted into the Sacramento streets; some were sold at auction, some to private bidders. In the end, his fortress salvage brought him less than $40,000.

Then the crops were ready for the cutting and the mares. Only, in a short week, the crops ceased to be. Armed men beat John Sutter's harvest down for feed; their horses slashed and flailed with sharp hoofs in the fields, grinding the golden stalks into the soil; oxen and sheep were driven in to feed on his grain-lanes, grim men with rifles sitting beside the trampling herds; his Indians dropped as they worked, leaden slugs in their bellies, death's cloud in their staring eyes.

John Sutter came and saw and raged, almost inarticulate in his passion. He was very close to death in those moments. Then he rode back to Hock. Evil days had fallen on his valley.

"It can't go on!" he cried savagely. "By Jupiter, it can't go on!" His body drooped in the silvered saddle. As long as men labored out there in the foothills for the golden flakes the drama would go on. . . .

In that winter a quintet of rascals formed an illicit partnership, with headquarters on an island in the river near Marysville. Armed with rifles and equipped with boats, butcher's tools and helpers, they slaughtered animals and sold meat to the Sacramento City inhabitants all through the rainy season. Relying on their inaccessible position, they paid heed to no man. In the spring they declared a net dividend of $60,000 and moved casually on. Every animal slaughtered had belonged to John Sutter.

EACH DAY saw the gold-fields expanding. Men went on and on, passed proven diggings, sought others. So swift in birth, so swift in death, those old camps. Only a few have beaten the conquering years. Their names were legion, intriguing, bizarre. Murderer's Gulch, Mad Mule, Churn Creek, Lost Cabin, Plugtown, Pinchemtight, Dogtown, Negro Hill, Diamond Springs, Sailor's Claim, Georgia Slide, Condemned Bar, Horseshoe Bend, Whiskey Flat, Rattlesnake Bar, Milkpunch, Shirt-tail Canyon, Deadman's Bar, Bogus Thunder, Yankee Jim's, Humbug Cañon, Grizzly Flat, Euchre Bar, Squirrel Creek, Boston Ravine, Malay Camp, Sucker Flat, Poverty Bar, Lousey Level, Henpeck's Flat, Graveyard, Red Hill, Rich Gulch, Kanaka Bar, Coyote Diggings—these and a hundred others.

Out of Sierra City came the Monumental Nugget,141 pounds; at Calaveras a 161-pound nugget was found; many chunks of yellow metal weighing from twenty to fifty pounds were discovered. Out of the fabulous region more than a half billion of golden dollars was to be garnered in ten years. It was wealth that was to exert an incalculable effect upon world history, stimulate universal trade, and even cause men to make discoveries of the precious stuff in a dozen other countries. All begun by a tiny flake in John Sutter's mill-race.

EARLY IN THAT YEAR OF 1850 a Squatter's Association was formed in San Francisco, its avowed purpose to nullify John Sutter's claims. Criminals and shyster lawyers were the principals in the new organization. This group chose to hold the land they had appropriated; by force, if necessary.

Immediately, the resolute citizens formed an Anti-Squatters Association to combat the lawless element. Where squatters had abruptly moved in and claimed city lots, they were summarily ejected. Many men died, shot down in the grim game.

Robber bands—some whispered they were closely allied with the land-stealing organization—preyed upon the citizenry at night. Peril was ever present in the streets after sunset. A night watch of ten men was finally appointed by the city council. They were to fill the prison brig with miscreants—if possible. A recently formed military company was to aid the night guard in case they were attacked by overwhelming numbers.

The land-grabbers were not confined to the valley. In the Ross and Bodega region they rushed in and squatted on what territory they desired. William Benitz, Sutter's agent was as powerless as his chief in the emergency.

The feud between Sutterville and Sacramento was hot, the tide sweeping slowly in favor of the *Embarcadero* town. Buildings were springing up to meet the swift demands of commerce. Lots leaped from $500 to $3,000. Hotels were erected, magical sky-jumping structures; the Sutter House, one of the first, was the most popular. By March 1850, Sacramento had thirty stores, a printing office, bakery, blacksmith shop, tin-shop, billiard-room, bowling alley, and six saloons combined with houses of prostitution. Hubbard's obscene Round Tent was a popular resort rivaled only by the game of monte in Jim Lee's famous Stinking Tent. Several store vessels were tied up along the river bank, also doing a brisk business.

That year's flood put four-fifths of the growing city under water. Boats could enter the second story of the City Hotel. A small steamer navigated the streets. Hundreds of animals were drowned and their decomposing bodies tainted the air for miles. The valley was a lake for many leagues. But, when the river subsided, the town seemed to take on new life.

River traffic picked up. Soon a dozen big steamers were nosing up and down the river from San Francisco to the *Embarcadero*. Speculation surged into a frenzy and the town was crowded with men and supplies for the mines. In April it became a port of entry. Profits ranged a hundred per cent over the incredible San Francisco prices. Rents ran as high as $5,000 per building a month. Lots stratosphered to $30,000 each. Eight thousand people now lived in the rocketing, gold-mad town.

John Sutter, Jr., re-conveyed all property and real estate to his father in June. All debts were paid and there was no longer necessity for the arrangement.

Since Governor Burnett could no longer handle his legal affairs, Sutter chose Henry A. Schoolcraft as his Sacramento agent; a man named Peachy was also appointed as his San Francisco representative. Then the Swiss placed the remaining bloc of his Sacramento City lots in Schoolcraft's hands for sale; later on, Peachy was also given lots to dispose of.

Choice of irresponsible persons to transact his business in these later moments of stress was a glaring stupidity on John Sutter's part. "The swindlers," he wrote, "were very different from Bidwell, Reading and Hensley, the men who had been my trusted employees in the days before the gold discovery. These first associates so inspired me with trust and friendship that I was ready to welcome every unscrupulous sharper who came my way after the gold madness."

Peachy was reputed to have made at least $80,000 in a suspiciously short time while handling Sutter's affairs. Later, when Sutter's land troubles were continually in the courts, the Swiss sought out Peachy's law firm to defend him. Very neatly his shyster aide crawled out of the matter by pleading he was too busy at the moment to represent the Captain's interests.

After Peachy and Schoolcraft, came General A. Winn. He, in turn, sold a large number of lots and rendered no accounting to his employer. Winn's family had their portraits painted at a heavy cost and paid for the canvases in Sutter's city lots. Besides this, Winn borrowed $5,000 at ten-percent-a-month interest, and made no mention of it to Sutter.

The Swiss did not learn of Winn's act until the note had reached the sum of $35,000. "I expected," said Sutter, "to meet honesty in business transactions and to find honor in all men of good address. It was necessary for me to trust someone—I could not attend to my tremendous holding alone—and the men to whom I granted my power of attorney swindled me on every side."

So it went, agent after agent, men who considered the Swiss fair game. No redress was possible. The law had not yet come; only its semblance. Cunning and might were still in the saddle.

LATER IN THE YEAR, about the time the new home at Hock was completed, Sutter had a visitor whom he had not seen for months. It was Marshall, he of the yellow flakes and the morose manner. Things had not gone well with him at Coloma; the swarm of seekers had buffeted him sorely, made him more surly.

He was more of a Spiritualist than ever now—the spirits were going to guide him to fortune. Patiently, Sutter listened to his wild tales, gave him provisions, pack-animals and Indians. Away he went.

This was the first of many such visits. Finally, Sutter's Indians refused to go with the eccentric fellow who stooped so historically in the golden mill-race.

"We will not go with that man," they said firmly to the Father of the Fort—he who no longer had a fortress. And the Swiss did not urge them.

"His spirits never led him to fortune," wrote Sutter, in retrospect. Years later Marshall was to die near Coloma, a recluse in a tiny cabin. Other men than he were to find an abundance of the precious metal; but not the frenzied fellow who rode with the first flakes to Sutter's Fort.

All 1850 saw disorder and bloodshed in the feverish city—born of the squatter riots. In time the condition shook public confidence in all land titles; floods and an increased taxation brought an abrupt lowering of real-estate values.

A financial crisis came in September. The chief bankers and merchants closed their doors, bankrupt. Thieves grew bolder, more predatorially persistent.

Cholera came to the valley in October. Five hundred people died in sixty days. Many fled away from the plague. The Odd Fellows organized and built a hospital; the Masons bought medicine and coffins. The old building near the fort was also used as a hospital during the epidemic. It was one of the tragic, seething eras of an empire's building.

A DELEGATION waited on John Sutter at Hock.

"Captain Sutter," their spokesman said, "we have come to ask a favor. Every day scores of people are dying in the town. We have no place to bury them. We thought perhaps you might donate a plot of ground for such a purpose."

Sutter glanced about him at his visitors. Many in that circle were his avowed enemies; off there, in the town, men were dying who had sought to steal both his goods and his land; to destroy all the things that such possession assured the owner. Now he was asked to bury them.

The Swiss shrugged wearily. His courtesy was worn thin these days.

"I shall deed the city a ten-acre tract at once," he answered them. The spokesman opened his mouth to thank the donor.

A sudden twinkle came into Sutter's eye.

"By Jupiter, gentlemen," he said, "if you can fill that graveyard I'll be glad to give you tracts as long as you need them."

Chapter XLV

ARRIVAL

GOVERNOR PETER BURNETT resigned his post 1u January 1851. It may be that he saw a whip-hand could not be held over some of his choice underlings in the legislature. His public reason was that press of private matters demanded his immediate personal supervision, which was merely a retiring gesture made from an increasingly difficult position.

The Great Madness of 1849 made security a myth in the new state. For five years the ruthless reign of disorder continued; indeed, up to 1860, there were few men who obeyed any written or moral covenant. A transitional tempest it was, reeking of brigandage, corruption and collusion in the political cockpit.

Beyond the law-making and law-enforcing circle of leeches was an arena of wholesale terrorism and bloodshed. Gold had brought the dross residue of all lands and seas to California; their counsel and wolfish example drove the drama as they wished it.

To the Swiss it was to be a battle to the death, an endless conflict with suborned politicians, cunning tricksters, and land-jumping pistol-jugglers. Doggedly, he set himself to stand upon the highest hill until the deluge retreated, baffled by time and circumstance. It was astounding, this fetid wave; but the Swiss had almost lost the faculty to feel astoundment. What was, must be faced. Without complaint he entered into calculating opposition. Peace and permanence seemed dead stars set in an undying night.

In that five-year period between '49 and '54 more than four thousand two hundred people were murdered in California. Callous souls called her Murderer's Paradise. A man who carried a gun was supposed to be able to take care of himself: if he was shot in the back and his gold dust stolen, it was his own affair. Certainly, no one took the trouble to inquire into the incident.

San Francisco alone had a total of twelve hundred murders in that half-decade span. Only one conviction was secured in the courts. Hunger, accident, cholera or Indians accounted for five thousand three hundred more fatalities within the state borders; two thousand two hundred lives were lost at sea enroute to the gold-fields; one thousand six hundred perished on the overland trail through Indian stratagems; one thousand four hundred committed suicide; one thousand seven hundred went insane. An appalling record for five years.

Facing such conditions, it is obvious that a great land-holder would be lucky to escape with his life—regardless of his loss in herds, property and real estate. In every way that a man might fight for security, John Sutter fought. He mined with his Indians; he entered into trading partnerships; he sold more city lots; he carried freight in his launches; in every legitimate manner he attempted to bolster his personal fortunes. But as fast as he accumulated wealth some shyster lawyer or agent or bandits or squatters despoiled him.

John Sutter was not a fool. He was merely illy-equipped, emotionally, to ride on the crest of such a frothy tide. Generous, hospitable, eager to befriend, swift to believe every man honest—no matter how often he discovered the contrary—these were the human handicaps John Sutter carried with him in that unequal struggle. The only wonder of the thing is the fact of his miraculous physical survival.

In that year of 1851 John S. Fowler had in his Sacramento law office for safe keeping the three original Mexican grants issued to John Sutter—the New Helvetia, Sobrante, and "general title" documents. One night someone set fire to the office. In thirty minutes the structure was ashes; and somewhere in the ashes lay the precious records, lost forever. Another disappointment for the Swiss. Another triumph for the lawless interests.

When Peter Burnett resigned, the lieutenant governor became chief executive of the new state. This John McDougall was a talented, charming crook, given to drink, carousals, ruffled white shirt-fronts, buff coat and pantaloons, brass-buttoned blue coats, and frequent attempts to commit suicide while in his cups.

"There are but two things I fear," the new governor often declared fiercely—"God and Mrs. John McDougall!"

With this dissolute wastrel at the helm no man was bold enough to predict a speedy creation of law and order. Especially John Sutter. The two men had never been friends. McDougall had tried to secure control of the Sacramento River lots through intimidation and messenger-carried threats. The bluff had not worked. Yet the Swiss could look forward to little square-dealing as long as McDougall sat in the executive chair of the swiftly flitting capital.

The same year brought Sacramento's first vigilance committee into being. Conditions had become unbearable for those citizens who earnestly wished for some show of security. The committee worked well, in its way. But the mere hanging of a few criminals was not the answer to the problem. A deterrent, yes, but not of sufficient magnitude to swerve the codeless hordes from lust and pillage.

RUMORS CAME VAGUELY from Washington that a land commission was soon to be functioning in California— Federal-appointed and unbiased, it was affirmed. John Sutter received the news with a calm hope. "At least," he said, "it must come sometime."

So the year wore away. . . .

The men at the mines were still beset by hunger and cholera and scurvy and rheumatism. Even the straight-legged Swiss of late had known rheumatic twinges. It was no uncommon sight to venture into a scurvy-tortured camp and discover long rows of human heads, beards flapping in the breeze, seemingly set in the ground to grow. Miners believed that contact with the earth had a beneficial effect on the disease. Often entire camps were buried up to their necks, only a few men being left above ground to discourage the grizzlies and coyotes from becoming head-hunters.

In December 1851, came a beloved visitation to the graying Captain and his impetuous, quick-tempered first-born. A hard-ridden horse came dashing up to the new Hock home. The tired rider swung off his mount and met Sutter on the slightly raised stoop.

"Yer folks is in San Francisco, Cap Sutter," said the man. "Comin' down on the *Sacramento* right away. I've rid hard but I come by San José and they ort to be here soon."

"Great news! Great news!" beamed John Sutter. "Come in, Sicard. Have dinner with me. By Jupiter, you are really a messenger of glad tidings. . . . Come in! Oh, John! John! Did you hear? . . ."

Sicard followed the happy Captain in to where the younger Sutter lay on a settee. The boy was but shortly risen from an attack of fever. Sutter held his son's shoulder in a tender grip.

"They will soon be with us, dear son," he said softly.

THREE DAYS LATER the *Sacramento* bore its four excited passengers to the home on the Feather River. John Sutter stood upon the bank and waved his huge hat as the white sails of the schooner came beating up the shore. At his side stood his son.

It was the moment John Sutter had been visualizing for seventeen long years. . . . Now they had really come, his loved ones, come to share his empire. *Ach Gott*, the empire that was so sorely beset. . . .

"My dears! My dears!" cried the Swiss and held out his arms to them across the narrowing tide. . . .

They came ashore like people in a dream. It was as if the man on the bank was a stranger. . . . It had been four years since they had seen the elder brother; it was an eternity since they had seen the big man with the graying temples.

Then his arms were about them and suddenly tears came to everyone.

"At last!" cried John Sutter. "I can ask little more than this. . . ."

Anna was older; yes, and her lips were thinner and her face was lined and her eyes did not laugh the way they used to do. . . . and Anna Elisa, a lovely young woman. . . ." "So like her mother—long ago," he thought; and suddenly found himself giving a silent curse to lost years . . . . and Emil Victor, a man . . . little William Alphonse—nineteen years old. "Only babies when I left them," thought John Sutter. . . .

Chattering, laughing, crying, they came at last to the house he had prepared for them. They scrambled happily through the wide door. As they passed under his roof-tree John Sutter's heart sang as it had not done for an incredible space of years. . . . The battle, no matter what its ending, would not be so bitter now. . . .

THIS SAME YEAR George McKinstry, Jr., late Sutter aide, wrote a letter to young Lieutenant Kern, he who had commanded the Fort Sutter military garrison in 1846. . . .

San Diego, Dec. 23rd, 1851.
Dear Kern:

Immediately on the discovery of gold I wrote you and advised you to hasten out. Yet I presume if you *had* come, and made the almighty pile, you would have lost it as most of us have.

Since you left this country a most astonishing change has taken place. The new Yankees would say for the better, but not we old fellows from Captain Sutter down to old Bray!

The *Embarcadero* is now the large city of Sacramento. The old fort is rapidly going to decay; the last time I was there I rode through, and there was not a living thing to be seen within the walls. Ah, what a fall is there, my fellow!

The lovely Sacramento, which in our time was only disturbed by "the well-known, fast-sailing, copper and copper-fastened Clipper-Schooner *Sacramento*, Youckmomney, Master," is now ploughed day and night from San Francisco to Marysville (old Theodore Cordua's farm) to the Yuba and to Colusa (Larkin's farm) on the Upper Sacramento by most magnificent steamers. These last are generally termed "floating palaces" and are crowded with hungry gold-hunters and speculating Yankees. Times are not what they "useter was."

Due to my long sojourn in the Western Wilds I do not feel at home and I have journeyed down here to San Diego to look at the country. I may purchase a ranch and settle here for life. From what I have seen of this part of the state I don't think the damned Yankees will crowd me out much. Yet, to my astonishment, the Jews are on the ground doing battle in the "old clo" line. Old San Diego is full of them. . . .

The old Sacramento crowd has been much scattered by death and disaster since you left. William Daylor by cholera; Jared Sheldon shot in a row with miners; Perry McCoon by a fall from his horse; Sebastian Keyser drowned; Little Bill Johnson—woeful x—Kin Sabe?; Captain "Luce" missing in the mountains; Olimpio shot by miners; old Thomas Hardy, *rum*; John Sinclair, cholera; William E. Shannon, cholera; old William Knight, *rum*; Charley Heath, *rum* and missing; Bob Ridley, fever, I think; and others too numerous to set down.

Our good friend Captain John Sutter has fitted up the Hock Rancho in superb style but I regret to say his reign seems smashed to flinders; old Theodore Cordua, tom bien; Daylor and Sheldon estates both said to be insolvent; our old and particular crony, John L. Schwartz, still inhabits the Fishing Rancheria and has finally built that two-story house to escape the mosquitoes which he talked so much about. God knows how he stands the present pressure; he goes it, though, more than ever on the rum. Old James McDowell was shot down by miners some two years since—his widow is the owner of Washington, the town opposite Sacramento City; many fine buildings there but at present it is no go—some five hundred inhabitants, however.

Old Kitnor is Captain Sutter's mayordomo at Hock—he made a fortune and went bust; William A. Liedesdorff, dead; old Eliab Grimes, dead; Jack Fuller, ditto—also Allen Montgomery. Montgomery's widow married the man who called himself Talbot H. Green, formerly with Larkin at Monterey and afterwards W. D. M. Howard's partner in San Francisco. His real name was found to be Paul Geddes some years since, a bank-robber from the United States. He departed to clear up his character; which was the last of him. I have not seen her for a long time but am told she is the same "black-bottle" woman.

Old Louis Keseberg, the Donner Party Man-Eater, has made a fortune and is now running a restaurant on K Street in Sacramento City. I would like to board there, I wouldn't. Pierson B. Reading is on his farm raising wheat and pumpkins in abundance—I camped on his rancho some six weeks last summer. He was the Whig candidate for Governor, but could not make it. It was said his friendship with Captain Sutter cost him the squatter votes. He has been wounded twice in Bear-Hunts since you left—shot in the hand two years ago and broke his leg badly two months ago. Next time it will be his head if he doesn't quit. He plans to go to Philadelphia on the 1st of April next and marry; about time, I think—squaws and niggers won't do. Old Snyder and Sam Hensley both married. Bidwell too damn prosperous to speak of.

Sam Norris has made two or three hundred thousand, but is reputedly hard up and thought to be busted. Samuel Brannan, ditto. In fact, I could fill a foolscap sheet with the names of the busted Old Guard in this community, including your humble servant.

I purchased the Chico Rancho of old William Dickey, who went to the States or Ireland—I don't know where the hell he is. Old John Yates went to England. Sam Neal is on his farm; he has built a large frame house and still loves horses—still rides the little grey.

Doctor Bates and his brother made a snug fortune—lost it—gone to practicing again. Old Nicolas Altgeier made a city on his farm. The city blew up and I think the explosion bent him some. By the by, he is married to a white woman, or rather, a Dutch woman. Nye made some seventy-five hundred thousand; don't know how he stands. Hicks made a hundred and fifty thousand and is an exception—still got it, I hear. "Ellick McDowell" (Selim E. Woodworth) is a State Senator at Monterey—left the Navy—Great Country this, eh?

Farming is carried on to a great extent. Vegetables raised here would astonish you both as to quantity and size—cabbages 53 pounds per head, Irish potatoes 33 inches in circumference, etc. You ought to visit the country once more "before you die." Short trip by Steamers or by Vera Cruz and Acapulco, which I am told, is a very pleasant one; a new line of stages and packs has been established on that route, full as cheap and quick. I came down on the Steamer the other day with one of the owners of the line; he has lived in Mexico sixteen years and thinks it is *the* country.

Well, I must bring this Dick Sniveler history to a close. I have been writing it down in a room filled with high-strung officers going it loose, full of music and "otard dupy"—some just in from Gila, others from Santa Fe and Colorado. . . . I shall expect a long letter from you. . . .

Yours,

George McKinstry, Jr.

To
Edward M. Kern
3 Logan Square
Philadelphia
Pa.

Chapter XLVI

TRAVAIL

THE UNITED STATES Land Commission met in San Francisco for the first time in January 1852. They had been appointed at Washington to deliberate upon nearly five hundred Mexican grant land titles and confirm or reject, as their findings dictated. Seven commissioners sat on that board and it was the most painstaking and painsgiving collection of judges ever to officiate in the state. At the end of four years only three claims had been settled. Sutter's was not among them.

Besides this major struggle between the claimants and the United States there was always a complicated litigation in progress between private individuals over the same tracts. Even when the minor skirmishes had been concluded the battle had to be fought all over again in the Supreme Court of the nation.

Costly, distressing procedures, all of them. To maintain his title, his occupancy, and make improvements, John Sutter spent a fortune. Fifty thousand dollars went in cash and services which formed the original consideration of the grant; a like sum went for taxes and surveys; the cost of litigation for ten years was $125,000, including fees for counsel, witnesses, traveling expenses, and incidentals; more than $100,000 was paid out to legalize the covenants of "deeds of grant," a sum over and above that received from sale of real estate. Thus a total of over $325,000 was expended by the Swiss in the bitter controversy.

Louis Saunders, Jr., represented Sutter as counsel for a time during this period. But he accepted fees from both sides in many of the Sutter-Squatter cases; at all events, the Swiss never won a case under Mr. Saunders's expert manipulation.

"Eugene F. Gillespie, a son-in-law of General Winn," writes Sutter, "was a member of a company that had been organized to secure and legalize land grants through the United States Land Commission. They bled me freely and stole a great deal of land from me which they divided among themselves. My association with them derived me nothing but unrest and loss.

"Gillespie now owes me $15,000 (1878). I exempted a piece of land designated as the Yuba City tract which I intended to present to my son, J. A. Sutter, Jr. However, I was swindled out of the tract in question. Judge Field aided my despoilers and he was no better or more honest than they were. . . ."

There is no reasonable doubt but that the United States robbed seven out of eight claimants seeking justice before that commission. The very people who had been assured of their land titles were thus deliberately despoiled. It is an evil blot on the honor of a great republic —that is, if you care to take a matter of public honor seriously. It was probably the most flagrant government confiscation of property in modern times.

For more than twenty years the individual had to defend his title, at great expense, against powerful opposition that had no costs to pay. It was simply robbery; not in the real interests of this republic or the American settlers, but in the interests of speculating land grafters.

This government action was incalculably stupid. Spoliation of the grant holders was only one facet of the affair. Unsettled land titles and unending court wrangles were another. Every occupant of land felt that his possession was threatened, whether he was squatter or grant-owner. No man, grant-claimant or squatter, could sell or dared invest in expensive improvements; why put money into land that the courts might deed to another? Population was driven away by such conditions, industry and development were stifled; for two decades the state was prevented from utilizing her natural resources.

A sad résumé of imbecilic incompetence that bred a harvest of murder, disease, hatred, pillage and despair.

Such a stern daily drama would have beaten down most adventurers; but not the Swiss. There was greatness in the man; and weakness. His family was with him now, a trust to fight for; they were present with the cheery word for the slowing warrior in dark days. There was no faltering or dismay at Hock Farm; only the eternal idea that the tangle would straighten itself soon to the confusion of all enemies of the Sutter clan.

Then the Swiss received a hundred-thousand-dollars-worth of notes, signed by purchasers of Sacramento City lots. He entrusted James King of William with these notes for safe keeping. When the real estate depreciated during the banking crisis both King and Peachy gave up the notes to the various signees and released these purchasers from their contracts. Naturally they had no legal right to sanction such a procedure. Peachy had received his commissions on all these sales and not a cent was returned to Sutter.

Next, the $5,000 note at ten percent a month, negotiated by his ex-agent Winn, came to the Captain's notice. "I was resting tranquilly at Hock Farm with my family," Sutter states, "not knowing I owed a dollar in the world. Then came the sheriff to serve an attachment, the original note having mounted to $35,000, being held by Hastings and Hensley, the banker.

"The two waited at Nicolas, the county seat, to see how the sheriff would fare with his mission. I was forced to go to Nicolas and satisfy them by surrendering a $30,000 note which I held against Captain Simmons."

IF SUTTER'S PERSONAL LIFE was troubled, his "Embarcadero" city was no less so. In March 1850, a terrific flood had again inundated two-thirds of the town structures, taking a week to subside. Then, in November, came the greatest catastrophe. Fire swept away most of the city at a loss of $5,000,000. No sooner had the mush-

room buildings once more arisen than the great floods
of December 1852, and January 1853, made the site an
unhealthy plague spot. Yet always a fierce stuff of existence gave it rebirth—the lust for the yellow flakes.
Moreover, in 1854, the dignity of state capital was added
to the city with the erection of a suitable legislative
structure. The *Embarcadero*, where John Sutter's venturesome feet had first trod only fifteen years before, had
taken on stature and continuance.

"ONE SPRING AFTERNOON in the early fifties," wrote
William Heath Davis, "I made a visit to San Francisco.
On the corner of Montgomery and Sacramento streets I
accidentally met Captain John A. Sutter. Our greeting
was most cordial and spontaneous, for we had not seen
each other since January 1845, in Los Angeles, just after
the capitulation of Micheltorena.

"The Captain said: 'Come, let us go to some private
place. There is a room in the rear of Barry and Patten's
resort where we will be away from the noise of the
street.'

"Captain Sutter was faultlessly attired and looked
young and fresh. He ordered us an excellent luncheon,
together with a cold bottle of Heidseick. As we ate and
sipped the sparkling beverage, we indulged in many
reminiscences of the trip in which I had commanded one
of his schooners to the American River on his first
venture in 1839.

"His conversation ran over his association with the
early merchants, especially Nathan Spear; Spear, said
the Captain, had stood by him in the beginning of the
Sacramento Valley settlement, when the very existence
of New Helvetia wavered in the balance.

"After the severe winter of 1839-40, the success of
Sutter's undertaking was assured. He had familiarized
himself with the unknown wealth of the region in
beaver, salmon and sturgeon; also the plains in bear,
elk, deer and other fur-bearing animals. The tallow

derived from the elk was an article of commerce and in great demand at two dollars per *arroba*. Beaver and land otter were plentiful in the tule flats and streams. The savages were also a source of revenue and aid; he paid them so much a skin for their catch and many of them were skillful hunters. In this and other ways Sutter emerged into prosperity and supreme influence which was recognized by the merchants afloat and ashore, also by wealthy *hacendados* of the province.

"Sutter appreciated Spear's faith in his integrity and ability as a leader and had sent him huge shipments of furs in payment for supplies which Spear had cheerfully booked against the Captain in his critical financial days.

"We talked and sipped, and sipped and smoked. Finally we veered to the gold discovery. The Indians from a very early period had learned something of its value. They had obtained this knowledge from the mission padres. It was from the rich finds made by Indians and deposited in the missions that some six or seven thousand dollars was secured by church officials. The yellow offering was placed in a fine silk purse made especially for the purpose and sent to Rome as a gift to the Pope. This occurred years before the finding of the San Fernando placer diggings. Bishop Garcia Diego, first Bishop of the Roman Catholic Church in California, was the donor.

"Captain Sutter continued the story of his experiences in his long years spent in conquering the great Sacramento Valley. He remarked that they were the happiest years of his life because he had been in a position to be of service to the emigrants and others in need, with plenty of food and supplies to be generously handed out and no compensation asked or expected."

Chapter XLVII

HOLOCAUST AT HOCK

Nᴏᴛ ᴜɴᴛɪʟ 1857 did the United States Land Commission reach a decision on the Sutter grants. Rejoicing came to Hock Farm. For all the documents—having been laboriously reproduced from memory and accompanied by affidavits—were pronounced legal and valid, sacrosanct under the Treaty of Guadalupe Hidalgo.

"At last, by Jupiter!" exulted Sutter, voice aglow. His family were more cautious in their enthusiasm.

The squatters were furious. Their shyster lawyers at once appealed the case to the United States District Court of Northern California. Again the whole business was aired and adjusted with voluble ceremony.

Not until 1858 did the higher court reach a verdict. Again wild joy reigned on the Feather River estate. "These grants are perfect and legal in all respects. . . ." affirmed the tribunal.

But even this did not satisfy the squatters and their legal talent. Again came an appeal to that last august body, the Supreme Court of the United States. For another year the tiresome struggle went on. . . .

Then came the final word. The New Helvetia grant was confirmed; but the Sobrante and "general title" grants were discarded and declared invalid. Deep gloom fettered John Sutter and his brood; but only for a stunned moment.

"Surely something can be done," he said.

The Supreme Court had admitted his grants "meritorious and just" and the grounds for the adverse decision were only vaguely proscribed. The attorney general's argument was almost naïve—"It is against the public policy for one man to hold the fee of so much land," he declaimed. Which statement has no bearing on the case whatsoever.

By the Treaty of Guadalupe Hidalgo all of John
Sutter's grants were valid; even if he had acquired them
from the Mexican government through collusion—which
he had not—the only honorable legal action possible by
the Supreme Court was to confirm his holdings. The
decree which reversed the lower court decision was
robbery of the most bald-faced nature—a pitiable commentary on justice.

The nation that he had befriended in a moment of
need had now turned Shylock for a group of squatters.
To say that Sutter was astounded leaves much to the
imagination; it was long before he could even bring
himself to believe the blighting truth.

"Are all my labors to come to nothing?" he exclaimed wrathfully at last. "I cannot believe the United
States capable of such action. Surely something must be
misunderstood. . . ."

On went the struggle, kept alive by the unbeatable
Swiss. He was more impressive in defeat than victory.
For he could not see that he was defeated.

In addition, he had given titles to much of the
Sobrante grant under deeds of personal warranty. After
the Supreme Court decision favoring the squatters, he
was obliged to make good those deeds, at an unfair
sacrifice, from the New Helvetia grant. So, in reality,
the confirmation of his original eleven leagues was of
little advantage to him. No longer was he a great
landed baron—the unsubtle sages in Washington had
seen to that. Even Hock Farm began to be eaten up by
debt and attachment.

Desperate, John Sutter strove to save the Feather
River Rancho. In 1859 he sold his Fort Ross and Bodega
real estate to William Muldrow, George R. Moore and
Daniel W. Welty. He did this regardless of the fact that
Mexican authorities had made various grants in 1844
which overlapped his Russian holdings.

The Mexicans were at legal fault in the matter. They
merely issued grants on territory which was most clearly

the property of the Swiss at the time the grants were made.

Sutter's late sale stirred up a mare's nest for a time. The men who purchased the holdings attempted to dispossess squatters then on the land. The attempt was unsuccessful and the Mexican grants approved as valid. Once more the squatter interests had scored.

The so-called pension of $3,000 a year for ten years accorded by the State of California to John Sutter was hardly a gift. For ten years he had paid taxes on the Sobrante Grant; when it was taken from him no restitution was ever made. This "pension" did not amount to one half the sum Sutter was forced to pay for taxes on his confiscated tract in that decade.

The famous Sutter Rifles were formed, under the Swiss' honorary command, during this period. The Captain was commissioned as a major general of state troops.

When golden-voiced Kate Hayes came to Sacramento, General Sutter was at his Hock estate. Every seat for the celebratory affair was sold at auction. The Sutter Rifles, in a burst of civic and patriarchal pride, bid in the first seat for their absent commander at $1,200.

On the day of the concert a deputation of the company sailed up to Hock and escorted the General to Sacramento as a guard of honor. As he landed, his entire company was drawn up in military formation at the dock to greet him.

A great round of applause met him at the theatre. With his officers on either hand the happy Swiss sat, the principal guest of the evening, on a red plush settee in the first row.

That night he was again an emperor, his subjects mummers in the world of Make-Believe. But for the night only. In the morning he sailed back to his remaining acres, ready once more to begin the eternal jousting.

That self-faith of the Swiss held an invincible quality that was almost monotonous. The fast-sweeping years swarmed by and heaped a whiteness on his head, a certain slowness in his stride, a hint of *embonpoint* at his middle. But the spark of surety was unquenchable, serene.

" Congress will do something about it," he would repeat. " By Jupiter, there will be some restitution made. . . ."

JOHN SUTTER'S CHILDREN were no longer young when they came to his side. Somehow, he had always seen them as children, visualized their life in his new home as the joyous playtime of Youth. . . . But his sons were men and his daughter was a lovely woman when the schooner adventured up the Feather River.

Soon his eldest boy married Maria del Carmen Rivas and went to Acapulco, Mexico, as United States consul. Next Dr. Francis Xavier Link married the charming Anna Elisa and carried her away from the Hock home. Emil Victor drifted away, the wanderlust in his heart. William Alphonse married the graceful, brown-eyed Pauline Stootz and left the valley. John Sutter and his Anna stood alone, buffeted and scourged, unyielding.

He watched the Civil War flame into being; saw his gold act as the life-blood which held the Union indissoluble; bore in tears with his Anna the news that his youngest son, Colonel William Alphonse Sutter, had died from battle-wounds in Nevada City—wounds received while leading his company against Southern troops; saw the struggle of Blue and Gray come to an ending.

The Father of the Fort was sixty-two years old in 1865. He was still sure that Congress would do the just thing, make some compensatory gesture, designed to aid and comfort. It would have to come soon, though—bit by bit the Feather River Rancho was being filched from him by greedy, rapacious hands and scheming minds.

JUNE 7th, 1865. Stars silvered the stretching valley, painted the redwood and adobe mansion with a soft sheen. The moon was a curling crescent, clutched in the hands of night. For two hours the house had been darkened, lightless. John Sutter and his Anna slept; their servants slumbered in the outhouses, also.

It was two hours beyond midnight. Far off, the sound of horses' hoofs came down the night wind. Then they ceased. Soon a number of figures came stealthily through the starlight, bundles in their arms. They advanced slowly, furtively, dropped their burdens beside the rancho home.

Then all of them went away, but one. He waited a long, long time. Then he, too, was gone, a black phantom pacing the unreal halls of darkness.

Above, the moon still showed its curved blade; it might have wavered, as if the burnished scimitar hung by a tiny thread.

A red tongue laughed up out of the dark bundles along the redwood walls, grew more maliciously sure in a breathless instant. The tongue found voice, sang some crackling song of conquest, the song of a flame not cowed by man. The night wind came and beat the glowing crimson into consuming life.

John Sutter and his wife slept on. The servants did not waken. The red laughter had grown now, began to dance upon the redwood walls. The crackling chant was more perceptible. All about the south wing was a rising radiance, cloud-reaching, breeze-aided.

Still a mile away, rode a single horseman, bound for Hock Farm. He was an officer of the law and he came in the night because he wished to place a certain final writ in John Sutter's hands. He was tired and sleepy and irritable, was this night-riding deputy sheriff. . . . Suddenly his eyes caught a flashing reflection before him. A wavering wall of beauty showed off in the direction of his destination.

The rider stared, cursed suddenly.

"Fire, by God!" he shouted. Spurs bit deep into his startled mount's flanks. "Cap Sutter's place!"

The horse gathered under him; sharp hoofs began to beat upon the flying ground.

As the deputy sheriff rode the radiance broke into billowing banners of lashing crimson; and suddenly the countryside held a rose-glow for stretching leagues.

From a quarter mile the rider's frantic voice sped to mingle with the flame-voice.

"Fire!" he cried monotonously. "Fire! Fire! Fire!"

In a moment he was there, out of the saddle, crashing huge knuckles down on the door.

Inside were voices, an awareness upon them now. Anna was screaming. The barrier flew open. John Sutter came out, still struggling with heavy pantaloons, shoelaces flapping in the redness.

"*Ach, Gott!*" he cried. "My home!"

The scene took on kaleidoscopic vividness. Indians came running now, eyes shaken from stolidity, yowling discordantly. Once more John Sutter dashed through the doorway, smoke-wreathed now. The deputy followed him. In a moment they came out, almost carrying Anna. A streamer of red curved over the door as they passed beyond it.

"My papers! Deeds!" shrilled Sutter suddenly and turned to enter again.

But a fierce red hand barred the way. No man would pass that portal save a man who would remain within. The Swiss raised his hand and cursed. . . .

An hour later John Sutter stood before a pool of glowing ashes; his left arm was about Anna's waist. She was weeping. His eyes were on the embers; and yet they seemed to continue on, beyond. . . .

The deputy, grimy, exhausted, came limping up. "Sorry, Cap," he said awkwardly. "Mighty tough."

He drew out a creased document with a sheepish uncertainnesss. Thrusting the paper into the Swiss' hands, the officer turned away, speechless.

His horse's hoofs moaned away into the breaking dawn.

Absent-mindedly the Father of the Fort thrust the paper into his right-hand trousers pocket. He did not look at it. Anna was watching him, misery in her eyes.

"My *Liebchen*," he said, his voice clear and ringing, "we will go to Washington, you and I. Justice will be done us there. That is sure."

He patted her shoulder tenderly, his eyes still on the hot ashes, ashes that would soon be dead embers. All his records and documents had been eaten up in that holocaust. . . . More than a million acres of his Empire had dropped away in nothingness in the hindering years. . . . Hock Farm, too, was gone. . . .

THAT VERY DAY, in the East, a soldier sat writing a letter to a friend. His name was General William Tecumseh Sherman, analyist, tactician, idol of the nation.

"To General John A. Sutter," he wrote, "more than to any single person, are we indebted for the conquest of California and all her treasures. . . ."

under guard, in the night he eluded his captors and
escaped.

"My corporal," wrote Sutter, "upon finding the spy
missing, immediately jumped on an unsaddled horse and
hotly pursued. He caught up with the man and lassoed
him. Back they came. I then had handcuffs placed on the
prisoner, informing him I would probably release him
when we reached his home near San José."

Perhaps Sutter was tempted to treat the fellow as his
own courier had been treated. They were coming to San
José; the same cottonwood on which Pablo Gutierrez
had been hanged was not far off; indeed, summary action
might have been wise. But Sutter set the man free. . . .

"Next morning," the Captain continues, "we
reached Mission San José, having sent forward twenty-
five riflemen as an advance guard. Accompanied by my
staff, I called upon the padre in charge, who received us
in a friendly manner. . . . He then told me that General
José Castro had visited the Mission briefly, retired from
San José, and was now believed to be in the general
direction of Santa Clara.

"The padre set refreshments before us. But some of
my men followed the *mayordomo* as he was serving wine,
discovered its abundant source, and soon drank more
than they should. . . ."

Captain Sutter states the case lightly. Though he
gave a swift command to move on, those orders came a
bit late. For some hours after leaving the hospitable
mission the infantry column may be described as staggering after the enemy; the mounted portion, though
given to raucous song, were more orderly, owing to the
fact that the horses had not followed the *mayordomo*.

"That night we camped five miles from San José,"
reads Sutter's account. "A strict guard was kept during
the hours of darkness for fear of a surprise attack. Reports placed Castro not far distant. Here the thoughtful
padre sent us provisions and I had two bullocks killed
to supply my men with meat.

Chapter XXII

RIDERS TO THE SOUTH

JOHN SUTTER's army marched at dawn. It was January 1st, 1845—New Year's Day. Two-hundred-and-twenty strong, they were. With drums sending rolling volleys of sound toward the hills they paced or rode through the main gateway of the fort. On a silver *palomino*, in the very van, came Sutter. He was advancing to one of the most stormy scenes of his untranquil career.

He turned in his saddle, saluted from the column's head. Pierson B. Reading, standing to the left of the great gate, raised his own hand smartly. He had been left in command of the fortress until the Captain's return.

Sutter's chief military threat was the company of one hundred foreign riflemen under the leadership of John Gantt. Then came his hundred trained Indians, infantry and cavalry, under Ernst Rufus. A large brass field piece wheeled groaningly along, intent on battle, attended by a dozen pompous artillerymen. John Bidwell was Sutter's chief aide-de-camp. Jasper O'Farrell was quartermaster; Samuel J. Hensley was his assistant. A few subordinate officers completed the roster.

Past John Marsh's rancho near Monte Diablo ran the line of march. There the voluble owner insisted on joining the force, this despite his well-known sympathies for the insurgent cause. Marsh's action was unexpected. But the pseudo doctor was cunning. . . .

On hastened the troops to the Governor's support. At Don Antonio Suñol's rancho, ten miles from Mission San José, the cavalry caught a spy. The man had been sent on by Castro from his San José headquarters to report on the strength of the approaching column.

The captive was brought before Sutter. For an hour he was cross-questioned, but the fellow, evasive and clumsily contradictory, admitted nothing. Finally placed sailed for the *Embarcadero* to bear the news to the owner. . . .

Now Sutter was incensed by a more serious affair. Pablo Gutierrez was acting as a special courier carrying important missives between the Swiss and the Governor. Special boots had been made for him in Sutter's shoeshop; a double sole had been designed which securely held the dispatches while the rider was enroute to his destination.

One December morning Gutierrez galloped away, capital-bound, waving to Sutter as he went. That night his body swayed on a cottonwood in San José, making restless shadows in the moon glow. Alvarado and Castro had found the dispatches and made their answer.

At the time the ruler of the fort received news of the strangely burdened tree in San José, came a visitor riding boldly from that village. He was Charles W. Weber, making an unwelcome appearance to look things over. Since he was a friend of Castro and Alvarado—Bidwell had seen him in their company—the purpose of his reconnaisance was discernible.

With great abruptness he was seized and thrown into the fort calaboose, that dark chamber usually reserved for recalcitrant savages. There he stayed until released, some three months later.

ONE MORE PRIVATE conflict ends the year on the eve of dark days. Jacob Leese is reputed to have fought thirty thrilling minutes with Colonel Victor Prudon in the Sonoma public square. This contest ended with a balled fist smacking the immaculate Colonel flush on the chinwhiskers. Which ended his interest in the affair for the moment.

Reason for the disagreement: not recorded. Aftermath: Leese lost his position as alcalde; Prudon offered to renew hostilities with pistols; and both of them finally tapped fingers and made up.

gave Bidwell an official order for Captain Sutter; this communication directed the Swiss to gather his forces and proceed at once to Monterey. The Governor assured Bidwell of his ability to handle the situation and sped him on his way; his parting words assured best wishes and friendship for the Americans of the Valley.

At San José Bidwell rode directly into the ranks of the rebel army, then encamped near the village. Castro and Alvarado met him with smiles and soft words. They sent their most cordial greetings on to Captain Sutter. So much for the facial conformities of all *Californio* hostilities.

Thus detained only a few minutes, the messenger pressed on. . . . In time he galloped his lathered mount through the fortress gates. Sutter read his orders and speeded his plans. He sent agents over the whole northern frontier in search of military supplies, even requisitioning some horses at Soscol and Petaluma, a procedure which drove Vallejo frantic.

THE SACRAMENTO made her appearance at Yerba Buena on December 22nd with a small cannon and other arms on board. Sutter had thought it advisable not to dispatch the craft without some means of defense at the crew's disposal. That arrival of the New Helvetia boat caused much comment, some derisive, some calculating and some stormy.

One night, Francisco Guerrero and a number of Californians captured the schooner and smuggled the armament across the bay for the use of Castro's army. They left the boat at its moorings, using the customs-house craft for the actual transfer.

Sutter had yet made no hostile move. So, for some indeterminate reason, the leaders of the revolt deemed it politic to let the New Switzerland captain commit the first overt act. Accordingly, his cannon and small arms were returned to Yerba Buena.

George Patterson regained possession of the gun and firearms. Placing them once more in the *Sacramento* he

Chapter XLVIII

THE TRAIL LEADS ON. . .

WHEN GENERAL JOHN AUGUSTUS SUTTER left California in October 1866, he was sixty-three years old. Physically, the years had dealt graciously with the Swiss; only a twinge of rheumatic pains plagued him infrequently. Heavier now, slower of movement he was; but his blue eyes were as laughingly keen and his self-faith as sure as when he found his wilderness domain more than a quarter-century before.

With him he took his wife, and Carmen and Anna Elisa, his granddaughters, and John A. Sutter III. At his insistence, these three children of his eldest son came by steamer from Acapulco; their father had been United States consul there for more than a decade.

A friend had told the General of the marvelous schools of Lititz, Lancaster County, Pennsylvania; and also recommended the curative qualities of Lititz Springs for rheumatic ailments. He wanted his grandchildren well educated and he wanted to present his case to Congress. "Perhaps the springs will chase away this stiffness, too," he said hopefully.

So he made the pilgrimage with Anna and the three children. He carried with him many letters to Congress from important Californians; even Governor Frederick F. Lowe insisted on his bearing documents to both houses pressing the justice of his claims.

LITITZ IS A tiny town of peace. Its inhabitants are Moravians, simple, honest, quiet-loving folk whom a rushing world cannot chain to the chariot of speed and turmoil. To this placid place came the General and Anna and their charges. With the trifle of money he possessed he bought a brick colonial house in the village, a two-storied structure of spacious rooms. There he took up the business of living and planning again.

Carmen and Anna Elisa were sent to famous Linden Hall; John A. Sutter III was a student in Beck's Academy. The General himself found relief in the springs. His two dogs, Watch and Bijou, wandered with him on many long strolls or walked more sedately with him in the large garden behind the house. He rode his favorite saddle-horse for miles about the countryside, his figure a familiar sight to the laborers in the fields.

John Sutter's home stood opposite the Springs Hotel —now the General Sutter Hotel—and the Swiss often took his meals there. The French chef was a jewel of his kind and prepared many special dishes for his affable patron. The General was over-fond of rich gravies; and Antoine Dubois knew gravies of a taste to delight an epicure.

On occasion the rich foods played havoc with a digestion which had valiantly endured the unsubtle fares of the wilderness. "By Jupiter, I grow a shade older," laughed the General. But he refused to desert Antoine and his incomparable dishes. . . .

Old friends sought the Swiss out. General Sherman, who had been Sutter's friend and guest in California, came frequently; General Phil Sheridan, another old friend of Hock days, came often; General H. Gates Gibson was another visitor. This trio and a score of others aided the white-haired fighter to plan the presentation of his claims before both legislative houses. Through them he was able to secure reputable legal counsel and forge ahead to what he saw was certain fulfillment—a settlement where justice would prevail.

Each session of Congress found him in Washington, eager and ever sure. Congress always seemed complaisant. But somehow or other they never got around to do anything about it. . . . Great men wrote and personally pled before both houses in his favor. Memorials were presented, full of data and explanation. Reams of paper setting down the facts were studied by committees. . . . And the years strode on, each dropping a heavier milestone as they passed, seeing the Swiss grow older, slower, grayer. . . .

His FRIENDS were many in the little town. The staid Augustus Beck of Beck's Academy was an intimate; cheery Dr. Levi Hentl, Dr. J. H. Shenk, the genial storekeeper Hayden H. Tshudy, the Rev. Charles Nagle, pastor of the church—all knew and loved the aging General. He walked and talked with them; and his wit and humor were as sparkling as ever.

The other Lititz folk paid little attention to the General; they merely accepted him. Not one of them beyond his little circle was more than dimly aware of who John Sutter was; or in what stirring drama he had played the leading rôle. They had some vague idea he was a great man; but that sufficed them.

ONE SUMMER DAY, the master of Beck's Academy caught his friend, the General, in conversation with a passing vagrant. Moreover, his eyes had caught the gleam of a half dollar passing from clean blue pantaloons to grimy, tattered ones.

The tramp went on, hurriedly.

"John," exploded Dr. Beck irascibly, "why do you persist in giving money and talking to such unkempt people?"

"Ah, my friend," observed the General, "he was hungry and weary and disheatened. I have always aided such men. I shall do so until I die. . . ."

Early in 1875 the Associated Pioneers of the Territorial Days of California was founded in New York City. General Gibson, Sutter's friend, was the first president, an honor soon to pass to the Swiss. Headquarters for the organization was named as Sturtevant House. All Californians then in the East became members of the association.

On September 9th, the society assembled at Pacific Coast Centennial Hall in Philadelphia, there to celebrate the twenty-sixth anniversary of California's admission day. Every Californian who could possibly get there stormed the hall on that occasion. Most enthusiastic of the lot was John Sutter.

From the hall they swarmed to the Globe Hotel on Belmont Avenue, the official meeting place. The reunion dinner was a colorful success. Speeches were eloquent and plentiful. The music by McClurg's Cornet Band was a volume of wonder, designed for sympathetic ears. The General sat on President Gibson's right hand and reveled in the dashing display and good food and gay fellowship; not forgetting to tilt an amber-colored glass at ecstatic intervals.

Each year thereafter the Associated Pioneers held a grand reunion and dinner, usually in Sturtevant House. John Sutter and Anna never missed an affair, both present always as the society's honor guests. Those meetings always made the General younger, more buoyant. It was good to sit at table with men who remembered him as a benevolent, absolute ruler over a great valley.

In June 1880, the General made his yearly trip to Washington. As usual, he put up at Charles Mades' Hotel, on the southwestern corner of Pennsylvania Avenue and Third Street. Of late he had been bothered more by the plaguing rheumatism.

"I get tired too easily," said the General to Dr. Smith Townshend.

"Now, John, take it a little easier," cautioned the physician. "You're not a youngster any more."

"Plenty of jump in the old body yet," said the General.

He had come alone this time. Usually, Anna and even Carmen and Anna Elisa came with him. General Sherman happened to be in the city, heard of his arrival, and sought Sutter out at once.

"I'm sure your claim will be allowed this session, General," he said exultantly. "Everything seems sure at last."

"I knew it would come." The blue eyes twinkled. "It was only a matter of waiting. . . ."

Only a few days before, he had written: "Fourteen years I have presented my claims to Congress, seeking only simple justice. I asked only $1.25 an acre for the Sobrante tract—$122,000.

' The request is now before Congress. The Committee was afraid to allow me the entire amount for fear it might excite opposition. Therefore they have decided on $50,000 as the sum to be asked for, an amount I am sure I will receive.

"To get it I have already spent $25,000 and must pay $10,000 more to my lawyer. So there will be little left. Yet it will be enough to keep Anna and myself from need. . . ."

This was the sum which John Sutter was to receive for land worth hundreds of millions of dollars. . . .

On May 31st the General wrote a letter to an old friend, Johann Jakob Jenny-Roth, in Basel. It read:

"Dear old friend:

"Your letter of April 23rd was very much appreciated. It reached Lititz in due time and my dear wife forwarded it with my other mail. Nothing could have given me greater pleasure than to hear you were still among the living. Mr. George Kramer, son of our friend Johann George Kramer who married your cousin and lives in New York with his family, told me that you had died. It made me very sad and I rejoice to hear it is not true.

"The reason for not answering you for such a long time is that for a few weeks I was very ill. I suffer from frequent and acute attacks of rheumatism, the result of long years of campaigns and exposure; often I spent the night *a' la bell' étoile* and often I sat on horseback for several days and slept in wet blankets at night.

"Very often I have thought of our childhood and of how we played at being soldiers. . . . I am sending you two photographs of myself, one taken here which I do not like so much, the other taken in New York a year ago. I must have changed greatly these last eighteen months. Well, one gets older. . . .

"They are about to grant me $50,000—not much but I shall be satisfied to have done with the affair. I have been coming here every year for fifteen years and always there was something in the way of success. But that is all changed now.

"I hope to be able to journey home in about two weeks for it is quite terrible for my dear wife to be quite alone. We own a large and beautiful home with every modern comfort and a pleasing garden which we built eight years ago to please my wife. The house cost $10,000, the furniture $3,000. Thus we manage to live modestly, decently and retiringly. I am not rich but it is scandalous the way the little German papers have described us as living in the most bitter poverty. My niece in Burgdorf, Julie Schläfly, spinster, could not stand this any longer and wrote denunciatory articles to many of them. My son, Emil Victor, also wrote from San Francisco.

"If occasional papers in America say I am poor now they do not mean it in the German or Swiss sense. Today they call anyone a poor man who has not $100,000. If the United States Supreme Court had not defrauded me of my thousands of acres in the most unjust manner, I would have been worth millions. . . .

"I was happy when my family arrived in California. August, the eldest, had already served his apprenticeship with the firm of Schnell in Burgdorf. He became a clever business man and has been U. S. Consul in Acapulco for years. We assumed care of his children—our grandchildren—in order to give them a good education in the United States. Their mother is Spanish.

"The children spoke only Spanish at first and my wife learned Spanish from them and the servants. The son of August—J. A. Sutter Third—owns a business in New York. When I was there on January 19th he visited me with his wife, J. A. Sutter Fourth, and a tiny little great-granddaughter who delighted me very much. The two daughters are also married and the elder lives in Lititz; she has two sons—her husband is a civil engineer —and one son lives up in Yankeeland.

"Such is the way of the world as one grows older. My daughter, Anna Elisa, married a German doctor named Link. They went to Acapulco and are still making money there; their two sons, Emil and Victor were educated in San Francisco under their uncle's care. Emil, the elder, has a brilliant position with a Swiss firm in Guatemala; he is only nineteen years of age and wants his brother to join him. They are both good-looking, well-trained, alert youths.

"My son Emil Victor has for years been a notary public in San Francisco. He fares well because of his knowledge of languages, since Frenchmen, Italians, Germans, Spaniards, etc. seek him out to ratify their business transactions. He is also Greek consul—nothing very remunerative, but an honor. He is also interested in a copper mine which should bring him good dividends.

"My youngest son, Alphonse, died from wounds received while a Colonel in the Civil War. He commanded eighty men from Sutter County against the rebels. He married a Miss Stootz of Berne, whose father was a minister of Roggwyl. They had one son, Alphonse—his uncle Emil raised him—and he is now entering his uncle's business in Acapulco.

. . . "We could long have celebrated our golden wedding, my dear wife and I, but our family has been so scattered—we had not the heart. I am most pleased, dear friend, that your life's evening has been so happy and content. I shall be pleased to hear how you fared in the long years—please tell me which of our old friends are still living.

"The Weber family in Leipzig informed me promptly of the death of our old associate, which is a pity—yet each of us leave in turn. My greetings to your dear wife and family, and to your eldest son—I still remember him

as a little boy—Hans Jakob. Is your sister still living?—
I cannot write as well as I should like to, but I shall write
you such fragments of my story as come to mind. The
reason that I did not write you before is that up to ten
years ago we were still hoping to be able to travel back
to Europe and surprise our friends. But it proved so difficult to get my money from Congress that the plan was
dropped and I had not the heart to write until now—
when I am sure of success.

"Neither did I write to my niece in Burgdorf for four
years. When you write me, address me at Lititz, as I
shall soon be home again.

"Meanwhile, I close with most cordial greetings.
"Your old friend
"John A. Sutter

"P. S. It is still surprising how beautifully you still write
—such a firm, steady hand. J. A. S."

Washington was hot that June; and getting hotter.
Perspiring members of both houses were eager for ad-
journment. John Sutter's claim found itself, as customary,
on the tag-end of the session's business.

On the afternoon of June 18th, Representative
Dickey of Pennsylvania rose up in the House to give a
eulogy on his old friend, General Sutter; incidentally to
present his claim for final approval. Mr. Dickey was, it
must be set down, a trifle mellowed by a beverage of
some potency. His words dragged eloquently on. General
William Tecumseh Sherman sat in the gallery, mopping
his face with a handkerchief, waiting to carry the good
news to the Swiss. The General was at his hotel, resting;
he had been there in the morning but the heat had sent
him away at the noon hour.

In his hotel room, Sutter lay upon his bed and slept.
He was very weary; happy, too, that this was the last
journey he would have to make to Washington. It was
all settled. The pittance was to be finally allowed.

Five o'clock came; a knock on his door awakened the General. He sat up, put his feet over the edge of the bed.

"Come in," he invited, a smile of surety on his lined old face.

The door opened. Sherman came in. There was bleakness on him and his lips were straight.

Sutter stood up, expectant. ' The claim?" he said, the blue eyes certain.

"It's a damned shame, General!" burst out Sherman. "They're adjourned. Your claim didn't even go to a vote."

A strangeness came into the blue eyes. They seemed to grow cold and old; blue ice they seemed to be, ice from a far-off Swiss glacier that suddenly ceased to know the sunlight.

"Next year," he said clearly, "next year they will surely—"

He fell suddenly, like a stricken thing, back upon the bed. Sherman ran forward with a cry, shifted him slightly, held up the white head tenderly.

John Sutter had passed beyond caring for any earthly claim; or for the task of sifting the ashes of Empire.

They carried him back to the peaceful village and the people of simple heart. Famous men came to the church where Charles Nagle preached the burial service. Sheridan and Sherman and Frémont and Gibson and a hundred others were there. Some had hated the sleeper; but most of them had loved him.

At the end they bore him to the churchyard. Into the earth of which he had dreamed his glory of empire would rise up, they consigned him. His stone of memory bears the Sutter Crest, a crest that had been used by the Clan of Sutter before the days of the Swiss Independence. . . . In another year, his Anna was to sleep beside him. . . .

A woman who had been a child of the famous Donner Party whom John Sutter had succored in the snows and brought to the refuge of the fort, writes him his last salute. Her name was Eliza Donner.

"I have been very sad," she wrote, "since news flashed across the continent bidding the friends of General Sutter mourn his loss. In tender and loving thought I have entered his home, looked down upon the sleeper, brushed back his white locks. It is still difficult to realize that he is dead, that my childhood's idol of all that was generous, noble and good has come at last to the long rest of God's peace; that the last paragraph has been written in his kindly, adventurous life. . . .

"As long as California has a human history the memory of General Sutter will warm the hearts of her people. It was he who fed the hungry, clothed the naked, and comforted the distressed children of California's pioneer days. Surely his name glows eternally in vivid letters of sunlight on Sierra mountain crests; and no man can fail to see it etched in the sunset glory of the Golden Gate."

THE END

ACKNOWLEDGMENTS

To Dr. HERBERT BOLTON, Miss Edna Martin, Mrs. Eleanor Ashby Bancroft and J. J. Hill for their invaluable and gracious aid at Bancroft Library; to Carlie Wallett, Research Secretary of the Henry E. Huntington Library in San Marino, California; to Captain and Mrs. Frank Sutter Link for the privilege of inspecting and using the Sutter family records and the Sutter Albums; to Dr. Erich Schultz-Ewerth of Berlin for his remarkable data on the General's continental existence; to Templeton Crocker for his permission to use the superb pencil sketch of Hock Farm, the only pictorial original in existence; to Miss Dorothy H. Huggins of the California Historical Society; to Mr. Howard Hull of Lititz, Pennsylvania; to Victor Link for further Sutter records; to Mr. Phil B. Bekeart who so affably aided me with his extensive knowledge of Gold Days and who has contributed many unique pictures from his private library to this volume; to Mr. Harry C. Peterson, genial curator of Sutter's Fort Historical Museum, whose assistance and counsel have meant much to me and whose deft photographic artistry is responsible for the reproduction of most of the art in these pages; to Harry van Winkle, secretary of the Society of California Pioneers; to Henry Kirk, friend and playright; and to the following authors of original MSS. and books without whose aid this biography could not have been written:

William Baldridge. "The Days of '46." MS.
N. B. Ball. "Sketch By a Pioneer." MS.
T. A. Barry and B. A. Patten. "Men and Memories of San Fransciso." Published 1873.
D. P. Barstow. "Recollections of 1849–51." MS.
Washington Bartlett. "Sentiment of a Pioneer of '49." MS.
John Russell Bartlett. "Personal Narrative of Exploration And Incident in California." N. Y. 1851. 2 vols.
Bear Flag Papers. 1846. MS.
Henry J. Bee. "Recollections of California from 1830." MS.

Josiah Belden. "Historical Statement." MS.
Josiah Belden. "Letters of a Pioneer of '41." MS.
Calhoun Benham. "Testimony in the Behalf of the United States vs. Sutter, New Helvetia." Pub. San Francisco, 1881.
George Berry. "The Gold of California." Pub. London, 1849.
John Bidwell. "California in 1841 to 1848." MS.
John Bidwell. "Journey to California." 1841. MS.
Henry W. Bigler. "Diary of a Mormon in California." MS.
Wm. M. Boggs. "Reminiscences of 1846." MS.
Edmund Bray. "Memoir of a Trip to California." MS.
Patrick Green. "Diary of One of the Donner Party." 1846. MS.
Charles Brown. "Early Events in California." MS.
Edwin Bryant. "What I Saw in California."
Peter H. Burnett. "Recollections and Opinions of an Old Pioneer."
Peter H. Burnett. "Recollections of the Past." MS. 2 vols. "Notes on California." Pub. New York 1850.
California Textbook. Published San Francisco. 1852.
J. H. Carson. "Early Recollections of the Mines."
Francis Cassin. "A Few Facts About California." MS.
Enrique Cerruti. "History Note Books." 1821-1846.
Enrique Cerruti. "Ramblings in California." MS.
John Chamberlain. "Memoirs of California Since 1840." MS.
E. R. Chapin. "Reminiscences of a Surgeon." MS.
Joseph B. Chiles. "Visit to California in 1841." MS.
James Clyman. "Note Book." 1844-46. MS.
Walter Colton. "Deck and Port." New York, 1850.
Walter Colton. "The Land of Gold." New York, 1860.
Walter Colton. "Three Years in California." New York, 1850.
John Connor. "Early California Recollections." MS.
John Coulter. "Adventures on the Western Coast." 2 vols.
Henry J. Dally. "Narrative from 1840." MS.
William Heath Davis. "Glimpses of the Past in California." MS. 2 vols.
Peter Dean. "Occurrences in California." MS.
Sir James Douglas. "Voyage From The Columbia To California, 1841." MS. 2 vols.
Job F. Dye. "Recollections of California." MS.
James A. Ford. "Letters 1833-48." MS.
John Forster. "Pioneer Data from 1832." MS.
Talbot H. Green. "1841-48." MS.
James Gregson. "Statement 1845-49." MS.
John Grigsby. "Papers of 1846-48." MS.
David N. Hawley. "Observations of Men and Things." MS.
William R. Grimshaw. "Narrative of Events 1848-50." MS.
William Hargrave. "California in 1848." MS.
F. G. Hearn. "California Sketches." MS.

Josiah S. Henshaw. "Historical Events." MS.
William S. Hinckley. "Letters of a Sea Captain." MS.
Charles Hopper. "Narrative of a Pioneer of 1841." MS.
William Kelley. "An Excursion to California."
Sebastian Keyser. "Memoirs of a Pioneer." MS.
Leonard Kip. "California Sketches." MS.
Thomas Knight. "Early Events in California by a Pioneer of 1845."
    MS.
Thomas Knight. "Recollections." MS.
Wm. H. Knight. "Scrapbooks." 40 vols.
Thomas O. Larkin. "Description of California 1845." MS.
Thomas O. Larkin. "Notes on the Personal Character of Califor-
    nians." 1845. MS.
Thomas O. Larkin. "Documents for the History of California
    1839–56." MS. 9 vols.
Jacob P. Leese. "Letters from 1836." MS.
William A. Liedesdorff. "Letters of a United States Vice Consul."
    MS.
J. M. Letts. "California Illustrated." Pub. 1852.
J. M. Letts. "Pictorial View of California." 1853.
Robert Livermore. "Occasional Letters from 1825." MS.
Jim McCue. "Twenty-one Years in California." MS.
W. D. McDaniels "Early Days in California." MS.
George McKinstry, Jr. "Papers on the History of California." MS.
John Marsh. "Letters of a Pioneer Doctor." MS.
Henry Marshall. "Statement 1843." MS.
Francis Mellus. "Diary 1838-40." MS.
J. F. Morse. "Illustrated History of California."
Timothy Murphy. "Letters from 1824." MS.
Samuel Neal. "Notice of a Pioneer of 1845."
J. L. Ord. "Reminiscences of 1847." MS.
George F. Parsons. "Life and Adventures of James Wilson Marshall."
George Patterson. "Adventures of a Pioneer of 1840."
G. Payson. "Romance of California." New York, 1851.
"PIONEER SKETCHES." A Collection. MS.
R. H. Thomes. "Life of an Emigrant of 1841." MS.
W. J. Tustin. "Recollections of an Emigrant of 1845." MS.
Davis' Glimpses. MS.
Joseph Warren Revere. "A Tour of Duty in California."
William A. Richardson. "Letters of a Pioneer Sailor." MS.
Thomas M. Robbins. "Diary 1843-46." MS.
Alfred Robinson. "Life in California 1846." MS.
Alexander Rotscheff. "Deed of Ross to Sutter." MS.
Napoleon B. Smith. "Biographical Sketch of a Pioneer." 1845. MS.
Nathan Spear. "Loose Papers of an Early Trader." MS.
David Spence. "Letters of a Scotchman in California." MS.

David Spence. HISTORICAL NOTES. 1824-49. MS.
Abel Stearns. "Correspondence of a Merchant." MS.
J. D. B. Stillman. Overland Monthly. ii. 257. Ob. on Diseases in the
    Sacramento Valley.
Wm. A. Streeter. "Recollection of Historical Events." MS.
John A. Sutter. DIARY. Scrapbook from the Argonaut. 1839-48. MS.
John A. Sutter. "Examination of the Russian Grant." Sacramento,
    1860.
John A. Sutter. "Statistical Reports on Indian Tribes." MS.
John A. Sutter. CORRESPONDENCE. 1839-48. MS.
John A. Sutter. "Personal Reminiscences." MS.
John A. Sutter. Correspondence of the Sub-Indian Agent, '47-48. In
    California and New Mexico, Messages and Documents 1850.
John A. Swan. "Monterey in 1842." In *San José Pioneer*, March 30th,
    1878.
John A. Swan. HISTORICAL SKETCHES. 1844. MS.
William F. Swasey. "California in 1845-46." MS.
Bayard Taylor. "At Home And Abroad."
Bayard Taylor. "El Dorado."
Francis P. F. Temple. "Recollection of '41-47." MS.
James L. Tyson. "Diary of a Physician in California." MS.
"VERITAS" Examination of the Russian Grant.
Jean Jacques Vioget. "Letters of an Early Trader." MS.
Joel R. Walker. "Narrative of a Pioneer of 1841." MS.
J. J. Warner. "Reminiscences of Early California." MS.
Frank Watson. "Narrative of a Native Pioneer." MS.
William Weeks. "Reminiscences of a Pioneer of 1831." MS.
Michael White. "California All The Way Back To 1828." MS.
William Wiggins. "Reminiscences of a Pioneer of 1840." MS.
Henry F. Williams. "Statement of Recollections." MS.
Benjamin D. Wilson. "Observations of Early Days." 1841. MS.
Edward Wilson. THE GOLDEN LAND. Boston. 1852.
William Wolfskill. "Story of an Old Pioneer." In the *Wilmington
    Journal*.
James Woods. "Recollections of Pioneer Work in California." San
    Francisco, 1878.
VALLEJO DOCUMENTS. 36 Volumes.
FORT SUTTER PAPERS. MSS.
Robert von Schlagintweit. "California Land und Leute."
John A. Sutter. Petition to Congress.
Thomas O. Larkin. Official Correspondence. MS.
Sutter-Suñol Correspondence. 1840-46. MS.
Stewart Edward White. "Ranchero."
T. J. Schoonover. "Life and Times of General John A. Sutter."
William R. Castle, Jr. "Hawaii, Past and Present."
C. L. Andrews. "The Story of Sitka."

Sir Edward Belcher's "Voyage Around The World."
Sir George Simpson's "Voyage to California Ports in 1841-42."
Cyril P. T. Laplace. "Campagne de Circumnavigation." 6 vols.
William A. Slacum. REPORT ON OREGON. March 26th, 1837. 25th
    Congress, 3rd session; House Report 101. Washington, 1838.
Juan Bautista Alvarado. "Historia de California." 5 vols. 1876. MS.
Juan Bandini. HISTORIA DE ALTA CALIFORNIA. MS.
Berreyessa and Carrillo, "Quarrel at Sonoma." 1846. MS.
Domingo Carrillo. "Documentos Para la Historia de California."
    MS.
José Carrillo. "Documentos para la Historia de California." MS.
    2 vols.
Manuel Castro. "Documentos para la Historia de California." 2
    vols. MS.
M. Coignet. "Rapport sur les Mines de New Almaden." Paris, 1866.
John Conway. "Early Days In California." MS.
John Currey. "Incidents in California." MS.
Nicolas A. Den. "Letters of a Pioneer Doctor." MS.
Narciso Duran. "Informe de Actual Estado de las Misiones, 1844."
    MS.
Etholin. "Letters on Ross. 1841." MS.
Frémont's Report. 1845.
Alexander Forbes. "A History of California." London, 1839.
Fourgeaud. "The Prospects of California." In *California Star*. April
    1848.
James R. Garniss. "Early Days of San Francisco." MS.
Archibald S. Gillespie. "Correspondence of a Government Agent."
    MS.
Francisco Guerrero. "Cartas—1839-46." MS.
Wm. E. P. Hartnell. "Convention of '49." Original Records. MS.
Wm. E. P. Hartnell. "English Colonization in California 1844." MS.
Wm. B. Ide. "Bear Flag Revolt." MS.
Jacob P. Leese. "Bear Flag Revolt." MS.
C. F. McGlashan. "History of the Donner Party."
Ross. "Contrat de Vente. 1841." MS.
Ross. "Propuesta de Venta é Inventario. MS."
Wm. H. Russell. "General John A. Sutter." Pamphlet.
Mariano G. Vallejo. "Historia de California." 5 vols. MS.
Yate's "Sacramento Valley. 1842." MS.
G. M. Sandel's MS. "The King's Orphan." Visit to California. '42-
    43. Scrap Book Collection.
Eldredge's "History of California."
Dr. William Maxwell Wood. "Wandering Sketches in California."
J. B. McMaster's "History of the United States."
H. H. Bancroft's "History of California."

SUTTER'S FORT TODAY

By Harry C. Peterson, Curator

There was but one Sutter's Fort in 1849, the most talked of frontier fort in America that year—Sutter's Fort, the gateway to the realization of golden dreams of great wealth, to romance, to achievement, to life's desires. Through its gates poured the stream of the world's most red-blooded adventurers, men of character, men of intellect, sturdy and unafraid. They came to dig gold, they stayed to create the most romantic history of any place on the globe, a history so replete with wondrous stories of accomplishment in every line of endeavor that the world still looks at us in amazement.

In 1849 Sutter's Fort was the gateway to the future hopes of a hundred thousand history makers—today the old fort is the gateway to the memory of that hundred thousand men of adventure, the gateway to the past—a monument to Captain John Augustus Sutter, to his foresight, to his vision, and to their fulfillment by the men brought here through his instrumentality.

For today Sutter's Fort is again becoming the objective point of hundreds of thousands of visitors to California, that they may see within its walls the historic mementoes of those olden days of 'Forty-nine, those romantic days of the Great Gold Harvest, the days when man reaped the wealth of the earth with a pick and shovel.

There is an almost uncanny similarity in the fate of our pioneer empire builders: they who struggled against almost unbelievable obstacles in the wilderness to succeed, they who prepared the way for others, less hardy, to follow.

The pioneer trail blazer only too often died unheralded, penniless, neglected and unappreciated by the very generation that profited most through his sacrifices. Then, years later, the succeeding generation recalls his deeds, lauds his memory, and erects costly monuments to commemorate the greatness of the very man for whom their fathers had shown scarcely a neighborly appreciation.

The fate of Capt. John A. Sutter was no exception to this rule; but his public recognition by the State of California, belated though it was, is of the kind that would have most pleased the genial old Swiss gentleman.

His old fort, practically abandoned in 1850 after Sacramento City was established at the river front, soon became an almost forgotten place "out in the country." The citizens of the new City had stripped it of its doors and windows, of all the lumber that could be pried loose. Only the height of the Central Building prevented the removal of its roof and timbers, for its heavy oaken floor joists and roof rafters were so crudely chopped and uneven that no one took the trouble to remove them.

Stripped of its protecting shingles, the wind and the weather eroded the outer fort walls. The wide slough just north of it needed filling in, that a roadway might be constructed. The adobe walls provided the material.

The Central Building was occupied for short periods by squatters, but finally the last one, a hog raiser, abandoned it.

Thus it lay, unkept, no longer fit even for picnicking parties until 1890, when the Sacramento Parlors of the Native Sons of the Golden West raised a fund of $20,000, bought the two blocks of land upon which remained the ruins of the most famous fort in American history, then deeded it to the State of California, "for public use."

A restoration committee was appointed by the Governor to supervise its reconstruction, and $20,000 was appropriated for that purpose. The restoration committee went very thoroughly into the details of its original construction, but the amount appropriated was insufficient to carry out their plans completely. They had hoped to restore the walls with adobe brick, but found the cost prohibitive, so second-hand bricks were used to finish up with, after the available adobe bricks were utilized. The garbage-filled sloughs were cleaned out and converted into two beautiful lakes, the grounds were laid out under the supervision of John McLaren, of Golden Gate Park.

For some time no particular use was made of the fort, then it was decided to turn it into a museum. Unfortunately, only a caretaker was provided. Cheap pine cases were put in, and a general collection of curios resulted.

In 1925, George Radcliffe, then chairman of the State Board of Control, a Native Son, secured an appropriation of $10,000 from the legislature for the purpose of reorganizing the fort. A professional museum curator was employed to formulate an administrative policy, which was adopted by the State for its future guidance.

The policy is, briefly, "that the reorganization, classification and exhibition of the collections at Sutter's Fort be made with the dominant idea in mind of making it essentially an historical museum of the so-called 'American invasion of California;' that its exhibits be restricted exclusively to the events leading up to the establishment of the fort by Captain Sutter, and to those events that lead up to its acquisition by the United States and particularly covering the gold discovery, better known as 'The Days of 'Forty-nine.' That, so far as possible, the buildings, interior and exterior, be handled in such manner as will best retain and impart that romantic atmosphere of the Days of 'Forty-nine."

It is the intention to re-create in every way possible, and keep that romantic atmosphere of '49 at the fort. All the exhibits, the labels and the cases are planned with the one idea of carrying across to the visitor that elusive flavor of those old days. To enhance this interest, many of the old rooms will be rehabilitated to conform as nearly as possible to their original state. Lack of funds has seriously delayed much of this work.

Though depending entirely upon donations, the collections have increased from a few cases to several large rooms full of rare historical exhibits, many of priceless value.

Just inside the main gate stands the A. J. Weldon hay press, made by a farmer and his hired man far up in the Sierras, from trees chopped down on his farm, seasoned and fashioned into a press with a hammer, saw and chisel.

In the Central Building are five large rooms containing rare relics of Sutter; Marshall; Frémont; Kit Carson; P. B. Reading

Sam Brannan; Senator and Mrs Leland Stanford; John A. Chase, descendant of Salmon Portland Chase; the Gregson family, and scores of other well-known California pioneers.

Marshall's first wooden gold pan (a Mexican batea), his gold rocker, iron baby cradle, his tools and saddle are exhibited. Also Sutter's magnifying glass which he used to inspect the first gold brought down to the fort by James W. Marshall in 1848. Sutter's mirror, that has reflected the countenances of Frémont, Carson, Gen. Vallejo, Gov. Castro, and the majority of the early explorers of his day is shown along with a piece of timber from the original Coloma saw mill.

Pioneer costumes in variety, old bed spreads, shawls, laces, household utensils, ornaments and early sewing machines attract the feminine interest. The fort possesses several rare spinning wheels, with textiles that were made from thread spun on them. One of the rarest items is the first pair of ladies' silk stockings made in California, made from the raw silk spun from cocoons raised by the lady who knitted them. There is enough silk in these two stockings to make two dozen of the modern type.

Heavy, square-toed ladies' shoes, "for Sunday wear," are indicative of the rough trails the pioneer women travelled on their way to church.

In the basement rooms are the miners' relics; scores of firearms, from the small gambler's Derringer to the massive four-barrelled "goose-gun", with a record of 198 ducks at one shot. Guns owned by both Abe Lincoln and U. S. Grant before they became famous are on display.

A faro look-out's chair, an exceedingly rare item, is reminiscent of the old gambling halls where the look-out sat in this chair, a brace of six shooters held in his lap, ready for instant action, for delay on his part would have meant a new look-out the next evening, and a funeral the following day. For this risk he received $50 nightly.

One of the rarest and most interesting exhibits are parts of the original Reed wagon that was abandoned by the Reed family while crossing the Great Salt Lake Desert with the ill-fated Donner Party. For over eighty years historians had searched in vain for this camp site on the desert. It was found eventually by Capt. Chas. E. Davis, who spent three seasons locating the trail of the Donner Party who came across in 1846-7.

The Pioneer Art Gallery, located in Sutter's old distillery building, contains hundreds of portraits of California pioneers, early historical paintings and countless historical documents, including the original marriage records of the fort, as well as the cattle-brand records of early Central California. Letters of Sutter, Frémont, Bidwell, Reading, McKinstry and other early settlers are shown, along with original diaries, maps and record books.

The first three Concord stages that came to California around the Horn are preserved at the fort, along with a Conestoga "prairie schooner," the only one remaining of the 3,200 Conestogas that transported freight across the Plains from the Missouri River. Old ore wagons, oxcarts, fire engines, mowing machines, buggies and wagons remind the visitor that travelling in the days of '49 was no sinecure.

One room is devoted entirely to historical safes and trunks that came out in ox wagons or around the Horn. In the Malakoff safe, for several weeks, was kept a gold brick having a value of $114,000. This brick was the result of about ten days' run in the old Malakoff Hydraulic Mine in Nevada County.

The foregoing gives but a vague idea of the treasures now preserved in the fort museum. As rapidly as possible, new rooms will be opened up, specializing upon the early mining days, with models of some of the old mining camps as they were in their prime.

The fort is open free to visitors every week day in the year from nine until four. Sundays from ten until four.

Thus, through relics and records of the past, the State of California is keeping alive the memory of Captain Sutter and those other courageous men and women who made this the glorious State that it is.

INVENTORY
OF
SUTTER'S PURCHASE OF FORT ROSS AND BODEGA.

REAL ESTATE

The estates are: (A) at Fort Ross, (B) Kostromitinoff Rancho, (C) Klebnikoff Rancho, (D) Gorgy Rancho, and (E) at Bodega.

(A) FORT ROSS

Square Fort, made of planks, 1,032 feet in circumference, 12 feet high; it has two turrets at the angles.

IN THE FORT ARE:

Commandant's House. (old) made of thick wood, 48 feet long, 36 feet wide, roofed with double boards. It contains 6 rooms, corridor and kitchen.

Commandant's House (new) made of thick wood, 48 feet long, 24 feet wide, containing six rooms and corridor.

Commissioned Officers' House. 10 rooms, 2 corridors; 60 feet long, 21 feet wide.

Barracks. of 8 rooms, 2 corridors, 48 feet long, 24 feet wide.

Warehouse. (old) 2 stories, 48 feet long, 24 feet wide, has an open gallery with pillars.

Warehouse. (new) of thick planks, 42 feet long, 24 feet wide.

Kitchen. (new) 24 feet long, 21 feet wide.

Warehouse. (for food supplies) of thick planks, 48 feet by 18 feet; a prison here.

Chapel with cupolas. 36 feet long, 24 feet wide. A bell tower here.

Well. 15 feet deep.

OUTSIDE THE FORT AT FOOT OF HILL.

A Forge, Anvil, and Shop for a blacksmith; of thick wood, 33 feet long, 18 feet wide.

Tannery. 30 feet long, 18 feet wide; here a machine to compress tanned hides.

Bathhouse for troops. 18 feet by 15 feet.

Shop for coopers. 60 feet by 30 feet.

Shed. for the fishing boats, on rafters; 60 feet by 30 feet.

IN THE VICINITY OF THE FORT:

Barrack's Kitchen, a *Bakeshop* here; 30 by 18 feet.

Two Cattle Barns of thick planks, 120 feet by 21 feet wide; also a corral here 168 feet by 120 feet.

8 Sheds, 8 Pools, 10 Kitchens. The houses have plank roofs, windows with glass, and wooden floors.

WITHIN 5,000 FEET OF THE PRESIDIO ARE:

Wooden Threshing floor with floor of planks, 60 feet in diameter; here a shed 30 feet by 15 feet.

Orchard with fruit trees: 330 feet by 144 feet.

It has more than

260 fruit trees	10 pear trees
207 apple trees	10 quince trees
29 peach trees	8 cherry trees

also some vines.

The Orchard has a new house with 4 rooms, 27 feet by 24 feet, roofed with planks; here a *kitchen* 15 feet square.

Nearby is a little *orchard*, 84 feet by 63 feet. It has 20 fruit trees and vines. Also a glass *summer house*.

Ross has 70 acres of cultivated land. This larger part is fenced.

The Fort has a vegetable garden 420 feet by 120 feet; also a hot bed.

(B)
KOSTROMITINOFF RANCHO.

Barracks: 48 by 18 feet, roofed with planks. 3 rooms and 2 corridors with roofs.

Warehouse: 42 by 18 feet, roofed with planks; of wood for washing wheat in the river.

House. 18 by 12 feet.

Two Threshing floors: one 60 feet in diameter; one 48 feet; the floors made of planks; the walls made of boards.

Floor for winnowing wheat: 12 feet square, made of thick wood and beams.

Houses for Indians. Made of planks, 45 feet by 15 feet.

Kitchens: with 2 ovens.

Bathhouse: of planks, roofed, 18 by 12 feet.

A boat to travel on the *Slavonika* (Russian) River. The rancho has 100 acres of cultivated land.

(C)
KLEBNIKOFF RANCHO.

Adobe House: 3 rooms, 21 by 15 feet, roofed with lapped boards. A sundial here.

Barracks: 60 by 21 feet. 3 divisions roofed with boards.

Warehouse: 45 feet by 21 feet. Wooden floor.

Wooden floor: large. 72 feet in diameter; floor of planks.

Kitchen: Bread oven; forge. 36 feet by 15 feet.

Bathhouse: 21 by 12 feet.

4 Houses of Various Sizes: 1 for food; 2 for Indians; 1 for tobacco.

Mill: worked by horses with one stone. Can grind 4 *fanegas.* There is farming land here suitable for beans, corn, tobacco, etc.

(D)
GORGY RANCHO

Barracks: 6 rooms. 42 feet by 18 feet.

Kitchen: 24 by 12 feet.

Bathhouse: 18 by 12 feet.

Warehouse: for supplies. 42 by 18 feet.

Floor for winnowing wheat: of planks, 108 feet in diameter.

Two Houses: for supplies.

Two Hot Beds.

Vineyard: with 2,000 plants and some fruit trees. The cultivated land is fenced. Suitable for chili, onions, beans, corn, etc.

(E)
BODEGA

Warehouse: 60 by 30 feet.
House: 18 feet square. 4 rooms. A stove.
Bathhouse: 24 feet by 18 feet.
Corral.
A Boat.
A House with a stove. 12 feet square.
A large corral.
A Hut and Corral: where the horses are pastured.
A 20-ton launch: excellent for the coast.
A four-oared boat.

CHATTELS
Farm Machinery.

Steel machine for cleaning wheat.
Rake with steel teeth.
26 horse plows.

19 ox plows.
2 native plows.
19 rakes with iron teeth.
10 rakes with wooden teeth.
25 harnesses for horses.
18 harnesses for oxen.
15 halters.
20 reins.
Five carts with four wheels.
Ten carts with two wheels.

CATTLE:

2,000 head.
1,000 horses.
1,000 sheep.
70 mules.
4,000 head in all.

DESCENDANTS OF

GEN. JOHN A. SUTTER. Born midnight Feb. 23, 1803, at Kandern, Baden. Died June 18, 1880, at Washington, D. C.

ANNA DUBELT. Born Sept. 15, 1805, in Switzerland. Died Jan. 19, 1881, at Lititz, Pennsylvania. Married 1823.

Issue: *3 sons, 1 daughter*

A. JOHN AUGUSTUS SUTTER, JR. Born Oct. 25, 1826, Switzerland. Died 1897, Acapulco, Mexico.
B. ANNA ELISA SUTTER. Born 1828, Switzerland. Died March 1895, Acapulco, Mexico.
C. EMIL VICTOR SUTTER. Born 1830, Switzerland. Died July 3, 1881, Ostend, Belgium.
D. WILLIAM ALPHONSE SUTTER. Born 1832, Switzerland. Died Nevada City, Aug. 14, 1863.

DESCENDANTS OF
(I)

JOHN AUGUSTUS SUTTER, JR. Married MARIA DEL CARMEN RIVAS. *1 Son, 2 Daughters*

A. JOHN A. SUTTER III. Born in Acapulco, Mexico. Died (date unknown). Married Fannie Salt of New York.
3 sons, 1 daughter

    1. JOHN A. SUTTER IV. No children.
    2. VICTOR ALPHONSE SUTTER. Died in infancy.
    3. ALPHONSE VICTOR SUTTER. 1 child.
       a. *John A. Sutter V.*
    4. JAUNITA SUTTER. Married twice: 1st Frank Earle; 2nd Wm Kleinschmidt.
       a. *Jaunita Earle.*
       b. *Natalie Earle.*

B. ANNA ELISA SUTTER. Born Acapulco, Mexico, 1856. Died San Francisco, California, July 1914. Married twice.
1st husband HOWARD J. HULL, Lancaster, Penna.

1. HOWARD JOSEPH SUTTER HULL. 35 Cottage Ave. Lancaster, Penna. Born (date unknown). Married Susan Eshelman, daughter of John Eshelman of Lancaster, Pennsylvania: *1 son.*
   a. *Howard J. S. Hull, Jr.* Born (date unknown).
   Note: more complete information concerning dates etc. for the above family could probably be had by writing to Howard J. Hull, 35 Cottage Ave., Penna.
2. RICHARD HULL. Married (name of wife unknown).
   1 son, 2 daughters.
   a. *Richard Hull, Jr.*
   b. *Ysabel Hull.*
   c. *Annie Hull.*

2nd husband VICTOR ALPHONSE LINK, her first cousin

3. VICTOR ALPHONSE LINK. Born July 3, 1889, San Francisco, Calif. Not married. Chief Engineer.
4. CAPT. FRANK SUTTER LINK. (Francis Xavier Sutter Link). Born April 26, 1891, San Francisco, Calif. Married, November 26, 1921, Berkeley, California. Wife's Name: Aida Wanda Verdi (born Nov. 9, 1899, Berkeley, Cal. Wife's Parentage: Anthony Frederick Verdi and Katharine Camilla Nave. *1 daughter.*
   a. *Aida Anna Link.* Born August 25, 1922, 9:23 a.m., Berkeley, California.
5. EUGENE FREDERICK LINK. Born January 2, 1895; San Francisco, Calif. Not Married. Staff Sgt. U. S. Army.

C. CARMEN SUTTER. Born Acapulco, Gro. Mexico (date unknown). Died May 3, 1890, Woonsocket, Rhode Island. Married JESSE SMITH: *3 children* (Have been unable to trace them).

DESCENDANTS OF
(II)

ANNA ELISA SUTTER. Married Dr. FRANCIS XAVIER LINK.

2 sons

A. VICTOR ALPHONSE LINK. Born Acapulco, Mexico (date unknown). Died 1914, San Francisco, California. Married his first cousin *Anna Eliza Sutter*, daughter of J. A. S., Jr.

3 sons

1. VICTOR ALPHONSE LINK. Born San Francisco, July 3, 1889. Unmarried.

2. CAPT. FRANK SUTTER LINK. Born April 26, 1891, San Francisco.
3. EUGENE FREDERICK LINK. Born Jan. 2, 1895, San Francisco.

B. EMILE LINK. Born Acapulco, Mexico (date unknown). Died in Guatemala. Not married.

DESCENDANTS OF
(III)

EMIL VICTOR SUTTER. Was not married. No descendants.

DESCENDANTS OF
(IV)

WILLIAM ALPHONSE SUTTER. Married PAULINE STOOTZ: *1 son.*
A. ALPHONSE SUTTER. Born (date unknown). Died, San Francisco, California. Married Emma Perry, San Francisco. *No Children.*

INDEX